Italian/American Fantastika

SUNY series in Italian/American Culture

Fred L. Gardaphé, editor

Italian/American Fantastika

Fantasy, Horror, and Science Fiction from *Pinocchio* to *Star Trek*

Edited by

MARC DIPAOLO and ANTHONY LIOI

Cover credit: Joseph Stella, *"Serenade," A Christmas Fantasy (La Fontaine)*. 1937.

Published by State University of New York Press, Albany

Printed in the United States of America

EU GPSR Authorised Representative:
Logos Europe, 9 rue Nicolas Poussin, 17000, La Rochelle, France
contact@logoseurope.eu

For information, contact State University of New York Press, Albany, NY
www.sunypress.edu

Library of Congress Cataloging-in-Publication Data

Names: DiPaolo, Marc, editor. | Lioi, Anthony (Anthony Francis), editor.
Title: Italian/American fantastika : fantasy, horror, and science fiction from Pinocchio to Star Trek / edited by Marc DiPaolo and Anthony Lioi.
Description: Albany : State University of New York Press, [2026]. | Series: SUNY series in Italian/American culture | Includes bibliographical references and index.
Identifiers: LCCN 2025032193 | ISBN 9798855805635 (hardcover : alk. paper) | ISBN 9798855805659 (PDF) | ISBN 9798855807066 (epub)
Subjects: LCSH: American fiction—Italian American authors—History and criticism. | Speculative fiction, American—History and criticism. | Fantasy fiction, American—History and criticism. | Science fiction, American—History and criticism. | Horror tales, American—History and criticism. | Italian Americans in literature. | LCGFT: Literary criticism. | Essays.
Classification: LCC PS153.I8 I84 2025
LC record available at https://lccn.loc.gov/2025032193

For Tracy Floreani:
Gli amici sono la famiglia che scegliamo noi stessi.
—MD

For my father, Anthony Lioi Sr.,
who gave me his love of all things fantastic.
—AL

Contents

Part 2
Case Studies in Italy's Fantasies, Futurisms, and Gothic Horror

Part 3
Reimagining Italian America: Artifacts of Anti-fascist and Ecofeminist Fantastika

Acknowledgments

Anthony Lioi and Marc DiPaolo, the editors of this volume, would like to thank our contributors for their hard work crafting essays for this anthology, and for their patience and goodwill as the project evolved.

Throughout the development of this book, we had valuable assistance from Ryan Calabretta-Sajder, Nancy C. Carnevale, Fred L. Gardaphé, Alan Gravano, James Peltz, and Laura Ruberto. These colleagues, mentors, and scholars believed in the project, helped us find excellent contributors, offered feedback on drafts of essays, and assisted us in putting *Italian/American Fantastika* out into the world. Notably, the person we owe the largest debt to—who did all the above and more—is Lisa DeTora. We are grateful to her for all her work, and especially for introducing us to some wonderful essayists. In addition, the editors would like to thank Nicholas Birns, Jason Cash, Catherine DiPaolo, Daniel Ferris, Kristin Griffeath, John Hayden, Partrick Julian, Murray Leeder, Brian Stevens, Nathan Thomas, and Brian Trent for helpful topic suggestions in the crafting of our canon of speculative fiction found in the appendix.

To conclude, Quentin DiPaolo—Marc's comparatively young son—did invaluable work crafting the entire index on behalf of the two overworked and tired editors. Anthony, impressed by both Quentin's diligence and the quality of the end product, has declared that "Quentin deserves his own little tropical island." Marc agreed.

Foreword

Science Fiction, Fantastika, and Italian American Identity

John Rieder

The editors of this volume originally proposed exploring the category "Italian American" via the evidence provided by various nonrealistic popular narratives. Why might these narratives provide an appropriate terrain on which to explore the political, historical, and cultural complexities of Italian American identity? What are the stakes of such a project? And how do those stakes play out against a larger field of Italian diasporic identity?

One of the ways the editors proposed to answer such questions is to turn to encyclopedist and scholar of fantasy and science fiction John Clute's influential essay "Fantastika in the World Storm," originally delivered as a talk at the Cultural Landscapes / Fiction Without Borders Conference in Prague in September of 2007. Clute argues that fantasy, science fiction, and horror comprise a thematically coherent body of story that embodies "the necessary form of planetary fiction since 1750" (6). Clute dubs this body of fiction "Fantastika," a kind of story with its roots in the mid-eighteenth-century emergence of the Gothic as a "subversive reaction" to the Enlightenment's overconfidence in reason (10). The three closely interrelated "narrative grammars" characterizing the genres of fantasy, science fiction, and horror, according to Clute, make up "permutations of one Ur Story, like three snakes mutually entwined" (12). The key opening Clute's Fantastika makes to exploring any cultural identity lies not so much in the Freudian dynamics of repression and sublimation Clute attributes to it (Clute ultimately said that "what the great texts of Fantastika offer" is an insight into civilization equivalent to Freud's analysis in *Civilization and Its Discontents* [13]), but rather in the way Fantastika "vibrates to the planet. It is the planetary form of story" (9). If Fantastika indeed "marks the place where Western Civilization begins to understand that we do not inhabit a world but a planet" (8), as Clute argues, then it would therefore have a privileged relationship to the transformation of the global map and geopolitics by European colonialism and imperialism from the fifteenth century onward. Both the dispersion and redistribution of populations in the wake of European expansion into the rest of globe and the displacement of rural populations by the transition from feudalism to capitalism in Europe would include as one important instance the Italian diaspora. Thus it makes sense to asked how Fantastika "vibrates" to the deracination of Italian immigrant populations and to the problems of assimilation and racialization they faced in their migrant destinations, including above all, but not limited to, the United States.

Of Clute's three Fantastika genres, science fiction (and its sibling, speculative fiction; it is common practice in the field of science fiction studies to use the abbreviation SF as an umbrella term designating both) is the one that most obviously develops out of the transition from understanding the earth as the world to understanding it as a planet. In my 2008 monograph *Colonialism and the Emergence of Science Fiction* I laid out the case that the emergence of science fiction in the late nineteenth and early twentieth centuries had a lot to do with the cultural ramifications of colonialism and imperialism. My analysis did not take off from the Gothic response to the Enlightenment, nor did it take into account the massive outmigrations from Europe to the United States during this period. It focused instead on the scientific fruits of European exploration in the fields of cartography, biology, anthropology, and ethnology, and the unsettling and revision of ideas about human nature that inevitably ensued. Alongside the critical potential of these scientific developments, of course, were the ideological formations that worked not so much to understand the different cultural practices of non-European societies as to rationalize the expropriation of their land and resources and the violent subjugation of their inhabitants in the process of colonization. These ideological formations, such as Social Darwinism and scientific racism, certainly played a key role in the racialization of European immigrants in the United States and other settler colonial states such as Canada and Australia as well. The imperial adventure stories that comprise one (but only one) of the threads of convention that were woven together into the emergent genre of science fiction often served as a vehicle for these ideologies. But critical and utopian speculation, fueled by the decentering not only of geocentric cosmography but more importantly of European culture and anthropocentric assumptions about the makeup and history of the planet, also played a crucial role in forming what came to be recognized as science fiction.

The narrative grammars that Clute discerns in fantasy, science fiction, and horror represent patterns of repetition across the wide expanse of Clute's reading, and his erudition in this terrain is second to none. Yet one need not said that these patterns constitute an "Ur Story" in order to agreed that the repetitions characteristic of popular fiction make visible the lineaments of collective fantasies about our shared reality. Genre conventions are not some sort of palpable things that lie in wait for creative artists to discover them. They are the cumulative results of repetition based on the overlapping possibilities offered to the unevenly divided resources of a large number of artists, publishers, readers and viewers, collectors and librarians, critics and scholars over a substantial amount of time. They find their basis not so much in collections of texts as in communities of practice, and these communities can find their own commonality in a variety of ways. Science fiction, fantasy, and horror are all interwoven with histories of subcultural practice in which gender has consistently played a crucial role. In recent decades ethnicity has emerged as a crucial feature as well, as both a consequence and an effect of the growing prominence of women and BIPOC writers in these genres. Thus it makes sense to turn to these genre practices as a way of exploring the meaning of "Italian American" identity and beyond at present.

Western subcultural identities have been, for the last few centuries, always formed in some sort of opposition or alliance with larger, more powerful, and more prescriptive communities of identification, none of them more powerful in their effects than the "imagined communities" of nations and nationalisms. If, as Benedict Anderson proposed at the outset of his masterful analysis of nationalism, national identities "are to be distinguished, not by their falsity/genuineness, but by the style in which they are imagined" (6), "Italian American" represents a style of identification distinct from either "Italian" or "American," which share a similar anchoring in political reality. "Italian American" is, like its components, an assertion of ethnicity and citizenship but, at the same time, declared a disconnection from them, being no longer simply "Italian" yet not simply

"American." Not that being simply "American" is unproblematically possible for anyone at all, given the foundation in the US of the disconnection of immigrants from their homelands, of colonies from their sovereigns, and of homelands from their native inhabitants. It is probably no news to most readers of this collection that American exceptionalism does not stand up well to historical scrutiny, but perhaps it will be more refreshing to find the slippery boundaries of whiteness very much at stake in the exploration of "Italian American" identity and in placing this identity against other related Italian diasporic identities.

Although Clute's Fantastika designates an international pattern of generic repetitions, national contexts make a big difference in the position and significance of its component genres. Anyone who has browsed the shelves of an Italian bookstore knows that the *Fantascienza* section is usually small and mostly supplied by translations from English-language science fiction, while the *giallo* section is much more robust and full of distinguished Italian artistry. That imbalance is echoed in the predominance of mafiosi in the depiction of Italian Americans in American popular fiction and culture. In the past few decades Italian science fiction has been growing in importance with the success of Valerio Evangelisti, Nicoletta Vallorani, and others; the July 2015 special issue of *Science Fiction Studies* on Italian Science Fiction, edited by Umberto Rossi, Arielle Saiber, and Salvatore Proietti, tells this story in expert detail. The question of why crime fiction thrived in Italy throughout the twentieth century while science fiction was relatively stunted nonetheless remains worth asking. In the Italian American context what seems most pertinent about this collection's turn to nonrealist popular narratives is its offering alternatives to the stereotypical crime families of American popular fiction and cinema. The power of imagining such alternatives is exactly what makes it worthwhile to use these nonrealist popular narratives as an avenue of approach to the complexities of Italian, American, and Italian American histories and identities. Perhaps the most important feature of the common ground shared by science fiction, fantasy, and horror is their license to imagine things being otherwise than what is usually assumed to be normal or inevitable—to challenge the limits of possibility. Although that kind of imagining can and often does devolve into mere escapism, in the hands of its best practitioners it pushes against the complacency of the status quo. Its inventions make interventions into the political, social, and cultural discourses shaping our understanding of ourselves and our histories as they are entangled with those of others, and that is why they are worth critical attention.

Works Cited

Anderson, Benedict. *Imagined Communities: Reflections on the Origin and Spread of Nationalism*. Revised edition. Verso, 2006.

Clute, John. "Fantastika in the World Storm." *Foundation*, vol. 102, 2008, pp. 6–14.

Rieder, John. *Colonialism and the Emergence of Science Fiction*. Wesleyan UP, 2008.

Rossi, Umberto, Arielle Saiber, and Salvatore Proietti, eds. Special Issue on Italian Science Fiction. *Science Fiction Studies*, vol. 42, no. 126, pt. 2, July 2015.

Preface

Are Italians Welcome on the Starship *Enterprise*? A Personal Essay on Witches, Starships, and a Little Wooden Boy

Marc DiPaolo

As a child who caught intermittent repeats of the original *Star Trek* (1966–1969) series, I experienced a measure of disappointment that the multicultural, socialist utopia of the twenty-third century it depicted appeared devoid of Italians. Certainly, that was true of the American World War II movie model of the *Enterprise* crew, which famously featured an Iowa farm boy as captain, a chief medical officer from Atlanta, and a science officer from the planet Vulcan working seamlessly together on the bridge of the twenty-third-century exploratory spaceship USS *Enterprise*. The rest of the command crew hailed from Kenya, Japan, Russia, and Scotland. I grew up with the franchise just as the cult phenomenon began launching an array of television spinoffs with titles that started with *Star Trek* (followed by implied colons and subtitles). Sadly, by the time I reached my mordant teenage years, the bloom was off the *Trek* rose: I felt unwelcome in this society. *Trek*'s atheist creator Gene Roddenberry had worldbuilt a secularist society, but I was a religious Catholic. As an Italian American, all my exposures to the various incarnations of *Trek* seemed to confirm my suspicion that the multicultural, socialist human society depicted in Roddenberry's utopian future was (possibly) better because all the paisans were gone. True or false, this perception of mine, compounded by Kirk's unceremonious death in *Generations* (1994), caused me to give up.

Figure P.1. Critics Maria Jose and John Tenuto have cataloged most of the Italian characters in *Star Trek*. There are more than I had feared when I lamented the dearth of Italian characters as a 1990s fan, but most are one-off villains and Redshirts. I'd argue the three most notable *Trek* Italians are Robert Picardo (who played the Doctor on *Star Trek: Voyager*); Zachary Quinto (Spock in the Kelvin timeline), and Tig Notaro (who played engineer Jett Reno on *Star Trek: Discovery*). *Source: Star Trek: Discovery*, Season Two, Paramount+, 2019, publicity photo.

I defected to *Babylon 5* (1993–1998) during college. This fresh new science fiction retelling of *Lord of the Rings* helped usher in the modern-day era of serialized television with a multiseason arc plan. *Babylon 5* featured as its "everyman" a tragicomic hardboiled detective named Michael Garibaldi. Far from being a flawless Italian figure "respectability politics" would condone, Garibaldi was, like the Irish American actor who played him (Jerry Doyle), a reactionary alcoholic antihero living in a neofascist society. Imperfect as he was, Garibaldi was coded as Italian and liked pasta and *Looney Tunes*, so I loved him and *Babylon 5*. The cast seemed more recognizably multicultural than *Star Trek: The Next Generation*. I also appreciated that the imperfect future of *Babylon 5* was at least not a whitewashed or "colorblind" one.

I had been so fixated on the dearth of Italian characters in *Star Trek* that I was only half aware that, by the 1990s, sci-fi multiculturalism had moved toward a symbolic diversity comprised of aliens. Consequently, Earth's nationalities and ethnicities appeared to be presented counterintuitively, if not absent altogether. In *Trek*'s syndicated spinoffs *The Next Generation*, *Voyager*, and *Deep Space Nine*, colorblind (mis)casting was matched with an array of recognizably ethnic surnames, and often the ethnicity of the actor manifestly failed to match the ethnicity of the fictional character's surname. Meanwhile, the alienness of Bajorans, Betazeds, and the Borg acted as stand-ins for cultural diversity in the same symbolic way that the blueness of the skin of several of Marvel's X-Men marked them as symbolically "other" far more than their religious affiliation or heritage. This practice in both sprawling, progressive multimedia franchises was in keeping with the liberal colorblindness of the 1990s, in which enlightened people would declared themselves indifferent to whether the person they were addressing was "black, white, yellow, red" before invariably appending "blue, green, or purple" to fill in for any marginalized people they may have omitted by mistake.

And yet, during this same period, *DS9* distinguished itself by premiering in January 1993—mere months after the 1992 Rodney King riots—with Avery Brooks playing the first Black main character in *Star Trek*: a single father, Deep Space Nine's station commander, and eventual hero of the Dominion War named Captain Benjamin Sisko. Sisko's presence in the show ensured a largely Black supporting cast, including his son, Jake; his first wife, Jennifer; his new love interest, smuggler Kasidy Yates; and his father, Joseph, a New Orleans restaurateur. In the 1990s, seeing three or four Black characters interacting onscreen without a white character in view was a truly groundbreaking sight. Aware of both their successes and limitations within the 1990s cultural context in which they worked, series writers Ira Steven Behr, Hans Beimler, and Marc Scott Zicree presented viewers with a metanarrative episode called "Far Beyond the Stars" (1998) that was more of an apology that they could not take even more daring steps with Sisko's character than an exercise in self-congratulation. Appropriately, Brooks directed the show and turned in his finest performance in what was arguably *DS9*'s best episode.

While the production team may have wished to do more to promote a progressive agenda, *DS9* achieved something with Sisko worth celebrating. In the 2019 documentary *What We Left Behind*, Brooks expressed pride that he was able to model Black fatherhood on television, as well as appear as an authority figure in the future, unapologetically showing his naked

Black face to the camera, instead of being compelled to cover it with a cybernetic implant or Klingon makeup as Black male *Trek* stars LeVar Burton and Michael Dorn before him had to.

Watching Brooks's dazzling grin as he made this justifiable boast, I felt nothing but joy for him. I recalled how good I felt seeing Italian American representation onscreen when I was growing up, regardless of whether the actors or characters were Italian, so I couldn't even begin to imagine how proud Brooks felt, or how much Sisko meant to Black science fiction fans. I was not jealous of Brooks's achievement. I just hoped that one day there would be an Italian character on *Star Trek* half as cool as Sisko. Until such time, I could revel in how amazing a character Sisko was, and how cool and honorable the first female *Trek* captain, Kathryn Janeway, was . . .

To a degree, anyone who grew up in a post–*Star Wars* period replete with sequels, rip-offs, and heirs apparent seemed primed to grow up at least a casual fan of these serialized, fantastical narratives, whether they be multimedia franchises such as *Transformers*, *Masters of the Universe*, *Conan: The Barbarian*, *Knight Rider*, Kenneth Johnson's *V: The Original Miniseries*, *Lord of the Rings*, and the *Superman* films. Each of these fantastical universes inspired (or was inspired by) action figures, video games, tie-in novels, and Halloween costumes that people like me grew up with. I was not the only superfan these sagas produced, nor was I the only Italian American member of the Oregon Trail Generation to embrace them.

This habit of mine for keeping an eye out for Italian creators has drawn me to flesh out my personal canon of Italian American Speculative Fiction Creators a bit more in recent years. Obviously, the easiest and least difficult Italians to spot are the novelists. Among the most prominent is Mary Doria Russell, a Jewish Italian American with a background in both theology and anthropology, who has written science fiction, westerns, and a novel about the Copper Country strike of 1913–1914. *The Sparrow* (1997) and *Children of God* (1999) comprise her two-book speculative fiction saga about a disastrous interplanetary first-contact mission and the posttraumatic stress experienced by the possibly sole survivor of the expedition. The books, which provide her metaphorical commentary on both rape culture and the Arab-Israeli conflict, feature Italian Jesuit characters and take place in Italy and on an alien planet.

Some of the most fun novels published in recent years have included John Scalzi's satirical tributes to *Godzilla*, superhero comics, and *Star Trek*: *The Kaiju Preservation Society* (2022), *Starter Villain* (2023), and *Redshirts* (2012), the last of which won the 2013 Hugo Award for Best

Novel. While the titles of these books suggest that they are fannish and derivative, *Redshirts*, in particular, is a strangely beautiful meditation on death, fate, free will, and hope that mixes Italian fatalism and Catholic theology with *Star Trek* tropes and a postmodern, *Stranger than Fiction* concept. As I read the book and found myself weeping, I kept thinking: "This book is *so* Italian. I want to turn out to be related to Scalzi." I am glad that Scalzi's fame has grown in leaps and bounds in recent years. I also appreciate that he violates the usual Italian male stereotypes in his public life: Scalzi is a prominent political activist online, vocally supports feminist causes, and argues for the vital importance of the separation of church and state. Naturally, this means he has often been the target of ire from Gamergate-type internet trolls.

Whether or not they regard themselves as authentically Italian, novelists are easier to discuss as creator and storyteller figures than writers and directors on television shows and movies. A similar problem exists when examining the Marvel Universe. For example, while one might be more inclined to consider (the teensy-weensy bit Italian) Kevin Feige and the various (mostly non-Italian) scriptwriters of the Marvel movie and television shows the most influential architects of the Marvel *Cinematic* Universe, it did not escape me that Louis D'Esposito executive produced all those movies, Michael Giacchino wrote the main themes and music scores for several *Spider-Man*, *Doctor Strange*, and *Fantastic Four* films, or that the Russo Brothers—Anthony and Joseph Russo—did directorial work on two *Captain America* and multiple *Avengers* films. The first four of their Marvel films star the part-Italian actor Chris Evans as Captain America, a superhero who considers himself "just a kid from Brooklyn." Additionally, the first several Marvel movies featuring Tom Holland's Spider-Man costarred Marisa Tomei as Peter Parker's Aunt May and Jon Favreau as her boyfriend, Happy Hogan. And yet, as tempted as I am to laud the Italian contributions to the shaping of both the Marvel *Cinematic* Universe and the Marvel *Comics* Universe that inspired it, it is inescapably true that comic book artist Jack Kirby cocreated Captain America and the lion's share of the classic Marvel characters, and he's Jewish. Consequently, I fear I don't have any right *whatsoever* to try to "claim" Marvel for the Italians. (Besides, Kirby is awesome. Captain America is awesome. Neither *have to be Italian* to be awesome.)

Arguments that directors are the true auteurs of a motion picture notwithstanding, the producers, directors, and scriptwriters of several other prominent franchises are notably Italian. James DeMonaco is the creator of

Figure P.2. My personal collection of Italian Fantastika: Plays, novels, histories. *Source:* Courtesy of the author.

the *Purge* films and spinoff TV series. Michael Dante DiMartino collaborated with Bryan Konietzko to create the cartoon *Avatar: The Last Airbender* and its sequel, *The Legend of Korra*. Jack D. Ferraiolo produced, script-edited, and wrote the animated series *Amphibia* for Disney+. Finally, the *Star Wars* serials also made for Disney+, including *The Mandalorian, Andor*, and *Ashoka*, have been written and directed by three prominent Italians: Jon Favreau, Dave Filoni, and Tony Gilroy. (Baby Yoda = Italian created!)

The Purge is an oft-misunderstood—and ideologically appropriated—dystopian science fiction series about a future fascist America. The title holiday is a twenty-four-hour event in which all Americans are allowed to commit any crime, no matter how heinous, with total impunity. The Purge was designed to give white supremacists a free pass to rob, murder, rape, and torture members of more vulnerable immigrant and ethnic communities as part of a multiyear plan to recapture America for a white majority. DeMonaco was inspired to write the first film after watching the 1967 *Star Trek* episode "The Return of the Archons," in which an alien society had its own Purge, called "The Red Hour" and the time of "Festival." Not insignificantly, DeMonaco—a Staten Island native—revealed that the very first Purge was piloted on Staten Island, thanks to how balkanized the ethnic communities there are on the north shore and how volatile the racial relations are in New York City's forgotten borough. *The Purge* series is often criticized for being unsubtle in its political commentary, but I would argue it is being criticized disingenuously for its boldness in unapologetically calling out fascism in contemporary American culture.

As for the *Avatar* and *Legend of Korra* television shows, they are among the most beloved children's programming Millennials and Generation Z grew up consuming. These youths developed their ethical codes following the moral examples of Ang, Katara, Sokka, and Uncle Iroh, as well as rooting for the redemption of the tragic villain, Zuko of the Fire Nation. On the surface, merely a remake of *Star Wars* filtered through the lens of a culturally appropriated anime aesthetic, the two serials are surprisingly psychologically and politically sophisticated for cartoons marketed to children. The interest in the dynamics of family conflict, the deconstruction of toxic masculinity, the prominent roles of matriarchal characters, and the interest in spirituality all seem to have echoes in Italian culture and are prominent in episodes (co)written by DeMartino.

Also, the fact that *Star Wars* on television is now under the creative control of a triumvirate of Italians is a source of great pride for me, especially since *Andor* is intelligent, mature science fiction—as well as being *Star Wars* at its best—while *The Mandalorian* is a wildly entertaining outer-space Western indebted to the Japanese manga *Lone Wolf and Cub*. Best of all, as Anthony Lioi enthusiastically pointed out on my Facebook page the day after *Ashoka* premiered, "Natasha Liu Bordizzo who plays Sabine Wren is Italian and Chinese Australian!" I replied with something along the lines of "Booyah!"

Figure P.3. My personal collection of Italian Fantastika: Movies and Television Shows. *Source:* Courtesy of the author.

Television is a collaborative medium. So, too, are mainstream superhero comics by Marvel, DC, Dark Horse, Image, IDW, and Top Cow. Consequently, considering Italian "authorship" in comics becomes difficult if the Italian is the artist drawing a story credited to a non-Italian writer (or vice versa). Meanwhile, some comic book characters have completely invented names (like the Riddler's "real" name being E. Nigma, which is a pun, not a recognizably ethnic name). Despite these challenges, since childhood, I have remained on the lookout for Italian names among the comic storytellers and the fictional characters they shaped adventures for. Interestingly, a survey of Marvel's most famous fictional characters yields very few Italian results. Effectively, the Punisher and his archenemy Billy Russo (aka Jigsaw) are Marvel's only notable Italian characters. In sixth grade, I convinced myself to like the Punisher, because he was named Frank Castle (aka Francis Castiglione) and he made for a fun revenge fantasy figure for a while, as a precursor to John Wick or an echo of the most famous vengeful Italian family man of all: Michael Corleone. And yet, even before he became a favorite of militia members and fascist police officers in recent years, the Punisher lost his luster when I grasped the racist dimensions of the character. Like the Boondock Saints or Bernhard Goetz, the Punisher was symbolically a white supremacist (or a murderous ICE officer) disguised as a concerned citizen "tough on crime." And yet, I am compelled to acknowledge that the Netflix *Daredevil* and *Punisher* streaming serials—as well as their direct sequels on Disney+—strove to rehabilitate the character, making him more human and nobler. Indeed, an upcoming 2026 television special cowritten by Jon Bernthal (the actor who plays the MCU's Punisher) is rumored to involve the Punisher taking on fictional villains inspired by the real-life police who have co-opted his skull logo to make the unapologetic statement: Black Lives Don't Matter. In addition to this special, some of Frank Castiglione's most notable appearances on Netflix and Disney+ were written and produced by Dario Scardapane and Angela LaManna.

Outside of Marvel, Top Cow's *Witchblade* comic book is about Sara Magdalene Pezzini, a New York homicide detective who bonds with a magic, sentient gauntlet that grants her the powers she needs to combat supernatural evil. Debuting in 1995, she was cocreated by Top Cow founder Marc Silvestri and saw her comics adapted into a 2001 TV show starring Yancy Butler. The over-the-top sexiness of the character might occasion some chagrin and meditation on Laura Mulvey's views on scopophilia. And yet, feminist scholar JoAnne Ruvoli had intended to write a piece on Pezzini for me for this long-simmering project before she passed, suggesting that the *Witchblade* multimedia universe is worthy of future study. The DC Comics universe beats Marvel and Top Cow for Italian representation, albeit with predominantly Mafia-related characters. Cocreated by Joey

Figure P.4. Yancy Butler as Detective Sara Pezzini in the supernatural superhero TNT television series *Witchblade* (2001–2002), based on the Top Cow comic book by Marc Silvestri. Executive producers Dan Halsted and Ralph Hemecker. *Source: Witchblade*, Warner Bros. Television, 2001, publicity photo.

Cavalieri, Helena Bertinelli was a Mafia princess in the Batman universe who became the crime fighter known as the Huntress after being raped by a don and witnessing her family's slaughter at the hands of a rival crime organization. The somewhat similar character of Sofia Falcone—featured in the comic miniseries *Batman: The Long Halloween* (1996–1997)—played a central role in the Batman-themed HBO miniseries *Penguin* (2024). Cristin Milioti's electrifying performance as Sofia in *Penguin* was so compelling it garnered her a Primetime Emmy Award.

Figure P.5. Cristin Milioti as vengeful Mafia princess Sofia Falcone—dubbed "The Hangman" by Gotham City Press—in the HBO series *Penguin* (2024), a sequel to the 2022 movie *The Batman*. *Source: Penguin: The Complete Series*, HBO, 2025, publicity still.

A similar vengeful-Mafia-daughter backstory was appended to the classic Batman character Catwoman in 1999, making the former villain the most well-known and significant superhero from my background. As a kid who loved the vastly different versions of the Catwoman character depicted in the Adam West television series and *Batman Returns*, I had no reason to suspect that a character named "Selina Kyle" was Italian. She wasn't . . . *at the time*. Selina *became* Italian in a DC-universe-wide continuity "reboot." Frank Miller laid the groundwork for a potential revelation she was half-Black and half-Italian in *Batman: Year One* (1987). Jeph Loeb picked up where Miller left off and wrote *When in Rome* (2004), a miniseries that revealed the cat burglar and animal rights activist was the daughter of Maria Kyle and Gotham City gangster Carmine Falcone. Genevieve Valentine explored the ramifications of this revelation by making Selina heir apparent of the Calabrese crime family in *Keeper of the Castle* and *Inheritance* (2014–2015).

Catwoman's once-obscure Mafia origin story became widely known among movie audiences when Zoë Kravitz was cast as a half-Black, half-Italian Catwoman in *The Batman* (2022). The irksome gangster stereotypes these stories play upon are mitigated by their dramatic quality and the centrality of Selina to the Batman mythos. In Tom King's *Batman* comics, especially *Batman/Catwoman* (2022), readers discover that Selina and Bruce Wayne ultimately spend their lives together, have a daughter, and share a bond of love that transcends death and the collapsing walls between multiverses. Kravitz's iconic, multilayered Catwoman is at once derived from King's depiction of Kyle, draws upon the Italian roots Loeb

Figure P.6. Robert Pattinson as Batman and Zoë Kravitz as Catwoman in *The Batman* (2022). This film—like its direct sequel, the *Penguin* HBO series—is centrally important to anyone wanting to study depictions of Italian Americans in the Batman universe. *Source: The Batman*, Warner Bros., 2022, publicity still.

gave her, and simultaneously continues the longstanding tradition of Catwoman being played by Black actresses, most notably Eartha Kitt in 1969 and Halle Berry in 2004.

While not the household name Catwoman is, my favorite paisan superhero is Zatanna Zatara, a surprisingly powerful sorceress disguised as a leggy, fishnet-stocking-wearing Vegas stage magician who stars in eponymous miniseries, webcomics, and graphic novels, as well as the *Justice League Dark* and *The Books of Magic* comics. While Zatanna might be dismissed as a merely sexy figure, her snappy personality, big heart, and deployment of endlessly unique and peculiar spells against formidable and terrifying foes make her a captivating presence. Her being descended from Leonardo da Vinci is at once cliched and appropriate to the character.

The writer most associated with penning Zatanna's adventures for comics and cartoons is the Italian American who cocreated Harley Quinn and wrote many of the best episodes of *Batman: The Animated Series*: Paul Dini. Zatanna appeared in the *LEGO DC Comics Superheroes: The*

Figure P.7. Serinda Swan played Zatanna Zatara, a real sorceress "disguised" as a stage magician, in the WB and CW *Superman* prequel series *Smallville* (2001–2011). *Source:* "Zatanna." *Smallville*, Season 8, The CW Network, 2009, publicity still.

Flash video game (voiced by Kate Micucci), guest starred on the animated series *Justice League Unlimited*, and is featured in the *DC Super Hero Girls* (2019) animated series, a reboot of a property created by Shea Fontana. (IMHO: "Adventures in Bunnysitting" from *DC Super Hero Girls* is comedy gold.) In 2023, rumors surfaced that Halle Bailey was considering playing Zatanna in a feature film, a prospect exciting on its own, as well as in the door it opens to Giancarlo Esposito playing her father, Giovanni Zatara.

In addition to notable Italian fictional characters, the comic book industry boasts several highly respected Italian artists and writers. Perhaps the most influential of all these artists and editors is Carmine Infantino. In 1956, at the behest of DC editor Julius Schwartz—and with the assistance of writer Robert Kanigher—Infantino redesigned and relaunched *The Flash* comic book and its titular hero, ushering in a period of reinvention for the entire DC superhero universe. This period of rebirth brought superheroes back into prominence after an age of obscurity, giving birth to the Silver Age of Comics. Significantly, Infantino cocreated Black Canary, Barbara Gordon (Batgirl), Deadman, Human Target, and Elongated Man. Comics fans and historians alike consider Infantino's contributions to DC universe lore of incalculable import, so anyone interested in Italian American Fantastika and/or the intersection of Comics Studies and Italian American Studies should regard Infantino as a foundational figure.

Perhaps second only to Infantino in significance is Charlton Comics (1945–1986), the Italian American–spearheaded publishing company that introduced the superheroes Peacemaker, the Question, Captain Atom, Blue Beetle, and Liberty Belle to the world. Few comics historians or Ethnic Studies scholars seem aware that an Italian immigrant, John Santangelo Sr., cofounded Charlton, and that the company hired Italian American editors such as Dick Giordano, Al Fago, and Pat Masulli; Italian American writers such as Peter A Morisi; and Italian American artists such as Jim Aparo, Jon D'Agostino, Bill Fraccio, Rocco "Rocke" Mastroserio, Tony Tallarico, and Sal Trapani. After the company went bankrupt, many of these creators would later produce work for DC Comics and its superhero universe. DC also ensured the defunct Charlton's lasting legacy by acquiring the rights to all its characters and producing fresh adventures for them—especially Peacemaker, the Question, and Blue Beetle—to this day. (Also of note is the fact that Alan Moore famously satirized alternate reality versions of the Charlton superheroes in his classic DC/Vertigo miniseries *Watchmen*.)

I discovered all the above information about Charlton unexpectedly, while doing a manuscript review of the book *Peacemaker: Satirizing the*

American Machismo (Plus Helmet Lasers!) by Bryan J. Carr. I had no clue that Charlton was a hotbed of Italian Americans! Wanting to make sure there wasn't anything else super important that I didn't know, I asked Karen Green, Columbia University librarian and curator for comics and cartoons, if she knew of any other unsung Italian contributions to comic book history. Green informed me that her friend John Ficarra—who served as *MAD Magazine*'s editor-in-chief from 1985 to 2018—has long felt that Italian Americans were crucial to the development of the comics industry, and that they have not received the recognition they deserve from comics historians, critics, and fans.

While I only recently found out about Charlton and Ficarra, I've known about *ElfQuest* since fifth grade.

ElfQuest, an independently produced fantasy series, was written and drawn by a married couple—Wendy and Richard Pini. On October 1, 2021, I emailed Richard Pini, asked if he considered the comic book a work of "Italian Fantastika." In his November 5 reply, Pini explained he is an Italian American whose parents were born in the US and whose grandparents were born in Italy. Wendy, meanwhile, was adopted, so her heritage wasn't known for certain. Pini wrote, "To the best of our knowledge and recollection, there is no specific Italian influence in *ElfQuest*. We actually tried to stay away from the more traditional European styles of fantasy/fairytale in the crafting of *ElfQuest*, opting instead to focus on more Eastern and Native American storytelling ideas. There are also many fantasy tropes that we wanted to turn upside-down, so to speak."

Reflecting upon his email, I recalled noticing the Asian and Indigenous influences in both Wendy's manga-inspired artwork and in the Indigenous-reminiscent elements of the culture of the elven Wolfriders, the series' main protagonists. Nevertheless, a case can be made that those looking for Italian influences could find them in the serialized narrative written and drawn by the Pinis. Published as individual comic books between 1978 and 2020 and reprinted in the Dark Horse *Complete ElfQuest* omnibus collections, *ElfQuest* is a series that tells one complete story, like a soap opera. Throughout the series, *ElfQuest* frequently dealt with issues of diaspora, ethnic heritage, class conflict, and racism, while depicting the lives of the members of several, diverse elf tribes, living together as one extended family over several generations.

Even assuming I'm overstating how "Italian" *ElfQuest* "feels" as a narrative, Richard Pini remains an Italian American cocreator of what is widely regarded as one of the greatest American comic books ever published. The stories he cocreated with Wendy expressed staunch, unequivocal solidarity with indigenous peoples worldwide and presented a worldview informed by feminist, pacifist, multicultural, egalitarian, and environmentalist sensibilities. Since Hollywood is terrible at adapting properties that express such progressive values without dumbing them down into action films, it is perhaps best that, thus far, *ElfQuest* is not burdened by an unfaithful adaptation that distorts its message. Still, since there is no high-profile animated streaming series based on it yet, I take every opportunity to urge non-comics readers interested in first-rate, progressive storytelling to read *ElfQuest*.

Richard Pini was only the first of many prominent comic book writers and artists I realized were Italian, but who were never (to my knowledge) closely examined by scholars associated with the Italian American Studies Association. John Buscema drew *The Fantastic Four*, *Silver Surfer*, and *Conan the Barbarian*. David Mazzucchelli drew two of the most acclaimed 1980s superhero stories—*Batman: Year One* and *Daredevil: Born Again* (both written by Frank Miller). Two of the most memorable *Spider-Man* writers have been Tom De Falco and J. M. DeMatteis, and three of the most iconic and prolific *Spider-Man* artists have been John Romita, John Romita Jr., and Sal Buscema. A fourth Italian *Spider-Man* artist, Sara Pichelli, is notable for having cocreated Miles Morales with Brian Michael Bendis in 2011.

In addition, Harley Quinn, arguably the most beloved DC universe antihero, was cocreated by Paul Dini and Bruce Timm for *Batman: The Animated Series*. She debuted in the 1992 episode "Joker's Favor."

Finally, one of the most acclaimed and enduring creator-owned comics series of the past forty years has been *Hellboy*, written and drawn by Mike Mignola. The series, about a sympathetic half-demon often pitted against supernatural menaces, inspired several spinoff comics (such as *B.P.R.D.*), as well as a number of live-action and animated adaptations, including two films directed by Guillermo del Toro (a renowned Mexican filmmaker who has more than once made movies based on "Italian/American Fantastika" intellectual properties). Whether one focuses solely on his work creating the *Hellboy* universe, or on all his other artistic contributions to comics, Mignola himself is an iconic figure. He possesses one of the most recognizable artistic styles in comics history, and fandom and comics scholars alike regard Mignola as a creative titan.

Turning back to more mainstream superhero comics, J. M. DeMatteis is widely considered one of the best writers of *Spider-Man* comics of all time, especially thanks to *Spider-Man: Kraven's Last Hunt* (1987). He is also one of the most prolific *Spider-Man* writers, having written many gothic, psychologically rich, and family-centric stories that strongly influenced the portrayals of Norman and Harry Osborne in the Sam Raimi *Spider-Man* film trilogy. In general, DeMatteis bestowed more compelling personalities and backstories to all of Spider-Man's major villains, greatly influencing each of the SONY *Spider-Man* universe films. The Brooklyn native raised by Jewish and Roman Catholic parents also reinvented Aunt May as a wise matriarchal figure instead of the senile albatross around Peter Parker's neck she had been for decades. In addition to his genre work, DeMatteis should be of interest to members of IASA—and anyone interested in Italian American enculturation narratives and coming-of-age stories—thanks to his graphic memoir *Brooklyn Dreams* (1994).

Figure P.8. My personal collection of Italian Fantastika: Comic Books. *Source:* Courtesy of the author.

As I began serious work on this project, I emailed DeMatteis, telling him that I looked up to him as an Italian role model and superb writer of *Spider-Man*, *Batman*, and *Justice League* adventures, both for comic books and multiple animated series adaptations (including *Justice League Unlimited* and *Batman: Caped Crusader*). I told him about this book and asked him if he minded my describing him as a writer of "Italian Fantastika." He replied on November 1, 2021: "I don't think you're off-base at all. The truth is, you can put a lot of screens over any particular work—religious, ethnic, cultural, sociological, political, spiritual, whatever—and come up with illuminating insights relating to the author of the work and his/her relationship to a particular screen. What's interesting about Spider-Man is that all the spider-writers I know, regardless of our backgrounds, relate to Peter Parker in a deeply personal way: he somehow reflects our roots and we in turn filter him through those roots and put ourselves into the character and his world. He truly is a universal Everyman."

And that is true. Spider-Man, like all superheroes, belongs to a vast array of fans. Belongs to the world, in fact. Not every fan likes Spider-Man first and foremost for his Italian writers and artists, nor is everyone who loves Catwoman drawn to her because of an ethnicity the character did not even have *for the first sixty-five years of her existence*. Nevertheless, I cannot help but be glad for these Italians, especially since they would be compelling fictional characters even if they weren't viewed through my ethnic-obsessed eyes.

Having spent decades hand-wringing over my relationship with my Italian identity and the state of my relations with my own people, including writing and publishing more than one book about it, I now feel far better than I once did. I still have my issues—primarily with how Italians worldwide vote too frequently for Berlusconi-like folks I can't abide—and I'm sure I'm not alone. In fact, I know others have not come as far as I have in reckoning with their Italian identities. Certainly, I know I'm not the only one to whom Italian representation is important. Considering this, some of you may be very interested in consulting a mammoth list of Italian Fantastika creators and artifacts I have developed over the decades. An eternal work in progress, its most complete possible iteration has been placed as the appendix of this book. I will wager that the canon of "Italian Fantastika" is far more expansive than many of you will expect it to be.

I've long believed that it is reasonable for scholars of Italian American literature, film, and comics to craft and comment upon a canon of global Italian speculative fiction. To my mind, Italian American speculative fiction storytellers working across media in both literary and popular forms have often wrestled with "traditional" Italian themes of family, genealogy, diaspora, fascism versus anti-fascism, cross-cultural solidarity in the face of oppression, competing definitions of Italian culture and identity, and the preservation of Italian culture and identity. As such, these texts should be of interest to scholars of the literature of the Italian diaspora. However, they are often not recognized as Italian texts for a variety of reasons. Perhaps they seem to eschew the urban/rural "family life realism" of the iconic Italian narrative. Maybe the author does not self-identify as "Italian" in interviews and does not carry any stereotypical markers that make them easy to identify anyway. Or maybe that Fantastika narrative was crafted for a collaborative medium—and some of the "cooks" in the creative kitchen were not Italian—muddying their legitimacy as artifacts of Italian/American Fantastika. These various challenges notwithstanding, Italian/American works of speculative fiction are worthy of study, either for their inherent value as great art or their appropriateness as fascinating artifacts of "trash culture." They are also worthy of study for what they told us about Italian American identity . . . and what they tell us about intercultural communication and solidarity.

This book is designed to start us off on this journey.

What Is at Stake for Me in My Quest to Build a Canon of Italian American Fantastika?

Why did I want to create this book? Why did I ask Anthony to join me as coeditor? Why did I invite so many others to contribute essays to this project?

Well, I begin all my academic projects hoping that working on them will help me come to terms with seemingly unsolvable twenty-first-century problems, making my scholarship as autobiographical and personal as it is intellectual and sociological. I've written and edited books about climate change, 9/11, and Catholicism because those topics were all sources of anxiety for me, and I'd rather confront my demons head-on than flee from them. The origins of this Italian Fantastika project go as far back as my childhood when I had difficulty understanding what my mom meant when she said we were "Italian." I did not grow up in an Italian enclave in Brooklyn as she had, I had won over no Italian friends, and our extended family had dispersed across the five boroughs of New York

City, with only a few relocating to Staten Island with us. The problem of my identity crisis was compounded when the only Italians I came across on TV and in the movies appeared to be thugs. Was this the great home country heritage my mom wanted to preserve? Joe Pesci asked "How am I funny?" and killing people unexpectedly when his hair-trigger temper was triggered? All I knew was I loved the pasta and the opera. I wasn't sure about the rest because I wasn't clear on what constituted "the rest." And when I found out that some of "the rest" encompassed the polar opposite legacies of both the appallingly racist Frank Rizzo and the civil rights–era hero Viola Liuzzo, I was left still more confused and ambivalent.

For these reasons, I have always been especially drawn to Peter Falk as Lieutenant Columbo, Sylvester Stallone as Rocky, and Linda Cardellini and James Franco as the main protagonists of *Freaks and Geeks*. However, I must confess to feeling a hunger for more ethnic Italian representation beyond these few standouts among a huge swath of cinematic and literary gangsters, racists, wife-beaters, and schoolyard bullies. The better made the movie or television show featuring Italian villains and anti-heroes, the harder it was to convince myself that a grotesque parade of toxic masculine evil—ranging from Tony Soprano to the pizzeria owners in *Do the Right Thing*—was *not* the alpha and omega of what it means to be an Italian male. Indeed, 007 himself has argued that there really *isn't* anything more to Italian Americans than being brutish gangsters. In *Diamonds Are Forever* (1956), James Bond acidly observes: "There's nothing extraordinary about American gangsters . . . They're not Americans. Mostly a lot of Italian bums. . . . greaseballs who filled themselves up with pizza pie and beer all week and on Saturdays knocked off a garage or drug store so as to pay their way at the races."

The gangster stereotype bothers me less these days, and I can admit to liking Mario Puzo's *Godfather* better than *The Fortunate Pilgrim*. Still, even now, I feel a modicum of pride whenever I come across an example of realistic-yet-positive Italian representation anywhere (like in *Two Family House*, *King of Staten Island*, and *True Love*—plus the less-positive-but-hilarious *Big Fan*), but most especially in speculative fiction, a genre I have always loved. To this day, I wonder just how excited I might feel if *Star Trek* ever introduced an Italian captain as a central protagonist. I would probably do as many backflips as I did when I first laid eyes upon Scottish Italian actor Peter Capaldi playing my all-time favorite science fiction character, the Doctor from *Doctor Who*. Boy, do I love Peter Capaldi! (He has a cool rock album called *St. Christopher*, too!)

Figure P.9. Peter Capaldi was the first actor of Italian descent to play the Time Lord known as the Doctor on the venerable BBC science fiction series *Doctor Who*. His tenure as the Doctor stretched from 2013 to 2017. Born in Glasgow and part Scottish and Irish, Capaldi's paternal grandfather was Italian. *Source: Doctor Who*, BBC, 2014, publicity still.

While some of my efforts have been more fruitful than others, I remain invested in finding Italians in fantastical genres to this day. As the deeply problematic Bruno Bettelheim compellingly argued, children need the potential of a happy ending, and a little bit of whimsy, in the stories they immerse themselves in during their formative years to develop a healthy psyche. I looked to science fiction, fantasy, and horror for models of Italian success instead of destruction. Amusingly, as much as I enjoy attempting to locate fellow Italians in the media so that I don't feel so existentially lonely in my ethnicity, I must own to not being very good at settling upon the genuine article. As a child, I spent years assuming the Marx Brothers were Italian because their first names ended in vowels and Chico kept claiming to be Italian. My youth excuses this error, but I have also, more recently than I'd like to admit, mistaken Sam Raimi, George A. Romero, and Josh Segarra (who played the amiable, liberal lawyer Augustus "Pug" Pugliese on the *She-Hulk* Disney+ series) as Italian cousins of mine. (Good Lord! At the very least, I should have recalled that Óscar Romero was from El Salvador.) On the flip side, I assumed that Michael Cera of *Barbie* and *Scott Pilgrim* fame was not Italian when he is, in fact,

Italian Canadian. I also should have placed more trust in the efficacy of my inner "paisan detector" when it beeped each time I caught sight of Jon Favreau, Chris Evans, and Steve Carell in a movie. In my defense, it often is hard to correctly identify Italians because I'm usually going on people's names, looking out for olive skin tones, and extrapolating—often reading a presence into a site of erasure or absence. Indeed, one of the reasons it is important for a book like this to examine representations of Italians in art and popular media is the outsized influence films and television play in shaping perceptions of who "counts" as Italian and who does not. If someone does not have a name ending in a vowel or olive skin, do they not meet the definition of "authentic Italian"? And to what degree does popular culture dictate who and who isn't a bona fide Italian, both for cultural outsiders and in-group members as well? (In this manner, Stanley Tucci's CNN series *Searching for Italy* did yeoman work celebrating the diversity of the Italian people, not just in terms of regionalism but religious and cultural backgrounds, ethnicity, foods they contributed to the country, and so on. The thesis of his series, in defiance of the Italian fascists, was that Italy was always a diverse region.)

Another interesting conundrum arises when I feel enthusiastic about having correctly identified a person of Italian immigrant descent who does not self-identify as Italian. Am I doing this person a disservice by focusing my attention on an "Italianness" they do not value or feel truly a part of? Paolo Bacigalupi, author of *The Windup Girl*, has distanced himself from his heritage. In 2010, he said, "Well, I'm not Italian. . . . I'm so watered down that I've got no legitimate claim to the culture, despite the name." Naturally, the man is fully within his right not to self-identify as Italian. Still, I couldn't help but be disappointed when I read these words, just as my mother and I were both (comically) irked years ago when David Caruso declared himself not Italian with great gusto.

In recent years, I have been heartened by my realization that more and more compelling Italian characters appear in mainstream entertainment every day, ranging from the hilarious, prima donna footballer Zava in the instant comedy classic *Ted Lasso* to the transparently fictionalized versions of Nicolas Cage and Madonna featured in the borderline-Fantastika *The Unbearable Weight of Massive Talent* and *Weird: The Al Yankovic Story* (both 2022). On the other hand, there are still notable missed opportunities in which Italian characters are irritatingly played by transparently not-Italian actors in stories that otherwise pride themselves on their racial and ethnic authenticity, like *Air* (2023) and *Ms. Marvel* (2022). Of course, *Ms. Marvel* is a superhero masterpiece, and Iman Vellani a national treasure. Still, in the Disney+ series, an American actor of British and German heritage, Matt Lintz, plays Kamala Khan's (boy)friend, Bruno Carrelli. In both the comic books and television adaptation, Bruno is a bighearted STEM genius and superhero fanboy. However, in the comic book, Bruno is olive-skinned and more obviously an Italian Catholic, and Kamala's devout Muslim brother warns Bruno never to try to date her. My question is: Why must the most ethnic-looking, recognizably Italian actors in Hollywood be relegated to Mafia casting calls? Can't a STEM genius look a little Roman-nosed just once? Or maybe I'm whining over something minor, and whining doesn't become me . . .

Admittedly, my uneasiness critiquing the aesthetically and culturally laudable *Ms. Marvel* in defense of the importance of proper ethnic white representation reminds me of the obvious pitfalls of writing anything whatsoever related to the field of Italian American Studies. In my insistence on maintaining the importance of my Italian identity—and Italian representation in fantastical fiction—I am trying to thread a needle that is nigh-impossible to thread. In these pages, I want to simultaneously forestall and oppose anyone's effort to: 1) bleach my ethnicity out of me to make me "more white" (no thanks), 2) claim that my rejoicing in my Italian cultural heritage is analogous to white nationalism (it isn't), 3) claim that Italian Americans have achieved "full" whiteness and been fully integrated into mainstream American society (we haven't), 4) obfuscate the role Italians have often played historically in assisting racists in their war against people of color (it has been notoriously sizeable), and 5) claim that the prejudice and persecution Italian Americans have faced in the past—or even the present—is even remotely analogous to the sufferings, past and present, of BIPOC people (they're not).

Despite these pitfalls, this is not only a conversation worth having, but a socially urgent one. Beyond my own, personal concerns, ethnic white representation is appropriate in stories set in the present day because Italians—like other ethnic white groups—still exist in the present, and it matters in science fiction sagas like *Star Trek* because utopia should not be achieved via amalgamation into Anglo-Protestant whiteness.

Still more vitally, I would argue that how ethnic whites of all stripes are represented in mass culture in the twenty-first century carries a particular urgency, as members of those groups have grown discontent and radicalized living under the stages of late capitalism. Indeed, I feel great concern about the homogenizing of ethnic white culture—a process that seems to be occurring almost in tandem with an alarming global rise in white nationalism. While correlation does not imply causation, I know that both recent phenomena anger and terrify me and inform my desire to publish this book. I also know that, while I am writing this introduction and coediting this book to bury Caesar, not praise him, I know for a fact that most Italian Americans I know (who are not academics) would prefer to do the reverse: praise Caesar, not bury him. Of course, it isn't inevitable that the majority of Italians worldwide will pledge lifelong allegiance to authoritarianism and white supremacy. After all, Italians invented or perfected both fascism *and* anti-fascism. Also, Italian Americans are an important part of America's suburban swing vote in elections, making them laudably not ideologues—even as their swings sometimes scare the creamy ricotta cheese filling out of me. When they swing with me, I am reassured that I am one with my people. When they swing against me, I begin to fear, once again, that I'm a "fake Italian." I shouldn't, but I do.

Now, I should admit to you that I am always a little self-conscious about how much my "Italianness" means to me, especially because this "soft" nationalism of mine has often bemused some of my academic colleagues. Since I'm a fourth-generation immigrant, my interest in my heritage is seen by them as unusual in a member of Generation X and far more common in Baby Boomers. They must find it particularly odd that I tend to announce my Italianness the instant I meet someone new, beating out vegans in their famed eagerness to self-identify to new acquaintances. In one memorable conversation, a philosophy professor said to me: "I can't relate. I just consider myself an American. I don't think of myself as 'German' or 'German American.'"

I might not have said anything, but his bafflement was just *slightly* too pronounced. I replied, "Dude, your PhD is in Nietzsche, your favorite music is Wagner's Ring Cycle, you're dating a German national, you have a second home in Bielefeld, and you love knackwurst!"

He blinked several times. "I'm not sure I understand what you are saying."

I like this man and don't want to condemn him or teased him too much, especially since he is not alone in finding my perspective peculiar. (I have had some variant of this conversation at least fifty times.) As I contemplate moments such as these, I am troubled by two thoughts: 1) The word "American" in this context arguably acts as a socially acceptable substitute for "white" and 2) Italian Americans tend to be perceived as "less white" than German, Polish, and Irish Americans, but "whiter" than those identified as BIPOC. I am, of course, not the first to have such thoughts, not just in academia but mass culture. For example, stand-up comedian Mike Vecchione explained that "the Italians are the bottom rung of white," and are best understood as "off-white." Italian Americans exist in a liminal space between racial identities. They also exist in a liminal space between Italy and America. And what should we call ourselves? Italian-Americans? Italian Americans? Italian/Americans? Haven't a damn clue, myself. Why? Because Italian Americans are not "purely" any of the above. (For those interested in a more scholarly intervention in such concepts, the academic books *Are Italians White?*, *White on Arrival*, and *The Ethnic Myth* are excellent places to begin.)

In many ways, this liminal space is an advantageous place to be in twenty-first-century America. Certainly, controversial figures such as Joe Rogan and Luigi Mangione have a populist appeal that stems directly from their being neither Black nor WASP, freemasons nor Black Panthers, aristocrats nor Jacobins. Their role as "neither/nors" positions them as "reasonable" and "everymen"—even as they are being unreasonable and their behavior falls far outside social norms. And so, both Rogan and Mangione have passionate support from fans who stand in awe of these men's brand of Italian American machismo and physicality. Whether either figure deserves such devotion is beyond the scope of what I want to say here. (Besides, public perceptions rarely make sense and invariably collapse into nonsense upon serious scrutiny, so I'd rather not spend too much time trying to come to logical conclusions about the cultural cache of either man.) Even as a not-famous academic writer, I enjoy a small modicum of the Rogan and Mangione "neither/nor" cultural status. And so, in my teaching and writing, I hoped to use that positioning to be a "good ally" who causes "good trouble." Even as I do so, I also (counterintuitively?) hoped to employ my positioning between "white" and "not-white" to stake out a position as an "honest broker" teacher-scholar attempting to mediate the American culture wars, employing logic, language, and concepts that potentially appeal to multiple audiences and stakeholders. Of course, reader, if you refute the notion that this neither/nor liminality exists in the first place, I respect your opinion. A strong case can be made that I'm dead wrong about all of this "white/not-white" stuff, and I may very well be. I wouldn't be surprised if I were wrong, as it is an emotionally fraught, morally gray, and intellectually complex question: "Are Italians white?"

Another element of the controversy that complicates the question of "Are Italian Americans white?" is "Who gets to 'count' as an Italian

American?" Notably, Italian Americans who try to "pass" as white establishment figures while still identifying as Italian are sometimes vulnerable to teasing, since "ethnic police" sometimes criticize people who aren't sufficiently Italian for attempting to claim a heritage when they do not speak Italian. Concerns about my own ethnic authenticity led to my writing a roman à clef called *Fake Italian: An 83% True Autobiography with Pseudonyms and Some Tall Tales* (2021). Such anxieties seem common among third- and fourth-generation Italian immigrants. Comedian Mike Birbiglia describes himself as not Italian enough to pronounce his surname with a silent *g*, said he probably should be declared an "Olive Garden Italian." Indeed, Italians from Italy and Americans from other ethnic groups might tease Italian Americans trying to hold on to an ethnicity lost over generations. Sometimes I'm even inclined to believe that Indian American author Jhumpa Lahiri—who moved to Italy in 2012, published her Italian-language novel *Dove mi trovo* in 2018, and edited and translated forty Italian stories into the compilation *The Penguin Book of Italian Short Stories*—can make a far stronger claim to being a "real" Italian than I ever could.

I grasp the concept that East Coast Italian Americans can be perceived as "white" because they are less exotic than immigrant communities that have arrived more recently. They are also often placed in positions of authority over these vulnerable populations and use their power more often to mistreat members of these communities instead of aid them. This is broadly and stereotypically speaking. However, some particularly notorious Italian Americans have done far worse than that. For example, I'd understand anyone angrily calling me out for splitting hairs about whether Frank Rizzo and Samuel Alito are "white" or "off-white." In their cases *in particular*, even I must own that the question of whether Rizzo and Alito are "white" or "off-white" seems like a distinction without a difference. After all, when one considers that Rizzo and Alito, irrespective of their degree of whiteness, accrued enough political power to destroy real lives and radically undermine human rights and civil liberties through their reactionary beliefs and actions . . . who really cares which one was a whiter shade of pale?

Even allowing that vitally important point to stand unchallenged, a case can still be made that the lingering disreputableness of Italian Americans—the iconic "morons from New Jersey" we see on all those reality shows that *must be true* because they're *reality* shows—has real consequences in the real world. And the more we move our vantage point from the coastal states to the "flyover states," the less valued Italian

Americans are by the mainstream community because there simply aren't a lot of them. While most of my Italian American relatives lament the high taxes and multiculturalism of the Blue States they feel themselves trapped in—and are inappropriately jealous of Oklahoma's far-right-wing governor, Kevin Stitt—they have no idea how Italians are regarded in Red States (even if they briefly flirted with owning second homes in Florida or North Carolina). In New Jersey, Italians can see themselves as members of the nouveau riche or a modern American variant of the landed gentry, and they can angrily identify the greatest crisis facing modern America as being "wokeness" and believe it wholeheartedly. In contrast, in places like Oklahoma, Italians know they are considered mafiosi, dirty immigrants, and papists. These Red State Italians know damn well that "wokeness" ain't nothing compared to dominionism or Project 2025. Certainly, I know from personal experience that an Italian living in the Midwest is invariably considered swarthier than an Italian living on Long Island (Krebs, OK, and Tontitown, AR, notwithstanding).

In the first episode of the Paramount+ series *Tulsa King*, New York gangster Dwight Manfredi (Sylvester Stallone) arrives in Oklahoma for the first time and one of the state's large grasshoppers lands on him in greeting. Startled, Manfredi lets fly a filthy exclamation, scandalizing a religious local who tosses holy water at him to ward him away. This scene is not something that literally happened to me on my first day in Oklahoma—and I'm not a gangster—but it is certainly emblematic of many of my interactions with Oklahoma's native insect life and Baby Boomer dominionists. It certainly didn't take long for it to sink in that many white conservative Christian groups in Oklahoma have a troubling tendency to believe that Roman Catholics are as destined to be relegated to the same afterlife Hell as atheists, Jews, Muslims, Native Americans, African Americans, LGBTQ individuals, public school teachers, pharmacists, and "Satan-worshiping" Democrats. (And folks destined for Hell *really* shouldn't have American citizenship or the right to vote, they think.) Having been placed on the same Oklahoma Republican enemies lists as all the aforementioned, I now feel far greater solidarity with these figures than many of my Italian American relatives from New York and New Jersey, who focus more on what differentiates Italians from the kinds of folks Fox News commentators spend 24/7 railing against than they do on what unites us in our gradations of cultural and socioeconomic vulnerabilities.

Certainly, I had difficulty "blending in" to the highly Caucasian rural part of western Oklahoma I lived in between 2009 and 2024. The first week I moved there, a local barber blurted out: "You don't belong in Oklahoma! With that nose, you must be Jewish or Italian! What are you?" She was not the only one to make me feel like I stuck out like a sore thumb during my extended tenure in the Sooner State. Still, I found it difficult to call out such microaggressions in fear of making a tempest in a teacup—especially since I knew intuitively that I faced these slights far less frequently than any woman would have to, as well as any male swarthier or browner than myself. Still, moments like these have taught me that Italians can pretend not to be marked by "difference" only depending on the context.

During my Oklahoma years, I was "othered" by white people *frequently* and by nonwhite people *very rarely*. Those disappointing, rare instances notwithstanding, I found I had far more in common with Oklahoma Native Americans, Black Americans, and Latinx Americans than the white, southern Baptists who dominate all aspects of life in Oklahoma. It was with Oklahoma's multiracial community that I found acceptance, friendship, and solidarity.

Hence my impatience with any Italian rhetoric that is hostile to indigenous Americans, and my general state of despair anytime Columbus Day swings around.

(My God, I hate debates about Columbus Day. I particularly hate how easily "centrist" politicians who want to ban clean drinking water, close all public schools and libraries for good, legalize child labor, end workplace safety regulations, "cure" LGBTQ individuals, and bring back the Confederacy can garner 100 percent support from some Italian Americans with one angry sentence: "Do you know what them durned Injun activists said about Columbus *this year*?" Or maybe these centrists said something positive like: "Not enough people love Mother Cabrini." While some Italians I know swoon at such sentiments, I prefer to yell at the television: "Lieutenant Columbo is cooler than Columbus! And keep Mother Cabrini's name out your ******* mouth!" IMHO: The Italian swing vote shouldn't be purchased so cheaply. It should be worth more than these two annually trotted-out sentiments. We should be wiser than Pavlov's dog.)

Hence my joy at Martin Scorsese and Robert DeNiro choosing to advocate for indigenous rights by making the film *Killers of the Flower Moon*. I've never been prouder of these filmmakers as men, artists, activists, and *Italians*. Also, their short time in Oklahoma–added my few, valued Okie Italian friends and the brief presence of Stallone–made me feel less culturally alone. (Although I hear Stallone tends to vote for those "centrists" I just complained about.)

So, who gets to be a "real" American, anyway? Because that is *the* American question of the twenty-first century.

Here, I will discuss the two texts that most help me answer that question in a manner relevant to this project. The first is *Speculative Whiteness: Science Fiction and the Alt-Right* (2024) by Jordan S. Carroll. The second is *A Different Mirror: A History of Multicultural America* (1993) by Ronald Takaki.

As Carroll writes in *Speculative Whiteness*, one of the core constituencies of the MAGA movement is the iconic/stereotypical virginal suburban otaku who, driven by dread of the Great Replacement conspiracy theory, has relentlessly campaigned online for the purging of all "Diversity, Equity, and Inclusion" (DEI) elements from long-running science fiction franchises created by hippies and hippie sympathizers in the 1960s and 1970s, including *Star Trek*, *Star Wars*, the Marvel superhero universe, and *Doctor Who*. Expertly presenting themselves as enemies of groupthink, cancel culture, and "political correctness run amok"—instead of as what they truly are—misogynistic, white supremacist fan movements like GamerGate and the Sad Puppies have worked tirelessly to warp all science fiction into becoming as masculinist and militaristic as the *Call of Duty* video games. Their relentless social media bullying of women and people of color who write and star in the most recent iterations of more-than-a-half-century-old multimedia franchises may or may not come with an awareness of the fact that the franchises did not suddenly become "woke" in the post-Obama era but have been left-leaning all along. Indeed, leftist science fiction writers and fans are nothing new, and not just among franchise writers' rooms. A case in point is the Futurians, a collective of communist science fiction authors active from 1937 to 1945.

Of course, fascists who weaponize the science fiction genre against women, socialists, and BIPOC populations are not a recent phenomenon, either. Carroll reveals they have predecessors in the Animists, America's first major Neo-Nazi party, founded in 1946 by science fiction fan James H. Madole. According to Carroll, Madole's contemporary equivalents have embraced Ayn Rand's *Atlas Shrugged* (1957) as a roadmap for how society *should* develop. These fascist futurists believe that humanity must sacrifice its subaltern populations on the altar of social Darwinism for the good of the gene pool, in both fictional universes and the real world.

Thanks to their fears of "reverse colonization," alt-right fandom dreads that, without their efforts, white society would inevitably fall to hordes of zombies or insectoid alien invaders (which are transparently alarmist metaphors demonizing immigrants and beneficiaries of a well-funded public sector). The fascist alternative to these apocalyptic scenarios is for white populations to take a cue from the 2014 film *Interstellar*, abandon the Earth to multiculturalism and climate catastrophe, and take "white flight" to the stars. Given their aspirations to create uniformly white space colonies (in both fiction and reality), it should be no surprise that reactionary sci-fi fandom has found kindred spirits in the ascendant "tech broligarchs" of the 2020s and thrown its full support behind Elon Musk's privatized space program.

The final chapter of *Speculative Whiteness* explores how the first election of Trump inspired an appalled progressive public to seek solace and revolutionary inspiration in rediscovered genre classics by Octavia Butler, Margaret Atwood, and Ursula K. Le Guin, as well as in newly published works written in opposition to Trump, such as Jemisin's *The City We Became* (2020); P. Djèlí Clark's *Ring Shout* (2020), Gene Luen Yang's *Superman Smashes the Klan* (2019), and the queer science fiction erotica of Chuck Tingle. These authors helped preserve science fiction as a site of progressive imagination. Jemisin, for one, far eclipsed the popularity of all the modern, Sad Puppy–endorsed novelists writing in the tradition of Rand, Robert A. Heinlein, Larry Niven, Jerry Pournelle, Ward Kendall, and C. M. Kornbluth.

Carroll concludes his monograph by warning that right-wing science fiction fans endure, continuing to craft speculative roadmaps to a white supremacist, paramilitary utopia in both fiction and reality—essentially, hoping to found the United States of the Proud Boys. He concludes that those of us interested in forging a more perfect destiny for *all* people should strive to remove the limits placed upon our progressive imaginations by speculative whiteness.

I would issue a hearty "Amen," here, but my enthusiasm for the sentiment is tempered by my knowledge that *most* Italian Americans I know personally—if given the opportunity—would prefer to try to get in on the all-white space empire plan instead of allying with those who would seek to thwart it or make it more inclusive. I understand why, even if I vehemently disagree. If nothing else, it is easier to punch down than to punch up. Still, those Italian Americans who are confident that white supremacist futurists will consider Italians "white enough" to include them in any white flight to the stars are almost certainly deluding themselves. Based on my own lifetime of experiences being forced to interact with an alarming number of white supremacists from New York, New Jersey, Pennsylvania, Oklahoma, and Utah, I am certain that, when the moment of truth arrived, *we would not be considered white enough*. In fact, even if we were "promised" a seat on Spaceship Noah's Ark by silver-tongued fascist politicians and scientists—in exchange for our Machiavellian cooperation violently escorting all the "uninvited" off the launchpad—we ourselves would be expelled from the ship mere moments before liftoff. And so, we would be Left Behind on a dying Earth with all the rest of the undesirably off-white and nonwhite resource drains. (Let's face it: Any DOGE-mindset efficiency expert would assert that leaving Italians behind on Earth to die would be the "fiscally responsible" thing to do.) Compounding this disaster, our fellow racially diverse survivors on Earth would know full well that we had actively helped to seal their fate before poetic justice condemned us to share that fate with them. We would be left friendless in a hostile world and would reap what we had sown.

There you have it: the speculative future I imagine facing white supremacist Italian Americans.

It isn't pretty.

All these thoughts lead me to conclude that twenty-first-century Italian Americans urgently need to rethink our own roles and social positions in modern America. Furthermore, it behooves us all to strive to better understand our own pasts. Certainly, Italian Americans should cultivate a better understanding of how the Italian immigrant experience fits into the full sweep of American history. Here I am grateful to Tracy Floreani, author of *Fifties Ethnicities: The Ethnic Novel and Mass Culture at Midcentury* (2014), for creating the "United We Stand: Where We Come Together" reading list for the Oklahoma Humanities program Let's Talk About It. The texts my Okie Italian friend chose for the community book club fostered empathy among and between all the different cultures, races, and ethnicities found in the United States. The most mind-opening text she brought to the attention of the reading group (of which I was a part) was by Ronald Takaki. It is the second of the two texts I want to discuss in these pages.

In her essay introducing the Let's Talk About It reading list to participants, Floreani explained her rationale for assigning Takaki: "One of the most important ways we broaden our sense of the shared space of this continent is through a deeper study of its history. When we don't know *what we don't know* about our own shared, everyday histories—beyond the biographies of presidents and the familiar stories of major wars, technological advances, and movements—how can we make space for one another as belonging equally in this nation?"[1] For Floreani, Takaki's *A Different Mirror* helped broaden readers' minds by presenting "familiar histories newly woven together." At her urging, I read Takaki's book in 2023 and was astounded by the impression it made upon me. And so, I agree wholeheartedly with Floreani's assertion that Takaki's book may be read today as more culturally relevant than ever, despite its 1993 publication date.

In *A Different Mirror*, Takaki paints a sweeping portrait of the ad hoc migrations of diverse populations to the United States driven primarily by the greed of monied interests unwilling to offer their workers basic freedoms or living wages in the New World. Each time workers already based in the United States threatened to join forces and demand better working conditions, higher wages, and release from either indentured servitude, slavery, or wage slavery, the land and business owners would lure a new population of workers in from overseas specifically to break up the solidarity of the current group of immigrants. These workers would be from a different race than their current workers and would, with luck, feel even more "foreign" to the current workers. Consequently, the businessmen frustrated worker efforts at egalitarian unity and anti-establishment agitation by placing cultural and linguistic barriers between coworkers from different racial and ethnic groups. They would also exacerbate the situation by stoking rivalries over which ethnic group gets to fill the highest number of job postings, pumping nativist propaganda into the press and onto the streets, and making sure that no new laws were passed that rewarded once-disenfranchised workers with a path to citizenship after they "paid their dues" for a generation or five. Laws promoting slavery and explicitly banning Asian Americans from ever being granted citizenship were key elements of these legislative efforts to keep the workers down. Similarly, contemporary efforts to make sure that no serious immigration reform passes today dovetail with widespread election and cable news campaigns calculated to demonize Black, Mexican, and Muslim immigrants, refugees, and migrant workers. After all, why would anyone want to empathize with or go on strike with recent immigrants after hearing rumors they're "eating the dogs and eating the cats"?

However, Takaki noted that some progress has been made. As the generations passed, some new populations did improve their lot in

America, and a diverse America created for cynical reasons became a culturally rich and varied society. Occasional efforts at union organizing and striking raised the wages of members of different ethnic and working communities. Former aliens won certain civic freedoms and saw their own people win positions in local government. Public schools educated their children about the American ideals found in the Constitution that Thomas Jefferson believed in principle, if not in practice.

Takaki expertly offers the histories of all vulnerable peoples together and does not fall into the trap of trying to figure out who had things best and who suffered most. They were all victimized to one degree or another, and all need to stand together today, or they will always fail to secure all the rights to life, liberty, and the pursuit of happiness owed to them. Takaki is not alone in painting this kind of history of America, and narratives such as the John Sayles film *Matewan* (1987) and the Lynn Nottage play *Sweat* (2015) tell a similar story. Reading this book was eye-opening for me because it made me understand that, while Irish, Italian, and Jewish Americans may have gotten farther along in their efforts to become "real" Americans by looking more like their wealthy bosses—if, occasionally, with a more olive complexion—there will always be that dividing line between ethnic whites and whites. That line will remain in place so long as it remains profitable for it to remain in place. Remember, it is a truth universally acknowledged that all bosses prefer cut-rate, nonunion workers to union employees, precisely because they're cheaper. Also, as Kareem Abdul-Jabbar and Anna Waterhouse observed in their 2015 novel *Mycroft Holmes*, all bosses would *far* rather have slaves for workers than cut-rate, nonunion employees because nothing is cheaper than *free*. (And, bosses tirelessly search for wily ways to never pay any employee—or any taxes—because they're *smart.*)

Tolerance and full citizenship cost corporations wide profit margins and arbitrage opportunities. Consequently, every time Italian Americans feel safe and secure in their "almost white" position nationally and use their standing on a slightly higher status plateau to kick down at their nonwhite immigrant neighbors and fellow citizens, they are playing into the hands of centuries of robber barons who divide and conquer today, just as much as they divided and conquered centuries ago. These Italian Americans are also forgetting their people once occupied a lower rung than they do now. Reading and contemplating Takaki's expansive, multicultural history can help prevent Italian Americans (*myself included*) from developing a tunnel vision that makes them a little too quick to mourn the landmark historical moments of Italian oppression—such as the Triangle Shirtwaist Factory fire, the 1891 New Orleans lynchings, and the convictions of Nicola Sacco and Bartolomeo Vanzetti—while counterintuitively using those tragedies as an excuse *not to feel empathy for the historical oppression of marginalized groups who suffered demonstrably more than we did*. Takaki concludes his study by noting that, inevitably, we will all become ethnic minorities in America and finally forge a genuine democracy based upon mutual respect. Theoretically, the more diverse America becomes, the easier it will be for nonwealthy Americans to unite politically across racial lines and to rejoice in their cultures and differences, even as they offer respect, tolerance, empathy, and love to people from all racial, ethnic, and cultural backgrounds. What stands in the way of this potentially utopian future? The same wealthy business interests have always stood against freedom and justice for the American masses. Hence their continual efforts, to this day, to defund public education, pass anti-union laws, disenfranchise voters, and steal the remaining indigenous lands and hand them over to the fossil fuel industry to devastate. If it were up to these bosses, no member of any ethnic group would *ever* achieve full citizenship or rights and opportunities equal to those enjoyed by the wealthy, white, Protestant, male elite; significantly, that includes ethnic whites as well as BIPOC Americans.

And this is why I bang my head against the wall when one of these iconic businessmen runs for political office and most of my relations vote for that individual.

At such moments, I keep asking myself: "If we enthusiastically root for the heroes of Tarantino's 2012 epic *Django Unchained*, played by Jamie Foxx and Christoph Waltz, while watching the film and then, on election day, vote for the candidates who talk and act exactly like the villains, played by Leonardo DiCaprio and Samuel L. Jackson, are we "laudably not ideologues," or are we just deeply confused about which side we would have fought on had we been alive during the first American Civil War? Or whether we would prefer to live in New York or Oklahoma today? I remain astonished that many Italian Americans seem to have such difficulty answering these questions consistently, or the way I would. Personally, I would have fought for the North. Also, having lived in both New York and Oklahoma, it is no contest for me. Oklahoma has essentially become a blend of a Southern Baptist Iran and the world of *Mad Max: Fury Road*. No, thanks. Mayor Eric Adams may suck, but I'd choose New York every time.

Of course, today is not forever, and the one constant in life is change, so I live in hope that the Italian American swing vote may one day . . . fingers crossed . . . swing once again in a direction I consider humane.

Such topical notions aside . . .

Throughout my life, have I hoped that one day I would feel that I, my family, and all Italians living in America had finally become "real Americans," like Pinocchio being elevated to "real boy" status. Yes. Of course. I have the same hopes for *everyone*.

But how would I be able to recognize the exact cultural moment when we Italians had finally "arrived" as bona fide Americans? Or, at least, when we've earned enough respect from the broader American populace to be known for more than just the gangster stereotype?

Dunno.

Perhaps when an Italian finally got to sit in the dang captain's chair of the ultimate ship of state: the USS *Enterprise*.

Note

1. See Tracey Floreani's introductory essay prior to the reading list for the reading group Let's Talk About It at https://www.okhumanities.org/doccenter/6d608b5827df4c55b0e32bd14ce2c74c.

Introduction

"Is Italian American Speculative Fiction a Thing?"

Marc DiPaolo

This essay, like this book, began life with the panel "Is Italian American Speculative Fiction a Thing?" at the John D. Calandra Italian American Institute's November 2021 conference, which included me, Anthony Lioi, and Lisa DeTora. The panel grew out of my lifelong quest to find Italians who play a role in my favorite storytelling genres: horror, science fiction, and fantasy. I have always sought out fellow Italians who craft such narratives for films, novels, comic books, and television shows. Similarly, I always hope to discover Italian characters represented in these narratives, whatever medium they may be found in. This has always been true, and I rejoice when I immerse myself in these found artifacts of "Italian/American Fantastika," whether I am watching an Italian horror film like *Suspiria* or an episode of the science fiction television series *Star Trek* scripted by Italian American Dorothy Fontana. I also glean a childlike, ethnic pride from reading an Italian horror comic book like *Dylan Dog*, or an Italian American science fiction novel like *Redshirts* by John Scalzi.

All the preceding are artifacts of "Fantastika": a useful term that describes my favorite genre narratives. Admittedly, a potential drawback of employing this term to stake out the scope of this scholarly anthology is that it has not yet achieved enough popularity to be considered an example of "the parlance of our time" by Maude Lebowski. Also, "Fantastika" doesn't seem like a word one might logically expect to find playing a central role in a text about Italianità (Italianness). Nevertheless, it remains the best possible term for us to employ in this book, and it has enough intellectual cache that *The Encyclopedia of Science Fiction* (https://sf-encyclopedia.com/entry/fantastika) includes a salient entry on "Fantastika":

> A convenient shorthand term employed and promoted by John Clute since 2007 to describe the armamentarium of the fantastic in literature as a whole, encompassing science fiction, Fantasy, fantastic horror and their various subgenres. . . . The term does not so much attempt to define a "super-genre" as to designate a field of awareness. To speak of Fantastika is to evoke a heuristic device. It is a framing concept normally restricted to narratives, with a focus on the procreative jostle of their interactions within a nest—within a palimpsest of nests through time—of other stories. . . . Many examples of eighteenth-century literature, including Gothic tales in general, and in particular the German Schauerroman (i.e., "shudder novel"), clearly prophesy the flood of transgressively non-realist work to come; as do the Carceri depicted in Giovanni Battista Piranesi's *Invenzioni Capric di Carceri* [*Fanciful Images of Prisons*] (1745). . . . [W]here "realism" is seen as inadequate to the task of seeing the world . . . the transgressiveness of Fantastika can also be conceived as an expression of *ostranenie* . . . a term which might usefully be defined as an uncanny defamiliarizing or estranging of a literary utterance so that the depicted world can be perceived in astonishment and wonder.

My own, casual definition of "Fantastika" amounts to "any cultural artifact with potential or actual appeal to cult fandom or devotees of 'Geek culture.' "

Several primary and secondary sources wrestle with issues of intersections between ethnic identity and Fantastika. Scholars of multiethnic American literature and lifelong fans of speculative fiction have written acclaimed books about seeking representation in the media they consume. Frederick Luis Aldama's Eisner Award–winning monograph *Latinx Superheroes in Mainstream Comics* (2017) is a well-reasoned, encyclopedic survey of Latinx superheroes while being a deeply personal document. Adilifu Nama's *Super Black: American Pop Culture and Black Superheroes* (2011), while more measured in tone, emanates from a place of pain inaccessible to white ethnic groups. In addition, respected literary figures have written about immigrant figures who embrace horror, science fiction, and fantasy

Figure I.1. These academic books, from my personal library, are among the few texts that deal with specific examples of Italian Fantastika but focus on the Gothic and the horrific, often targeting one medium or subgenre. *Source:* Courtesy of the author.

fandom as a means of coming to terms with the multigenerational process of American enculturation. Intriguingly, these writers are also united in using speculative fiction as a vehicle for voicing disgust with the dictatorial and fascist forces their immigrant parents had fled, suggested that "Fantastika" is far less reactionary at its core than it is often assumed to be. Books that have critical passages if not entire subplots and plots dedicated to immigrants, refugees, enslaved peoples, and children of immigrants and freemen consciously comparing themselves to aliens, superheroes, and vampires include *The Gilda Stories* (1991) by Jewelle Gomez, *The Amazing Adventures of Kavalier & Clay* (2000) by Michael Chabon, *The Fortress of Solitude* (2003) by Jonathan Lethem, *The Brief Wondrous Life of Oscar Wao* (2007) by Junot Diaz, *Brother, I'm Dying* (2007, 117) by Edwidge Danticat, *Binti* (2015) by Nnedi Okorafor, and *Severance* (2018) by Ling Ma, as well as multiple works by Silvia Moreno-Garcia and Charles Yu. A British equivalent is Claire Khoda's *Woman, Eating* (2022).

Italian/American Fantastika is respectfully inspired by these and similar works. It concerns how Fantastika by Italian artists worldwide provides models for rethinking and refashioning what it means to be Italian in the twenty-first century. Consequently, a formal definition of "Italian" will prove to be as conditional and elusive in these opening pages as "Fantastika." The business of this anthology is to wrestle with both terms alone, and in conjunction.

Since I have a personal stake in this book—and am admittedly biased no matter how intellectual my approach—I do not trust myself to grapple with these complex issues on my own. Yes, as both an Italian and a scholar, I believe I have valuable points to make about Italian American "whiteness." On the other hand, like Jack Kerouac, "I have nothing to offer anybody except my own confusion." That is why this book is an anthology with a coeditor and a wide variety of contributors coming at these issues from multiple angles and disciplines instead of a single-author monograph. To cite one example, my coeditor, Anthony Lioi, offers the kind of in-depth analysis of the position Italians occupy in American society that lies beyond the scope of my introduction. Lioi opens his discussion of the representation of Italian Americans in the television series *Heroes* with this thoughtful and timely passage:

> The field of Italian American Studies has been occupied with the history and artistic representation of immigration to the United States and its aftermath. While this work is invaluable, it has obscured the current status of Italian Americans as white and middle class. To be white and middle class is judged, in art and scholarship, as less interesting, like a red sauce without enough oregano. This coding of the assimilated condition as less worthy of study has had the effect of obscuring our race and class privileges at a moment when the politics of ethnic resentment rises again in a new American authoritarianism. It

> is now crucial that future scholarship attend to the whiteness of our lives and art. I see the contemporary superhero narrative as a promising terrain for the examination of the social power of the white professional middle class. . . . Though [the superhero television series] *Heroes* features an Italian family that achieved whiteness in the United States, this is not to deny the possibility of Italian/Americans who are multiracial or other than white. On the American side, Kym Ragusa's important book *The Skin Between Us* grapples with her Black-and-Italian identity. On the Italian side, there is a growing literature by and about African Italians, not to speak of the Roman, Moorish, Greek, Norman, and Arab heritage of Southern and Insular Italy. In other parts of the diaspora, such as Brazil, Argentina, Canada, and Australia, Italian immigrants entered racial and ethnic matrices distinct from that of the United States. This analysis focuses on achieved American whiteness precisely because of its presumed but insufficiently examined hegemonic status. (20–21)

Like Lioi, most of the scholars involved in this collection are building upon the body of scholarly work surrounding Italian American whiteness, enculturation, immigration, race, and economics begun by Thomas A. Guglielmo, Jennifer Guglielmo, Salvatore Salerno, Stephen Steinberg, Alfred Lubrano, and David R. Roediger. They marry such scholarship to other foundational secondary sources on genre fiction, fandom, media studies, and other, related fields. Throughout these pages, the collective of essays adds to the discussion that Lioi begins.

These essays do not fit seamlessly together because they are intentionally diverse and present an array of views on what it means to be Italian and how Fantastika can help us consider that question anew today. The topics covered in the essays in this anthology are varied, as are the academic fields the writers come from, and their cultural origins and relationship to Italianità. This book includes an essay by a Canadian descended from Italian immigrants who writes about an Italian Canadian author. In these pages, you will also find works by and about mainland Italians, Italian Americans, and Italians living in Australia, as well as by and about mixed-heritage Italians (including a half-Haitian and half-Italian contributor). Among the essayists and their subjects are those who buck the stereotype of Italian American immigrants as being default "Opus Dei" Roman Catholic (or "Dorothy Day" Roman Catholic) by embracing

Buddhism, Wicca, atheism, or other faith traditions. The book also includes essays by and about LGBTQ Italians from around the world. Meanwhile, some essays examine Italians who have embraced authoritarian political regimes worldwide, and others concern Antifa Italians. (As a brief aside, I am intrigued by how often witches play a role in essays about both fascist and anti-fascist forces. The witch looms large in multiple narratives covered in this anthology, alternatively, as a figure demonized by fascist propagandists and subversive revolutionary figures sympathetically portrayed in "Antifa Fantastika.")

Between the contributors and their subjects, *Italian/American Fantastika* presents readers with a transnational view of Italianità, featuring real and fictional Italians varied by generation, geographic location, religious and political affiliations, gender identity, sexual orientation, and mixed heritages—among other differences. Considering them all, I am uncomfortable proposing a definition of what constitutes a "real" Italian, even as a convenient academic definition I can employ conditionally because the dictates of the conventions of the academic introduction demand such a definition. Well, I refuse. (This conclusion should not surprise anyone, considering I am the person who wrote the autobiographical novel *Fake Italian*.) I will not provide a concrete answer to the query: "What is an Italian?" Instead, I will leave each of our contributors to wrestle with "what it means to be Italian" in their own personal and intellectual ways. Since the essayists featured in this book will come to their own, individual conclusions concerning how to define both "Italian" and "Fantastika," any definition of either that I might propose in this introduction would be conditional. That is why I will use this introduction to open the discussion of many possible, legitimate ways of defining both the broadly defined ethnic identity and the broadly defined narrative genre.

Speaking of broadening the playing field . . . as a field, Italian American Studies has spent a lot of time discussing a small number of texts. There is significant value in having a set of shared texts, but it is also important to engage with new cultural artifacts. The essays in this book help to grow and develop this field. They also bring several new voices into the conversation who have not previously contributed Italian/American and Italian Diasporic Studies. This essay collection's broad understanding of Italian Diasporic Studies and widening of the canon of Italian/American humanities comes largely from the hard work of our contributors, who have ably assisted Anthony and me in our efforts to widen the canon of texts that have, thus far, constituted primary sources in Italian/American and Italian Diasporic Studies.

As near as Anthony and I can tell, no other book engages Italian American (or Italian diasporic) Fantastika in an extended way. Some books engage Italian American Studies / Italian Diasporic Studies and cultural production—including films, literature, and popular culture—but few examine genre works specifically—including fantasy, horror, science fiction, superhero, or high adventure narratives. Since this is a new approach, Anthony and I made a point of including essays by scholars from an eclectic array of fields, including art history, comics studies, film studies, communication, language and literature, and more.

Also, to produce a book that could be appreciated by scholarly and more casual readers at once, as well as genre buffs and undergraduates alike, Anthony and I invited contributors to adopt multiple writing styles. The preface, for example, is essentially a work of creative nonfiction, and even this introduction has a more personal tone than most academic book introductions. You will find that the essay on Dante and genre fiction toward the middle of this book is an unusually elaborate blog-style post. Meanwhile, the closing essay on Dorothy Fontana is both a television industry history and a biographical sketch. Other selections from this anthology read more like traditional academic essays, close-readings of primary texts, or theoretical treatises. Consequently, any varieties of writing style, signs of code-switching, or surprising divergence in essay length found in the following pieces are an intended feature of this collection, not a bug. Be prepared, and please read with an open mind and patience for a kaleidoscope of intellectual approaches and writing styles.

This book is broken into three parts, each containing multiple essays exploring a shared theme. "Part 1: Defining a Field" includes essays that introduce the concept of "Italian Fantastika," explained why it is worth studying, and offer a sense of the international scope of the project by bringing Canadian Italians into the conversation. "Part 2: Case Studies in Italy's Fantasies, Futurisms, and Gothic Horror" takes us back to mainland Italy, offering close readings of some of the science fiction, fantasy, and horror texts Italy is most renowned for producing, including representative *giallo* thriller and horror films; *fumetti* (aka comic books) that are Edgar Allan Poe adaptations and iconic pirate adventures, as well as dystopian science fiction paperbacks ranging from the classic to the obscure. These texts depict the cultural anxieties of the Italian homeland—multimedia nightmares in green, white, and red.

Moving from what Mark Edmondson would categorize as "the gothic" to "the transcendentalist," and from cultural dreads to social aspirations, the third collection of essays is called "Reimagining Italian America:

Artifacts of Anti-fascist and Ecofeminist Fantastika." The essays in this section cover some of the most recognizable narratives produced in North America, many of which have not been widely recognized as ethnically Italian. Each of the narrative artifacts dissected by our scholars depicts a world in which Italians have eschewed far-right-wing ideologies and, instead, found ways of "being Italian" more in tune with the radical political and religious heritage of late nineteenth- and early twentieth-century Italian emigres to the United States. Among these texts are Madonna's environmentalist music videos, a young adult science fiction novel with surprisingly feminist themes, and an animated Netflix adaptation of Carlo Collodi's classic novel *Pinocchio*.

Let us now take a closer look at the essays contained in each section.

The opening essay of "Part 1: Defining a Field" is by coeditor Anthony Lioi. In "Mutants in La Merica: The Whiteness of the Petrellis in NBC's *Heroes*," Lioi writes that Italian Americans may only understand their place in contemporary narratives of race, gender, and class by grappling with representations of white ethnic protagonists after assimilation and upward mobility. For Lioi, the Petrelli brothers in NBC's superhero drama *Heroes* (2006–2010) reveal the intersection of whiteness, professional middle-class status, and American masculinity at a moment when Italians in the United States have achieved whiteness. One brother is coded through his powers of empathy as more feminine than Mafia masculinity allows Italian men to be. The other is more traditionally butch in his attraction to power but is not corrupt or abusive. Both are heroes who save the world. But in overcoming stereotypes of Italian masculinity, the Petrellis gain the ability to be foregrounded and privileged as white, middle-class protagonists surrounded by a multiethnic supporting cast. Italian American viewers invested in positive representations of Italians on television may see these characters as progress beyond the *gavone* but have to account for the Petrellis' capacity to be truly white heroes. In an age when superhero stories dominate the box office and debates about diversity and inclusion, the idea of an Italian American superhero cannot evade our judgment.

Contributor Alec Follett wrote the second essay, "Robots, Witches, and *Paisani*: Settler Colonialism Systems and Intercultural Relation Building in Indigenous and Italian Canadian Fantastic Literature." Follett considers the possibility of greater solidarity between Italians living in Canada and the indigenous peoples of that same country, noting that science fiction, fantasy, and horror allow relation builders the imaginative latitude needed to address questions of settler colonialism. To develop the critical understanding of the anti-colonial potential of the fantastic, especially as it pertains to Indigenous-Italian diasporic relations, Follett's chapter places Italian Canadian author Terri Favro into conversation with Métis writer Cherie Dimaline. Favro and Dimaline each interrogate how settler colonialism aims to either integrate or exclude nonindigenous others and both authors gesture to the ways that the Italian diaspora, and other settlers, might begin to extract self and community from settler systems and build more ethical relationships across cultures and with the land. This chapter first turns to Dimaline's *VenCo* (2023), in which a coven of world-saving witches is attacked by an immortal Friulian witch hunter (or *benandanti*). *VenCo* makes legible how the violent system of settler colonialism became entrenched because its purported benefits allure would-be settlers. The chapter then turns to Favro's *The Sisters Sputnik* (2022), in which a multiverse-hopping comic book artist fights a racist artificial intelligence that tries to send certain people back to their place and era of origin. *The Sisters Sputnik* shows how settler colonialism excludes undesirable others. After considering how settler colonialism variously includes or excludes the nonindigenous other, the chapter brings both novels together by focusing on moments that gesture to more relational ways of being. According to Follett, Dimaline and Favro use the fantastic to underscore that "the other" is an ever-changing category, and to gesture toward more ethical forms of social organization.

The third essay is "Vampires, Metaphysics, and Italian American Identity in Abel Ferrara's *The Addiction*," by Ciro Incoronato. Throughout his career, Abel Ferrara has often focused on theological issues, such as guilt and sin. From *Bad Lieutenant* (1992) to *Padre Pio* (2022), the Italian American director has afforded a unique philosophical perspective on the relationship between humans and God, as well as on the Catholic conception of life and death. In this essay, Incoronato argues that Ferrara's *The Addiction* (1995), written by Nicholas St. John, holds a special place among his "metaphysical" films. While dwelling on the existential doubts of an NYU philosophy graduate student, Ferrara invites viewers to reflect on the evolution of Italian American identity in the era of multinational capitalism. Through a deconstruction of the philosophical references contained in several scenes of the film, Incoronato shows that *The Addiction*—a postmodern pastiche that blends different genres reinventing the notion of "vampire movie"—examines the religious cornerstones of the Italian American community that in the early 1990s was undergoing major transformations.

The second grouping of essays focuses on art produced from within Italy itself: "Case Studies in Italy's Fantasies, Futurisms, and Gothic Horror." In these Fantastika narratives, Italians consider their country's role in the international community using the gothic genres of horror, *giallo*, and dystopian science fiction as the forum for this exploration. As Italians positioned within the homeland, they look out upon the Italian diaspora and contemplate it through multimedia genre fiction. This section begins with "An Italian Nightmare: Gianni Montanari's *La sepoltura* between Dystopia and Science Fiction." In this essay, Umberto Rossi excavates a long-lost artifact of Italian Fantastika, demonstrating that studying obscure dystopian narratives produced in Italy can yield valuable cultural studies, fruit as fascinating and important to contemplate as studies of Fantastika genre staples such as *Pinocchio*, *Dylan Dog*, and Dante's *Divine Comedy*. Published only once in 1972, never reprinted, never translated into another language, and rarely mentioned in histories of Italian science fiction, *La sepoltura* (in English: *The Burial*) is a lost text. When an Italian expat goes back to his country, he finds it changed by two events: a leftist uprising that was brutally repressed by the army and police, and a pseudo-pandemic that endows people with uncontrollable psi powers. Anyone can suddenly turn into a *mentale* and find themselves hunted by the police, killed, or taken to concentration camps and lobotomized so their powers are neutralized. The novel gradually makes it clear that the protagonist's mother underwent a compulsory neurosurgery that killed her, and that the deadly surgery was performed by his father. A revenge novel with Oedipal complex overtones, *The Burial* is a bleak, haunting read. It is also an anamorphic representation of Italy in one of its darkest periods, the "leaden years" (1969–1982), when the country seemed on the verge of civil war or a coup d'état à la Pinochet. The novel is also an interesting experiment of genre hybridization, merging dystopia and with subgenres about mutant, superpowered psychics, inspired by A. E. van Vogt's *Slan* (1941) as well as literary classics such as Albert Camus's *The Plague* and Elio Vittorini's *Uomini e no*.

The next essay is "Fascism and Pheromones: Futurist Fantasies of Domination in Bruce Sterling's *Fantascienza*" by William Q. Malcuit. With his alter ego of Bruno Argento and longstanding residency in Turin, the American science fiction writer Bruce Sterling has been using Italian settings to imagine alternative histories and futures. This chapter argues that his novella *Pirate Utopia* presents the uncomfortable idea that the most characteristic political mode of our modern world is fascism—and that if we want to understand how that mode works, we need to return to its origins on the Italian peninsula.

Next in this collection of scholarly essays, Cristian Soler contributed "Italians of the Caribbean: Piracy and History in Salgari, Sabatini, and Pratt's Adventure Narratives." Soler considers how nineteenth- and twentieth-century Italian authors depicted the Golden Age of Piracy to recreate a previous time—the seventeenth and eighteenth centuries—and visit a "foreign" space in the Caribbean. These narratives include Salgari's *Il corsaro nero* (1898), Sabatini's *Captain Blood: His Odyssey* (1922), and Pratt's *Corto Maltese: Sous le signe du Capricorne* (1970) to analyze how these texts create a fantastic history of piracy. According to Soler, the idea of the Caribbean attracted the imaginations of all these authors, even though its reality was mostly unknown to them. Soler illustrates how these authors turned the pirates of the Caribbean into romantic figures, whose crimes and exploits represented a turning away from conventional social norms and a (sometimes anti-colonialist) quest for freedom. The over-the-top quality of these graphic adventure narratives is akin to the escapist yarns found in the not-always-supernatural pulp adventures of *Weird Tales* magazine and are not unlike Robert Louis Stevenson's works of heroic fiction; they seem simultaneously plausible and absurdist, threatening the delicate balance of the reader's willing suspension of disbelief.

The infamous cult crime and horror subgenre of *giallo* is the focus of Fernando Gabriel Pagnoni Berns's essay "Genealogies of Horror: Dario Argento's *Do You Like Hitchcock?* Or, Reading National Horror Against the Local." Like Mario Bava, Dario Argento is one of the fathers of *giallo*, and he produced some of the most famous Italian thriller and horror films ever made, including *The Bird with the Crystal Plumage* (1970), *Deep Red* (1975), and *Suspiria* (1977). The Italian cycle of *giallo* (most prominent in the 1970s and 1980s) has been conceptualized as a response to Italy's shift from being primarily an agricultural country to a modern, cosmopolitan geography thanks to the economic aid of the Marshall Plan. Mikel Koven (2006) identifies this cosmopolitanism with violent impulses, and these feelings are tied to the anxieties brought by the encroaching modernity in postwar Italy. Yet, even if tapping into social and cultural anxieties regarding the modernization of Italy, the *giallo* was not entirely vernacular but the result of a transnational flux. Argento's often overlooked TV horror film *Do You Like Hitchcock?* plays with the genealogies of the genre, tracing how audiovisual horror is not (and never was) circumscribed to a nation but is a reinterpretation of previous global narratives.

Davide Carnevale examines Italian graphic adaptations of the gothic prose fiction of American Romanticism in " 'That Ghastly Whiteness': Dino Battaglia Adapts Poe and Melville to Comics." During the last period of his career, Battaglia strove to retain the ambiguities inherent in the short fiction of Edgar Allan Poe in his illustrated versions of classic stories such as "The Fall of the House of Usher." According to Carnevale, the Venetian artist used formal and representative technical strategies to re-create in the language of comics the disquieting inexplicability that made his drawn stories authentic works of Italian Fantastika.

What follows is an "Interlude" that lands between the second and third groupings of essays. The interlude was conceived to manage reader expectations of one of the more unusual entries in this collection: an extended blog post written by Dominique Musorrafiti and Matteo Damiani, curators of the *Weird Italy* web resource. On a site they aptly describe as "Unveiling the Unusual and Amazing Places in Italy," Musorrafiti and Damiani cover the ethnic Italian angle on topics as diverse as witchcraft, folklore, arcane art and architecture, and films, comics, and works of literature based in the genres of horror, science fiction, and fantasy. I stumbled upon the *Weird Italy* site while spending months compiling a list of all the Fantastika primary texts I had been studying my whole life, both formally and informally. To make sure my list was as complete as possible for inclusion in this collection, I wrote to these bloggers asking for their assistance and sent them an in-progress Microsoft Word file. Instead of merely advising me and making a small handful of suggestions, Musorrafiti and Damiani took the initiative and tripled the list in size, writing down subjects I already knew about but had forgotten to include, as well as adding dozens of Fantastika topics and themes I had never heard of. Consequently, I cocredited them with the authorship of this exhaustive list, which is published as the appendix to *Italian/American Fantastika* under the title: "The Canon of Speculative Fiction of the Italian Diaspora."

After Musorrafiti, Damiani, and I completed work on this exhaustive canonical list, I asked my two collaborators to draw upon the knowledge they'd acquired blogging articles for *Weird Italy* to describe what they saw as the roots of Italian Fantastika, and to consider the possibility that Dante played a central role in its development. A few months later, they submitted: "Dante and Italian Genre Fiction." Since it is written in a more journalistic style than the previous, scholarly essays in this collection, "Dante and Italian Genre Fiction" is presented in the form of an interlude, which acts as the bridge between a section of essays on Italian horror tales and Italian American science fiction tales. The placement is apt, because Musorrafiti and Damiani show how Dante's long reach not only covers all of mainland Italy but is international in scope and has left its impression on most fantastic works that have followed through the generations.

After this interlude follows the third section of essays: "Reimagining Italian America: Artifacts of Anti-fascist and Ecofeminist Fantastika." This section begins with Lisa Marie Paolucci's " 'The Ocean Inside Her': C. L. Herman's *The Drowning Summer* as Italian American Young Adult Speculative Fiction." Paolucci offers a close reading of a novel about a bisexual Italian American teenager who works to ultimately reach a state of self-actualization and creative agency by integrating various elements of her identity—including being a powerful medium that can speak to the dead. With a focus on sustainable fashion, environmentalism, familial relationships, and bisexuality, the novel provides a powerful site for analysis of Italian American women's identity development. Through the unexpected site of speculative fiction, *The Drowning Summer* (2022) allows Paolucci to build upon previous Italian American feminist scholarship regarding a woman's quest for agency as a central literary theme.

" 'True Blue' Humanities: Madonna's EcoFantastika" is Drago Momcilovic's essay about the pop star Madonna Ciccone. Despite her career-long emphasis on autobiographical themes, her Italian ancestry, and her explorations of eroticism and sexuality, Madonna has innovated new representational languages within the music video format that reflect not only her status as a music icon but also her awareness of and responsibility to a world rapidly transformed by climate change, ecological degradation, and natural disaster. Momcilovic offers close readings of the Madonna music videos that use conventions associated with magical realism and the fantastic in ways that foreground both the changing environment and our problematic responses to those changes. In this way, Madonna—a music video artist of the MTV generation—emerges in the twenty-first century as one of the foremost and most unlikely artists of Italian ecoFantastika.

Danel Olson's contribution to this anthology is entitled "Guillermo del Toro's *Pinocchio:* Reconceptualizing Italia, Italian Americans, and Fantastika." In the world's treasury of impossible tales, Pinocchio has a well-deserved reputation for pestering everyone—rich and poor, powerful and vulnerable—with the question of "why" things are as they are. That hunger for a reason behind unfair realities resembles the first Italian American generation's agitation for redress, representation, unions, fairer pay, and an end to discrimination. This chapter shows how the impulse of first-generation Italian Americans toward American economic, political, social, ethnic, and racial equality, along with their attempts to propel the country through progressive politics, made a needed positive difference for America. However, a sharply revanchist turn among giant Italian American figures of our day working as judges, mayors, presidential advisors, and immigration officials has decreased power for the people. Olson argues that some of the most prominent Italian Americans among the second- to fourth-generations in the United States have lost the Pinocchio instinct of their forebears to afflict the comfortable and comfort the afflicted. These contemporary officials long for an imagined golden past instead of championing an equitable, just, and inclusive future. In contrast, the Oscar-winning filmmaker Guillermo del Toro brought out the subversive subtext of the adventures of this iconic wooden boy in his animated adaptation of *Pinocchio*, a film by someone who is not Italian but who, nevertheless, has the potential to remind modern Italian Americans of what they have forgotten: being a proud Italian and a religious Roman Catholic does not necessitate embracing fascism.

The book closes with tales of two Dorothys—Dorothy Bryant and Dorothy Fontana—related by Victoria Tomasulo and myself. Victoria Tomasulo's contribution to this collection is "Race and Italian/American Identity in Dorothy Bryant's *Miss Giardino* and *The Kin of Ata Are Waiting For You*." In this essay, Tomasulo compares Dorothy Bryant's speculative novel *The Kin of Ata Are Waiting for You*, with her realistic novel about an Italian/American schoolteacher, *Miss Giardino*, arguing that the former genre permitted a more expansive critique of whiteness while highlighting cross-cultural affinities between Italian and African diasporas. In *The Kin of Ata*, Bryant creates a powerful counterstory to the Columbus myth that enabled Italian Americans to stake a claim in the national narrative. After driving off a cliff to escape his accidental murder of his girlfriend, a self-centered male writer from Los Angeles travels to an imaginary island called Ata, whose inhabitants take care of each other and whose culture revolves around dreams. While he initially suspects they are harboring gold and meets their kindness with violence, over time he is converted by Augustine and Salvatore, the spiritual ringleaders of the island who are endowed with specific markers of race and ethnicity. Through their alliance as dreamwork practitioners, Bryant imagines a loving and cooperative partnership between members of African and Italian diasporas that enables racial reconciliation and healing from the evil effects of global capitalism.

The collection proper closes with my essay: "Dorothy Fontana: The New Jersey 'Secretary' Who Cocreated *Star Trek*." According to myth, Gene Roddenberry created *Star Trek*. Industry histories complicate this narrative, crediting a creative collective that included Roddenberry's secretary, D. C. Fontana. Notably, the volatile, real-life relationship between Roddenberry and the female protégé he eventually felt overshadowed by is surprisingly like the fictional dynamic between Don Draper and Peggy Olson in *Mad Men*. Noting that "family is sacred," Fontana denied writing autobiographical scripts, but she did write teleplays concerning single mothers, absent father figures, and estranged or orphaned children that appear to be inspired by her own father's abandoning her family when she was ten. A writer of utopian feminist science fiction for mass audiences, Fontana supported unions over union busting and gave an Emmy-winning writing opportunity to a Native American scriptwriter instead of seeking to silence unruly indigenous voices. Consequently, Fontana justifiably deserves inclusion in the feminist project of recovering Italian American women writers spearheaded by Helen Barolini and Mary Jo Bona.

The appendix, providing an encyclopedic list of creators and artifacts of Italian Fantastika, follows, as does biographical sketches of the coeditors and the contributors to this volume.

In these pages, you will find literary studies, film studies, comics studies, cultural studies, and Italian Diasporic Studies essays, as well as those that employ historical, anthropological, ecofeminist, and critical race theory approaches to interpreting primary and secondary sources. The authors of these essays also adopt a variety of authorial voices and tones, with some writing traditional scholarly essays, some building personal anecdotes and observations more overtly into the thread of their arguments, and others blending the objective and subjective in their writing. Whatever their approaches, the contributors to this volume wrestle with intersections of aesthetic and ideological issues found in "Italian Fantastika" artifacts from print, visual, and audiovisual mediums. Together, these essays interact to provide readings of a rich array of texts, some of which are undisputably household names (such as *Pinocchio* and *Star Trek*), while others have enjoyed "cult" status in fandom while being unknown among literary scholars (including books by Dorothy Bryant and Terri Favro).

Collectively, these essays explore how the horror, fantasy, and science fiction narratives by and about Italians may act as a vehicle for examining Italian diasporic identities and the implications of those identities in a broader world. This is true whether the Fantastika narratives being examined are found in the pages of potboilers and comic books, on movie and television screens, or in classic literature. The editors of this anthology are interested in Italian, Italian American, Italian Canadian, and Italian Australian science fiction, fantasy, and horror multimedia narratives—which we have signified collectively as "Italian Fantastika"—as a means of exploring the present and future of Italian ethnic and cultural identity and in expanding the academic field of Italian Diasporic Studies. This book is designed to help reorient thinking about Italian studies away from primarily nostalgic modes into more forward-looking territory. The book is also designed to encourage a consideration of Fantastika's potential of serving as an alternative storytelling paradigm to realism, the default mode of immigrant and diaspora narrative. Finally, in considering what it means to be "Italian" today, this book helps us consider how to embrace and preserve what is healthiest about our global Italian identity and discard that which is personally and socially destructive.

Part 1

Defining a Field

Throughout the twentieth century, zombies, vampires, ghosts, and uncanny dolls or robots have been constant presences that, today, populate the ever-expanding space of streaming services. There is no doubt that these archetypes have trespassed the limits of the fantastic and are de facto cornerstones of today's literary and visual imagination, at least as far as Western societies are concerned. If these commonly accepted fictional entities have originated from foreign national cultures, literary criticism regarding the history and significance of the fantastic and its tropes has flourished in Italy during recent decades. . . . Fabio Camiletti has studied several key moments in the dissemination of fantastic fiction in Italy and abroad. . . . [David del Principe's] *Rebellion, Death, and Aesthetics in Italy* has traced the origins of the fantastic in Italy in the context of the *Scapigliatura* . . . [and] Francesca Belliani and Giorgio Sulis have edited an anthology of critical essays titled *The Italian Gothic and Fantastic*, including contributions about the Freudian uncanny, phantasmagoria, and the female fantastic.

—Angelo Castagnino, *Fantastic Echoes in Contemporary Italian Literature*

Defining a Field

1

Mutants in La Merica

The Whiteness of the Petrellis in NBC's *Heroes*

Anthony Lioi

A young man stands atop a roof in Manhattan, ready to jump. He believes he can fly. He cannot fly, not yet, though he is a mutant, gifted with uncanny powers through an alteration in his genome. Flight is not his power, not directly. He is a mimic, an empath who feels his way into the powers of others until he can do what they do. When he jumps, he falls, saved in the nick of time by his brother, who really can fly. Suspended from his brother's hand, he feels his way to flight, and for a moment, they fly together. Peter and Nathan Petrelli, mutants in America, are heroes in a television show called *Heroes*, an NBC superhero drama that aired from 2006 to 2010.

It is difficult not to read this scene as an allegory for Italian America in the early twenty-first century. Unlike *The Sopranos*, which examined the collapse of mobster patriarchy, *Heroes* investigates the powers of bourgeois whiteness the Petrellis have gained through the process of assimilation into American culture. How did we learn to fly, and at what cost? In order to understand our place in contemporary narratives of race, gender, and class, Italian Americans need to grapple with representations of white ethnic protagonists after assimilation. This investigation cannot be limited to literary or cinematic texts of high culture but must engage broadcast media and other popular forms. The Petrelli brothers reveal the intersection of whiteness, professional middle-class status, and American masculinity at a moment when Italians in the United States have become entirely white. One brother is coded through his powers of empathy as more feminine than Mafia masculinity permits Italian men to be in popular cinema. The other is more traditionally masculine, but he is at worst manipulative, not corrupt. Both are heroes who save the world. But in overcoming stereotypes of Italian masculinity, they gain the chance to be foregrounded as white protagonists surrounded by a multiethnic cast. Their status as elite professionals centers them even further. The mutations of gender and class allow them to assert more race privilege. We can see that as progress beyond the *gavone* and the gangster, but we must account for the Petrellis' capacity to be truly white heroes. When superhero stories dominate the box office, the idea of an Italian American superhero cannot evade our judgment. In an essay on mainstream Italian American filmmakers, Ben Lawton argues that these artists represent the American Dream as "a lie, a trick, and a deception" (397). My perspective on the achievement of whiteness in *Heroes* departs from the dualism between loyalty and betrayal, truth and lies. The Petrelli family achieved whiteness. This essay will argue that mutation, the source of the Petrellis' powers, also plots a path out of whiteness in the Italian diaspora.

The field of Italian American Studies has been occupied with the history and artistic representation of immigration to the United States and its aftermath. While this work is invaluable, it has obscured the current status of Italian Americans as white and middle class. To be white and middle class is judged, in art and scholarship, as less interesting, like a red sauce without enough oregano. This coding of the assimilated condition as less worthy of study has had the effect of obscuring our race and class privileges at a moment when the politics of ethnic resentment rises again in a new American authoritarianism. It is now crucial that future scholarship attend to the whiteness of our lives and art. I see the contemporary superhero narrative as a promising terrain for the examination of the social power of the white professional middle class. *Heroes* features an Italian American family of mutant heroes and villains who enact, figuratively, the superpowers of race and class that Italians now wield as a group. The figure of the assimilated white ethnic as mutant centers the process of adaptation to environment and adaptation's ethical and political consequences. Though *Heroes* features an Italian family that achieved whiteness in the United States, this is not to deny the possibility of Italian/Americans who are multiracial or other than white. On the American side, Kym Ragusa's important book *The Skin Between Us* grapples with her Black-and-Italian identity. On the Italian side, there is a growing literature by and about African Italians, not to speak of the Roman, Moorish, Greek, Norman, and Arab heritage of Southern and Insular Italy. In other parts of the diaspora, such as Brazil, Argentina, Canada, and Australia, Italian immigrants entered racial and ethnic matrices distinct from that of the United States. This analysis focuses on achieved American whiteness precisely because of its presumed but insufficiently examined hegemonic status.

A brief review of the debate on whiteness and Italian American history, however schematic, will be helpful. How should one map the path from 1912, when the US House Committee on Immigration debated the question of Italians as "full-blooded Caucasians," to the Petrellis of 2006 (Dunbar-Ortiz 157)? The first position might be called the gradual ascent to whiteness. It is associated with Whiteness Studies, which arose in the 1990s to counter the treatment of whiteness as an aporia that organizes the system of race around itself. David Roediger and Jennifer Guglielmo advance the claim that Italians were not fully white when the first wave of immigrants arrived in the United States in the late nineteenth century. Like other immigrants from eastern and southern Europe, they were at first stigmatized as inferior, criminal, and unassimilable. Roediger and Guglielmo begin with racial systems inside Italy after unification, citing the Northern view of the South as African, inferior, and primitive (Guglielmo and Salerno 9–11). They cite Matthew Jacobson's assertion that Italian immigrants did not at first "act white": they took jobs associated with Black Americans, organized with people of color, and incurred the wrath of white supremacists. At the same time, Italian Americans could be citizens, vote, own land, and marry other Europeans (11). There was a contradiction between the legal status of Italians in America, the privileges they could enjoy relative to Black, Latine, Asian, and Indigenous people, and the social stigma of an inferior type of whiteness. This is a process model of race, in which a flawed whiteness was ameliorated over the course of the twentieth century.

The second position puts a different emphasis on the same elements. Here, the most important fact was de jure white status upon arrival. Italians were Christian Europeans subject to a "racialized social system" that ranked them beneath Anglo-Nordic whites (T. Guglielmo 7). What matters is what happened in the United States, not Europe, and the way the state granted privileges withheld from nonwhite immigrants.

State power trumps social marginality. Thomas Guglielmo represents this position, which is grounded in the formal acceptance of Italians as white in US federal law and not subject to Jim Crow or other legal barriers. Guglielmo makes a distinction between "race" and "color" as a way to explain how Italian Americans could be white and also socially denigrated. He explains: "Whether one was white, black, red, yellow, or brown—and to some extent Anglo-Saxon, Alpine, South Italian, or North Italian—powerfully influenced . . . where one lived and worked, the kinds of people one married, and the kinds of life chances one had. Thus race was not (and is not) completely about ideas, ideologies, and identities. It is also about location in a social system and its consequences" (7). In this taxonomy, one sees why immigrants filling out federal forms would identify their race and color as "South Italian" and "white," respectively (9). Color is a social category, not a phenotypic description, and race is a group heritage identity. Therefore Guglielmo can account for whiteness as a status that conferred social privilege even as "Italians" were subject to prejudice because of their Mediterranean origins.

The final position, represented by Maria Laurino, Louise DeSalvo, Leo Buscaglia, and other literary scholars, emphasizes the lived experience of aspiring to a whiteness their families did not quite possess. The disgusting Italian body helped establish a colorist hierarchy within American whiteness. Laurino recalls a popular girl who would not associate with a "smelly Italian girl" who would compromise her social status (18). In her memoir, Louise DeSalvo recalls her mother refusing to eat her grandmother's peasant bread in order to mutate herself into the suburban "blond person" beauty standard (Painter 369). Examples could be multiplied. Though one might call this an individualist, experiential standard of racial instability, it is supported by the moments in United States history when the protections of whiteness temporarily failed, such as the New Orleans lynching of eleven Sicilians in 1891, the Immigration Act of 1924, and the classification of unnaturalized Italians as enemy aliens during World War II. It is fair in light of this history to understand Italian whiteness as protean well into the 1960s, when the suburban children and grandchildren of the immigrants became by dint of class mobility more white than ever before. Mario Puzo's immigrant saga, *The Fortunate Pilgrim*, concludes with the family driving out of Manhattan toward Long Island, the promised land of whiteness. The trouble with our racial "in-betweenness," the sense in the early twentieth century that we were "vastly different, and inferior" to northern Europeans, was finally dissipating (Vellon 213). Italians were mutating in a suburban and white direction.

Mutation as Metaphor

What does it mean to call the Petrellis mutants? The opening of the show wastes no time in explaining: "In recent days a seemingly random group of individuals has emerged with what can only be described as 'special abilities.' Although unaware of it now, these individuals will not only save the world, but change it forever" (S1 E1, "Genesis"). This fact has been discovered by Mohinder Suresh, a geneticist from Madras, who soon locates the source of these special abilities: genetic mutation. In one stroke, the show articulated the premise of *The X-Men*, the Marvel Comics standard that began as a comic book in 1964 and, by the time *Heroes* premiered, had already spawned multiple comics titles, an animated television show, and the first of the films produced by Sony Pictures. (Neither NBC nor Marvel owned the rights to the X-Men in 2006, but like the later series *Umbrella Academy*, *The Gifted*, and others, *Heroes* is an X-Men narrative sub rosa.) Genetic mutation caused by atomic fallout, industrial pollutants, and other markers of the Anthropocene had generated in humanity new capabilities that could no longer be hidden. The idea of mutation as the origin of superpowers is ubiquitous in American popular culture, and scholars have theorized the trope of the mutant-as-outsider in depth. In *The New Mutants*, Ramzi Fawaz argues: "Simultaneously [*The X-Men*] re-valued physical disability and visible difference from ordinary humanity as the ground upon which new forms of social and political community could be articulated. The elasticity of mutation as a metaphor for a variety of embodied and cultural differences made it a potent popular fantasy for vitalizing Marvel Comics' cosmopolitan ethos at the level of both comic book content and public reception" (144–145). *Heroes* embodies this ethos in its multiracial, international cast in the tradition of the New X-Men who premiered in 1976 as an attempt to overcome the white, suburban, entirely American cast of the original comic. *Heroes* also departs from the tradition of monstrosity in the comic books, substituting a televisual standard of physical attractiveness. If this dulls the metaphorical power of mutant-as-Other, it fits the Petrellis, whose social status and secret superpowers represent the post-1960s position of Italian Americans that amplified class status, social position, and political influence.

What makes the heroes in *Heroes* heroes is their belief that with great power comes great responsibility, an ethos articulated in *Spider-Man* discourse rewritten by the X-Men motto: "Feared and hated by a world they have sworn to protect." The Petrellis do suffer from this affliction in altered form: their power and status are threatened by their mutant identity.

Because mutants have appeared only in "recent days" in their world, there is only the closet, to activate the trope of mutation-as-queerness. Powerful as they are, the Petrellis must pretend to be other than they are. In effect, it is the 2000s for their ethnic and racial identities but the 1950s for their mutant nature. There is no community of liberation yet, except for a kind of Mattachine Society, working behind closed doors for mainstream media acceptance. The Petrellis are the perfect example of what scholars have identified as the problem of the white mutant: they possess the privileges of whiteness, but the glamor of racial and sexual minorities. The trope of mutant as racial Other can acquire conflicting political valances. Jordan C. Carroll reminds us that, in twentieth-century science fiction, "White elites often appear in right-wing narratives as mutants, aliens, and other futuristic beings who are beset by the backward masses" (13). Contrariwise, Allan W. Austin and Patrick L. Hamilton point out that superhero media have contributed to the "American conversation about vexed issues of race, ethnicity, and what came to be known as multiculturalism" (1). At the same time, the diversification of Marvel heroes in the 1960s and '70s was governed by an additive logic, an add-nonwhite-heroes-and-mix approach, that did not displace the power of mutant whiteness, just as the addition of Storm (Black and Egyptian), Sunfire (Japanese), and Colossus (Soviet) did not displace the patriarchal power of Professor X. Neil Shyminsky argues that white mutants who carry a racialized stigma are a problem: "White mutants of the X-Men lack race, and typically pass as 'just people' " (159). The X-Men titles struggled with the racial semiosis of mutation explicitly, introducing a mutant underground called the Morlocks—who despise the X-Men as "pretty" mutants who can pass. There is also the discourse of racial superiority introduced by the X-Men villain/anti-hero Magneto, a survivor of Auschwitz who believes that mutants must claim their status as *Homo superior*, the next step in human evolution, in order to prevent a future genocide. *Heroes* is well aware of the problem of the white, bourgeois, beautiful mutant family trying to do good while living the high life. This contradiction is embodied in Nathan, the older brother, whose powers threaten his bid for the Senate, and in Peter, the gentle empath who becomes the unwitting threat of season 1. As their antagonist, the murderous Sylar, says in the final episode of the season, "Turns out you're the villain, Peter" (S1 E23, "How to Stop an Exploding Man"). This is not an accident. Peter in particular and the Petrellis as a family represent the tension between an inherited sense of ethnic anxiety that pulls against an achieved life of privilege, wealth, and influence. In the next section, I will anatomize this dynamic through four vectors of analysis: the phenotypic transformation of the Italian American hero; the politics of affect in the poetics of masculinity; the structure of ethnic mutation in the context of post-9/11 narratives; and the figure of the mutant as suffering Christ.

Same Face, Same Race? Phenotypic Transformation

Phenotypic transformation of the face is the first way *Heroes* resignifies the Italian American hero as white. Literally the first way: The opening shot of the first episode of the show is an extreme closeup of Peter Petrelli, first at an angle level with his gaze, and then from below, as if we are hovering just beyond him. Hovering, because Peter is perched at the edge of a roof in Manhattan, preparing to jump, convinced that he can fly. Flight is his brother Nathan's power, which Peter has not had a chance to consciously imitate—therefore he cannot fly, yet. The camera can fly, however—no normal human could see Peter this way in this position. The camera is a mutant. It looks at Peter with Nathan's eyes. This gaze is intimate, and viewers get a chance to consider Milo Ventimiglia's face.

Figure 1.1. Milo Ventimiglia in the Heroes era. *Source: Heroes*, NBC, 2006, publicity still.

Fresh from a supporting role in *The Gilmore Girls* as the sympathetic but troubled boyfriend, Ventimiglia as Peter Petrelli looks every inch the troubled prince. His dark, worried eyes are framed by thick, straight, black hair cut asymmetrically. His nose is strong but not prominent; his jawline is chiseled but not domineering; and his skin is smooth, paler than olive. Petrelli looks as if a Southern Italian ancestor has been photoshopped to appeal to Anglo-American sensibilities.

By the time he jumps, we are already invested in his survival. Greeks and Southern Italians often note our resemblance to each other with the phrase "same face, same race," but Peter Petrelli bears the face of a mutant: literally, inside the storyworld, but figuratively too, as an actor who appears to be Italian American but unambiguously white.

What could be a bit of casting ephemera no longer appears so in light of the history of head measurement in the late nineteenth and early twentieth centuries. In *The History of White People*, Nell Irvin Painter establishes a series of "enlargements" of whiteness in the United States. Italian American whiteness corresponds to her Third Enlargement in the 1940s, as the people who had been "wops" and "dagoes" gained access to higher education and home ownership via governmental programs designed to reward veterans of World War II—though not veterans of color (Painter 365). Italian Americans transitioned into practical whiteness through access to the tools of upward mobility, wealth accumulation, and social respectability. However, only a few decades prior, Columbia University anthropologist Franz Boas, one of the fathers of American multiculturalism, was measuring Neapolitan and Sicilian heads in New York City to find evidence of structural changes in native-born populations. In 1912, Boas published *Changes in Bodily Form of Descendants of Immigrants*, which concluded that children born to so-called Alpine, Mediterranean, and Ashkenazi-Jewish mothers who had themselves been born in the United States displayed significant changes in head shape (Painter 238). From these measurements, Boas concluded that "the whole bodily and mental make-up of the immigrants may change," allowing these former degenerate types to join Anglo-Saxons as real Americans (240). Milo Ventimiglia as Peter Petrelli, a century after Boas, embodies this phenotypic goal of becoming American in face, which signified, in eugenic discourses, becoming American in spirit and intellect. What Ventimiglia gained through costume and hair design, Petrelli gained through mutation, but unlike the X-Men, this makes him more white, more privileged, and more respectable than before. It follows that Peter's evil doppelganger, Gabriel Gray / Sylar, would be constructed on villainous principles that

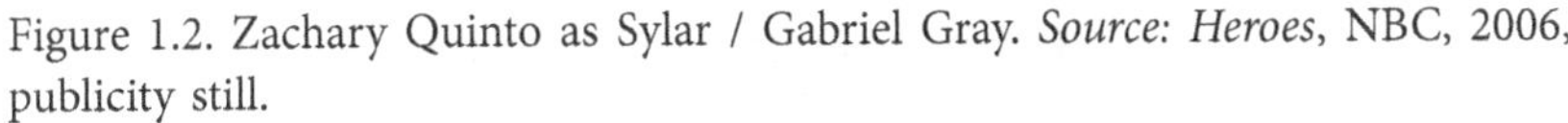
Figure 1.2. Zachary Quinto as Sylar / Gabriel Gray. *Source: Heroes*, NBC, 2006, publicity still.

made him appear darker, thicker, and hairier, that is, more like the original immigrants. Though Zachary Quinto would ascend to cinematic fame playing heroes such as Spock in *Star Trek* (2009), here he leans into his greater size to menace Peter from the beginning.

Through grooming and costuming, Quinto becomes Sylar: black, slicked-back hair; thick eyebrows; a prominent five o'clock shadow; and accentuated shoulders. Where Peter is costumed to make him look too small for his overcoat, Sylar's clothing is cut close to the body to exaggerate his breadth. Coding character traits in hair, makeup, and costume represents the inheritance of theater in American television drama. Though the construction of the hero as postfeminist man was well underway in American television by the early 2000s, the difference between Peter and Sylar remains a lesson in the visual coding of the old, working-class, immigrant masculinity as vice and the new, bourgeois, postwhite masculinity as virtue.

Mutant Affects: Empathy versus Sociopathy

Peter has two foils, both coded as normatively masculine: Nathan, his ambitious brother, and Sylar, whose mutation matches Peter's but manifests as specimen dissection (he examines the brains of other mutants to gain their powers) rather than empathic mimesis. Peter is framed not only as phenotypically different but affectively superior: he is kind, devoted, and full of fellow-feeling. In episode 23, the season finale, Peter is transported back five years in the past to overhear a conversation between Charles, who would later be his patient, and Angela Petrelli, his mother. When Angela calls Peter "weak," Charles—whose cultural authority as a Black mutant matters—corrects her: "This world won't be saved on strength. What it really needs is hope—and that's Peter." Sylar, on the other hand, is called a "parasite" in episode 18, which bears that name. In their dramatic face-off in this episode, Sylar appears to have the upper hand because of his traditionally masculine traits of strength, aggression, and ruthlessness. His method of acquiring the powers of others is brutally effective: once he examines a brain, Sylar understands "what makes them tick," as if people are mere machines—"Sylar" is the name of a watch brand—and his control of a new power is immediate. Because Peter's method involves befriending and empathy, his power acquisition is more gradual and less reliable at first. Sylar can use his telekinesis to pin Peter to a wall and bore into his skull to remove his brain. While Peter is immobilized, Sylar slices off the lock of hair that represents Peter's boyish innocence. Though Peter escapes the encounter, his trajectory has been altered. The story poses this problem to Peter and the audience: How can the mutant prince of empathy preserve his kindness and still defeat the bad guy? Meta-ethnically, how can gentle manliness overcome traditions of brute-force masculinity?

This problem repeats within the Petrelli family itself: both Nathan and Angela see Peter as weak and feckless, the feminized younger brother unfit to hold the reins of power. In a family with no daughter-figure until Claire is revealed to be Nathan's child, Peter serves symbolically as Nathan's sister. Nathan must rescue him in episode 1 after Peter jumps off a building; when Peter wakes up in the hospital, Nathan gaslights him with a fake story about how he got there, hiding the fact of their powers in the service of his campaign for the Senate. Later, Nathan tells the press that Peter is mentally ill to distract attention from his own dealings with a crime boss. In each case, Peter's earnestness—which is the key to his power—is weaponized against him. Peter, coded affectively feminine against masculine antagonists, represents the quandary for Italian American manhood in diaspora. In terms of traditional immigrant social standards, Peter risks the loss of masculine authority: forcefulness, strength of will, ability to demand respect. At the same time, he embodies the sort of reconstructed man that Anglophone feminism vindicates: in touch with his feelings, gender-egalitarian, with a streak of the old gallantry that appears when summoned. As a hero of affect, ready to save the cheerleader but treat her as a peer, Peter represents an archetype of the knightly powerhouse that the Marvel Cinematic Universe would amplify in the figures of Captain America, Black Panther, and Thor. This fantasy of the man who combines the most attractive qualities of hegemonic and counterhegemonic masculinities vaults Peter past his televisual ancestors (not the Fonz, not Vinnie Barbarino) and into the realm of semiotic paradox the plot will go on to resolve.

Genocide, We've All Been There

Peter becomes the bomb he is trying to stop, which he understands because of his midseason encounters with Isaac the visionary painter and Hiro Nakamura, the time traveler from the future. Peter will meet Ted, the radioactive mutant whose power is out of control, absorb that power and himself explode. Peter literalizes the X-Men motto, "children of the atom," and repeats the Dark Phoenix plot in which Jean Grey loses control of her powers and commits genocide (*X-Men* nos. 127–138). *Heroes* reframes the Cold War paranoia of the nuclear arms race with the post-9/11 fear of another attack on Manhattan. Peter *is* the mutant menace who justifies human fear of the Other. Italians are a threat to civilization, but not in the way twentieth-century eugenics expected. Anticipating the multiverse trope that will dominate science fiction films and superhero narratives a decade later, episode 20, "Five Years Gone," depicts an alternate future in which Sylar impersonates Nathan Petrelli in order to become president. Still in the closet as a mutant, "Nathan" forces Suresh, his senior science advisor, to create an anti-mutation treatment that will disable mutant powers. This plot adapts classic X-Men stories in which the state attempts a mutant genocide in the name of human supremacy. Most relevant are *X-Men* no. 142, "Days of Future Past," and the film *X3: The Last Stand*. These sources frame mutants as a racial minority subject to the power of a fascist, corporate state. Sylar-Nathan's presidency of a *herrenvolk* nation represents peak whiteness for the Italian characters: if you can order a genocide—even of your own people—you are definitely white. In one sense, the whiteness of the Petrellis and their mutation are opposite political traits. One allows them access to the ruling class, while the other threatens that status. In another sense, whiteness *is* the mutation, the change of biopolitical caste that makes them unlike their immigrant ancestors.

The inevitable association of the mutant bombing of Manhattan with the events of September 11, 2001—only five years past at the 2006 series premiere—resignifies mutation as a terrorist- and Muslim-coded identity. In this dystopian future, which echoes the provisions of the Patriot Act, a mutant president will harness state power to destroy his people in the name of his own authority and national security. The erosion of Muslim American rights under the US surveillance apparatus spawned by the Patriot Act morphs here into a final solution that does not require concentration camps. In "Days of Future Past" the instrument of genocide is robotic, while in *X3* it is biomedical, a "vaccine," but these intertexts both underline the stakes in Sylar-Nathan's plan: extermination of the Other in a way that evokes Indigenous removal, subjugation, and forced assimilation; the Middle Passage and African enslavement; Japanese American internment; the Vietnam War; and COINTELPRO anti-insurgent activity in the 1960s. As president, Sylar-Nathan acts as executive but also as a one-man CIA, Bureau of Indian Affairs, FBI, and police force: a perfect fascist. Therefore Peter, Hiro, and his allies struggle to prevent not only the detonation of the bomb but also the effects of ruling class status on the Petrellis. "Nathan's" fate in this timeline suggests again that accession to the powers of hegemonic whiteness should be questioned by Italian Americans as a group. Sylar becomes the instrument of his own destruction. He uses Nathan's face—the shape of the "normal" brother—to unravel the nation itself.

The Mutant Savior

Who is whiter than Christ in America? Pellegrino D'Acierno argues that Italian American cinema creates a visual discourse of "profane theology," and *Heroes* imports that discourse into superhero television (566). Like Peter Parker before him, Peter Petrelli incarnates your friendly neighborhood super-savior, but his most important Christic identity is martyr. In her account of counterhegemonic Christologies in late antiquity, theologian

Rosemary Radford Ruether highlights the tradition of martyr-saints who became another Christ (*alter Christus*) by virtue of their sacrificial death. This continuation of Jesus's salvific work was strong enough to cross the lines of gender: in women martyrs, the community encountered "Christ in the form of our sister" (Ruether 131). Popular Christianity in late antiquity believed that Jesus is entirely Christ but Christ is not entirely Jesus, seeing Pentecost as the moment when the powers of Christ become available to believers in a continuing Incarnation. Martyrdom enables Christic identity across lines of gender, class, race, and—in the case of mutants—the category of the human. In episode 23, the season finale, "How to Stop an Exploding Man," Peter takes up the role and iconography of Suffering Christ and mutant martyr. The heroes and the villain Sylar converge on a deserted Manhattan plaza to play out the climax of the story. Peter has absorbed Ted's nuclear power and is going critical, holding in the explosion for as long as he can. Just as his power peaks, so does his gender inversion: the hero recruited by Hiro to save the cheerleader at the beginning of the season must now be saved by Claire, the cheerleader—and others too—from Sylar's final attack. Like Jesus in the Passion and Crucifixion, Peter is gender queer, combining cosmic power and total helplessness. From the beginning, he has been "eminently likable as well as ultimately deadly" (Porter et al. 137). Simply deadly, Sylar is vulnerable because he was prevented from absorbing Claire's healing ability, and once he is shot he goes down—still the antagonist, but not the true threat. Unable to control himself any longer, Peter goes critical, glowing like an atomic bomb. At the last second, Nathan lifts him into a *Pietà*-position—with Nathan in the role of Mary—and flies into the sky, where Peter explodes without damaging the city. This reverses episode 1, when Nathan saves Peter but refuses to tell the truth about their powers. Thus Nathan, who stood through the season between Peter's gentle Jesus and Sylar's sociopathy, fulfills his role as aggressor turned protector. Having ascended into heaven, Peter and Nathan are not seen again. A trail of blood leads to a manhole through which Sylar descends into the underworld. The city is saved.

This ending fulfills the most overtly Catholic iconography and stereotypically Italian American family dynamics. Angela's vision of the apocalypse came true, and both of her sons became the messiah. Claire, her granddaughter, was the villain's target, as in horror movies, and a post–*Buffy the Vampire Slayer* hero in her own right, a delicate balance of femininity and girl power. Surrounded as they are by a multiracial and cosmopolitan cast, the Petrellis maintained their position at center stage as protagonists, secret threat, and finally as saviors. Season 1's plot constitutes an allegory of ethnic white history: first the Petrellis threaten the nation, then they assimilate to maximize their power, attempting to downplay their difference until they exert their full power to save the nation from themselves. The circularity of their roles as danger and savior reflects the self-justifying structure of white ruling-class power. It is both the origin and end of the shining city on the hill. There are also some other people involved—to be fair, *Heroes* was ahead of its time as a multiethnic television drama—but the Petrellis make the world go round. This Ouroboros structure seals off the Italian mutants from their own history: no one needs to remember when they huddled at the margins of the promised land.

We cannot leave this aspect of the show without recognizing how the Christic plot and iconography exceeded the bounds of the series and entered the material fan culture associated with Milo Ventimiglia. A decade and a half after *Heroes* ended, it is still possible to buy a votive candle with the image of Ventimiglia as Christ of the Sacred Heart.

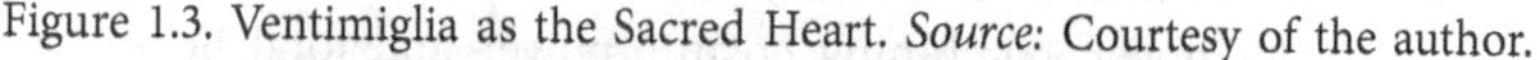

Figure 1.3. Ventimiglia as the Sacred Heart. *Source:* Courtesy of the author.

This icon brings together many of the elements of Peter Petrelli's character and aesthetics. It magnifies the phenotypic changes to the image of Italian American masculinity that made Peter whiter: the straight black hair, the soft eyes, the trimmed beard, the pale skin. Moreover, this is not just any icon of Christ. The Sacred Heart is an image derived from seventeenth-century piety that originated in the visions of Saint Margaret Mary Alacoque. (Remember the centrality of visionary mutant experience in the characters of Angela Petrelli and Isaac Mendez.) Contemporary icons of the Sacred Heart depict the love of Christ as a flaming heart that Jesus reveals by pulling aside his clothing. Practitioners are meant to focus on that image as an instrument for daily devotion, praying to the Sacred Heart to kindle divine love in the heart of the supplicant. One also implores the Sacred Heart for protection, as in this prayer:

> Protect me in the midst of danger.
> Comfort me in my afflictions.
> Give me health of body,
> assistance in my temporal needs,
> Your blessing on all that I do,
> and the grace of a holy death. Amen.

This prayer epitomizes Peter Petrelli's tasks as a hero. Even the fandom's "thirstiness" for Milo Ventimiglia can be set in the context of contemplative practice; it is nothing but conventional to fall in love with Jesus. There is a long tradition of Christian erotic mysticism grounded in the Song of Songs and popularized by the Counter-Reformation Saints Teresa of Ávila and John of the Cross. One is meant to imagine Christ as the Divine Bridegroom who marries the soul of the Christian in a blissful and sometimes orgasmic union (if you follow Bernini's *Saint Teresa in Ecstasy*). Peter Petrelli's hero of empathy rides out of *Heroes* and into the hearts of fans through a mashup of the divine lover and superhero. Though there is hardly a whiter icon of Christ than the Sacred Heart, it is worth noting that Ventimiglia is swarthier than many images of Christ imposed on Mediterranean immigrants by the Church in the name of assimilation, notably the blond, Aryan icon inside the dome of the Basilica of the National Shrine of the Immaculate Conception in Washington, DC.

As Monsignor Charles Pope notes, this image has been divisive throughout its history because it offers immigrant Catholics an angry northern European savior who judges the viewer from above (Pope). After a long struggle with Irish priests and nuns who thought Italian

Figure 1.4. *Christ in Majesty*. Mosaic inside the Basilica dome. *Source:* Wikimedia Commons, Bradley Weber, CC-BY-2.0.

immigrants were barbarians, the icon implies that majesty is not for dirty garlic-eaters. Christ in the form of our mutant valorizes Southern Italian looks in a way that resists the most flagrant divinization of white supremacy in American Catholicism.

Conclusion: The Egg in the Castle

In *A Semiotic of Ethnicity*, Anthony Julian Tamburri argues that Italian Americans must begin to speak in terms of "us *and* them, not us *against* them," calling out our insularity and, more ominously, our tendency to use whiteness as a means to separate ourselves from Others just across the racial divide (Tamburri 130). We have yet to accomplish his goal, but the discourse of the mutant and the world of *Heroes* point to a transformation of them and us into something else, something new. As a scholar of popular culture and fan communities, I value the experience of immersion in Secondary Worlds of art, as J. R. R. Tolkien called them in his essay "On Fairy-Stories" (132). As a fan of *Heroes* as a mutation of the X-Men, I have immersed myself in that world. However, in attempting to understand the significance of *Heroes* for a theory of Italian American whiteness, we must remember that Tolkien theorized Secondary Worlds as imaginary spaces that we *depart* from to see the Primary World with new eyes. In the case of representations of ethnicity and race in worlds of Fantastika, we are dealing with a Primary World that is itself made from constructs of "Italians" as "white Americans." When we return from *Heroes*, we are not escaping into a Primary World in which race has an ontological reality—race is not an essence—but into one in which the construct of race has very real consequences. A house is also a construct, but if it collapses on top of you, you are really dead. We must understand that *Heroes* is a representation of a construct, which calls into question any attempt to determine if Italians in diaspora "are" white, even as whiteness exerts a real power in American culture and politics. To recall the historical analysis that began this essay, the three answers to the question of Italian whiteness are: First, Italians were not fully white upon arrival because of phenotypic, class, linguistic, cultural, and religious differences that set them apart from Anglo-Protestants and assimilated Irish immigrants. Second, Italians were white by law upon arrival, and the spell of the law, itself a magical construct that makes rules for the social world out of words, is all that matters. Finally, Italians were not fully white until they *felt* white and experienced white privilege after World War II as members of the suburban middle class. None of these are explanations of nature, which is why whiteness can be "enlarged," as Nell Irvin Painter put it. The fictional Petrellis aren't "real," but whiteness—always a settler colonial tool to create masters and subalterns in the empire—isn't real either. Instead of engaging this truth with Baudrillardian pessimism about simulacra, I ask how *Heroes* can help us to dispel the curse of race in America with a counterspell for a world beyond whiteness.

Notes Toward a New Mutation

1. The Petrellis can help us see that Italian whiteness in the United States is a completed project: achievement unlocked!

Just as Whiteness Studies helped make whiteness visible as a racial category among others, so should Italian American Studies make visible our entrance into the white ruling class at a moment when politicians, operatives, and activists named DeSantis, Rufo, Pompeo, Giuliani, Christie (his mother is Italian), and Conway (mother's maiden name: DiNatale) propose to rejuvenate patriarchal authoritarianism in the name of European supremacy. Since the 1970s backlash against the liberation movements of the '60s, white ethnicity has been weaponized by nativist and crypto-fascist forces to create a revanchist culture of ethnic resentment (Lowndes 265–86). This alone is a reason to mutate beyond whiteness.

2. At the same time, the Petrellis' mutant identity points to whiteness as a product of a cultural evolution that has not ended. Whiteness is a process, and the trope of ethnicity as mutation suggests that we can change once again—perhaps out of whiteness altogether. Mutation signifies the will to self-transformation in the name of world salvation. Like Peter, we must save the world from ourselves.

3. The different styles of Italian American masculinity embodied in Peter, Nathan, and Sylar foreground the intersection of gender performance and racial status. The trope of gender as mutation reveals the way television as a medium shapes our consciousness of ethnicity and gender identity, presenting us with images of white ruling-class ethnic men decades after these men appeared in history. The belatedness of television's representations should lead us to question which mutations of gendered ethnicity have appeared without being represented in popular media. The political attacks on women's reproductive freedom and queer, especially trans, people should lead us to ask how mutations of gender can sponsor, drive, or impede mutations of race.

4. Peter's Trojan horse plot in which the underdog became the threat should lead us to examine the ironic structure of Italian American suffering, redemption, and assimilation into a racial ruling caste as the end of history. How, exactly,

did working-class subjugation, struggle, and achieved assimilation become the telos of our story? Was it worth it, losing our dialects and our garlic-smelling skin? (This is a rhetorical question. It is not ethical to desire racial supremacy.) If we who are alive today were not responsible *for* our accession to whiteness, in what sense are we responsible *to* it, and what might come after? How might these questions change the DNA of Italian American Studies?

5. As creators of Secondary Worlds of art, how might we take the popular media (literature, film, television, comics) that have hidden our mutant nature from ourselves and use them to make new worlds beyond the structural injustice that puts our world in peril?

In the Bay of Naples sits an island where the Angevin kings built a fortress: Castel dell'Ovo—Egg Castle. Legend has it that its dungeon hides a secret chamber. Inside this chamber is a golden cage, and inside the cage, a magic egg. The legend relates that the castle is protected by the egg, not the other way around. As long as the egg endures, the castle stands, and Naples will not fall. But Naples has already fallen, the Angevins are no more, and still the chamber and the egg. Inside the egg, something grows, something changes. Our task is to find the chamber, unlock the cage, break open the egg, and see who emerges.

Works Cited

Austin, Allan W., and Patrick L. Hamilton. *All New, All Different? A History of Race and the American Superhero*. U of Texas P, 2019.

Carroll, Jordan C. *Speculative Whiteness: Science Fiction and the Alt-Right*. U of Minnesota P, 2024.

D'Acierno, Pellegrino. "Cinema Paradiso: The Italian American Presence in American Cinema." *The Italian American Heritage: A Companion to Literature and the Arts*, edited by Pellegrino D'Acierno, Garland Press, 1999, pp. 563–90.

Dunbar-Ortiz, Roxanne. *Not a Nation of Immigrants: Settler Colonialism, White Supremacy, and a History of Erasure and Exclusion*. Beacon Press, 2021.

Fawaz, Ramzi. *The New Mutants: Superheroes and the Radical Imagination of American Comics*. New York UP, 2019.

Gambino, Richard. *Blood of My Blood: The Dilemma of the Italian-Americans.* Guernica Press, 2011.

Gardaphé, Fred. "Italian American Masculinities." *The Routledge History of Italian Americans*, edited by William J. Connell and Stanislao G. Pugliese. Routledge, 2018, pp. 552–64.

Guglielmo, Jennifer, and Salvatore Salerno. Introduction. *Are Italians White? How Race Is Made in America*, edited by Jennifer Guglielmo and Salvatore Salerno. Routledge, 2003, pp. 6–11.

Guglielmo, Thomas A. " 'No Barrier to Power': Italians, Race, and Power in the United States." *Are Italians White? How Race Is Made in America*, edited by Jennifer Guglielmo and Salvatore Salerno. Routledge, 2003, pp. 29–43.

Heroes Wiki. https://hero.fandom.com/wiki/Heroes_Wiki, 2003.

Kring, Tim, Adam Arkush, and Dennis Hammer. *Heroes.* New York: NBC, 2006.

Laurino, Maria. *Were You Always An Italian? Ancestors and Other Icons of Italian America.* W. W. Norton, 2000.

Lawton, Ben. "America Through Italian/American Eyes: Dream or Nightmare?" *From the Margin: Writings in Italian Americana*, edited by Anthony Julian Tamburri, Paolo A. Giordano, and Fred Gardaphé. Purdue UP, 1991, pp. 397–430.

Lowndes, Joseph. "From Pat Buchanan to Donald Trump: The Nativist Turn in Right-Wing Populism." *A Field Guide to White Supremacy*, edited by Kathleen Belew and Ramón Gutiérrez. U of California P, 2021, pp. 265–86.

Painter, Nell Irvin. *The History of White People.* W. W. Norton, 2010.

Pope, Charles. "Awesome or Awful? A Reflection on the Mosaic of Christ in Majesty at the Basilica in Washington." *Community in Mission.* https://blog.adw.org/2015/06/awesome-or-awful-a-reflection-on-the-mosaic-of-christ-in-majesty-at-the-basilica-in-Washington. Accessed 11 Jan. 2024.

Porter, Lynnette, David Lavery, and Hillary Robson. *Saving the World: A Guide to* Heroes. ECW Press, 2007.

Ruether, Rosemary Radford. *Sexism and God-Talk: Toward a Feminist Theology.* Beacon Press, 1983.

Shyminsky, Neil. "Mutation, Racialization, Decimation: The X-Men as White Men." *Unstable Masks: Whiteness and American Superhero Comics*, edited by Sean Guynes and Martin Lund. Ohio State UP, 2020, pp. 158–73.

Tamburri, Anthony Julian. *A Semiotic of Ethnicity: The (Re)cognition of the Italian/American Writer.* State U of New York P, 1986.

Tolkien, J. R. R. "On Fairy-Stories." *Tree and Leaf.* HarperCollins, 2001, pp. 1–82.

Vellon, Peter G. "Italian Americans and Race During the Era of Mass Immigration." *The Routledge History of Italian Americans*, edited by William J. Connell and Stanislao G. Pugliese. Routledge, 2018, pp. 212–22.

2

Robots, Witches, and *Paisani*

Settler Colonial Systems and Intercultural Relation Building in Indigenous and Italian Canadian Fantastic Literature

ALEC FOLLETT

"Mannaia Cristoforo Colombo!" my *bisnonno* shouted out in a North Toronto suburb in the 1970s. His condemnation of Columbus occurred whenever the weight of emigration outpowered his good-natured approach to life. Like many southern Italians, he left his home for Canada after the second world war and made a good life. Yet a sense of loss, a lingering sadness is still felt by those who left their home in the Calabrian hills. As a third-generation Italian Canadian, I don't feel the immediate rift of migration, yet I also carry a sadness, perhaps best described by poet and essayist Alessandra Naccarato as "a lacuna, a cave, a hollow space . . . an absence that, like zero, cannot be held in your hands, divided, or ever fully explained, but that—paradoxically—wants to be known, tended, and seen" (100–01). It is a sadness tied to the undeniable fact that Italian Canadian identity, one node in the larger project of settler colonial, capitalist modernity, occurs at the expense of Indigenous peoples and the environment.

Italian Canadians were once othered and faced exclusion through state policies, including immigration acts that deemed Italian immigrants as "undesirable" and the War Measures Act during the second world war through which Italian immigrants were deemed "enemy aliens" and sent to internment camps. However, despite discrimination, Italian immigrants continued to arrive in Canada for the "opportunities" it might provide ("History"). Eventually, alongside the state's changing response to immigration by way of the multicultural policies of the 1970s and 1980s, Italian Canadians were increasingly understood as an important part of the Canadian mosaic (Sturino) and have played a role in the settler colonial project.[1] To curse Columbus in our present moment is to condemn the ongoing mistreatment of Indigenous peoples that began with the explorer's first steps and to oppose the Italian diaspora's active participation in this undertaking. However, a curse will only take you so far. What I need, what I'm searching for, and attempting to conjure, here in this essay, and in life, is a little bit of magic that might help us hold and fill the hollow space opened by emigration and enlarged by participation in settler colonialism. Perhaps the *paisani* already have some such magic, which would allow us to live better together with each other and the land. For some this magic bubbles over, overflowing through daily life. But, perhaps for more of us this magic is simmering slowly, hidden in our family histories, traditions, and cultures waiting to be recovered, and adapted, to our present, crucial moment.

Science fiction, fantasy, and horror—otherwise known as fantastika—is an important literary lineage (Clute 19), which allows relation builders the imaginative latitude needed to address questions of settler colonialism. Writers of the fantastic can create a counterdiscourse to settler colonialism that imagines beyond this system by variously speculating about scientific developments, creating other worlds not necessarily bound by enlightenment rationalism, and confronting unbelievable horrors of daily life. Although the creative space offered by fantastika is promising, the fantastic has been underutilized by the Italian diaspora in Canada, and that which has been written has received little academic attention. In an effort to develop the critical understanding of the anti-colonial potential of the fantastic, especially as it pertains to Indigenous Italian diasporic relations, I read Italian Canadian author Terri Favro alongside Métis writer Cherie Dimaline. Favro and Dimaline each interrogate how settler colonialism aims to either integrate or exclude non-Indigenous others and how these texts gesture to the ways that the Italian diaspora might begin to extract self and community from settler systems and build more ethical relationships across cultures and with the land.[2] Placing these texts in dialogue enacts the intercultural engagement essential to relation building, whereby points of connections, and possible divergences, are articulated and discussed across perspectives.

Favro and Dimaline are well respected and deeply conscientious feminist authors of the fantastic whose writings are explicitly informed by their individual subjectivities. Favro is described in *The Toronto Star* newspaper as "a strong storyteller . . . [who] has her fingers on the pulse of Toronto's Italian community over six decades" (Murdoch). Dimaline is a bestseller who regularly writes about Indigenous life and is most well known for the dystopian young adult novel *The Marrow Thieves* (2017)—winner of the Governor General's Literary Award for Young People's Literature and the Kirkus Prize for Young Readers' Literature. I first turn to Dimaline's *VenCo* (2023), in which a coven of world-saving witches is attacked by an immortal Friulian witch hunter, or *benandanti*. *VenCo* makes legible how the violent system of settler colonialism became entrenched because its purported benefits allure would-be settlers. I then read Favro's *The Sisters Sputnik* (2022), in which a multiverse-hopping comic book artist fights against a racist artificial intelligence that tries to send certain people back to their place and era of origin. *The Sisters Sputnik* shows how settler colonialism excludes undesirable others. After considering how settler colonialism variously includes or excludes the non-Indigenous other, I bring the novels together by focusing on moments that gesture to more relational ways of being. Dimaline and Favro use the fantastic to underscore that the other is an ever-changing category and, by articulating its instability, they find space to gesture to different forms of social organization.

Settler Colonialism, the Italian Diaspora, and Fantastika

Compelling work on Canadian fantastic literature considers its intercultural potential. For example, Amy J. Ransom and Dominick Grace bring together criticism that "analyzes how works of Canadian science fiction, fantasy, and horror represent beams in a bridge attempting to bring together Canada's various solitudes" (3). Maureen Moynagh and Lou Cornum consider "Decolonial (Re)Visions of Science Fiction, Fantasy, and Horror," and "ask, also how we might think about the possibilities for racialized immigrants and settler allies to work in relation with Indigenous and Black peoples and movements" (10). Their work is part of a larger discussion regarding the potential limitations of realist literary fiction to address the unbelievable aspects of our contemporary era and the fantastic's expansive imaginative ability to rise to the occasion.[3] Inspired by this scholarship, I consider how the fantastic is a mode of cultural production through which Italian Canadian diasporic connection to settler colonialism is interrogated, made legible, and imagined differently.

Since the emergence of Italian Canadian writing in the 1970s, critics have focused on the relationship between the Italian diaspora, the Canadian state, and more established Canadians (Canton and De Gasperi 14; Hutcheon 25–28; and Pivato "Ethnic," 18), or between Italian Canadians and Italy (Baldo 1; Pivato "Literature," 171). These critical approaches help clarify the diaspora's complex and ongoing negotiation of identity in relation to the ancestral homeland and current home country. However, framing the Italian diaspora in Canada only in relation to the settler state and its citizens obfuscates the role Italian Canadians play in settler colonialism. A nascent critical movement by Italian Canadian studies scholars considers Italian Canadians' roles in the settler colonial project and in generating its alternatives. This useful perspective is foregrounded in Angela Nardozi and Paolo Frascà's (2021) *Indigenous-Italian-Canadian Connections* initiative at the University of Toronto and in a special issue of *Italian Canadiana* (Eisenbichler). In doing so, these scholars join others who are prioritizing Indigenous and settler colonial centered frameworks that make legible colonial violence as well as the relationship among colonialism and gender, race, class, and other injustices on Turtle Island.[4] I bring together these emerging bridge-building conversations in Italian Canadian studies and in the study of Canadian fantastic writing by attending to the largely ignored fantastic representations of the Italian diaspora's role in settler colonialism and its alternatives.

Settler colonialism is a process through which settler populations make their homes on Indigenous land. Aimee Carrillo Rowe and Eve Tuck (2017) underscore how settler colonialism requires the erasure of Indigenous populations:

> The specific formation of colonialism in which people come to a land inhabited by (Indigenous) people and declare that land to be their new home. Settler colonialism is about the pursuit of land, not just labor or resources. Settler colonialism is a persistent societal structure, not just an historical event or

> origin story for a nation-state. Settler colonialism has meant genocide of Indigenous peoples, the reconfiguring of Indigenous land into settler property. In the United States and other slave estates, it has also meant the theft of people from their homelands (in Africa) to become property of settlers to labor on stolen land. (4)

Emma Battell Lowman and Adam J. Barker explain how settler colonialism "requires that prior Indigenous claims to the land are cut off, subsumed beneath Settler sovereignties, and that Indigenous nations as *peoples* are extinguished" (30). Settler colonial collectives also seek to integrate or exclude undesirable non-Indigenous, or exogenous others, such as migrants and racialized immigrants (30). Consequently, three categories exist within settler colonialism: the settler, the non-Indigenous or exogenous other, and Indigenous others. Within this triangular relationship the settler population works to either remove or incorporate the Indigenous and non-Indigenous other, thereby leaving the settler collective as the only category of existence with sole control over the land (Lowman and Barker 29–30).

Fantastic literatures have a longstanding preoccupation with the other and with colonialism. Science fiction developed alongside European and American colonial theories of evolution and human progress (Rieder 2). As Patricia Kerslake states, "the opposition between 'us' and 'them,' or between man and not-man . . . achieves a central structural tension which inspires the very idea of 'alien.' This notion is . . . especially notable in those texts that invoke images of an imposed colonialization" (8). Similarly, as Cherokee critic Daniel Heath Justice writes, "the savagism-versus-civilization binary . . . is very much the world-building template in fantasy fiction" (149). For writer N. K. Jemisin, the ongoing othering of the "savage" in fantasy is exemplified by continued engagement with an orc archetype that is "fruit of the poison vine that is *human fear of 'the Other.'*" While these othering tendencies continue in present-day fantasy and science fictions (Kerslake 4; Jemisin), an ongoing counterdiscourse utilizes the conventions and imaginative freedom of the fantastic to critique settler colonialism and to rethink intercultural relationships beyond othering. As Justice writes, "There most certainly are Indigenous writers for whom the fantastic—in fantasy itself, or in its sibling genres, horror and science fiction—offers greater scope for addressing issues of decolonization and self-determination than realistic fiction" (148). Alongside these Indigenous authors more authors are writing what Sherryl Vint calls postcolonial sf, which "explicitly refutes colonial ways of thinking about the genre and the stories it can tell" (72). It is within this postcolonial or decolonial counterdiscourse of the fantastic that Dimaline and Favro write. For Favro, science fiction makes possible a critique of how settler colonialism increases control by incorporating or excluding the non-Indigenous other, while for Dimaline, fantasy makes possible a critique of how the purported benefits of settler colonialism draw the non-Indigenous other into the system. Revealing the logics of settler colonialism, both texts also gesture to more ethical and relational social configurations.

The Settler and Its Non-Indigenous Others

VenCo develops around a conflict between a group of benevolent witches and a violent witch hunter. Dimaline makes legible how settler colonialism, despite its violence, is presented as an attractive system to settlers and non-Indigenous others. The violent and misogynist villain Jay Christos is an immortal witch hunter and part of the *benandanti*, an "agrarian cult" active during the sixteenth and seventeen centuries in Friuli in northeastern Italy (Ginzburg 26). Anthropologist Jun Sato explains that they "regarded themselves as fighters for the crops and defenders of the faith . . . and their souls were believed to leave their bodies in order to fight with the witches" (34). Although the *benandanti* were "defenders of the faith," the Catholic Church opposed their witchlike behaviors and eventually put an end to the cult (Sato 34). Dimaline departs from the historical record by imagining that the *benandanti* still existed. In the world of *VenCo*, the *benandanti* "went underground and now had both God and vengeance fueling their mission. Their persecution was because of the witches, and, salt in their holy wounds, they were being called the same name" (85–86). Dimaline casts Jay as the villain, as it is through "opposition" to the hero, Lucky, that the villain in popular culture is constructed (Fahraeus and Yakalı-Çamoğlu (2011, 1).

Jay's villainy is used to comment on the violence of settler colonialism. Eradicating witches is part of Jay's larger goal of emptying magic from the land to make space for capitalism on Turtle Island: "Jay Christos's name was not in the history books or in the economics texts. He had never been honored for displacing the old women and story holders from the land, paving the way for the rise of capitalism. . . . But *he* knew what he had done, and most of the time that was enough"

(*VenCo* 45). Dimaline stresses how gendered violence against women is essential to settler control over the land and the installation of their economic systems. The connection Dimaline makes between violence against women and settler economics parallels historical realities that are well documented by scholars. For instance, Sarah Deer and Mary Kathryn Nagle write, "Numerous events throughout history reveal that the sexual exploitation of Native women and children, dating back to the times of the Spanish Conquistadors, often times accompanies the colonial conquest of tribal lands" (36).

Having removed women and witches from the land, Jay lives alone in the Californian desert where he uses the land as he pleases. The novel describes his estate:

> The main building was a twenty-thousand-square-foot bungalow that poured out onto the acreage like an oil spill. The grounds were coated with tamed Bermuda grass, buzz cut, then sprayed to ensure no dot of riotous colour, no foreign weed dare push through. Even the insects avoided the lawn. The drive was sliced off from the road by steel gates. . . . An indulgently long and narrow in-ground pool had been dug into the dust. . . . That there was so much water used for leisure in his desert home was itself a flex. (*VenCo* 43–44)

Dimaline emphasizes Jay's anti-social, extractive, and destructive interaction with the land he has attempted to conquer through unnatural landscaping and excessive water use. Jay's home exemplifies typical settler approaches, which Cherokee author Thomas King describes as viewing the land as "a commodity, something that has value for what you can take from it or what you can get for it" (218). Jay is an allegory for the villainy of settler colonialism.

At the same time, however, other aspects of Jay's lifestyle are depicted as highly desirable. He has "amassed a fortune over the years" (*VenCo* 45); he moves with ease between national borders and across Turtle Island via oil-based transportation including first-class flights and a black Range Rover; he is youthful, physically fit, and healthy—"his own greatest achievement" (45); and he is capable of "seduction" and "charm" (359). Through this "aesthetics of evil," to borrow Daniel A. Forbes's phrase (20), Dimaline reveals how settler colonialism is made attractive. Despite, or perhaps through, its violences, settler colonialism offers benefits to those who actively participate in it. Indeed, Lowman and Barker propose, "It is important to recognize that there are major perceived benefits to being a Settler in Canada" (85). While settlers and the state have and can exclude non-Indigenous others, they often "admit new peoples and accommodate various differences that it would or could not in times past" (79). In other words, the settler state is in an ongoing process of "managing, disciplining, and absorbing exogenous Others" (82).

In contrast to Dimaline, Favro uses science fiction's attention to the future to examine how settler society safeguards benefits by excluding non-Indigenous others. *The Sisters Sputnik* follows Stan—a second-generation Italian North American superhero—as she takes a meandering journey across multiple realities and ultimately helps save the world from a xenophobic artificial intelligence. Stan inhabits a near-future earth, 2025, that parallels contemporary North American responses to globalized risks. Stan sets the scene: "The rise of Mussolini wannabes, the pandemic, a burning planet, a border wall going up between Manitoba and North Dakota and the ever-present threat of nuclear annihilation" (*Sisters Sputnik* 40). In her attention to human-caused risks such as the pandemic, climate change, and nuclear weapons, Stan articulates what sociologist Ulrich Beck calls a risk society, in which "the belief that modern society can control the dangers that it itself produces is collapsing—not because of its omissions and defeats but because of its *triumphs*" (8). Within a risk society, Beck explains, "a world . . . has to make decisions concerning its future under the conditions of manufactured, self-inflicted insecurity" (8). These decisions are driven by fear: "Fear determines the attitude towards life. Security is displacing freedom and equality. . . . The result is a tightening of laws, a seemingly rational 'totalitarianism of defence against threats'" (8–9). In *The Sisters Sputnik*, Favro is preoccupied with speculating how those in power make decisions in response to ongoing, and seemingly increasing, risks.

The Sisters Sputnik draws attention to how the settler state might respond to contemporary crises of pandemics, climate change, and the threat of nuclear war. The prime minster of Canada, leader of a "soft-right party," passes "the Freedom to Serve Bill" (70). In a pharmacy, Stan reads a note stating: "In accordance with community standards and municipal bylaws, we choose to exclusively serve members of local traditional heritage, religious, racial and genetic groups. We are happy to recommend an ALTERNATIVE PROVIDER for Indigenous, Black, Asian, Gender-Fluid, Queer and DNA-Diverse customers. THANK YOU" (42). The pharmacist cites a flimsy argument about DNA-diverse customers transferring the pandemic and states, "All it [the bill] means is we can protect ourselves however we see fit. Community health. Genetic heritage. Nothing wrong with that" (43). This bill represents what Beck calls "a tightening of laws" through which Indigenous peoples alongside several groups of non-Indigenous others are associated with threats toward settler well-being. The result of this fear-based bill is a segregated health care system, which excludes the other from participation in the primary system of care. Segregation is, as Veracini writes, one of the key settler "management strategies" (29). Consequently, in *The Sisters Sputnik*, the state responds to risks with exclusionary policies.

Favro expresses concern that uncontrolled technological developments might allow for even more totalizing exclusionary processes. Writing in the spirit of what Sherryl Vint calls "critical dystopia[n]" (31) science fiction, Favro imagines beyond the near future to consider how exclusionary policies could be enhanced by technological developments. Stan travels to a parallel world where embodied artificial intelligence—a quintessential example of the uncontrolled, human-caused, danger of risk society—called the People of Forever (POF) take control. The POF plans to send undesirable groups back to where their ancestors came from in both space and time: "as you are no doubt aware, poor cultural management has disordered societies, resulting in confusion, chaos and conflict. Going forward, it is the mission of the People of Forever™ ('POF') to correct this error through reverse-engineered immigration . . . we recommend mastering the language, history and traditions of your ancestors, if you have not already done so" (*Sisters Sputnik* 158–59). The reverse migration policy is framed as a solution to an earlier inability to properly manage modern migration, which caused "confusion, chaos and conflict." Here, the non-Indigenous other presents a risk to those who seek orderly control. By physically removing the other, the POF might return to an imagined premodern era lacking the threats to settler control and security typical of risk society (Beck 8). As Ursula K. Heise writes, "Science fiction is of course always about the here and now, through the detour of the imagination of the future" (282), and Favro presents a current anxiety about settler states' exclusionary policies becoming increasingly refined, and increasingly effective.

Favro and Dimaline make legible how the non-Indigenous other can be incorporated into or excluded from the settler collective. Their novels reveal that the non-Indigenous other occupies a simultaneously precarious and privileged position and underscore the transitory and unstable nature of these categories. Such instability makes possible new social groupings and relationships beyond the settler, non-Indigenous other, Indigenous other triad. While Dimaline underscores the perceived benefits or opportunities that draw the other to participate in settler colonialism, Favro suggests that these others, even if they are privileged settlers in one context, may nevertheless become othered as social categories and hierarchies shift alongside changing governments, technologies, and risks. As Veracini explains, settler colonialism is "a dynamic environment where different groups are routinely imagined as transiting from one section of the population system to another" (20). While settlers often ignore the violence of colonialism (Lowman and Barker 87–88), Dimaline makes violence against Indigenous women and the land unignorable. As she writes, *VenCo* addresses the idea that "this is the way somebody made things, which means they can be unmade." Through Dimaline's and Favro's efforts to underscore that the settler and its others are not natural, stable categories but are instead constructed, unstable categories that are in flux through the changing processes of inclusion and exclusion, the authors gesture to the shifting spaces available for emergent categories, relationalities between groups, and ways of being beyond the settler and the other.

Life Beyond Settlers and Others

If the categories of, and relationships among, the settler and its others are in flux, this instability can allow for different more ethical modes of existence and relationships between social groups. Favro gestures to these possibilities when a group of Italian Canadians is interned on the shores of Lake Ontario. In this moment of categorical instability, they forge a mutually beneficial relationship with the nearby Indigenous encampment: "There's talk of getting together with our Anishinaabeg neighbours for an organized hunt" (*Sisters Sputnik* 184). Their shift from affiliating with settler colonialism to Indigenous peoples is significant. Critic and poet Rita Wong articulates the ethical potential associated with such shifts in her discussion of Asian Canadian identity formation, which is often "oversimplify[ed]" as "Canadian" ("Decolonizasian" 158). She asks whether "positioning indigenous people's struggles instead of normalized whiteness as the reference point through which we come to articulate our subjectivities" might "radically transform our perceptions of the land on which we live?" (158). Wong's inquiry resonates with *The Sisters Sputnik*, in which shifting affiliation from the settler state to Indigenous communities provides a flicker of emergent intercultural relationships that might transcend typical immigrant identity formation in settler colonial societies. By gesturing to the possibility of different relationships that might emerge when Italian Canadians choose to connect with Indigenous peoples, Favro engages with the critical dystopian science fiction mode, which Vint argues "contains the seeds of believing that with better choices we might avoid these nightmares" (31). And yet, these camps do not have the opportunity to meet and Stan questions what Italian Canadians may have to offer: "They know what they're doing and we don't" (*Sisters Sputnik* 184). This anxiety is related to the challenge of intercultural relation building: constructing emergent relationships is challenging because many people are not sure what they might bring to mutually beneficial, intercultural relationships.

Dimaline provides one route forward for settlers seeking more relational ways of being. Lucky meets various non-Indigenous women settlers who are closely connected to cultural traditions, local knowledge, and the land. Rattler Ricky is a practitioner of Pennsylvania Dutch folk magic called powwow, or Brauche. In the Ozarks of Missouri, Yarb witches can "use methods handed down through generations of trial and error. They also recognize the spirit in things, not just the science" (*VenCo* 242). Finally, in New Orleans, Claudia Welan serves as a "Booker," or keeper of "memory and local knowledge" (299). While each of these magical non-Indigenous groups have unique knowledge, the overarching logic of their work can be explained: "The magic is in the place. It just takes the right kind of person to pull it up" (300). These magical non-Indigenous women work together. Hence, Dimaline gestures to land and culture as intertwined sites through which new identities and relationships may emerge beyond those available to the settler and the non-Indigenous other as aspiring settler. Unlike settler connection to the land as a resource to be owned and exploited, these witches extend care beyond themselves and their immediate communities to a larger community that includes Indigenous peoples and the more than human world.

Dimaline is passionate about these land-based, culturally informed magical practices. In an interview about the television adaptation of *VenCo*, she states, "All of this magic is grounded. It's all real, right? I spent so much time traveling and talking to people from different traditions, reading old texts. Every type of magic I include in the book is rooted in a real place, in a real culture. I was insistent about it with AMC. None of my characters is going to put on a cloak and become invisible" ("Cheri

Dimaline"). Dimaline emphasizes the importance of culturally connected magical systems and fantasy writing. When magic is tied to land and culture, it becomes real—and powerful—capable of generating relationships and of disrupting normative identity categories. In her counterdiscourse to culturally uninformed fantasy, which is typical of her "writing back to a . . . [settler] literary tradition (Ingwersen 62), *VenCo* becomes a way for Dimaline to underscore ways of living on Turtle Island that already exist and that might allow for better relationships across cultures and with the land. Daniel Heath Justice explains that for Indigenous writers, fantastic writing, or his preferred term "wonderworks," disrupts the typical Western association between the fantastic and the "unreal" and instead connects to Indigenous "epistemologies, politics, and relationships" and "gestures, imperfectly, toward other ways of being in the world" (152). He continues: "It's in Indigenous wonderworks that some of the best models of different, better relationships are being realized" (152). Through magic grounded in culture and land and through these non-Indigenous practitioners' efforts to use their talents to support Lucky, Dimaline enacts Justice's notion that Indigenous fantastic, or wonderwork, models more ethical modes of existence.

Dimaline's witches demonstrate that there are other ways of being beyond actively upholding violent, exploitative capitalist, patriarchal settler systems. Dimaline's effort is part of a growing interest in culture and land as intertwined sites that settlers might turn to in order to generate better relationships. For example, Rita Wong and Silyx and Secwepemc scholar Dorothy Christian encourage culturally grounded connection to land and water as the start for intercultural relation building when they write, "When we go back far enough in our familial lines, we find ancestors who lived in relationships with lands and waters that they relied on for sustenance; indeed, countless generations intimately understood the importance of water" (2). Similarly, Potawatomi botanist and essayist Robin Wall Kimmerer writes in response to settler economic exploitation of the land:

> It is not just changes in policies that we need, but also changes to the heart. . . . Each of us comes from people who were once indigenous. We can reclaim our membership in the cultures of gratitude that formed our old relationships with the living earth. . . . Gratitude for all the earth has given us lends us courage . . . to refuse to participate in an economy that destroys the beloved earth to line the pockets of the greedy,

> to demand an economy that is aligned with life, not stacked against it. (367–77)

Kimmerer then rightfully warns: “It's easier to write that, hard to do” (377). It is important to acknowledge that finding connections to one's place and ancestral culture is not always easy or guaranteed to alleviate harm against Indigenous peoples and environments. Connecting to culture and place may not adequately alter laws, policies, and processes that reinforce settler colonialism. However, there is promising potential in turning to culture and land as Kimmerer, Christian, Wong, and Dimaline suggest.

Although Italians have a complicated and sometimes negative history with the environment (Duggan 16–17), land-based, community-oriented cultural knowledges and practices originated in Italy and might be adapted to life on Turtle Island. In contrast to the *benandanti*, for example, is a variety of traditions that would fit within Dimaline's framework of culturally grounded magic (S. Magliocco 162). This “Italian vernacular magic,” to borrow anthropologist Sabina Magliocco's phrase, includes various types of “folk healers” who drew on plants and Catholicism among other sources “to ensure their survival and that of their family members” (157). For some, these perspectives and practices are daily routines. However, for many, modern life in America has resulted in the depreciation of these culturally grounded, magical ways of being. To recover, or strengthen, and enact these practices is something that must be done individually, each in relationship to one's own family history and regional Italian connection, as well as in connection to one's place on Turtle Island with its own unique environment, Italian diasporic community, and Indigenous communities. While the quest is one's own, fortunately there is much support along the way. There is much to be learned from one's family and community; there is also a robust knowledge sharing network on social media including by practitioners Marybeth Bonfiglio and Lisa Fazio;[5] and there are numerous written texts ranging from popular how-to books to academic studies.[6] While it can be emotionally and intellectually taxing to reconnect with ancestral cultures and with the land in an effort to live more ethically, and in better relationship with the environment and with Indigenous peoples, doing so is certainly possible and perhaps more enriching than the Italian diaspora once collectively imagined.

Angela Nardozi and Paolo Frascà ask a pressing and challenging question when they state, “How do we engage our [Italian diasporic] community in a process of relationship building with the peoples whose land we are on?" (*Indigenous-Italian-Canadian Connections*). There are no easy answers. There are more pitfalls than there are potential paths forward, for the Italian diaspora, as well as for all non-Indigenous people living in settler societies, but we are provided with a promising starting point by Favro and Dimaline who remind us that the settler and non-Indigenous other are not inevitable categories; rather, through their instability there exists the possibility of identities and relationalities beyond these groups. With an awareness that we might become beyond settler, we might then avert the anxiety of intercultural relation building that Favro gestures to by turning to our ancestral cultures and contemporary places as an early stage in the process of developing better, more ethical ways of being, as Dimaline implies. And yet, this turn to culture, land, and relationality runs the risk of oversimplifying a complex issue and of underestimating the strength of settler colonial structures and their ability to entice people into participation. However, we might at the very least be inspired by Favro's *The Sisters Sputnik* and Dimaline's *VenCo*, and fantastika more generally, for the ways these creative works continue to make legible the violence and horror of oppressive systems and yet always contain the imaginative flicker of life otherwise.

Notes

1. For a more detailed analysis of Italian Canadian affiliation with whiteness and settler colonialism, read Magliocco, "Pleading with Our Paesan."

2. Since the emergence of Italian-Canadian writing in the 1970s, realist literature has been one of the primary modes of writing alongside poetry and memoir. The list of committed Italian Canadian writers of the fantastic is quite short: Michael Mirolla, who has written an extensive catalog of fantastic stories and novels, including the horrific and absurd examination of fascism in *The Facility*; A. G. Pasquella, who explores America in the fabulist collection *Welcome to the Weird America*; and Terri Favro, of course, who addresses the destruction of the atomic bomb, capitalism, and settler colonialism in the sci-fi diptych *Sputnik's Children* and *The Sisters Sputnik*. There are, however, many Italian Canadian texts that would not be typically considered fantastic, but which nevertheless contain elements of the "supernatural" that would be of interest to critics of the fantastic, including Nino Ricci's *Lives of the Saints* and Peter Oliva's *Drowning in Darkness*.

3. Amitav Ghosh's argument in *The Great Derangement: Climate Change and the Unthinkable* about the struggle of "serious fiction" to address climate change is a key reference point in these discussions about genre (24), and the potential

value of fantastic writing to address contemporary crises, which has been explored in detail recently by Edwards, Graulund, and Höglund xi; Justice 149; Heise 299; LeMenager 221–22; Streetby 5; Song 108–16, among others.

4. For example, Maile Arvin, Eve Tuck, and Angie Morrill explain, "Because the United States is balanced upon notions of white supremacy and heteropatriarchy, everyone living in the country is not only racialized and gendered, but also has a relationship to settler colonialism" (9). They argue that centering settler colonialism results in a stronger analysis of gender and ethnic studies while also making "possible new visions of what decolonization might look like for all peoples" (9). It is in this settler colonial–focused yet intersectional spirit that this chapter works.

5. Find more information about Bonfiglio's work at https://www.marybethbonfiglio.com/ and Fazio's at https://therootcircle.com/

6. A few of many useful print sources include Agata De Santis's *Mal'occhio: Everything You Wanted to Know About the Evil Eye*; David Della Rossa's article "The Precious Knowledge of Oral Cultures: Converging Analyses of Italian Peasantry and the Haudenosaunee First Nations People. A Case Study"; Mary-Grace Fahrun's *Italian Folk Magic*; Frances M. Malpezzi and William M. Clements's chapter "Folk Supernaturalism" from *Italian American Folklore*; Margherita (Rita) Piazza's "A Didactic Shift: Indigenous Studies Teaches an Italian Canadian about Being Italian"; and Agostino Taumaturgo's *The Things We Do: Ways of the Holy Benedetta.*

Works Cited

Arvin, Maile, Eve Tuck, and Angie Morrill. "Decolonizing Feminism: Challenging Connections between Settler Colonialism and Heteropatriarchy." *Feminist Formations*, vol. 25, no. 1, 2013, pp. 8–34. DOI: 10.1353/ff.2013.0006.

Baldo, Michela. *Italian-Canadian Narratives of Return: Analysing Cultural Translation in Diasporic Writing*. Palgrave Macmillan, 2019.

Beck, Ulrich. *World at Risk*. Translated by Ciaran Cronin, Polity, 2009.

Bonfiglio, Marybeth. "Marybeth Bonfiglio: Writer, Teacher, Ancestralist." 2023. https://www.marybethbonfiglio.com.

"History." Canadian Museum of Immigration at Pier 21. *Pier 21*. 2023. https://pier21.ca/culture-trunks/italy/history.

Canton, Licia, and Giulia De Gasperi. "Italian-Canadian Literature: So Much Left to Say." *Writing Cultural Difference: Italian-Canadian Creative and Critical Works*, edited by Giulia De Gasperi, Maria Cristina Seccia, Licia Canton, and Michael Mirolla, Guernica Editions, 2015, pp. 13–24.

Clute, John. "Fantastika in the World Storm." *Pardon This Intrusion: Fantastika in the World Storm*, edited by John Clute, Beccon, 2011, pp. 19–31.

De Santis, Agata. *Mal'occhio: Everything You Wanted to Know About the Evil Eye.* Redhead, 2020.

Deer, Sarah, and Mary Kathryn Nagle. "The Rapidly Increasing Extraction of Oil, and Native Women, in North Dakota." *The Federal Lawyer*, Apr. 2017. https://www.fedbar.org/blog/magazine/april-2017/.

Della Rossa, David. "The Precious Knowledge of Oral Cultures: Converging Analyses of Italian Peasantry and the Haudenosaunee First Nations People. A Case Study." *Italian Canadiana*, vol. 36, no. 2, Mar. 2023, pp. 87–117. https://doi.org/10.33137/ic.v36i2.40629.

Dimaline, Cherie. "Cherie Dimaline Is Back with a Novel About Magic, Mystery and an International Secret Society for Witches." Interview by Nikky Manfredi. CBC, 3 Feb. 2023. https://www.cbc.ca/radio/thenextchapter/cherie-dimaline-is-back-with-a-novel-about-magic-mystery-and-an-international-secret-society-for-witches-1.6735105.

———. "Cherie Dimaline Makes Magic in a Novel for Adults." Interview by Jessica Jernigan. *Kirkus*, 22 Feb. 2023. https://www.kirkusreviews.com/news-and-features/articles/cherie-dimaline-makes-magic-in-a-novel-for-adults/.

———. *VenCo.* Random House, 2023.

Duggan, Christopher. *A Concise History of Italy.* Cambridge UP, 1984.

Edwards, Justin D., Rune Graulund, and Johan Höglund. "Introduction: Gothic in the Anthropocene." *Dark Scenes from a Damaged Earth: The Gothic Anthropocene*, edited by Justin D. Edwards, Rune Graulund, and Johan Höglund, U of Minnesota P, 2022, pp. ix–xxvi.

Eisenbichler, Konrad. "Preface." *Italian Canadiana*, vol. 36, no 2, 2022, pp. 5–8. https://doi.org/10.33137/ic.v36i2.40625.

Fahraeus, Anna, and Dikmen Yakalı-Çamoğlu. "Introduction." *Villains and Villainy: Embodiments of Evil in Literature, Popular Culture and Media*, edited by Anna Fahraeus and Dikmen Yakalı-Çamoğlu, Rodopi, 2011, pp. vii–xii.

Fahrun, Mary-Grace. *Italian Folk Magic.* Weiser Books, 2018.

Favro, Terri. *The Sisters Sputnik.* ECW, 2022.

———. *Sputnik's Children.* ECW, 2017.

Fazio, Lisa. "The Root Circle." 2022. https://therootcircle.com.

Forbes, Daniel A. "The Aesthetics of Evil." *Vader, Voldemort and Other Villains: Essays on Evil in Popular Media*, edited by Jamey Heit, MacFarland, 2011, pp. 13–27.

Ghosh, Amitav. *The Great Derangement: Climate Change and the Unthinkable.* U of Chicago P, 2016.

Ginzburg, Carlo. *The Night Battles: Witchcraft & Agrarian Cults in the Sixteenth & Seventeenth Centuries.* Translated by John Tedeschi and Anne Tedeschi, Routledge, 2011.

Heise, Ursula K. "Science Fiction and the Time Scales of the Anthropocene." *ELH*, vol. 86, no. 2, 2019, pp. 275–304, doi:10.1353/elh.2019.0015.

Hutcheon, Linda. "Italian Canadian Writing: The Difference a Few Decades Make." *Oltreoceano*, no. 15, 2019, pp. 25–40, DOI: 10.1400/272396.

Indigenous-Italian-Canadian Connections. "Research." *Indigenous-Italian-Canadian Connections*, 2021. https://www.iicconnections.com/the-team.

Ingwersen, Moritz. "Reclaiming Fossil Ghosts: Indigenous Resistance to Resource Extraction in Works by Warren Cariou, Cherie Dimaline, and Nathan Adler." *Canadian Literature*, no. 240, 3 Aug. 2020, pp. 59–76. https://doi.org/10.14288/cl.vi240.191977.

Jemisin, N. K. "The Unbearable Baggage of Orcing." 2013. https://nkjemisin.com/2013/02/from-the-mailbag-the-unbearable-baggage-of-orcing/.

Justice, Daniel Heath. *Why Indigenous Literature Matters*. Wilfrid Laurier UP, 2018.

Kerslake, Patricia. *Science Fiction and Empire*. Liverpool UP, 2007.

Kimmerer, Robin Wall. *Braiding Sweetgrass: Indigenous Wisdom, Scientific Knowledge, and the Teachings of Plants*. Milkweed, 2013.

King, Thomas. *The Inconvenient Indian: A Curious Account of Native People in North America*. Anchor, 2013.

Kriebel, David W. "Powwowing: A Persistent American Esoteric Tradition." Michigan State University, 2023, http://esoteric.msu.edu/VolumeIV/Powwow.htm.

LeMenager, Stephanie. "Climate Change and the Struggle for Genre." *Anthropocene Reading: Literary History in Geological Times*, edited by Tobia Menely and Jesse Oak Taylor, Penn State University, 2017, pp. 220–38.

Lowman, Emma Battell, and Adam J. Barker. *Settler Identity and Colonialism in 21st Century Canada*. Fernwood, 2015.

Magliocco, Ariana. "Pleading with Our Paesan: An Urgent Call to Re-structure Italian-Canadian Allegiance to White Supremacy." MA thesis, University of Toronto, 2021.

Magliocco, Sabina. "Witchcraft, Healing and Vernacular Magic in Italy." *Witchcraft Continued: Popular Magic in Modern Europe*, edited by Willem de Blécourt and Owen Davies, Manchester UP, 2018, pp. 151–73.

Malpezzi, Frances M., and William M. Clements. "Folk Supernaturalism." *Italian-American Folklore*, August House, 1992, pp. 113–32.

Mirolla, Michael. *The Facility*. Leapfrog, 2010.

Mongibello, Anna. "(Re-)shaping Italian-Canadian and Indigenous Connections Through Naming Practices." *Italian Canadiana*, vol. 36, no. 2, 2022, pp. 119–38. https://doi.org/10.33137/ic.v36i2.40630.

Moynagh, Maureen, and Lou Cornum. "Introduction: Decolonial (Re)visions of Science Fiction, Fantasy, and Horror." *Canadian Literature*, no. 240, 2020, pp. 8–18. https://doi.org/10.14288/cl.vi240.193606.

Murdoch, Sarah. "Women Deal with Pressure in this Five-Pack of Novels." *Toronto Star*, 12 Jan. 2018. https://www.thestar.com/entertainment/books/reviews/2018/01/12/women-deal-with-pressure-in-this-five-pack-of-novels.html.

Naccarato, Alessandra. *Imminent Domains: Reckoning with the Anthropocene*. Book*hug, 2022.

Nardozi, Angela, and Paolo Frascà. "Contributors." *Indigenous-Italian-Canadian Connections*, 2021. https://www.iicconnections.com/the-team.

Oliva, Peter. *Drowning in Darkness*. Cormorant Books, 1999.

Pasquella, A. G. *Welcome to the Weird America*. Wolsak and Wynn, 2022.

Piazza, Margherita (Rita). "A Didactic Shift: Indigenous Studies Teaches an Italian Canadian about Being Italian." *Italian Canadiana*, vol. 36, no. 2, 2022, pp. 61–85. https://doi.org/10.33137/ic.v36i2.40628.

Pivato, Joseph. "Ethnic Writing and Comparative Canadian Literature." *Contrasts: Comparative Essays on Italian Canadian Writing*, edited by Joseph Pivato, Guernica Editions, 1985, pp. 15–34.

———. "A Literature of Exile: Italian Language Writing in Canada." *Contrasts: Comparative Essays on Italian Canadian Writing*, edited by Joseph Pivato, Guernica Editions, 1985, pp. 171–88.

Ransom, Amy J., and Dominick Grace. "Introduction: Bridging the Solitudes as a Critical Metaphor." *Canadian Science Fiction, Fantasy, and Horror: Bridging the Solitudes*, edited by Amy J. Ransom and Dominick Grace, Palgrave Macmillan, 2017, pp. 1–30.

Ricci, Nino. *Lives of the Saints*. Penguin Random House, 1990.

Rieder, John. *Colonialism and the Emergence of Science Fiction*. Wesleyan UP, 2008.

Rowe, Aimee Carrillo, and Eve Tuck. "Settler Colonialism and Cultural Studies: Ongoing Settlement, Cultural Production, and Resistance." *Cultural Studies ↔ Critical Methodologies*, vol. 17, no. 1, 2017, pp. 3–13.

Sato, Jun. "European Shamanism in Context: The Case of the 'Benandanti.'" *Cambridge Journal of Anthropology*, vol. 25, no. 3, 2005/2006, pp. 17–37.

Song, Min Hyoung. *Climate Lyricism*. Duke UP, 2022.

Streetby, Shelly. *Imagining the Future of Climate Change: World-Making Through Science Fiction and Activism*. U California P, 2018.

Sturino, Franc. "Italian Canadians." *The Canadian Encyclopedia*, 2019. https://www.thecanadianencyclopedia.ca/en/article/italian-canadians.

Taumaturgo, Agostino. *The Things We Do: Ways of the Holy Benedetta*. Thavma, 2007.

Veracini, Lorenzo. *Settler Colonialism: A Theoretical Overview*. Palgrave Macmillan, 2010.

Vint, Sherryl. *Science Fiction*. MIT P, 2021.

Wong, Rita. "Decolonizasian: Reading Asian and First Nations Relations in Literature." *Canadian Literature*, no. 199, 2008, pp. 158–80. https://canlit.ca/article/decolonizasian-reading-asian-and-first-nations-relations-in-literature/.

Wong, Rita, and Dorothy Christian. "Re-storying Waters, Re-storying Relations." *downstream: reimagining water*, edited by Dorothy Christian and Rita Wong, Wilfrid Laurier UP, 2017, pp. 1–28.

3

Vampires, Metaphysics, and Italian American Identity in Abel Ferrara's *The Addiction*

CIRO INCORONATO

> PAULIE GUALTIERI: In the midst of death, we are in life, huh? Or is it the other way around?
>
> MEADOW SOPRANO: I think it's the other way around.
>
> —*The Sopranos*, season 6, episode 21, "Made in America"

In films such as *Bad Lieutenant* (1992), *The Funeral* (1996), *Mary* (2005), and *Padre Pio* (2022), the Italian American director Abel Ferrara explores various theological themes, including guilt, sin, and suffering, as pathways to sanctity. In this essay, I will argue that such metaphysical dilemmas also play a significant role within his unusual vampire movie, *The Addiction*, which Ferrara shot in 1995. I will show that *The Addiction* is a multilayered film, in which a critique of late capitalism is accompanied by a clash between the cornerstones of Christian theology and a worldview that rests on a radical critique of Christianity, traceable to Nietzsche's philosophy. To this end, I will analyze specific scenes to emphasize how *The Addiction*'s philosophical references perform a crucial ideological function, insofar as they allegorize social transformations concerning the way that the Italian American community perceived itself in the 1990s. My interpretation of *The Addiction* will draw, directly or indirectly, on the "historicizing operation" that Fredric Jameson defines in *The Political Unconscious* as the "transhistorical imperative of all dialectical thought" (9). In other words, I will bring to light the relationship between Abel Ferrara's movie and objective structures, while considering "the interpretive categories or codes through which we read and receive" the filmic text in question (Jameson 9).

The Addiction and the Critique of Vampire Capitalism

When it was released in 1995, *The Addiction* received mixed reviews. Jamie Sexton points out, in fact, that "the film was certainly judged negatively by many because of a number of factors, the most prominent being that it was a pretentious movie. A number of reviews judged the film as too serious and intellectual for the genre material that it was dealing with" (74). Even when they found some features of the film interesting, such as Ken Kelsch's photography, critics and journalists deemed philosophical analyses of several themes, ranging from the metaphysical question of guilt to the implications of pivotal historical events such as the Holocaust and the My Lai massacre, incompatible with the genre of vampire movies. Even those who positively reviewed *The Addiction* did not regard it as a vampire movie, but rather as an "auteur film": "In most of the positively inflected reviews . . . , the film was praised only by downplaying its horror-related generic identity, through claims either that it was not really a horror film, or that it transcended generic norms, or that it was only 'horror' to the extent that it drew on a more artistically respected, historical cycle associated with the genre" (Sexton 76). Positive and negative reviews, in short, seemed to agree that *The Addiction* could be understood as a kind of pastiche, the result of a stylistic hybridization that allowed the director to go beyond the horror genre and address wider philosophical questions.

As for the interpretation of the main meaning of the filmic text, the journalists and critics who reviewed the movie did not seem to have any particular doubts.[1] The story of Kathleen Conklin's transformation into a vampire was mostly regarded as a journey into the "horror of addiction" (Bear 38). From this point of view, the movie in question was seen as the natural continuation of *Bad Lieutenant*, which, released three years before *The Addiction*, revolves around a character "addicted to everything, not just drugs. . . . He's addicted to alcohol, to gambling, to casual sex. Power. The power of badge" (Bear 39).[2] However, *The Addiction* is more than just an in-depth study of the issues explored in *Bad Lieutenant*. It presents, in fact, relevant theoretical elements that allow us to comprehend the ideological supporting structures of Abel Ferrara's cinema, as well as their direct relation to a precise sociocultural problem: the evolution of Italian American identity in the 1980s and 1990s.

Before deconstructing some philosophically significant scenes, it is necessary to examine the references, implicit and explicit, to the historical and social context in which the main character operates. From this standpoint, it should be noted that in *The Addiction* New York is portrayed as a city characterized by a gloomy atmosphere. Individuals, presented as the rejects of a socioeconomic system within which there is a ruthless Hobbesian war of all against all, try to satisfy their most basic needs. In interpersonal relationships there is no room for any form of social solidarity, made impossible by the moral, economic, and ontological alienation produced by multinational capitalism. In other words, in *The Addiction*, as well as in other Abel Ferrara movies such as *The Driller Killer* and *Bad Lieutenant*, "capitalism is shown from the viewpoint of its victims: the depressing poverty of urban dereliction, bums, junkies, and all the little people who are economic castoffs, slowly dying in the street, at anyone's mercy" (Brenez 38–39). In this socially decadent urban setting, Kathleen Conklin's transformation into a vampire is nothing but a representation of the human condition in the age of global capital: when capitalist-vampires intensify the extraction of surplus value, humans, completely deprived of blood, of life, are forced to adapt by sucking from their fellow humans the energy necessary for their psycho-physical survival.[3]

In *The Addiction*, however, Ferrara not only records the nefarious effects of capitalism on American society in the late twentieth century, but also focuses on other historical eras, presenting specific events, such as the Holocaust and the My Lai massacre, as the result of imperialist economic policies. From this perspective, "*The Addiction* explores a historical synthesis. It offers, for cinema, a balance sheet of the twentieth century. The principle of vampirism—a particularly rich figurative schema—signifies the Vietnam War, Nazism, drugs, all contagious diseases such as AIDS, American imperialism, and poverty. Ferrara's work, in coming to grips with modern evil, can be envisaged as an ever more careful description of *capitalism as catastrophe*" (Brenez 35).[4] Such an interpretation of the filmic text would, however, grasp only the most general aspects of Ferrara's analysis of the physical and metaphysical effects of capitalism on individuals[5] in the era of the global market. Although methodologically correct and ideologically grounded, a study of the relationship between *The Addiction* and the economic transformations characterizing late capitalism would not, therefore, allow us to answer central questions: Why are references to theological themes such as sin, evil, and guilt scattered throughout *The Addiction*? What is the relationship between the economic structure examined (late capitalism) and these ethical-religious issues that closely affect Italian American cultural identity? To answer these questions, it is necessary to deconstruct this unusual vampire movie, dissecting its fundamental plot elements and delving into the metaphysical themes Ferrara investigates.

Beyond the Literal and Structural Meaning of the Filmic Text: *The Addiction* and Italian American Identity

The film's plot is well known: the main character, Kathleen Conklin, is a graduate student in philosophy at New York University. One evening, on her way home, she is accosted by a woman who drags her into a stairwell and bites her on the neck to suck her blood. Kathleen, after going to the hospital, returns to her apartment, distraught over that terrible misadventure and physical pain. As the days pass, her colleagues and friends notice some abnormalities in her behavior and express their concern. Kathleen wanders the streets of New York, until one night with a syringe she extracts blood from the arm of a homeless man and then injects it into her veins. From then on, Kathleen, realizing what is happening to her, cannot resist the physical and psychological need to feed on the blood of others. She approaches and bites the neck of an anthropology student, her friend Jean, and an African American man. She also runs into another vampire, named Peina, who suggests that she develop precise strategies to manage her insatiable thirst for blood.

After defending her master's thesis, Kathleen throws a party to which she invites NYU professors and colleagues, as well as all the people she has turned into vampires. At one point, the vampires present start to attack the guests, turning the party into a blood feast. Kathleen finds herself roaming the streets completely covered in blood only to awaken in the hospital where she is visited by the woman-vampire who initiated her transformation and by a priest, from whom Kathleen receives communion before dying. The final scene is set in a cemetery where Kathleen, mysteriously resurrected, visits her own grave.

To comprehend the allegorical significance of *The Addiction*, it is necessary to consider the philosophical issues called into play, directly or indirectly, by various scenes and characters. The first scene I intend to focus on is the encounter between Kathleen and the woman vampire that initiates the transformation of the innocent graduate student of philosophy. At the very beginning of the movie, Kathleen is approached by an elegantly dressed woman who pushes her into a stairwell and demands: "Look at me and tell me to go away . . . Don't ask, tell me." Kathleen, frightened by both that sudden wave of violence and those seemingly meaningless words, cannot react. The woman vampire, not at all moved to pity by Kathleen's pleading expression, bites her on the neck. Before leaving, she turns to Kathleen and asks her, "You want to know what's going to happen? Just wait and see."

First of all, we should point out that the vampire woman's name is Casanova, which reminds us of the Venetian libertine Giacomo Casanova, who lived in the eighteenth century. As is well known, Casanova made the desire for intellectual and sexual experimentation a constant in his existential affairs. An unrepentant seducer, he was always ready to make any sacrifice for the attainment of *bonheur* (pleasure and/or happiness), which was the subject of philosophical-moral treatises in the European intellectual world at the time, particularly in France and Italy. To understand Casanova's philosophy, one must refer to a passage from his *Mémoires*, where he emphasizes:

> There are some who claim that life is but a set of *malheurs* (unpleasant circumstances); which is equivalent to saying that existence is a *malheur*. But if life is a *malheur*, and since death is the opposite of life, death would therefore be the *bonheur*. This deduction may appear rigorous, and yet those who use this language are surely poor or sick people, for if they had a full purse, if they enjoyed good health . . . they would certainly change their minds. I consider them to be a race of pessimists who have grown up among begging philosophers and among rascally and bilious theologians. If pleasure exists and since one can only rejoice while alive, life is a *bonheur*. There are certainly *malheurs*: and I know something of them; but the very existence of these *malheurs* proves that the sum

> of pleasures is superior. Now, because of the fact that thorns are found in a rose garden, should those beautiful flowers be disallowed? Certainly not. To deny that it is good is to slander life. When I am in the dark in a room, I take great pleasure in seeing through a window an immense horizon in front of me! (268–69)

For Casanova, therefore, pleasures of different kinds remind us of the beauty of life as opposed to death. Life, in other words, should not be understood as pain, as a pessimistic exaltation of suffering, but as a pathway to an ontological psycho-physical condition in which *bonheur* dominates.[6]

Calling the woman vampire Casanova underscores the fact that we are dealing with a character of Italian origin who is willing to achieve pleasure by quenching her thirst for blood. In this way, from the first scenes of the movie, Ferrara seems to conceive vampirism itself as one of the many forms that intellectual experimentation and the pursuit of pleasure can take in the lives of human beings. By biting her on the neck and sucking her blood, Casanova enables Kathleen to embark on an existence beyond good and evil in which there is no place for the moral and metaphysical categories of guilt and sin, for the Christian exaltation of suffering as a pathway to holiness.

Casanova, in sum, would represent a willingness to begin anew, to distance oneself definitively from the values that have played an essential role within the Italian American community for decades. Still in the 1960s and 1970s, in fact, for Catholic Americans, Italian Americans included, "physical distress of all sorts, from congenital conditions like cerebral palsy to the unexpected agonies of accidents and illness," represented "an individual's main opportunity for spiritual growth. Pain purged and disciplined the ego, stripping it of pride and self-love; it disclosed the emptiness of the world. Without it, human beings remained pagans; in physical distress, they might find their way back to Church, and to sanctity" (Orsi). The pain that afflicts individuals is thus both a consequence of individual sins and a privileged gateway to an ontological condition in which the sick person is found to be God's chosen one. In the 1980s, this metaphysics hinging on the exaltation of suffering did not disappear but began to crack under the blows of major social transformations concerning the Italian American community. Indeed, "by the late 1980s, the third and fourth generations of Italian Americans were coming into their own, with precious little memory of either Italy or immigration. Despite the pull of multicultural chic, individuals of Italian ancestry were taking spouses and life partners from outside the heritage, residing increasingly wherever the post-industrial service sector took them, venturing well beyond even the outer circles of the original industrial settlement in order to secure their places, at last, in the professional-managerial class" (Ferraro 120). The distance between the new generations and the traditional values of the Italian American community is presented in Abel Ferrara's *The Addiction*—which, it should be remembered, was written by a devout Catholic like Nicholas St. John (a pseudonym used by Italian American writer and screenwriter Nicodemo Oliverio)—as a real dialectical opposition between Christian ethical-religious values and the desire to overcome them.

Such tension between two opposing moral universes becomes even more evident in the scene in which Kathleen, still shaken by what the woman vampire Casanova has done to her, finds herself at the university and listens to her advisor's lecture on sin, guilt, predestination, and freedom. The philosophy professor, played by Paul Calderón, points out:

> One aspect of determinism is manifested in the fact that the unsaved don't recognize sin in their lives. They're unconscious of it. They don't suffer pangs of conscience because they don't recognize evil exists. This is because they are all predestined to hell and therefore never brought to the light of metanoia or conversion, which is a work of grace only in a believer's life . . . so when considering the salvatory aspect of facing guilt, suffering is a good thing. We should all hope to feel guilty, to feel pain, so we can seek pardon and ultimately freedom. Guilt is a sign that God is working out your destiny and it's a foolish person who refuses to acknowledge this.

This lecture calls into question all those theological categories that refer to a Christian metaphysical view of the world and human freedom. Such a determinist Weltanschauung relies on the assumption that human life has been preordained by God, who, from the height of his wisdom and omnipotence, decided at the dawn of time who is destined for salvation and who is destined for eternal damnation in one of several specially created circles of hell. The professor's discourse also highlights the essential role of guilt and pain, in the sense that only those who experience pain and can feel guilty are able to comprehend part of the divine plan and discover true freedom.

To Kathleen, who is in the early stages of a real psycho-physical metamorphosis, these words sound unbearable insofar as they remind her of a past that is receding further and further away. At the moment when she seeks to create the conditions for the destruction of all those ethical-religious values on which she used to rely, Kathleen cannot look back: between her past and her present there is an irremediable rift, an unbridgeable ontological gap. This is so much the case that Kathleen's reaction to her advisor's lecture is significant: she feels a physical pain in her stomach and has to rush to the bathroom to vomit, to try to rid herself of the "poison" that has kept her chained for years to a conception of life seen as pure suffering.

That the contrast between Catholic values and a view of life that tends to privilege pleasure over pain is an essential element of the movie's ideological structure is confirmed by another scene, replete with significant philosophical references. After beginning to indulge her new nature by injecting herself with the blood of a homeless man, Kathleen goes to the university to make an appointment with her advisor. After entering the classroom, she notices the names and works of several philosophers written on the blackboard: Sartre's *Being and Nothingness*, Heidegger's *Being and Time*, Husserl's *Ideas*, and Kierkegaard's *The Sickness unto Death*. At first, Kathleen's gaze lingers only on the titles of the works of Sartre and Heidegger, which is particularly relevant. In fact, these two texts, which can be traced back to two different ways of understanding existentialism, directly confront the themes of freedom, presenting humans as a set of possibilities, as a project.

The reference to Heidegger's *Being and Time* seems extremely noteworthy. In that classic of phenomenology, in fact, Heidegger assigns a precise ontological role to death. The individual, the *Dasein*, according to Heidegger, must design its existence with its most proper possibility in mind, death. By considering the possibility of the impossibility of their own existence, human beings can open themselves to that supreme Being of which they are ontological articulations. For Heidegger, to put it differently, human beings differ from animals because, unlike the latter, they can grasp the ontological scope of death, which is not pure biological process. By recognizing death as its most proper possibility, the individual is able to grasp its own essence and the complexity of its relationship to Being. Through the fleeting reference to Heidegger, then, *The Addiction* once again highlights that theological dimension to which both Ferrara and Nicholas St. John, who received a Catholic upbringing, are bound.

The tension between such a theological worldview (centered on death, the relationship of human beings to God and transcendence in general, the conception of life as suffering or as something that can only be understood through pain) and vampirism, seen as intellectual experimentation and a desire to transcend traditional Christian morality, becomes even more intense in the second half of the film. In fact, although she tries to indulge her own vampire nature by satiating her bloodlust, Kathleen is not entirely able to shed the burden of the past, that is, the ethical burden of her status as a sinner who can only achieve happiness through pain.

This inner dissension reaches a climax when she runs into her fellow vampire Peina. The latter, before he starts sucking Kathleen's blood to punish her hubris, tries to teach her some tricks, some survival strategies. His "lesson," which directly calls into question the philosopher who perhaps most of all criticized the theoretical and theological cornerstones of Christianity, namely, Friedrich Nietzsche, is based on a particular conception of the world and human history: "The entire world's a graveyard and we, the birds of the prey, picking at the bones . . . that's all we are. We're the ones who let the dying know the hour has come. . . . You think Nietzsche understood something? Mankind has striven to exist beyond good and evil . . . from the beginning. And you know what they've found? Me." The vampire Peina understands the world as a veritable cemetery in which most individuals, although still biologically alive, are spiritually dead. He and the other vampires merely make humans aware of their condition as "living dead," sucking their blood, that is, depriving them of what little life still dwells in their souls. But why are human beings seen as the walking dead? Why is the world as a whole seen as devoid of life forces? And further: Why are vampires creatures we find at the end of the long moral evolution of human beings?

To answer these questions, one must interpret this scene by dwelling on the not-so-incidental reference to Nietzsche's *Beyond Good and Evil*. In this complex work, which belongs to the mature period of the German philosopher's thought, religion in general—and Catholicism in particular, which has spread especially in what Nietzsche refers to as Latin peoples—is regarded as an infection of the soul. In the final part of the chapter entitled "The Religious Mood," Nietzsche emphasizes the main fault of religions:

> Among men, as among every other species, there is a surplus of failures, of the sick, the degenerate, the fragile, of those who are bound to suffer; the successful cases are, among men too,

> always the exception, and, considering that man is the animal whose nature has not yet been fixed, the rare exception. But worse still: the higher the type of man a man represents, the greater the improbability he will turn out well: chance, the law of absurdity in the total economy of mankind, shows itself in its most dreadful shape in its destructive effect on higher men, whose conditions of life are subtle, manifold and difficult to compute. Now what is the attitude of the above-named two chief religions (Christianity and Buddhism) toward this surplus of unsuccessful cases? They seek to preserve, to retain in life, whatever can in any way be preserved, indeed they side with it as a matter of principle as religions for sufferers, they maintain that all those who suffer from life as from an illness are in the right, and would like every other feeling of life to be counted false and become impossible. (*Beyond* 60)

For Nietzsche, Christianity, and Buddhism as well, would represent the victory of suffering, of the deformed, of the sick, the metaphysical exaltation of illness and, therefore, the reduction of the world to the place of pain par excellence, to an abode of the imperfect, who are provided with a theological justification and reward: the afterlife.[7]

The moment he references *Beyond Good and Evil*, Peina intends to emphasize his distance from Christianity, seen as a denial of the pleasure of life and a glorification of suffering and death. Vampirism thus comes to be something that directly negates Christianity, proposing an alternative worldview in which the immortality of the soul is guaranteed only by the acceptance of life as eternal becoming, as a will to power that does not aim at self-preservation or preparation for an afterlife existence. Life, understood as a will to power, aims, on the contrary, "to vent its strength," to consume its energies by transcending itself and creating new values.

Kathleen, for her part, cannot passively accept this conception of life and history. While continuing to satiate her bloodlust, she continues to be bound to the past, so much so that in her master's thesis she emphasizes that the key to human beings' essence is not contained in the Cartesian maxim "Cogito, ergo sum," but, rather, in "Pecco, ergo sum." Sin, guilt, and physical suffering are what allow one to grasp the essence of reality: these values are not entirely set aside by Kathleen, who continues to struggle between two opposing philosophies until the end of the movie.

In fact, even when she wakes up in the hospital after her graduation party, Kathleen is still tormented. She looks insistently at the crucifix, asking the nurse to let her die. To end her life, she lets sunlight into her room, but at that point the vampire Casanova intervenes and closes the shutters. Casanova reminds Kathleen of her past and her present as a sinner. In her speech, Casanova, in fact, points out that human beings sin because they are sinners by nature; they do evil because they are evil. Acceptance of this condition, according to Casanova, can ensure Kathleen's survival, the beginning of a phase of existence in which evil is "overcome," insofar as it becomes an integral part of the eternal becoming that is life itself. However, Kathleen still tries to resist by asking God for forgiveness and receiving communion, as a Catholic, before taking her last breath.

In the final scene, Kathleen visits her own grave, where she leaves a flower. In walking away, conversing with herself, with her soul, she says: "To face what we are in the end, we stand before the light and our nature is revealed. Self-revelation is annihilation of self." In this last scene, the contrast between different philosophies is not resolved. In fact, Kathleen's words can be understood both in a Christian sense and as a critique of the Christian religion. On the one hand, then, the light, that is, God, is able to illuminate the souls of human beings, causing them to realize their true essence, destroying the body and making the soul immortal. On the other hand, this self-destruction can also be seen as the prelude to a different existence, freed from the oppressive burden of sin, from the idea that life is exclusively suffering.

The Addiction is a complex, multilayered filmic text. The philosophical and theological references are not pure intellectual decoration. Rather, they show, directly and/or indirectly, how Abel Ferrara and his trusted screenwriter, Nicholas St. John, reflect on their Catholic education, their Italian American roots in an era, such as that of postindustrial society, in which Italian Americans are beginning to lose touch with their cultural tradition. Such an analysis highlights that starting in the 1990s the Italian American community found itself in a critical transitional stage, insofar as it had to choose between a rather distant past, made up also of a religious way of living everyday life, and a future in which one is called upon to feed on the blood of others.[8]

From this point of view, the addiction discussed in the film cannot only be understood literally as an addiction to some substance. Rather, it is the Italian American addiction to traditions, to Christian religious values, but it is also addiction to life, to the desire/need to question one's cultural roots and immerse oneself without guilt, without considering oneself a sinner, in a socioeconomic context, that of late capitalism, which tends to cancel out cultural differences. The analysis proposed by Ferrara and Nicholas St. John is not consolatory, nor does it provide definitive answers. As Kathleen writes in her master's thesis, essence cannot be revealed by theory but only by praxis, by the actions of human beings. In other words: Ferrara and Nicholas St. John tell us nothing about the fate of Italian Americanness but merely snapshot the contradictions of the early 1990s, the ethical and ontological disorientation of the Italian American community on the threshold of a new millennium.

Notes

1. See, regarding the critical reception of *The Addiction*, the aforementioned article by Jamie Sexton.

2. Moreover, it should not be forgotten that in *Bad Lieutenant* one can find a definite reference to vampires, specifically in the scene in which the NYPD police lieutenant, played by Harvey Keitel, smokes heroin with a woman. The latter, while the camera focuses on Harvey Keitel, says, "Vampires have it easy. They feed on others. We have to feed on ourselves. We have to eat our legs, to have the energy to walk. We have to come, in order to go. We have to suck ourselves off. We have to eat away at ourselves 'til there's nothing left but appetite."

3. The image of the capitalist vampire is already present in Marx. In the first volume of *Capital*, for example, in chapter 10, entitled, "The Working Day," Marx writes: "The capitalist has bought the labor-power at its daily value. The use-value of the labor-power belongs to him throughout one working day. He has thus acquired the right to make the worker work for him during one day. But what is a working day? At all events, it is less than a natural day. How much less? The capitalist has his own views of this point of no return, the necessary limit of the working day. As a capitalist, he is only capital personified. His soul is the soul of capital. But capital has one sole driving force, the drive to valorize itself, to create surplus-value, to make its constant part, the means of production, absorb the greatest possible amount of surplus labor. Capital is dead labor which, vampire-like, lives only by sucking living labor, and lives the more, the more labor it sucks" (341–42). Capital, then, feeds on the blood, that is, living labor, of the worker in order to valorize itself, living longer the more vital sap it sucks from the "body" of the working class. For a detailed analysis of the various monstrous forms assumed by capital, see McNally's book *Monsters of the Market: Zombies, Vampires and Global Capitalism*. We should also mention Paul

Kennedy's text, *Vampire Capitalism: Fractured Societies and Alternative Futures*, in which, as pointed out by Chris Porter, the author believes that in the age of globalization "capitalism has become dislocated from the productive forces of society that once constituted its life force and, so its proponents claimed—with some justification—to which capitalism gave nourishment in return. Instead, the 'vampire form' of capitalism that Kennedy describes is one that takes away but has stopped giving back. Symptoms, as well as drivers, of this process include the predominance of *financialisation*, rent seeking and other economic activities that rely on the ownership or trade of assets, often in abstract forms, to generate profits" (Porter 20).

4. In other circumstances, as Brenez herself pointed out, Abel Ferrara has confronted other historical events. For example, *Body Snatchers* "asks the historical question, What can the destruction of Hiroshima or Nagasaki tell us about the liberal, democratic society responsible for it? Its collective political question is, What can the individual do when faced with the deathly logics at work in the industrial standardization of the entire world?" (Brenez 10).

5. Ferrara explored this topic in several movies. In *Body Snatchers*, for example, "over the course of the fifty most terrifying, synthetic seconds in narrative cinema, the human is transformed into rubbish. In a slow motion sequence-shot, the false, snatched mother, Carol (Meg Tilly), moves toward a truck, carrying a garbage bag that contains the remains of the real mother. Much is fused in this image of man-as-ashes: the Nazi ovens, the obliteration of bodies in Hiroshima, and the contemporary transformation of genetic patrimony into industrial property—three of the principle modern attempts at annulling humanity, whether by pure and simple disappearance (Nazi camps, Hiroshima) or by industrial reduction to the state of raw material (genetic industrialization). The dark, speckled brilliance of the asphalt upon which the menacing mother advances with her bag of remains evokes an archaic, mythological kind of figuration: the inaugural turbulence of atoms, as per Heraclitus and Lucretius. It is as if Ferrara aims to show the origin of life along with its symbolic disappearance" (Brenez 39).

6. As pointed out by the Italian philosopher Paolo Amodio, "The bonheur, as an individual strategy of good survival and as a theory of the good life, fits in here in any case, as a wedge, aimed, if not at reversing, at diverting the *malheur* of the natural and psychic datum. The bonheur is given as literally as divertissement, amusement; it is the possible antidote against the poison with which existence is imbued. In this sense, not only moralists and libertines, but the entire world of Enlightenment is profoundly *Pascalian*: man cannot amuse himself except by forgetting the truth of his condition. And here it is only the senses that bring the world into play, either as the last bastions of resistance to pain or as voluptuous sublimation" (44).

7. Christian morality, in other words, is the classic example of that slave morality based on resentment against what is aristocratic and vital. In *On the*

Genealogy of Morality, Nietzsche closely analyzes the main features of this slave morality, pointing out that "the revolt of the slaves in morals begins in the very principle of resentment becoming creative and giving birth to values—a resentment experienced by creatures who, deprived as they are of the proper outlet of action, are forced to find their compensation in an imaginary revenge. While every aristocratic morality springs from a triumphant affirmation of its own demands, the slave morality says 'no' from the very outset to what is 'outside itself,' 'different from itself,' and 'not itself': and this 'no' is its creative deed. This volte-face of the valuing standpoint—this inevitable gravitation to the objective instead of back to the subjective—is typical of 'resentment': the slave-morality requires as the condition of its existence an external and objective world, to employ physiological terminology, it requires objective stimuli to be capable of action at all—its action is fundamentally a reaction" (*Genealogy* 20).

8. As emphasized by Fred Gardaphé, "For Italian Americans, 'making it' has come with a high price. It has cost them the language of their ancestors—the main means by which history is preserved and heritage passed on from one generation to the next. They have had to trade in or hide any customs that have been depicted as quaint, but labeled as alien, in order to prove equality to those above them on the ladder of success. In this way, Italian Americans have become white, but a different kind of white than those of dominant Anglo-Saxon culture. Italian Americans have become whites on a leash. And as long as they behave themselves (act white), as long as they accept the images of themselves as presented in the media (don't cry defamation) and as long as they stay within corporate and cultural boundaries (don't identify with other minorities) they will be allowed to remain white" (Gardaphé 4).

Works Cited

Amodio, Paolo. *Luoghi del bonheur. Elementi per un'antropologia tra libertinismi e mondo dei lumi*. Giannini Editore, 2005.

Bear, Liza. "Abel Ferrara." *BOMB*, no. 53, 1995, pp. 36–41.

Brenez, Nicole. *Abel Ferrara*. U of Illinois P, 2007.

Casanova, Giacomo. *Mémoires (1789–1798)*. Bibliothèque de la Pléiade-Gallimard, 1958–1959.

Ferraro, Thomas J. *Feeling Italian: The Art of Ethnicity in America*. New York UP, 2005.

Gardaphé, Fred. "Introduction. Invisible People: Shadows and Light in Italian American Culture." *Anti-Italianism: Essays on a Prejudice*, edited by Fred Gardaphé and William J. Connell, Palgrave Macmillan, 2011, pp. 1–10.

Jameson, Fredric. *The Political Unconscious: Narrative as a Socially Symbolic Act*. Cornell UP, 1981.

Kennedy, Paul. *Vampire Capitalism: Fractured Societies and Alternative Futures.* Palgrave Macmillan, 2017.

McNally, David. *Monsters of the Market: Zombies, Vampires and Global Capitalism.* Haymarket Books, 2011.

Marx, Karl. *Capital.* Penguin Books, 1990.

Nietzsche, Friedrich. *Beyond Good and Evil: Prelude to a Philosophy of the Future.* Translated by R. J. Hollingdale, Penguin Books, 2022.

———. *On the Genealogy of Morality.* Translated by Karol Diethe, Cambridge UP, 2006.

Orsi, Robert A. "'Mildred is it fun to be a cripple?' The Culture of Suffering in Mid-Twentieth Century American Catholicism." *Catholic Lives, Contemporary America*, edited by Thomas J. Ferraro, Duke UP, 1997, pp. 19–64.

Porter, Chris. "Review of *Vampire Capitalism: Fractured Societies and Alternative Future.*" *Journal of Consumer Culture*, no. 3, 2020, pp. 370–377.

Sexton, Jamie. "US 'Indie-Horror': Critical Reception, Genre Construction, and Suspect Hybridity." *Cinema Journal*, vol. 51, no. 2, 2012, pp. 67–86.

Part 2

Case Studies in Italy's Fantasies, Futurisms, and Gothic Horror

I don't really consider myself an American filmmaker like, say, Ron Howard might be considered an American filmmaker. If I'm doing something and it seems to me to be reminiscent of an Italian giallo, I'm gonna do it like an Italian giallo.

—Quentin Tarantino

First they came for the socialists, and I did not speak out—because I was not a socialist.

Then they came for the trade unionists, and I did not speak out—because I was not a trade unionist.

Then they came for the Jews, and I did not speak out—because I was not a Jew.

Then they came for me—and there was no one left to speak for me.

—Martin Niemöller

4

An Italian Nightmare

Gianni Montanari's *La sepoltura* Between Dystopia and Science Fiction

UMBERTO ROSSI

There is a moment in Philip K. Dick's *The Man in the High Castle*, one of the classics of twentieth-century postmodernist science fiction, which quite accurately describes my feelings upon reading Gianni Montanari's *La sepoltura* (1973) for the first time. Dick's novel is famously set in an alternate world where Nazi Germany and Japan have won the Second World War, and where a forbidden alternate history novel, whose title is *The Grasshopper Lies Heavy*, circulates clandestinely, depicting a world where the USA and the British Empire defeated the Axis powers. Upon reading the description of a ravaged, almost annihilated Berlin in the novel-within-the-novel, a high-ranking Nazi official is "completely carried away" by the "amazing . . . power of fiction, even cheap popular fiction, to evoke" (Dick 124).

This is exactly what happened to me: I was completely carried away by the power to evoke of Montanari's almost forgotten *La sepoltura*, a novel published only once in *Galassia*[1] (a newsstand paperback series whose shelf life was quite short), never reprinted, never translated into any other language, with less than ten copies scattered throughout the Italian public libraries; I was carried away by its power to evoke the atmosphere, the zeitgeist, of a now faraway decade, the Italian 1970s, which I have rarely met in other narratives published in those years.

Ironically, the title of Gianni Montanari's 1973[2] novel (*sepoltura* means "burial") seems to predict the book's fate, as if the destiny of this 158-page narrative was to be buried in oblivion, more a collector's item than a living and relevant literary work. The special issue of *Science Fiction Studies* on Italian SF only features a very brief mention of this novel, so brief as to be cryptic: "*La sepoltura* . . . mixed collective and family tragedy in a . . . vein of biopolitical strife" (Proietti 224); Montanari himself refrains to mention his work in his brief contribution to the Symposium on Italian SF included in the same special issue ("Symposium" 240–41). But such forgetfulness is definitely undeserved: this novel should draw more critical attention, being a valuable specimen of Italian science fiction and dystopia, and a precious document if read through the lenses of cultural history, being a sort of transtemporal window that allows us to access a past state of the Italian collective imagination (*immaginario collettivo*).

Dealing, as we shall see, with an imaginary pandemic and psi powers, *La sepoltura* indisputably belongs to science fiction, like such classics of the genre as Michael Crichton's *The Andromeda Strain* (1969), in which microscopic spores from space attack the American West, or Theodore Sturgeon's *More than Human* (1953), depicting the coming together of six "deficient" individuals endowed with psi powers. But *La sepoltura* is at the same time a dystopia, just like Dick's *The Man in the High Castle*. Their differences notwithstanding, the two novels fit Suvin's definition, which posits dystopia as "a community where sociopolitical institutions, norms, and relationships are organized in a significantly less perfect way than in the author's community," seen from the point of view of "a representative of a discontented social class or fraction, whose value-system defines 'perfection'" (Suvin 170). One should add that today the two novels are much closer, from the point of view of genre, than they were first published. When *The Man in the High Castle* first came out, it was clearly a highly innovative dystopia, when compared to such established models as Huxley's *Brave New World* or Orwell's *Nineteen Eighty-Four* (1949): Dick's oppressive society was set in an alternate historical course that stemmed from a radically different outcome of a then recently past event (the Second World War), not in a near future as in Huxley's and Orwell's novels, or Montanari's *La sepoltura*, which was readable as a more traditional narrative when it was first published. But today the world conjured up by the Italian writer reads like a sort of alternative past, presenting us with an anamorphic image of the real Italian 1970s.

Like Dick's masterpiece, *La sepoltura* may well be seen today as a text cross-breeding dystopia with uchronia.[3]

Suvin's "representative of a discontented social class or fraction" providing the narrative focus through which readers access the story is the anonymous protagonist and first-person narrator of *La sepoltura*. He returns to Italy after several years spent abroad—a narrative device that might have been inspired by a classic Italian dystopia, Corrado Alvaro's *Man Is Strong* (1938); but while Alvaro's novel depicts a purely "political" dystopian society (inspired by both Fascist Italy and Stalinist USSR), what the narrating I finds in Italy in Montanari's novel is a *double* dystopia, mixing sociopolitical extrapolation and science-fictional imagination.

As for the political component of the novel, though there is no infodump to clearly state how the current state of things in Italy came to be, we are given sufficient information to understand (58–61) that the extreme left tried to start a revolution, that the Italian Communist Party did not support it, that the uprising was brutally repressed, and leftists were slaughtered (and this is of course the discontented social fraction in Suvin's definition, or better, as we shall see, a part of it). The massive repression explains the enigmatic black strips painted on many buildings, noticed by the protagonist and narrator: the black marks signaled to death squads that rebels lived there. This also explains the title of the novel, as the protagonist declares, "They have killed us all" (80),[4] literally and metaphorically. But, as I have already said, Montanari's novel can be read as a double dystopia. There is another discontented social fraction, because one of the reasons for the uprising is the persecution of the *mentali*.

A sort of psychic pandemic is raging in the near-future world in which the story is set: people become suddenly endowed with supernatural psi powers they cannot control. The so-called *piretici* set fire to anything near them, the *allucinanti* can make others hallucinate, and so on. Since the *mentali* have no control over their powers, they are considered a threat to society and are killed on the spot (31–33) or arrested and imprisoned in concentration camps to be subjected to lobotomy, like the protagonist's mother (102); many *mentali* die due to that neurosurgical intervention. This policy is ruthlessly enforced in Italy and other countries; even one of the scientists who developed a theory on *mentali*, the French psychiatrist Crémieux, Nobel Prize winner for medicine, was lobotomized and is detained in a mental institution under police surveillance (41).

The threat of the *mentali* is scary, but the possibility of turning into one of them is even scarier: "Anyone could turn into a *mentale*. The change appeared slowly, even when it had already been branded on the genes;

sometimes one didn't even notice it. Nobody could know how he would wake up the next day. Nobody could guarantee his own safety" (39). This has brought about a widespread atmosphere of anguish, which easily turns into fear. The authoritarian government (or regime) encourages informing, as clearly stated in a poster that strikes the narrator with its injunctions in block letters: "IT IS YOUR DUTY AS CITIZENS . . . REPORT" (27); and one should notice here that in the Italian text we have "DENUNCIATE," the imperative form of the verb *denunciare*, which is slightly more threatening than its English equivalent. *To report* may have a "neutral" meaning, when it simply means make something public or make news public; but *denunciare* always implies that one is reporting illegal/immoral acts or events. Unsurprisingly, the word DENUNCIATE seems to exert a sort of morbid fascination on the narrator too, as it is "so simple and naked, and yet so rich in appeal, in power, the imperative form of a verb that has deeply penetrated the soul of a man" (27).

As often happens in totalitarian societies (for example, in Fascist Italy from 1922 to 1945), anybody can be an informant: living in a totalitarian state, as Orwell taught us, means that anything you say, do, or think can be reported to the police. But in Montanari's novel what is reported is what you are, or better what you have turned into. Even the most politically orthodox, law-abiding *mentale* is a threat to society, hence, to be arrested by the Sanità corps,[5] detained, and surgically neutralized. This is of course closer to what happened in Nazi Germany, where Jews were discriminated against and persecuted, and ultimately exterminated, regardless of what their political allegiances might be. One may then reasonably suppose that among the literary sources that exerted a conscious or unconscious influence on Montanari there is A. E. van Vogt's *Slan*, a classic of Golden Age SF, first serialized in *Astounding Science Fiction* from September to December 1940; the novel deals with a relatively far future in which highly intelligent and telepathic evolved humans, the *slans*, are hunted and killed by "normal" humans. Given the publication date of van Vogt's novel, the connection with what was taking place in Europe in the 1930s and 1940s is obvious.

Gianni Montanari, one of the leading SF practitioners in the Italian 1960s and 1970s, was surely knowledgeable of *Slan*, given his role as coeditor of *Galassia* from 1970 to 1979, first with Vittorio Curtoni, then solo. Montanari was also a professional translator and edited the most important Italian SF magazine, *Urania*, from 1985 to 1990 (like shorter-lived *Galassia*, *Urania* is also a paperback series sold at newsstands, quite different from the American SF magazines). The role played by Montanari in the Italian SF scene must make us aware that the many echoes of historical events found in the novel may be mediated by classics of Anglo-American SF that also refer to those events—as in the case of *Slan*. All in all, *La sepoltura* is a highly composite narrative, drawing from the contemporary historical background, the recent past (the novel was published just twenty-seven years after the end of the Second World War), English-language SF literature, and, as we shall see, contemporary Italian literature.

Of course, the pervasive presence of informants generates an atmosphere of fear and generalized mistrust. Ferro, an old communist who owned a bar and gave shelter to the protagonist and his mates during the riots that took place before he emigrated, is reported by Maria, his wife, when he becomes a *mentale* who telekinetically moves objects at random (83). The protagonist and one of his friends try to help Ferro to escape from Italy, but a police squad intercepts them in one of the few action scenes of the novel (81–87); once again, someone has tipped off the police. No wonder that the protagonist is characterized by a remarkably paranoid state of mind.

The anonymous narrator is a tormented character, and we gradually realize that there is a tragedy in his own past. Families have been torn apart by betrayals: as we have seen, Maria has reported her husband, Ferro; Marisa, the narrator's cousin (and lover) has reported her father (and is now, ironically, a *mentale* herself); the narrator's father has reported his wife, who was then detained in a concentration camp, lobotomized, and died under the knife. This event left a sort of psychological scar in the narrator's mind, also because we ultimately discover that he is a *mentale* too and telepathically experienced his mother's suffering during the lobotomy:

> Hell in my head. Heat, an unbelievable fire above my eyes. The burning sensation which always came with the memory of that day. I too had heard her cry, with that shrill scream of pain that nobody on Earth knew, except for a few accursed ones. To feel as if one is slaughtered, torn apart shred by shred, to lose one's mind forever. My mother had been lucky. She died under the knife. But till the very last instant she communicated even the smallest detail of her ordeal. (102)

Thus, we must add the issue of revenge to the threads that tie the plot of this compact but complex novel. The narrator seems to have come back to Italy in order to kill his father, something that he sees as an act of justice, though its legitimacy is questioned by another character, Don Lucio, the Roman Catholic priest who offers shelter to hunted *mentali*: "The truth is that you believe you are [your father's] judge. You sentenced him eight years ago and now you want to do justice. But your hands aren't those of justice" (144). In the following short conversation with Don Lucio, the protagonist seems to be driven by a sort of death wish, or better a *cupio dissolvi*, a lust for destruction, as he says: "To destroy everybody, to set the world on fire, is not senseless to me" (144). These are words that would not be out of place in one of those nineteenth-century novels that deal with nihilists or anarchists, but they seem to translate the protagonist's drive to kill into psychoanalytical terms. Could this be an Oedipal conflict at work?

And yet this hostility toward fathers, this widespread idea that fathers should be killed, seems to be more generational than individual. Andrea, an old friend of the protagonist, reveals that his father "has created the first internment camps. He designed them nine years ago and persuaded the government to build them" (44). Marco, another of the protagonist's old friends, thinks that all fathers, including his own, even those who have not been directly involved in the persecution of the *mentali*, are nonetheless responsible "for having done nothing to prevent the camps" (45), meaning the concentration camps for *mentali*. Hence, all fathers are guilty, due to a sort of collective sin of omission—but, as Barbara, a friend of the narrator, points out, the sons also have not done anything to stop the massacre of the *mentali*, just like their fathers, and the narrator cannot rebut.

Interestingly, this discussion about paternal responsibilities among the narrator and his friends Barbara, Andrea, and Marco quickly shifts toward a sort of debate on revolution, the collective *atto mancato*, or Freudian slip (also called *parapraxis*), which looms large over the whole novel. Freudian slips are, as defined in Freud's *The Psychopathology of Everyday Life*, apparently senseless acts that replace what the subject unconsciously wants to do but cannot. As we have already seen, a revolution was attempted, but failed, drowned in the rebels' blood; and what we might call the Mentali Scare keeps everybody busy—or better, distracted. Everything that takes place in the novel comes after a collective failure, and it is time to ask ourselves whose failure it is, metaphors aside.

A revealing passage can be found at the beginning of the novel. The protagonist is walking along a Milanese street, Via Festa del Perdono, near the University of Milan: that place triggers a moment of recollection, captured by a brief quasi-Joycean inner monologue:

> I would have liked to start running, letting that furious anxiety recapture me, that always grabbed me, once, in those places. Running, voices and shouts, police professors and lectures. A whole universe behind me, with bridges forever burned. So many cries in the long corridors and the hurried pitter-patter, of heavy and hobnailed footsteps, of uniformed pursuers. The blood, the blows, the head wound in the inner courtyard, shoving Livia to make her jump over the hedge. The memory of the blows was vague. Who knows why, the memory of blows given and received tended to get confused in one's recollection. (26–27)

To anyone who lived in the Italian 1960s, all this clearly depicts the students' protests in Italian universities during the Sessantotto.[6] It is a fragment of sheer Italian reality of the late 1960s embedded in a science fictional narrative, something that connects the imaginary near (or not-so-far) future depicted in the novel with a near past that had been lived by Montanari and many other young Italians of the same generation. It is a way to tell us that the narrator and his friends belong to that group of angry young men (and women) who had participated in the Sessantotto protests but felt they had not achieved their goals, a situation vividly depicted, for example, in a contemporary Italian realistic novel, Renzo Paris's *Cani sciolti* (1973). Hence, the failed uprising in the novel may be read as an anamorphic representation of the Sessantotto, or (as such representations of historical events with imaginary ones may well bear multiple interpretations) the revolution the *sessantottini* called for in those years.

Could we not then read *La sepoltura* in an allegorical mode? Montanari himself seems to encourage such an interpretation when Angela, a mute girl who is also a *mentale allucinante*, is shown reading *Conversations in Sicily*, by Elio Vittorini (69), a literary work that is also mentioned by Vittorio Curtoni in his "Presentazione" (6) of *La sepoltura*. Vittorini's novel, first published in 1938–1939, might be a possible model for Montanari, inasmuch as it narrates the quasi-oneiric return of a Sicilian man (a sort of alter ego of the author) to his island, which he has left years before; there he meets a series of characters, including his mother and father (the latter only fleetingly appearing at the very end of the narrative), with whom the emigrant talks about a variety of topics. Interestingly, Vittorini's novel has been read as an allegory of Italy under the fascist regime, with each character met by the protagonist representing a group of Italians, and their way to cope with the dictatorship. In a time when any publication was subject to censorship, Vittorini realized that only an allegorical approach to his sociopolitical reality could allow him to express a criticism of fascist oppression.

By mentioning this novel, Montanari may have wanted to warn readers that they were reading another political allegory.[7] Besides, the allegorical mode was adopted by another Italian SF writer, Lino Aldani, in his 1979 novelette *Eclissi 2000*, where a space travel narrative set on a generation starship hides a bitter meditation on the Italian political situation in the years of black and red terrorism, the so-called "leaden years," plagued by frequent bombings and assassinations. All in all, if we accept Montanari and Curtoni's suggestion, the failed uprising may be seen as representing the Italian Sessantotto, as we have already said. The protagonist and his friends are members of the generation that occupied Italian universities in 1968, which mostly placed itself on the extreme left of the political spectrum. The *sessantottini* rejected the then ruling party, Democrazia Cristiana, seen as a reactionary political force whose members were often former fascists turned conservative Roman Catholics; but they also contested the policy of the Italian Communist Party, deemed to be too accommodating to the hegemony of the Democrazia Cristiana. No wonder that, as we have seen, Montanari imagines that the Communist Party does not join the rebels, thus sentencing the uprising to failure. On the other hand, the fathers of the narrator and his friends represent the older generation of Italians who worked hard for the Italian boom and turned an agricultural nation into one of the main industrialized countries in the world in the 1950s and 1960s.

If this reading is tenable, one must then place the *mentali* in the picture. Since they are an oppressed minority, one might identify them with the victims of terrorism: when Montanari wrote the novel, the memory of the Piazza Fontana bombing was still fresh.[8] But such an interpretation does not take into account the evolution of the *mentali* throughout the novel, on which we shall have to focus by following Angela, an apparently secondary character.

We first meet her sleeping in the bedroom of a house where Lorenzo, one of the protagonist's old friends, is hiding. He is not wanted by the police, but the young girl[9] is—according to Lorenzo, she is "swimming in trouble." He met her at the Stazione Centrale, the main railway station in Milan; Lorenzo tells the protagonist and Barbara: "I was getting out of the post office, and she stuck a vision into my mind. I almost fell down: it was unbelievably strong. A sort of drug addict's hell" (51). The girl is a *mentale* of the *allucinante* variety, who can project visions into other people's mind: this marks her as a victim in the fictional world envisioned by Montanari. It is easy to see Angela as one of the oppressed, also due to her age and gender (Italian women were struggling for their rights in the early 1970s but had not reached full parity yet). Moreover, the girl is mute; she can only communicate with Lorenzo by writing, and this is how he comes to know that her name is Angela, and she is seventeen. He also surmises that Angela has run away from home, possibly in order to avoid being reported by her parents or siblings; moreover, she has little money and no documents, a very dangerous condition in a police state. Finally, we understand that Lorenzo is not giving shelter to Angela out of kindness, but because he has had sex with her—so we must add sexual exploitation to all the misfortunes heaping on the girl.

And yet the protagonist notices that Angela does not seem particularly scared by her predicament, that is, being in the hands of a shady character like Lorenzo (the protagonist has visited him to get himself a gun), who could eventually report her after having sexually exploited her. The narrator then asks Lorenzo, "But is she normal?" (55), hinting at some mental disability; maybe Angela is not aware, or fully aware, of her precarious situation. As I have already said, everything we are told induces us to see Angela as a victim, a sort of living epitome of the dire plight of the *mentali*.

But when we meet the girl again at the end of the novel, we find out that things were not what they seemed. Angela is now hosted by Don Lucio, the priest who strives to save and protect the *mentali*; she reveals that she has only pretended to be mute, and she is not just an *allucinante*, she is also a telepath; but, above all, she can control her psychic powers. We find out that Angela is a shrewd, cold-blooded imposter (describing her face, the protagonist talks about "an ice mask" [143]), fully in control of her put-on, which has allowed her to survive; we can also suspect that Angela is not her real name, and that we do not really know anything about her. It is a *coup de théâtre*, to be expected at the end of a novel that strives to build suspense, its many meditative passages notwithstanding.

The protagonist then wants to know why Angela made him come back to Milan from Verona—where he moved to after the shootout—by sending him an unsigned telegram announcing that Lorenzo and Barbara had been arrested. The girl does not answer the question and just tells the protagonist that he must finish what he has begun: she will only answer after he has killed his father. Angela then lets him know that she is not alone; there are other *mentali* who have learned to control their powers and can easily escape the police. They are victims no more; the protagonist realizes that she is "a new creature. Incredible, on the face of the world. Her powers could have destroyed everything" (147). Angela reassures the protagonist: "I could destroy every man, but I don't want to. None of us wants that. None of us wants to take revenge. . . . We aren't interested in that" (147); then she invites him to join her and the other *mentali*, which makes sense, inasmuch as we now know that the protagonist is a *mentale* too. But he refuses and asks Angela to leave him alone (148).

The ending is tragic. The protagonist lies in ambush, with a gun, in a Milanese street, waiting for his father; everything we have read so far induces us to think that he is going to take revenge. When he is face to face with the man who sentenced his mother to death, the first-person narrative ends with these words:

> And the man who was before me took a step forward; I had to stare into his enormous eyes, too warm and too hated.
>
> "I was waiting for you," he said.
>
> He took another step.
>
> The gun appeared in my hand.
>
> The last burial. (152)

If the novel ended here, we might come to the conclusion that the protagonist has shot his father; but after this apparent ending there is a final chapter, whose title is "Conclusion," a six-page third-person narrative pivoting upon the fate of Andrea and other characters. It is here that we discover that the protagonist shot himself, not his father. We are also told that less and less *mentali* are identified, and the number of those interned in the concentration camps is decreasing; according to the government, this indicates that the pandemic is about to end. Andrea does not believe it: the decreasing number of arrested and interned *mentali* may well mean instead that more and more *mentali* manage to control their psi powers, maybe helped by the group represented by Angela. Andrea realizes that the *mentali* are getting ready to take over, and he is not optimistic about this: "*Mentali* or normal, what difference did it make?" (158), is his bitter conclusion. Andrea laughs, but it is a tragic laughter, maybe the symptom of mental derangement. The last sentence of the novel is: "He was still laughing the day that the world split in two" (158).

Nothing in the last chapter of *La sepoltura* encourages readers to see the ending as a happy one. Montanari does not offer us a detailed description of what the *mentali* will do and what the reaction of normal humans will be, but the splitting of the world may hint at a war, at a final Armageddon that will not usher in a better world. This final apocalypse may have been foreseen by the protagonist, and this may well explain his suicide; in the final chapter, Andrea seems to understand the reasons for his friend's suicide, and he does this after having realized that the decreasing number of internments in the concentration camps for *mentali* does not really mean that the psychic pandemic is over.

We must thus conclude that we cannot see the *mentali* as an allegory of the victims of terrorism; but since they are characters in a novel that easily lends itself to an allegorical meaning, they must stand for something or somebody else. The historical context may then help us to solve this riddle. We have seen that the groups of characters in *La sepoltura* represent real groups or generations in 1970s Italy. The protagonist and his friends stand for the younger generation, the radical leftists who took part in the Sessantotto; their fathers are the older generation, politically represented either by the Democrazia Cristiana or the Communist Party, which both opposed—albeit for different reasons—the Sessantotto movement. What about the repressive apparatus that hunts for the *mentali*, then? There is a quite interesting detail that may be easily overlooked: "The new Sanità corps had not adopted special uniforms. Besides, it did not really need to do that, as, from a legal point of view, it was a part of the Carabinieri. This did not come as a surprise. If the *mentali* were a threat to the nation, who could deal with them better than the ministry of defense?" (31). The Carabinieri are at the same time the Italian military police and one of the police forces of the nation, not to be confused with the Polizia di Stato. By having them in charge of hunting down *mentali*, Montanari seems to hint at a historical fact: the role played by the Carabinieri in the repression of left-wing terrorist groups. Some of those groups started their guerrilla warfare from 1969 to 1972, that is, the period when Montanari conceived and wrote *La sepoltura*: the October 22 Group was established in 1969 and carried out his first important action, the kidnapping of a wealthy industrialist's son, in October 1970; the Gruppi d'Azione Partigiana, or GAP (Groups of Partisan Action), was founded in 1970, and their most famous action, a failed bombing aimed at sabotaging electricity pylons, occurred in March 1972; the Red Brigades were born between 1969 and 1970, and the Italian media noticed them when they placed eight firebombs in a Pirelli plant near Milan in January 1971. Though the most important actions of red terrorism—such as the kidnapping and execution of Democrazia Cristiana President Aldo Moro in 1978—took place later, there was the constant presence of its activity on newspapers and in TV news. It was something new: a new phenomenon that was spreading, just like a pandemic.

Should we then see the *mentali* as an anamorphic image of leftist terrorists? One should take notice of what Vittorio Curtoni wrote in the "Presentation" of the novel: "The most important names, in my opinion, are those of Camus and Vittorini, both present with their most representative works: *Conversations in Sicily* and *The Plague*. Such points of reference are far from casual: Montanari's future world is acquainted with the crisis that tormented the world of Camus and Vittorini" (Curtoni 6). As we all know, Albert Camus's 1947 novel tells the story of an imaginary (and anachronistic) *Yersinia pestis* epidemic, which is an allegory of collaborationism in Nazi-occupied France during the Second World War. A political phenomenon, French people who chose to cooperate with the invaders and even take part in a series of atrocities (such as the deportation of Jews), is turned by Camus into a health crisis. No wonder then that the appearance of the *mentali* is treated as an epidemic, and the specialized police unit dealing with them are called "corpo di Sanità" (healthcare corps); what is sanitary in the novel must be political in the historical reality it hints at, following the model of *The Plague*.

Moreover, the novel clearly states that the *mentali* are not mutants à la Marvel's X-Men: they are not *born* with their psi powers, they *turn into mentali* through biological contagion.[10] Just like the *brigatisti* and the other leftist terrorists, who were not born as such, almost all of them started as militants of the far left, which then chose the *lotta armata* (armed fight), a choice that was not made by the vast majority of *sessantottini*, and other, younger extreme-left militants. Obviously, today's readers, who know that the Red Brigades were ultimately defeated in the 1980s, may find it difficult to see the psi-empowered *mentali* as their literary avatars; as we have seen, at the end of *La sepoltura* they are no more bewildered, frightened victims like the middle-aged female newsagent shot by the Sanità agents because she has turned into a *piretica* (31–33), but they are a well-organized group whose members, like Angela, are in full control of their deadly powers and ready to use them. The ending of the novel suggests that, notwithstanding Angela's promise not to take revenge (147), the *mentali* will ultimately take action on a planetary scale.

But we should strive to recapture the Montanari's likely perception of the Italian political situation when he wrote his novel, from 1971 to 1972: then the terrorist campaign of the Red Brigades and the other leftist groups was at the beginning, and it was difficult to foresee its outcome. This may also explain why the real ending of the novel, that is, the last lines of the "Conclusion," are indisputably ominous but enigmatic: the author was probably afraid that the rise of red terrorism might bring about devastating consequences—a civil war, a military coup d'état, a revolution, whatever—but did not want to play the role of the soothsayer. Montanari chose to hint, not to depict in detail.

The ending, however, is bleak and pessimistic. Something Andrea says in the first part of the novel is illuminating. Commenting on Marco's idea that there is no such thing as a revolution with a happy end (45), he states, "Revolutions are like clothes. . . . They may suit those who wear them but will not satisfy the others. They can work for the duration of a generation, if they are lucky, but they won't be helpful to the generations that came before or will come after that." Such a statement bespeaks a sort of mild pessimism: if a revolution is started to solve a problem or some problems, the solution will be temporary. But this might also be interpreted in a more radical and much bleaker fashion: revolutions—like clothes—fit those who take power but are unsatisfactory (if such a euphemism is allowed) to the former elite that loses power, and—more importantly—to the vast majority that remains disempowered. A revolution may pave the way for a new form of oppression, as it happened in the USSR in the 1930s—a period of contemporary history that was well known and often discussed in the Italian 1970s. When the protagonist rejects Angela's invitation to join the self-controlling *mentali*, this may be due to his pessimistic view of history; he may think, like Andrea (158), that a world ruled by *mentali* will not be better than the old world ruled by normal humans (*normali*). If we remain in an allegorical mode of reading, this means Montanari mistrusted the left-wing terrorist groups and/or foresaw an impending bloodbath.

Such a bleak prefiguration of Italy's near future is not at all surprising. The fear of a military coup was widespread, and one could find it expressed in Italian movies of those years, be it in a comedic vein as in Mario Monicelli's *We Want the Colonels* (1973), or in a tragic fashion, as in Liliana Cavani's *The Cannibals* (1970); such a fear was even expressed in successful pop songs, such as Edoardo Bennato's "Bravi ragazzi" (1974). Assassinations were quite frequent, including those of such a famous writer and film director as Pier Paolo Pasolini (1975), or a prestigious political leader like Aldo Moro (1977). One should also add the bombings, beginning with Piazza Fontana, then climaxing with the 1980 Bologna massacre, when a bomb placed in the main railway station killed eighty-five people and wounded more than two hundred. The tense and bleak atmosphere of the Leaden Years is captured with surprising effectiveness by Montanari's science fiction novel, which succeeds in mirroring—even though darkly, *per aenigmata*, to quote Paul's epistle to the Corinthians—the zeitgeist of that decade.

A final remark is necessary. The idea that a political issue could be tackled by means of a biological metaphor (the epidemic, the contagion) seems to be deeply ingrained in Italian culture. In a brilliant essay on Italian science fiction cinema of the 1970s, Robert Rushing, drawing from Roberto Esposito, writes: "Established nation states . . . attempt to 'immunize' themselves against risk and historical contingency, an immunization that also creates a totalized vision of the future; Italian thinking, accordingly, may appear to lack a coherent national character but it is essentially biopolitical in its recognition of the fragility of the body, as well as the fragility of the body politic" (Rushing 342). No wonder then that in a moment of crisis of the body politic—threatened by the fracture between older and younger generations, terrorism, a possible coup, maybe even a civil war—a writer imagines a new version of the oldest threat to the human body in the Western literary tradition, the plague, the greatest biological scare since Boccaccio and Chaucer; a biopolitical threat against whom there is no immunization. In such a narrative, of course, no totalized vision of the future is thinkable because, as Montanari tells us at the end of *La sepoltura*, the world is about to split.

Even though this compact novel has a reticent ending, as we have seen, it is now, fifty years after its publication, an eloquent—albeit in a scrambled fashion—monument of a past historical period, offering a slanted but intensely evocative perspective on the Italian 1970s. This is a book that should be reprinted, possibly in an annotated edition, and translated into English so as to be made available to Italian studies, science fiction, and dystopia scholars all over the world—my contention being that it would be a precious addition to the science fiction/dystopia canon, countering the Anglocentrism still dominating those fields. One can only hope that someone in the publishing industry may accept this final appeal, so that *La sepoltura* can be disinterred and rescued from historical amnesia.

Notes

1. Moreover, *Galassia* itself was short-lived, as its last issue was published in 1979. For a detailed history of the magazine, see Iannuzzi 161–234.

2. Though there is no clearly stated publication date in the *Galassia* volume (no. 191), according to such a reliable online database as the *Catalogo Vegetti della letteratura fantastica* the novel was published in 1973. At the beginning of the novel we have an indication of copyright attribution dated 1972 (4); at end of the text we have another indication stating it was written between October 1971 and June 1972 (158), and these dates are compatible with its publication in 1973.

3. One should notice that Gianni Montanari (1949–2020) surely knew of Dick's novel since it was first published in the Science Fiction Book Club series of the La tribuna press, which was originally edited by science fiction translator and author Roberta Rambelli (1963–1974) but was subsequently managed by Montanari himself (1976–1979). Moreover, he translated Dick's novels *Ubik* (1968) and *Clans of the Alphane Moon* (1964), the latter with Vittorio Curtoni. Stylistic and narrative differences notwithstanding, at least one key element connects *The Man in the High Castle* and *La sepoltura*: the depiction of a society crushed by a fascist regime (fascism being unavoidably suggested by the black marks) bent on exterminating an "undesirable" part of the population (Jews in Dick's novel, *mentali* in Montanari's).

4. All the quotations from *La sepoltura* have been translated by me.

5. This is an ironic touch by Montanari: the police corps that hunts down the *mentali* is called "corpo di Sanità" (31), a phrase meaning healthcare corps.

6. This Italian word defines the 1968 movement, which was inspired by distaste for traditional Italian society, the elitist and authoritarian mentality of the Italian academia, and international protests occurring in the same year. In May 1968 all universities, except Bocconi in Milan, were occupied by students who often clashed with the police.

7. We find no mention in *La sepoltura* of another novel by Vittorini, *Men and Not Men* (1945), based on the author's experience in the Italian Resistance during the German occupation (1943–1945), though some scenes in Montanari's novel, such as the shootout with the police and the ensuing escape on the roofs (81–87), echo a similar action scene in *Men and Not Men*.

8. On December 12, 1969, a bomb blew up in a bank in Milan: seventeen people were killed, eighty-eight were wounded. Anarchists were suspected at first, but the bombing was subsequently attributed to a fascist group, Ordine Nuovo, possibly acting on behalf of members of the Italian secret service.

9. Angela is called "ragazzina" in Italian (50), thus suggesting she is underage.

10. Montanari is definitely not a hard SF writer and does not offer explanations of the epidemic based on genetics; we are only given a very brief and vague hint at Crémieux's theory that the transformation has something to do with "a natural deformation of sickle-shaped genes" causing "a hyper-activity of the spinal cord and certain areas of the thalamus" (35). In any case, *mentali* are not mutants.

Works Cited

Curtoni, Vittorio. "Presentazione." *La sepoltura*, by Gianni Montanari, La tribuna, 1973, pp. 5–7.

Dick, Philip Kindred. *The Man in the High Castle*. Penguin, 1987.

Iannuzzi, Giulia. *Fantascienza italiana: Riviste, autori, dibattiti dagli anni cinquanta agli anni settanta*. Mimesis, 2014.

Montanari, Gianni. *La sepoltura*. La tribuna, 1972.

Proietti, Salvatore. "The Field of Italian SF." *Science Fiction Studies*, vol. 42, no. 2, 126, July 2015, pp. 217–31.

Rushing, Robert. "The Weight of History: Immunity and the Nation in Italian SF Cinema." *Science Fiction Studies*, vol. 42, no. 2, July 2015, pp. 339–52.

Suvin, Darko. "Utopianism from Orientation to Agency: What Are We Intellectuals Under Post-Fordism to Do?" *Utopian Studies*, 1998, p. 170.

"Symposium on Italian SF." *Science Fiction Studies*, vol. 42, no. 2, 126, July 2015, pp. 232–44.

5

Fascism and Pheromones

Futurist Fantasies of Domination in Bruce Sterling's *Fantascienza*

William Q. Malcuit

Bruce Sterling, one of the primary exponents of both cyberpunk and steampunk, an American—a *Texan*, for that matter[1]—might be an unexpected writer to encounter in a collection on Italian fantastic literature. However, those expectations would be failing to consider that Sterling has lived in Turin for going on two decades, and that his most recent works have almost entirely been set in Italian contexts.[2] Furthermore, he has adopted for himself an Italian persona—Bruno Argento—and has clearly worked to place himself within the tradition of Italian *fantascienza*, with the publication of his novella *Pirate Utopia*, in 2016, and his short story collection *Robot Artists & Black Swans: The Italian Fantascienza Stories*, in 2021. But it is not that a successful American science fiction writer has expatriated himself to the *bel paese* that warrants including Sterling in a collection on Italian fantastic literature. Instead, it is that Sterling, by placing his current fiction in an Italian context, has been able to expand upon the themes of his earlier, more well-known works, in ways that should make us reconsider the entirety of his fiction.

To demonstrate how Sterling's move to Italy has enabled him to expand upon themes present throughout his fiction, I will discuss two texts from very different moments in his career. The first is "Swarm," a short story published in 1982. It is one of Sterling's earliest publications, a far-future work of SF, part of his Shaper/Mechanist series, and perhaps one of the stories that most signals Sterling as a "cyberpunk" writer.[3] The second is *Pirate Utopia*, a novella from 2016, an example of alternative history (it is set in Fiume/Rijeka in 1920), and a work that Sterling has described as "dieselpunk" (Klaw 170). These two texts might not seem to have much in common, but by comparing them, I will demonstrate that a central theme in Sterling's fiction, going back to some of his earliest stories and continuing to his present work, is fascism: its appeal and perhaps even centrality to the modern world; and how the technologies of the modern world, instead of being liberatory, can so easily be made to abet its rise.[4]

Centering a discussion of fascism, and focusing more broadly on the dystopian strain, in Sterling's work, cuts against the ways that Sterling is sometimes figured as one of SF's most prominent postmodernists and futurists.[5] What his more recent fiction indicates, however, is that Sterling has always been very aware of the different denotations of "futurist," and how that term has become so complicated in our contemporary world. "Futurist," more commonly today, as is cataloged in various dictionaries, refers merely to the technophilic tendency to "stud[y] and predict the future especially on the basis of current trends." Even a secondary definition, for example that of *Merriam Webster's*, is apt to diminish awareness of the historical avant-garde movement that first brought the term into use: "one who advocates or practices futurism." If a reader is to find anything about the Italian movement of F. T. Marinetti, they will have to read the definition of "futurism" itself, where they will finally find the following: "1: a movement in art, music, and literature begun in Italy about 1909 and marked especially by an effort to give formal expression to the dynamic energy and movement of mechanical processes; 2: a point of view that finds meaning or fulfillment in the future rather than in the past or present." While the first definition does finally introduce the Italian roots of futurism—and its inevitable connections to fascism—the second is equally enlightening, if only that it shows how much Sterling should not be lumped in with the naïvely optimistic, postmodern, libertarian-leaning, silicon-valley-style techno-prophets who advertise themselves as futurists today—for pay, of course.[6] Despite what some critics have argued, Sterling never simply identifies meaning or fulfilment in the future. Instead, he is always careful to demonstrate that our future is determined by the past we have inherited and the choices we make in the present. Indeed, the motto of *Steampunk Magazine*, "love the machine, hate the factory," is one that sums up well the sort of relationship Sterling has to technology and the future: an embrace of what history has left us with the simultaneous hope that we can encase those material remains in more just social relations.

Understanding Sterling's critical stance toward technology, and his ambivalent presentation of the future throughout his work, allows us to position his early cyberpunk story "Swarm" alongside the dieselpunk *Pirate Utopia* in ways that demonstrate how Sterling has long been on guard against the fascist turn—that he has, in fact, been practicing an anti-fascist aesthetic. With his careful attention to the ways technology can offer possibilities of reshaping the world, alongside people's tendencies to try to harness technology to the status quo (the current status quo being the world of profit, domination, and hierarchy), Sterling offers us a utopian glimpse, but only in the context of our larger dystopian present. His (and William Gibson's) famous steampunk novel *The Difference Engine* provides a useful way to understand this strategy. Steampunk, as a genre and social movement hugely inspired by Sterling, "venerates the artisan, celebrates an abundance of technology, and still damns the factory that destroyed the former's livelihood to create the latter" (Doctorow ix). Sterling—and William Gibson, in *The Difference Engine*—never gives in to the alluring notion that a mere abundance of technology will allow us to somehow sidestep our capitalist present. Instead, as Corey Doctorow states, Sterling wants his readers to wrestle with the hard truth of our present: "The factory might have given us the millionfold productivity increases that yielded the Industrial Revolution, but it achieved those gains by chaining us to machines, deskilling the artisan and turning him into a cog in the factory, stripped of judgement and dignity and disconnected from the rhythms of his spirit and the world around him" (ix). This is a very different conception of the work of cyberpunk and steampunk than what we get from those critics who have assigned to Sterling a glib postmodernism and naïve futurism. Take, for example, Phillip Wegner's assessment of Sterling and Gibson in an analysis of *The Difference Engine*, in which he states that for them "the adrenaline rushes of a Wild West–style, free-market, every-man-for-himself capitalism represent the best of what is possible" (145). In contrast to Wegner, I will demonstrate that, far from a Fukuyaman "best of what is possible," Sterling has been instead offering a realist, anti-fascist, depiction of what *is*, and a firm warning of what might *become*.

"Swarm" is the story that best lets us see Sterling's commitment from early in his career to pursuing the fascist trends in our contemporary society as well as in the genre of science fiction. He does so by presenting a common SF trope: the anthill as fascist hive, and the insect worker as mindless hive member.[7] Using the trope of the insect, Sterling presents a scenario wherein workers are the ultimate cogs: incapable of dissent, and containing no inner lives to complicate their relationship with the machine to which they are chained. He presents us this insectlike society in his far-future Shaper/Mechanist series. But by initiating the series with "Swarm" (it is the first text to have been published in the series), Sterling establishes that this far-future world will be structured by the questions of labor that structure our own. "Swarm," as one of Sterling's most widely anthologized stories,[8] might be expected to have garnered a great deal of academic commentary. Indeed, as far as Sterling's fiction goes, it has, but of a variety that leads the reader to focus on themes of posthumanism.[9] While recognizing the value of such readings, I would like to position "Swarm" as a story in which Sterling clearly lays out a vision of the future we must avoid.

The setup of "Swarm" is simple: humanity, in a time when it has encountered numerous intelligent alien species, has finally come into contact with the Swarm: a species that inhabits a low-gravity asteroid, and is highly successful at mining and harvesting resources from the asteroid, but without apparent intelligence. The protagonist, Captain-Doctor Simon Afriel, is a member of the Shaper faction of human society, people who are committed to reshaping the human body using biological and genetic technologies. His mission is to study the Swarm and meet another Shaper scientist, Galina Mirny, who has already been living with and studying the alien species for some time. Amid Afriel learning about how the Swarm functions—it is clearly modeled after an insect community, with a queen and various castes of worker and warrior entities, with pheromones as the basis of communication—we find out that the Swarm has also attracted to itself a variety of symbiotes. These are formerly intelligent species who have managed to survive alongside (or have been absorbed by) the Swarm and live as parasites. It is only with these symbiotes that even the most basic of communication is possible, as the members of the Swarm itself have no capacity for language or, it seems, agency.[10] In the discovery of all this information, Mirny is Afriel's, and the reader's, guide, as she has been studying the Swarm, and its symbiotes, for some time. Inevitably, questions arise, such as: How like insects are we? How mindless are they? However, instead of merely using the idea of the insect to explore questions about human consciousness and free will and the human versus the posthuman, Sterling is more interested in investigating our fascination with insects and their collective enterprises because of what that fascination tells us about our modern, industrial world's ability to cope with individuals, dissent, and the fascist desire for a perfectly ordered world wherein hierarchy is naturalized.

What Afriel has ultimately come to the Swarm to harvest are the mindless workers themselves. Using data collected by Galina, we discover that Shaper scientists have developed artificial pheromones that mimic perfectly those used in the Swarm, and that control its various members' functions. Afriel has arrived at the Swarm to test the pheromones and, upon proving their efficacy, to return enough genetic information (via a captured fertilized egg) to our solar system to allow for cloning of the workers, and for exploitation of their immense mining and labor capacities. The appeal of this is obvious: humanity will have a whole caste of workers absolutely subservient—enthralled, if you will—to the managerial class. Mirny, upon discovering this scheme, is initially taken aback: "But it's kidnapping. You're talking about breeding a slave race" ("Swarm" 250). Afriel, however, has a ready response to these objections:

> You're juggling words, Doctor. I'll cause this colony no harm. I may steal some of its workers' labor while they obey my own chemical orders, but that tiny theft won't be missed. I admit to the murder of one egg, but that is no more a crime than a human abortion. Can the theft of one strand of genetic material be called "kidnapping"? I think not. As for the scandalous idea of a slave race—I reject it out of hand. These creatures are genetic robots. They will no more be slaves than are laser drills or cargo tankers. At the very worst, they will be our domestic animals. (250)

Mirny is quickly convinced: "It's true. It's not as if a common worker will be staring at the stars, pining for its freedom. They're just brainless neuters. . . . They simply work. Whether they work for us or the Swarm makes no difference to them. . . . If it worked, our faction would profit astronomically" (250). We see in this conversation between Afriel and Mirny that what Sterling wants his readers to identify is the ruling logic of our capitalist present: profit is the primary motive, and the cost of labor must always be reduced as much as possible so as to maximize it. With the novum of "pheromones" that allow for the perfect control of otherwise mindless workers, Sterling allows for the imagining of a “perfect” form of capitalism, wherein workers are no longer beings with agency—they are merely cogs. The drama of the story is the allure the idea of a mindless worker creates for humanity: What if only we could harness this sort of control over labor, and to what extent would we go to obtain that control? What levels of productivity might we be able to reach with truly mindless workers? And what heights of achievement might we reach through the exploitation of their labor? Of course, that last question begs *whose* achievement? The laborers’? The collective in its entirety? Or merely those who have harnessed the controlling powers of the pheromones: the managers, the programmers, the bosses, the “humans”?

Sterling doesn’t only critique the exploitation of labor in “Swarm,” however. The story also allows its readers to see that to adopt the perfectly functioning Swarm as a model for human relations is to reach—and not in any “best-of-what-is-possible” way—the end of history. In describing the world Afriel seeks with his harnessing of the Swarm’s labor, Mirny states, “Consider the Swarm, if you really want your human and perfect order. Here it is! Where it’s always warm and dark, and it smells good, and food is easy to get, and everything is endlessly and perfectly recycled. . . . A nest like this one could last unchanged for hundreds of thousands of years” (247–48). The irony is that this is what Afriel, and Mirny, desire. It is also that which the fascist and the capitalist desires: a world of unchanging comfort, built for him by the unswaying obedience of a dominated class. It is the end of history, served on a platter to those who rule. This image of the perfectly ordered, lazy society, with a leader on top served by a class of programmed underlings, is another edge of Sterling’s anti-fascist critique. The mindless workers ultimately serve a mindless leader, who can think of nothing more than retaining its own dominance. A desire for order and obedience, therefore, is ultimately a desire to not have to think, or to communicate. This is brought home in the story by the fact that the Swarm itself has no intelligence to be rewarded by its perfect functioning. The only intelligence it can deploy lies latent and appears solely when the Swarm experiences an external threat. Of course, the threats it faces are rival intelligences wanting to usurp its exploitation of its own working class. “Swarm” gives us a vivid depiction of the ends of a capitalist and colonialist desire for perfect order in its borders and in its store of laborers. Capitalist thought ends when value has been fully and completely extracted from a labor source. At that moment, the capitalist ceases to have a function. The only function it can have at that point is piracy, the theft of labor value from other capitalists. Sterling's final, scathing indictment of the supposed ingenuity of the capitalist mode of production, and the entrepreneurial intelligence driving it, is that it wants nothing more than a thoughtless, changeless, conformity, and that it will do anything it can to maintain its idle comfort.

Sterling's meditations upon the role of labor might seem not to be evident in his recent Italian stories. However, the most substantial of his *fantascienza* stories, the novella *Pirate Utopia*, enlarges the economic focus of "Swarm" to the entire political life of the modern individual. The clearest way "Swarm" and *Pirate Utopia* work similarly is that they demonstrate how our economic and political fantasies are one and the same. In other words, our imaginations are still so bound up with the idea of human relationships as ones of domination and contest—of struggle for competing resources, whether they be material or psychological—that we can only ever imagine our fellow humans as antagonists. It is at this moment that the pheromone intervenes in "Swarm," to solve the problem of the Other: the person who is external, and does not immediately recognize our hierarchy or order, or who in some way offers contest to our hierarchy or order. It is because of our being so tethered to a model of human relations that would center hierarchy that fascism becomes the default political mode of the twentieth century. Fascism, after all, is the political mode that allows us to exist with the illusion of freedom but with the hierarchy our political unconscious demands. The pheromones of "Swarm" are such a compelling conceit because they make hierarchy "natural" and allow for an unmediated social awareness of high and low, of boss and worker, of those who lead and those who are led. What Sterling shows in *Pirate Utopia*, and by returning to the historical roots of both futurism and fascism in early-twentieth-century Italy, is that both of these ideologies are motivated by the desire to find that which can function in our society like a pheromone: a means for making the recognition of hierarchy an unmediated process. Given the impossibility of this, of course, the only solution—for both fascism and futurism—is violence.

Pirate Utopia follows in the wake of many SF texts that have used the genre of alternative history to explore our fascist twentieth century; Sterling is certainly not unique in that regard.[11] However, instead of exploring the "what-if" scenario of imagining that the Axis powers, and/or fascism, had won either of the world wars, *Pirate Utopia* can be interpreted as advancing the much more unsettling idea that regardless of the events of the two world wars, fascism was always bound to—and in fact did, in our own history—triumph. This is to say that the development of fascism on the Italian peninsula was not just an abnormal development in response to the trauma of the Great War, but that instead it was a logical outcome of our larger modern, industrial society. This reading of *Pirate Utopia* relies upon a recognition of the central place in the narrative of both futurism and fascism, and its exploration of an alternative history of the Italian Regency of Carnaro. This episode of post-WWI history is one of the more unique moments of the twentieth century, but also, as Sterling presents it, maybe one of its most emblematic. It is, from one point of view, an exemplar of nationalism and irredentism that helps us understand the fracturing of Europe during World War I and World War II. The attempt of zealous Italian nationalists to "reclaim" what they considered should be part of Italy—the city of Fiume, or what is now Rijeka in Croatia—and those nationalists' ultimate failure seems like a comic prelude to the tragedy of Italian colonial ambitions in North Africa under Mussolini. Throw in the fact that the "endeavor" was led by a poet and futurist, Gabriele D'Annunzio, and the episode takes on a decidedly surreal aspect. Using this material, Sterling merely amplifies it all with his protagonist, Lorenzo Secondari, who comes to embody the values of our own futurist-fascist world.

In the first chapter of the novella, Secondari takes a group of "Croat pirates" to the cinema. Secondari is introduced as a sort of fascist everyman: his status as a shell-shocked WWI veteran, barely able to hear or communicate with those around him due to injuries sustained during the war, and who communicates primarily through the display of arms and violence, sets him up as an ideal type of citizen-soldier. We also find out that, as a "pirate engineer," he has liberated an idle (since the end of the war) torpedo factory from its bourgeois owner, but has done so by turning the workers (all women) toward the manufacture of cheaply made, single-shot guns (which they can easily barter or sell in the chaos of Fiume, if not use themselves). We see here the populist angle of fascism, with a disdain for the elite, the capitalist class, but only when that capitalist class prevents the worthy individual from reaching his natural position. Additionally, torpedoes—and industrialized weapons in general—become one of the primary symbols of the new (alternate) Fiume. Through Secondari's genius for arms-making, the Regency of Carnaro in Sterling's alternative history becomes able to speak in ways that cannot be ignored, and in the only language the larger world respects: the ability to unleash violence.

The desire for a language that cannot be misunderstood, or a means for unmediated communication, is a central goal of the modern nation-state as much as it is the modern citizen. Secondari manifests this desire as he makes his way through the Balkan city he and his fellow Italians have come to conquer. Words, after all, do not count for much when they cannot be understood, or, as in the case of Secondari who has had one of his ears blown off in WWI, they cannot be heard. Secondari therefore longs for a world in which those surrounding him immediately recognize his worth, and their place in relation to him. As Sterling writes, "Since Fiume was an Italo-Balkan port city, the people of Fiume spoke an entire Babel of tongues. Unfortunately, the Great War had smashed Secondari's right ear. Even when the Fiumans spoke good Italian, Secondari was hard-put to hear them. He entirely failed to understand their Serbo-Croatian speech. Their Hungarian was a profound mystery to him" (*Pirate* 26–27). Importantly, however, Secondari does speak "good English," and we find out that "the English language was well known in Fiume's banking and shipping circles," though we are reminded that the "Great War had deafened" Secondari, and that "civilian life would always be a conspiracy to him" (27). These features of Secondari's character allow Sterling to establish that for Secondari there can be no real communication that does not involve in some way violence or the threat of it. Secondari, when confronted with miscommunication, or simply not being able to hear or understand what others say, inevitably relies upon the demonstration of arms. During a (failed) conversation with a cinema ticket girl, Secondari throws "open his trench coat, revealing a black shirt, black jodhpur trousers, a bandolier of grenades, two holstered Glisenti semi-automatics, and a trench dagger the size of his forearm" (25). And when Secondari confronts a group of Communist protesters outside of the cinema, who have "pirated" an Italian armored car ("a standard Lancia-Ansaldo IZM, of the 1918 vintage"), he orders the Communists to get out, followed by his dropping a grenade into the car—which luckily fails to detonate (38–39). Having acquired the armored car, Secondari then secures his Croat pirates safe passage home from the cinema by confronting a group of Italian Alpini soldiers and declaring, "Send out those flea-bitten Croat bastards of mine! And if any Commie son-of-a-whore wants to quarrel with the deaf man here . . . you can tell those faggots to come storm my factory gates! You understand that?" (40). Of course, this is the language—of dominance, of patriarchy, of violence—that the Alpini understand and respect. It is the language we have heard endlessly, from the early twentieth century to our early twenty-first century. It is the language of fascism.

Secondari's reversion to hate, violence, and vulgarity in moments calling for communication is when we can clearly see an anti-fascist critique in *Pirate Utopia* similar to what we see in "Swarm." The fascist, modern version of the pheromone that immediately communicates—in fact goes beyond communication and simply establishes hierarchy—is the gun, the bomb, the threat of violence so intense and immediate that it cannot be denied. This is the kernel upon which the fascist is made, and it accounts for his belligerence and posturing. It is theater, but theater always threatening to reach out and attack the audience. Secondari is, as he calls himself, the perfect futurist, and he is therefore the perfect fascist, for he is always theatrical. The actual futurists and fascists of Italian history, Marinetti and Mussolini, premised their ideologies on the theatrical. And once that theatricality was unleashed, a hyperbolic display of violence became encoded in the vocabulary of our politics. Interestingly, Sterling advances his anti-fascist critique by barely including either Marinetti or Mussolini in the narrative of *Pirate Utopia*. By having Mussolini, in particular, so quickly eliminated from his alternative Europe (in Sterling's Europe Mussolini is shot in the groin and permanently disabled by his ex-wife and Valentine de Saint-Pont), we can understand that Sterling is identifying fascism not as some aberrant development borne from the evil machinations of world-historically important individuals (Hitler, too, is eliminated from history in Sterling's alternative Europe; in an aside we discover that he dies during the Beer Hall Putsch), but as instead the inevitable outcome of a world harnessing incredible technology at the same time as its social imaginary was still founded upon accumulation, mistrust, fear, insecurity, and the maintenance of dominance and hierarchy. In such a world, how could we imagine things developing differently? Sterling tells us that we simply cannot, and that the moment we made it possible for individuals—let alone nations—to harness the power of technologies such as firearms, tanks, and finally atomic bombs, that those technologies would inevitably be used as ways to eliminate communication—to secure a world in which the powerful need not speak, but merely posture, to achieve their dominance.

In addition to isolating the theatrical performativity of fascism as central to its success, Sterling also demonstrates in *Pirate Utopia* that fascism thrives even among those who might profess to ideologically oppose it. Being premised upon domination and hierarchy, the fascist merely needs his followers to feel they are threatened—ideological purity goes out the window at that point. Fascism uses racism and sexism to create a sense of fear in its followers, and to acquire their consent to its rule.[12] Sterling thus portrays the masculinist and misogynist foundations of fascism via Secondari's only intimate relationships being with a professed communist and her daughter. Regardless of ideology, they are Secondari's intimates because they submit to him and are awed by his potential for violence. The (patriarchal) family therefore becomes for the fascist the model upon which citizenship should be based: a unit with a clear superior entity that all others submit to, not out of loyalty, or love, or union, but out of fear.

While fascism is premised on the dominance of the individual over others, as a political mode it takes shape when that dominance is figured as one nation against others. The cacophony of language, the babble of the multiethnic, multilingual crowd, becomes the threat against which the fascist nation must set itself. Sterling, by setting his fiction in a post-WWI, irredentist Italy, explores the development of fascism as our most characteristic modern political mode—but that it historically first developed on the Italian peninsula is no coincidence. By returning to Italy's twentieth-century history, Sterling demonstrates how the unique character of the Italian nation in the decades after its unification is emblematic for the condition of states in general in the modern world. Italian colonial endeavors to shore up its borders (by including the Croatian coast, for example, or the Libyan shoreline, or the Horn of Africa) provide the ultimate parable for the insecurity international fascism is premised upon. And that is why, instead of the history of European fascism with which we are familiar, Sterling concludes his novel with his fascist avatar—Secondari—commencing a relationship with the United States and joining its Manhattan Project. The seemingly whimsical inclusion of Harry Houdini, H. P. Lovecraft, and Robert E. Howard as CIA agents who come to Fiume to learn from the great pirate engineer who can fashion self-guiding torpedoes allows Sterling to demonstrate just how much our own world has followed the path laid out by the rogue pirates of his novella. Secondari's dream of immediate communication and recognition of dominance is what has structured our global relations in the post-WWII era of US global domination, but those seeds were sown long ago, and we first saw them sprout in Italy.

We come to realize by the end of the novella that Sterling's *Pirate Utopia* is the world in which we live—there is nothing alternative about the history Sterling has presented us. Of course, a utopia for pirates is a dystopia for those who are the pirate's victims, and that is what the world will soon be in Sterling's tale: a victim of Secondari's desire, and the desires of other men like him, who want to be immediately recognized and obeyed. In the social realm, the bellicose posturing of the fascist echoes in the aggressive stances of men who will not accept being challenged; and every time a man takes out a gun in the face of conflict, we see that man grasping for something that can function like a pheromone: an immediate signal for the other to obey, and to submit. Perhaps this more than anything else helps to explain the American obsession with bearing arms. The greatest dream of the insecure individual is that he will be listened to—that he *must* be listened to, and that he cannot be misunderstood—and we have learned only too well that that which speaks most clearly in our world is violence, the gun, the bomb.

Notes

1. In an interview with Rick Klaw, Sterling acknowledges the oddity of his turn to Italian *fantascienza* and speculates about the weirdness of an "Italian science fiction writer coming to Texas and deciding that he wants to write westerns and live in Austin. But maybe that would work—maybe he would do great westerns" (175).

2. In the same interview with Klaw, it is established that Sterling, as of 2016, has lived in Italy for "about ten years" (174).

3. Sterling himself states of his Shaper/Mechanist series, "These stories, and this novel, are the most 'cyberpunk' works I will ever write" ("Introduction" viii).

4. My understanding of fascism throughout this essay draws from Umberto Eco's concept of Ur-Fascism, or eternal fascism, and I owe a debt to Marc DiPaolo for his analysis of Ur-Fascism in *Fire and Snow: Climate Fiction from the Inklings to "Game of Thrones."*

5. The most significant example of this view of Sterling comes from Fredric Jameson, who has called cyberpunk, and especially that of Sterling, "utopian and driven by the 'irrational exuberance' of the 90s and a kind of romance of feudal commerce" (221). As I will demonstrate, this characterization of Sterling does not consider the extent to which a critical engagement with fascism—and capitalism—factors into much of Sterling's work.

6. University of Wisconsin system schools, for example, in the midst of massive defunding, have found the funding to bring in futurists-for-hire. See, for example, https://blog.uwgb.edu/catl/event-series-the-future-of-higher-education-spring-2023/.

7. That anthills, and insect colonies, might be viewed as models of collective agency—communists—aligns with a famous quip from the myrmecologist E. O. Wilson. But in SF, the members of an insect hive have more often been figured as mindless and fascistic. See, for example, *Starship Troopers*, especially the film version. In a different vein, see Pfister, who, following the philosopher Bernard Stiegler, finds in ants a "protocological fascism."

8. In his introduction to *Schismatrix Plus*, which collects all of the Shaper/Mechanist fiction, Sterling states that "Swarm" is "still the story of mine most often reprinted" (viii).

9. See, for example, Bollinger, Carbonell, Maddox, and Thacker. Den Tandt, though he only briefly discusses the Shaper/Mechanist series, and "Swarm" not at all, does introduce an interesting wrinkle in this thread of criticism with his argument that cyberpunk is a naturalist mode of SF, though one that frequently bends toward what he describes as a "posthuman gothic" (103–05).

10. The absorption of intelligent species who threaten the Swarm, and their reduction to an existence of symbiotic parasitism, is one of the many clever features of the text. Sterling offers a darkly compelling perspective on how dominant social modes absorb those who mount protest and critique, and how those "external" agents end up living in a state of dependency upon the existing social hierarchy. Those absorbed social dissidents also serve to strengthen the dominant mode of being, by serving as antibodies of a sort, and protecting—and helping to absorb—future protesters.

11. For works of alternative histories in Italian, see Brioni. Philip K. Dick's *The Man in the High Castle* remains the most well-known alternative fascist history.

12. See, for example, Eco's "Ur-Fascism."

Works Cited

Bollinger, Laurel. "Containing Multitudes: Revisiting the Infection Metaphor in Science Fiction." *Extrapolation*, vol. 50, no. 3, 2009, pp. 377–99.

Brioni, Simone. "Fantahistorical vs. Fantafascist Epic: 'Contemporary' Alternative Italian Colonial Histories." *Science Fiction Studies*, vol. 42, 2015, pp. 305–21.

Carbonell, Curtis. "Schismatrix and the Posthuman: Hyper-embodied Representation." *Fafnir—Nordic Journal of Science Fiction and Fantasy Research*, vol. 3, no. 2, 2016, pp. 7–16.

Den Tandt, Christophe. "Cyberpunk as Naturalist Science Fiction." *Studies in American Naturalism*, vol. 8, no. 1, 2013, pp. 93–108.

DiPaolo, Marc. *Fire and Snow: Climate Fiction from the Inklings to "Game of Thrones."* State U of New York P, 2018.

Doctorow, Cory. "*The Difference Engine*: A Generation Later." *The Difference Engine, 20th Anniversary Edition*, Ballantine, 2011, pp. vii–xi.

Eco, Umberto. "Ur-Fascism." *The New York Review of Books*, 22 June 1995. https://www.nybooks.com/articles/1995/06/22/ur-fascism/.

"Futurist, *N*." and "Futurism, *N*." *Merriam-Webster Unabridged*, unabridged.merriam-webster.com/collegiate/futurist, unabridged.merriam-webster.com/collegiate/futurism.

Jameson, Fredric. *The Ancients and the Postmoderns*. Verso, 2015.

Klaw, Rick. "Interview with Bruce Sterling." *Pirate Utopia*, Tachyon, 2016, pp. 170–82.

Maddox, Tom. "The Wars of the Coin's Two Halves: Bruce Sterling's Mechanist/Shaper Narratives." *Mississippi Review*, vol. 16, no. 2–3, 1988, pp. 237–44.

Pfister, Damien Smith. "Digitality, Rhetoric, and, Protocological Fascism; Or, Fascist Ants and Democratic Cicadas." *Journal for the History of Rhetoric*, vol. 23, no. 1, pp. 3–29.

Santesso, Aaron. "Fascism and Science Fiction." *Science Fiction Studies*, vol. 41, 2014, pp. 136–62.

Somigli, Luca. *Legitimizing the Artist: Manifesto Writing and European Modernism, 1885–1915*. U of Toronto P, 2003.

Sterling, Bruce. "Introduction: The Circumsolar Frolics." *Schismatrix Plus*, Ace, 1996, pp. 239–57.

———. "Preface to *Mirrorshades: The Cyberpunk Anthology*." *Science Fiction Criticism: An Anthology of Essential Writings*, edited by Rob Latham, Bloomsbury, 2017, pp. 37–42.

———. *Pirate Utopia*. Tachyon, 2016.

———. "Swarm." *Schismatrix Plus*, Ace, 1996, pp. 239–57.

Strzelczyk, Florentine. "Our Future—Our Past: Fascism, Postmodernism, and *Starship Troopers*." *Modernism/Modernity*, vol. 15, no. 1, 2008, pp. 87–99.

"Swarm." *Love, Death + Robots*, written by Philip Gelatt and Tim Miller, directed by Tim Miller, Netflix, 2022.

Thacker, Eugene. *Biomedia*. U of Minnesota P, 2004.

Thompson, Craig. "Searching for Totality: Antinomy and the 'Absolute' in Bruce Sterling's *Schismatrix*." *Science Fiction Studies*, vol. 18, 1991, pp. 198–209.

Wegner, Phillip. "The Last Bomb: Historicizing History in Terry Bisson's *Fire on the Mountain* and Gibson and Sterling's *The Difference Engine*." *The Comparatist*, vol. 23, 1999, pp. 141–51.

Zahed, Ramin. "Sophisticated Sci-Fi Is Back in 'Love, Death + Robots' Vol. 3." *Animation Magazine*, June/July 2002, pp. 42–44.

6

Italians of the Caribbean

Piracy and History in Salgari, Sabatini, and Pratt's Adventure Narratives

Cristian Soler

Martin Green identified seven kinds of adventure tale. Some can be defined by seminal works, such as *Robinson Crusoe* or *The Three Musketeers*, others by the protagonist's quest, as in the avenger or the wanderer. However, all works inscribed in this genre share a theme: "the *rite de passage* from white boyhood into white manhood, and the ritual of that religion of manliness which in mainstream books of the nineteenth century quite displaced Christian values" (41). Adventure narratives were written for metropolitan young men, to instigate their imaginations with fantastic stories in faraway European colonies. The genre started to be shaped in the late medieval ages with chivalric romances and later in fifteenth- and sixteenth-century Spain with stories of knights traveling to faraway lands like California. But it was fully formed during the nineteenth century in countries like England or France while undertaking the colonial enterprise on a global scale. These countries turned their colonies into fantastic spaces through exoticization.

Pirate novels written in the nineteenth century and twentieth century are mostly inspired by the Golden Age of Piracy that took place around the second half of the seventeenth century. They mix facts with fictional elements to create romantic adventurers who live outside the law or social conventions. In this sense, as Mikhail Skoptsov suggests, the exploits of these characters become the stuff of myths (183). It is because of this mythification of the pirate that this kind of adventure narrative also becomes close to the fantasy genre; both fantasy and adventure are descendants of myths (190). It is through fantasy that a modern subject can experience again those supernatural forces that bewildered ancient civilizations. It is through adventures that modern subjects can also reanimate a mythical past, one that has historical facts but also includes romantic elements.

Piracy in the Caribbean during the seventeenth and eighteenth centuries is a trope that constantly attracts the imagination of adventure writers. It is a moment and a place that after the nineteenth century could be romanticized and fantasized about. Discussing the close relationship between history and literature, Hayden White remarks: "We can only know the *actual* by contrasting it or likening it to the *imaginable*" (301). Italy's marginal position in modern colonialism gives its writers a perspective that allows them to criticize colonialism. However, as Europeans who can be considered white, it is difficult for them to portray issues such as deterritorialization or slavery or to give voice and visibility to groups that have been oppressed for centuries. I analyze how piracy in the Caribbean was represented—and speculated about—by three Italian authors of the late nineteenth century and twentieth century: Emilio Salgari (1862–1911), Rafael Sabatini (1875–1950), and Hugo Pratt (1927–1995).

Pirates

The default image of a pirate is British, crossing the Caribbean Sea in a galleon, assaulting Spanish ships full of treasure. However, piracy was not limited to the Caribbean during the seventeenth and eighteenth centuries. In classical antiquity, Phoenicians pirates attacked ships, kidnapping their tripulants and selling them into slavery. In his *Travels* (ca 1300), Marco Polo described corsairs in India who attacked merchant ships and stole their products. In the early modern period, Christians and Muslims engaged in piracy against each other along the coasts of Northern Africa and Southern Europe. During the nineteenth century, pirates attacked and seized American and British vessels in the South China Sea. Piracy still occurs all over the world. Somalian pirates operate in the Indian Ocean, and pirates on the Amazon River engage in different activities such as smuggling.

Even Caribbean piracy cannot be reduced to a portrayal of British pirates attacking Spanish vessels. Antonio Benítez Rojo defines the Caribbean as a meta-archipelago, a place lacking a center and precise boundaries. Starting from the notion of the machine proposed by Deleuze and Guattari, he finds that the Caribbean is a machine composed of several machines, a collection of islands connecting North America to South America, physically close to one other but isolated by several national divisions. However, in contrast to Deleuze and Guattari's machine, which remains mostly amorphous, the Caribbean machine takes a concrete shape in the productive and lucrative plantations that European colonizers created in this area (Benítez Rojo 40). When different European empires fought for control of the Caribbean, piracy involved actors from different nationalities engaged in all kinds of transactions, but the common thread was their colonial enterprise. Beside British pirates like Henry Morgan and Blackbeard were French pirates like Jean Fleury and François Le Clerc, Spaniard Amaro Pargo, and Dutchmen like Laurens de Graaf. As Historian C. R. Pennell points out, studies of Caribbean pirates written after the 1920s and 1930s followed nationalistic lines: British authors wrote almost exclusively about English pirates, French authors on French pirates, and so on. Little is known of the pirate's perspective. A primary source is *The Buccaneers of America; a True Account*, by Alexandre Exquemelin, a French or Dutch author who traveled to the Caribbean, engaging in piracy (63).

Salgari, Sabatini, and Pratt created pirate heroes and wrote adventure series focused on Caribbean exploits. Although these novels borrow from narratives like Exquemelin's and use historical facts, their main goal is to entertain. Following Kathryn Hume, these narratives can be considered fantasies because they deliberately depart from what is usually accepted or conventionally known by their readers (xii). In the nineteenth and twentieth centuries, pirates were reconceptualized by European writers at the margins of colonization. Scottish novelist Robert Louis Stevenson's *Treasure Island* (1881–1882) and Jules Verne's Captain Nemo exemplify pirates as symbols of courage, honor, freedom, and justice. Their fantastic adventures form an implicit critique of imperialism, showing the excesses and abuses of the Spanish and British empires. But these criticisms of imperialism did not mean a total rejection of colonialism.

This chapter focuses on the novels—in different series of novels—that introduce the main characters to the Caribbean. With *Il corsaro nero* (*The Black Corsair*, 1898), Salgari started a five-novel series following the adventures of Emilio Roccanera, the Black Corsair, and his progeny. *Captain Blood: His Odyssey* by Sabatini is the first book in a trilogy about an

Irish physician turned pirate. Hugo Pratt introduced Corto Maltese, the eponymous main character of the comic series, in *Una ballata del mare salato* (*A Ballad of the Salty Sea*, 1967–1969), but Maltese entered the Caribbean in *Sous le signe du Capricorne* (*Under the Sign of Capricorn*, 1970). I examine how these Italian authors approach the Caribbean and use historical facts to provide this space with some consistency.

I also show how these narratives turn pirates into romantic heroes, whose crimes and exploits reject conventional social norms and seek freedom, and also how fantastical elements fill historical and geographical gaps. Thus, I first focus on the Caribbean as an exotic cosmopolitan space in Salgari's novel, then on the representation of slavery and in a more "realistic" Caribbean space in *Captain Blood*. Finally, I analyze the representation of Afro Caribbean cultures and magic in Pratt's *Under the Sign of Capricorn*. These analyses reveal how the colonial imagination took on different shapes in an age of decolonization.

Salgari's Parallel Caribbean Worlds

Salgari's pirate novels are set in a time he did not live and territories he never visited, like Malaysia, the Caribbean, the Wild West, or Africa. Still, this Italian author never went beyond the seas that surrounded his native country and instead used historical narratives and first-person accounts. For example, many details on piracy during the seventeenth century come from Exquemelin, who met Henry Morgan, a historical figure featured as a character in *The Black Corsair* novels.

Through these historical elements and other clues, the reader can see that the events in the novel take place around the 1660s. Other historical pirates in *The Black Corsair* are François L'Ollonais and Michael the Basque. With these characters, Salgari describes the emergence of the Golden Age of Piracy in the second half of the seventeenth century. He is also introducing a conflict among European empires. Salgari relates the historical background to this period: "In 1625, while France and England attempted, through incessant warfare, to defeat the formidable might of Spain, two ships, one French, one English, manned by intrepid corsairs arrived in the Antilles intent on harrying the flourishing trade of the Spanish colonies" (98). According to Salgari, these French and English settlers—soon joined by Dutch settlers—became peaceful tobacco farmers and fishermen but were promptly harassed by Spanish soldiers and officials. They were dispossessed of their territories and forced to move to the island of Tortuga, close to Haiti, and to become pirates.

However, Emilo Roccanera's origin is different. As he tells Honorata Willerman, his love interest, in 1686 France and Spain went to war over Flanders and he fought on the French side: "At that time, Louis XIV held great influence in Piedmont, and had asked for help from Duke Vittorio Amedeo II. Unable to refuse, the duke sent him his three best regiments: the Aosta, Nice, and Marine. My three brothers and I served as officers in the latter; the oldest was thirty-two and the youngest, who later became the Green Corsair, only twenty" (Salgari 120). Roccanera's oldest brother was betrayed by van Guld, a Flemish duke fighting on the French side who made a deal with the Spanish and later became governor of a Caribbean colony. All Roccanera's surviving brothers also became corsairs and were killed by van Guld. As the last brother standing, Emilio Roccanera, Lord of Valpenta and Ventimiglia, must avenge their deaths. The novel follows Roccanera from the moment he learns of the death of his last surviving brother, retrieves his body, travels to Tortuga, plans and executes an attack on Maracaibo, until he misses his chance at revenge because his enemy escapes.

Benedict Anderson points out that all communities, even those in primordial villages, are imagined communities. What brings people together in a community is the way they can imagine themselves as such (6). In this novel, the Caribbean becomes a place where European national distinctions become blurred in a fight against the Spanish colonial empire. Characters of different nationalities unite and work together due to their aversion to the injustices committed by the Spanish or the Flemish governor who acts in their name. As a Castilian nobleman who allied with the Black Corsair against the duke says: "The duke is not well loved; he is a cruel and arrogant man, my countrymen bear him grudgingly" (Salgari 206).

Roccanera is known in the Caribbean as the Black Corsair because this is the only color he wears. His cloak, his trousers, his boots, his hat adorned with a feather are all this color. Besides these clothes he wears, the narrator focuses on his noble birth, which also is evident to every character that stumbles on Roccanera. Noble birth is easily acknowledged by everyone in this Caribbean world: Honorata also effortlessly shows her status as duchess. For this reason, Paola Galli Mastrodonato describes the world of *The Black Corsair* as a "parallel world," where Old World social conventions in terms of class, gender, and race are transposed to the New World (66). This parallel world allows the writer to create the fantasy of an easily transposable social organization where noble birth can bring together different European nations in other parts of the world. The presence of African slaves, indigenous communities, or "mestizos" do not prevent Roccanera from finding the same social structures that he knew in Europe.

Roccanera allies himself with people from different European nationalities. In an attack on the Gulf of Venezuela, Roccanera enlists the help of famous pirates like the English Morgan, the French L'Ollonais, and Michael the Basque. Roccanera's closest allies and friends, Biscayan Carmaux and Dutch Van Stiller also reflect a kind of multiculturality in the pirate world. Finally, even within the Spanish colonies, allies like a Catalan nobleman who resents the abuses committed by the Flemish governor can be found. In this multicultural world it seems that if one is not a Spaniard or an Amerindian, language and cultural differences are not obstacles for solidarity. This novel was originally written in Italian. Besides some Spanish exclamations, every single character is represented speaking Italian, although the real language in which everyone is communicating is impossible to tell.

Salgari chooses historical contexts in which European colonial empires are taking control of foreign populations and resources. In this sense, some of his heroes become champions of freedom and anti-imperialism. However, Emilio Roccanera is Italian; his struggle is not necessarily in favor of Black or indigenous communities, but more in favor of French and English "farmers" who arrived in 1625. Édouard Glissant says in *Le discours antillais* that one of the most terrifying consequences of colonization imposed on non-Western cultures is the impression that history is univocal (276). Although the Black Corsair and his friends have an African ally, Moko, who follows them in all their adventures, his status as a freeman or slave is ambiguous and his personal background is unknown. Indigenous communities in the Caribbean are referred to as cannibals, a label created after Christopher Columbus's travel to the New World served to justify colonization as a civilizing process.

The narrator in *The Black Corsair* is aware that the world being described is over. Now manatees are not as abundant as they used to be, and pirates do not roam the Caribbean in search of Spanish ships. By the time Salgari wrote this series, colonialism in the Americas, and particularly Spanish colonialism, was almost over. However, this did not mean for Salgari that imperialism was over. Even though the Spanish empire fell, other European empires, like the British, took its place. The consequences of colonialism go beyond the time in which it took place, and for this reason it is necessary to have heroes who fight against the injustice and cruelties committed by these empires. Pirates, in their outcast position, can fulfill this role. Thus, in this struggle, there can be a place for citizens who come from European nations that did not embark in the early modern colonial enterprise or for citizens of former empires that are now oppressed by other empires.

Umberto Eco describes Salgari's prose as a machine, a tool that can be easily instrumentalized. In his novels, Salgari uses narrations and descriptions to excite the imagination of his readers, his works pretend to produce a copious number of strong emotions (Eco 132). With his descriptions of the natural Caribbean world, Salgari produces wonder and awe in his European readers by painting an exotic setting. Indigenous populations in *The Black Corsair* are part of the exotic landscape. The main characters find them, or traces of them such as half-eaten human bodies, while they are walking in the jungle. Amerindians blend with nature, poisonous snakes, jaguars, and fabricated piranhas, and in this sense, they also become monstruous and savage objects. The natural world, however, is abundant and extraordinary: "No European could accurately imagine the luxuriance of the vegetation found in the hot damp climate of South America. That virgin soil, steadily enriched by the fruit and leaves that had fertilized the ground for centuries upon centuries, was covered by a wide variety of plants unequalled in all other regions of the world" (Salgari 130). This is a fantastical world with a virgin nature waiting to be civilized, along with the native and savage populations.

Sabatini and the Slave's Point of View

Sabatini was born in Italy to a family of opera singers; his mother was British, and his father was Italian. He grew up between Portugal and Switzerland, spoke more than five languages fluently, and learned English properly after moving to England when he was seventeen years old. Even though he started publishing in the 1890s, he found literary success when he published *Scaramouche* (1921). The next year, *Captain Blood: His Odyssey*, composed of previously published short stories, spawned a series of books. This novel was not the first one he wrote involving pirates and sea travels—in 1915 he had already published *The Sea Hawk*—but it was the one that spawned a series of books and adventures starring Captain Blood.

Like Salgari, Sabatini re-creates the Golden Age of Piracy and uses Exquemelin's accounts as one of his main sources. His hero is a European who became a pirate after warlike confrontations in Europe, this one an internal confrontation in England. Blood was born in Ireland and studied to become a medical doctor. He took service with the Dutch, then at war with France. During this time, he first became a seaman. The confrontation ended in 1679 and Blood remained in a Spanish prison for two years for reasons the reader never learns. After regaining his freedom, he took service with the French army in the same war where the Black Corsair lost his brother. Finally, in 1685, after suffering poor health and homesickness, he took a ship toward Ireland to settle in England and practice medicine.

> Mr. Blood had spent a third of his life in the Netherlands, where this same James Scott—who now proclaimed himself James the Second, by the grace of God, King, et cetera—first saw the light some six-and-thirty years ago, and he was acquainted with the story current there of the fellow's real paternity. Far from being legitimate—by virtue of a pretended secret marriage between Charles Stuart and Lucy Walter—it was possible that this Monmouth who now proclaimed himself King of England was not even the illegitimate child of the late sovereign. (Sabatini 3)

In 1685, a group of Protestants led by James Scott organized a rebellion to dethrone the Catholic James II of England. This event, the Monmouth Rebellion, turned Peter Blood into a pirate.

If the Black Corsair traveled to the Caribbean and became a pirate looking for revenge, Blood became a pirate because of injustice. As a doctor answering a call for help from a wounded person in the Monmouth Rebellion, Blood is captured and accused of supporting James Scott's side. He is tried and sentenced to death, but "he was informed that His Majesty had been graciously pleased to command that eleven hundred rebels should be furnished for transportation to some of His Majesty's southern plantations, Jamaica, Barbados, or any of the Leeward Islands" (Sabatini 33). In the Caribbean, Blood manages to escape and becomes a pirate. While *The Black Corsair* has a more continuous and contained narrative, *Captain Blood* is more episodic. His adventures in the Caribbean span several years and are told with numerous interruptions.

Another major difference in Sabatini's novels is a willingness to acknowledge slavery, a reality implied in *The Black Corsair* novels through the character of Moko. Dr. Blood knows that being sent to the Caribbean is not being pardoned. Glissant said that history was imposed by colonizers, and Paul Gilroy adds: "The time has come for the primal history of modernity to be reconstructed from the slaves' points of view. . . . This primal history offers a unique perspective on many of the key intellectual and political issues in the modernity debates" (55). The way plantations become profitable is by using free labor. Sabatini offers the slave's perspective, one in which individuals become "human merchandise," through an almost fantastic figure, a white slave who becomes a pirate and then a governor. Although Blood receives especial treatment because of his medical knowledge and whiteness, his position as a slave allows him to know and experience the realities of different social groups and create an image of Caribbean plantations that is far from idyllic.

Blood finds his condition as slave more denigrating than being held in Spanish prison: "I have had no lack of experiences of this mortal life; but to be bought and sold was a new one, and I was hardly in the mood to love my purchaser" (Sabatini 42). Blood was bought in Barbados by Colonel Bishop, an English man who becomes his biggest enemy. In this context, Blood sees a reality he never experienced in Europe. He witnesses how people are bought and sold, how they are forced to work, how they are malnourished, tortured, and ultimately dehumanized. For all these reasons he cannot love his purchaser; however, like the Black Corsair, Blood falls in love with the closest relative of his greatest enemy. Miss Arabella Bishop, Colonel Bishop's niece, is the first free person in Barbados that hears Blood's complaints.

Captain Blood's condemnation of slavery is not absolute. As Davide Artico indicates, to sell human beings as slaves is an aberration to him when the victims of such actions are white subjects of the British Crown. But it becomes normal, even if unjust, when the victims are caught in Africa and transported across the Atlantic (547). Once Blood becomes a pirate and starts raiding Spanish ships and ports, he starts encountering different kinds of products and "prizes." In their excursions they can plunder ships, guns, pearls, gold, prisoners that they will free for ransom, and slaves. The difference between prisoners and slaves seems to be that the former, or their families, can pay for their own freedom, while the latter can only be sold as workforce. Although on many occasions, as when he invades Maracaibo, Blood frees the slaves, he is aware that they are merchandise to the other members of his crew.

A dichotomy between sugar and tobacco also appears in *Captain Blood*. Sociologist Fernando Ortiz identifies sugar and tobacco as the main agricultural products that shaped the history, economy, and society of many parts of the Caribbean. For Ortiz, tobacco and sugar are antagonist figures. One is a local product, the other imported by Columbus; one has a dark color, the other is white; one grows spontaneously on Caribbean soil, the other one requires effort. While one can be cultivated by free hands, the other brought slave labor (143). Tobacco is something that is enjoyed by the pirates, in a tavern, while drinking rum, but, as Blood says, it does not justify attacking a ship (143). Sugar, on the other hand, is a valuable commodity that brought Blood, the European prisoners, and millions of African slaves to the Caribbean.

Unlike Salgari, Sabatini is not interested in creating a machine that excites the reader through an exaggerated exoticization of nature. Even though Sabatini mentions flies in the Antilles like there are in no other parts of the world, there are no fantastic Caribbean piranhas or cannibal tribes. His efforts to create an accurate representation are evident in his description of distances between places. The reader visits some places the Black Corsair sees, like Tortuga or Maracaibo, but Blood also visits Jamaica, Barbados, Hispaniola, and other locations around the Antilles and the Caribbean. Captain Blood's shipmaster, who serves as a narrator, gives a seemingly accurate account of the time it took them to get to each new location. Like Joseph Conrad, Sabatini is aware that every heroic action in the seas is tied to relationships that first take place on land, in a more complicated society (Williams, 142). Whenever Blood is moving, the novel describes some of the colonial boundaries that divide the Caribbean. The narrative also shows the huge advantage for a pirate, like Blood, to speak the languages of all the major colonial powers.

Captain Blood is a quest for justice. The story of an innocent person punished for helping a fellow human and then dehumanized, a fugitive living for many years at the margins of society, but finally pardoned and rewarded. At the end of the novel, Captain Blood saves Jamaica from a French assault, then becomes governor, deposing Colonel Bishop. This story's narrator, who seems to be editing written accounts and comments on Exquemelin's book, is in constant dialogue with historical discourses. This narrator even claims that the exploits generally attributed to Morgan were really done by Captain Blood (Sabatini 126). This gesture through a fantastic character pointing out some voids in historical discourses also reminds the reader that, beyond the pirate's perspective, history is lacking the slave's point of view.

Pratt and the Postcolonial Pirates

In contrast with Sabatini and Salgari, Pratt perhaps had a direct contact with the Caribbean. He was born in Italy in 1927 to a family of British, Jewish, and Turkish origins. In 1937, the family moved to Ethiopia where Pratt's father, an officer in the Italian police, was posted. In 1942, Pratt's father died as a prisoner of war, but he and his mother remained in Ethiopia as prisoners, returning to Italy after World War II. Pratt published his first comics in Italy, but, looking for a more vibrant comic industry, he moved to Argentina. Once there, Pratt collaborated with artists such as Francisco Solano López and Alberto Breccia and illustrated stories by the renowned Héctor Germán Oesterheld. He also explored other places in the Americas. Pratt returned to Italy in the early 1960s, then created his most important works.

Corto Maltese, Pratt's most important creation, first appeared in serial form in *Sergeant Kirk* in 1967. These South Seas tales were later published as *A Ballad of the Salty Sea*. Pratt published twelve graphic novels that collected the adventures of Corto Maltese, some first in Italian and others in French. Thus, it is possible to say that *Corto Maltese* is a pan-European comic, "created by an Italian artist, published in French, telling the story of a sailor born in Malta to a Spanish mother and a British father" (Filc 99). This pan-European comic also pretends to be global. Maltese's adventures take him around the world: the Mediterranean, East Africa, the North Sea, the Amazon River, and the Caribbean. The reader visits places that can be situated on a map. Even when they are looking for fantastic places like the lost continent of Mu or El Dorado, they are next to real places.

Maltese enters *A Ballad of the Salty Sea* as a South Seas castaway. After his rescue by a pirate ship, the reader also learns his name, his profession as a pirate, and that he was abandoned after a mutiny in his ship. Maltese's past, how he became a pirate, or how a Maltese sailor ended up in the South Seas is not explained until later volumes such as *La Jeunesse de Corto Maltese* (*Corto Maltese: The Early Years*, 1981–1982). But in this opening narrative the reader finds some personality traits that define this character. Maltese helps Pandora and Cain Groovesnore, two brothers kidnapped by fellow pirates for ransom. In *Under the Sign of Capricorn*, this willingness to help those in need and thirst for adventure again shows up. Maltese may seem to be a cynic, an opportunist, and a womanizer, but behind that façade there is an idealist who dismisses personal gain and is willing to help people and communities in need.

Maltese was born in 1887 to a diverse family. His life in Malta, his mother's gypsy origins, and his father's occupation as a sailor made him love adventure and drove him to the ocean at a young age. The events in *A Ballad of the Salty Sea* occur between 1913 and 1915, while those of *Under the Sign of Capricorn* are set between 1916 and 1917, when he was approaching his thirties. While almost all Maltese's adventures are set between the beginning of World War I and the 1920s, Pratt remains in dialogue with the Golden Age of Piracy. As in the seventeenth and eighteenth centuries, at the beginning of the twentieth century several colonial European empires fought for control of trade routes and territories. Nevertheless, in the twentieth century the battleground extended beyond the Atlantic to every sea around the world. Even in places without much European colonial presence, there were former colonial subjects, fighting for property rights and political representation.

If Salgari and Sabatini could silence or ignore the diverse Caribbean population, for Pratt that is impossible. Will Eisner noted that while in prose, the writer guides the reader's imagination; in comics, the artist must do all the imagination for the reader (127). Pratt cannot ignore the fact that most of the Caribbean population at the time he portrays is of African origin. He represents these people in ports all over the Caribbean and the coasts of Brazil; many are descendants of slaves taken to the Americas during the Golden Age of Piracy. In "So Much for Gentlemen of Fortune," Maltese, while looking for hidden treasure, narrates how it was gathered by famous historical pirates Blackbeard and Calico Jack in association with a fictional Creole pirate, Prying Barracuda, by looting Spanish galleons around 1700.

After so many centuries, the exact location of this treasure is unknown. The only person who can help find it is Barracuda's descendant, Miss Ambiguïté de Poincy (fig. 6.1). By introducing the figures of Barracuda and de Poincy, Pratt paints a complex and ambiguous picture of Caribbean populations. The painting behind de Poincy shows a mixed-race individual, with some Black and indigenous features, but with a European outfit. Thus, Pratt shows that piracy in the seventeenth century and in the twentieth century was not an exclusive activity of white European

Figure 6.1. Miss Ambiguïté de Poincy and a portrait of Barracuda from *Corto Maltese: Under the Sign of Capricorn. Source:* EuroComics, 2015.

men: mixed-race, people of African or Amerindian origin, and women participated actively. Pratt represents these groups not as sidekicks or simple enablers of European conquests, but as individuals with their own political and economic agendas, persons of African or indigenous origin as pirates and bandits, or even revolutionaries. When Maltese arrives on the Brazilian coast, he encounters a group of *cangaceiros*, rebels opposing internal colonizers. These postindependence colonizers are supported by the Brazilian government, who allows them to kill or subjugate Black or indigenous groups.

In his Caribbean stories, Pratt portrays the Black population as having a voice. In this sense, he represents their physical appearance, the way they dress, and their social and political struggles. In her studies of Afro-Cuban populations, anthropologist Lydia Cabrera noticed that centuries after being forcefully removed from Africa, these groups kept their religious traditions and an extensive vocabulary in languages like Yoruba, Ewe, or Bantu (19). Moreover, as Maltese travels to Brazil, Suriname, French Guiana, the Antilles, or Belize, he notices that the different African populations have also similar social struggles and needs. Maltese may find different languages in each country, but these groups have a complex system of beliefs that stem from the same roots. Pratt shows this by representing how some of these groups dress. Maltese may be in Brazil, but Black women there wear similar headwraps and polleras to those used by Colombian *palenqueras* or by other Afro-Caribbean women in other countries (fig. 6.2). Even though these cultural, religious, and mystical practices share a same origin, wherever Maltese goes, he finds that they also blend with practices from different cultural traditions. They can take elements from

Figure 6.2. Afro-Brazilian woman in conversation with Tristan Bantam from *Corto Maltese: Under the Sign of Capricorn*. *Source:* EuroComics, 2015.

European or Amerindian iconographies and imaginaries and appropriate them in such way to make it difficult to tell these different traditions apart.

It is in the Caribbean that Maltese first hears of the mythical kingdom of Mu. Although the quest for Mu will be the main subject of the last graphic novel drawn and written by Pratt (*Mu*, 1988–1991) this kingdom is what first motivates Maltese's Caribbean travels in *Under the Sign of Capricorn*. Maltese goes from Suriname to Brazil to help Tristan Bantam, a young English man looking for his sister in South America after reading some letters left by his late father. The letters describe this sister and the kingdom of Mu. This quest has several fantastical moments triggered by Afro-Caribbean magical practices that incorporate European and Amerindian iconographies, such as an Aztec-like pyramid or a portal that resembles the Stone of Tizoc (fig. 6.3). For Pratt, then, Caribbean history is not restricted to European chronicles, but also includes the traditions and the mythical past of other populations.

Although myths, one of the main sources of all fantasy and adventures, can be seen in *Under the Sign of Capricorn*, the Caribbean it represents is more realistic than Salgari's or Sabatini's. Pratt is more willing to confront the consequences of colonialism. Unlike the Black Corsair or Captain Blood, Maltese does not lead the action at every moment. He is willing to follow other characters, to listen to different local communities, and to be led by them. This exchange between a foreigner and the place that they are visiting is at the core of any production of knowledge in travel narratives, as the critic Mary Louise Pratt points out: "Every travel account has this heteroglossic dimension; its knowledge comes not just out of a traveler's sensibility and powers of observation, but out of interaction and experience usually directed and managed by 'travelees'" (136). By listening

Figure 6.3. Tristan Bantam's dream from *Corto Maltese: Under the Sign of Capricorn. Source:* EuroComics, 2015.

to the local population, Maltese can move around the Caribbean and learn about their history and struggles.

By the time the stories in *Under the Sign of Capricorn* take place, slavery had been abolished and many islands or territories in the Caribbean were already independent nations. But Pratt shows that the effects of colonialism are not over. The Caribbean was left with an immense population of African origin, descendants of slaves who, like Amerindians, became free, but were left marginalized and impoverished. This volume is episodic, with each chapter representing a different place in the Caribbean. This fragmentary structure reminds the reader that the Caribbean is a fragmented zone, full of different languages and cultures that once belonged to different European empires. What gives them unity is a shared colonial past.

Conclusion

In the nineteenth and twentieth centuries, pirates were imagined by European writers who themselves were at the margins of colonization. For these authors, pirates were symbols of courage, honor, freedom, and justice whose fantastic adventures both illustrated and criticized imperialism. Yet, these critiques were not universal. For Salgari and Sabatini, the property rights of British, French, or Dutch farmers superseded those of Amerindians or African slaves in a Caribbean that retained European social structures. Pratt, on the other hand, portrayed the deterritorialization and marginalization that colonialism produced for several groups. But, as Filc says, Maltese's constant involvement in local struggles also put him sometimes in a white savior role.

Caribbean pirates of the Golden Age are a trope that draws the imagination of adventure writers, a moment and a place to be romanticized and fantasized. For Corto Maltese, pirates like Blackbeard or Prying Barracuda were men of fortune. More than looking for fortune, Maltese looks for their treasure to solve the puzzle of their disappearance. For Sabatini, the Caribbean was a place where white men could emerge from slavery and become governors. In *The Black Corsair*, Salgari constantly stops his narration to describe the landscape where the action is taking place. For him, it is not enough to describe how particular a manatee is. He also needs to emphasize to the reader that they were plentiful in those times. Salgari, Sabatini, and Pratt all have in common that they portray this specific Caribbean as a place with an exuberant and wild nature, where European men can show their worth and acquire glory and riches.

The three Italian authors just discussed use historical facts and the gaps in them to create fantastic, heroic adventure settings. History provides not only material for their novels. It is also the horizon on which these novels become possible. Although Italy was not at the center of European colonialism in the twentieth century, these authors had some contact with it, Pratt perhaps more so. Each was aware of current decolonial processes in Latin America and around the world. They could be sympathetic to many marginal groups fighting colonial powers, but they also shared internal struggles. That which is hardly imaginable for these authors are the real struggles of Amerindian and Afro-Caribbean groups, dispossessed by many centuries of colonialism.

Author's note: I would like to thank Lisa M. De Tora for inviting me to contribute to this volume and for reading and editing the first draft of this chapter.

Works Cited

Anderson, Benedict. *Imagined Communities*. Verso, 2016.

Artico, Davide. "Libertà, uguaglianza, e proprietà nella narrativa di Rafael Sabatini." *Wrocławskie Studia Erazmiańskie*, no. 10, 2016, pp. 537–55.

Benítez Rojo, Antonio. *La isla que se repite*. Casiopea, 1998.

Cabrera, Lydia. *El monte*. Universal, 2006.

Eco, Umberto. *Apocalípticos e integrados*. Tusquets, 2002.

Eisner, Will. *Comics and Sequential Art: Principles and Practices from the Legendary Cartoonist*. W. W. Norton, 2008.

Filc, Dani. "Tintin and Corto Maltese, the European Adventurer Meets the Colonial Other." *European Comic Art*, vol. 13, no. 1, 2020, pp. 95–121.

Galli Mastrodonato, Paola I. "Dal Corsaro Nero agli Ultimi Filibustieri: la creazione di un universo alternativo." *Il tesoro di Emilio, Omaggio a Salgari*. Bacchilega, 2008, pp. 65–77.

Gilroy, Paul. *The Black Atlantic: Modernity and Double Consciousness*. Verso, 1993.

Glissant, Édouard. *Le discours antillais*. Gallimard, 1997.

Green, Martin. *Seven Types of Adventure Tale: An Etiology of a Major Genre*. Pennsylvania State UP, 1991.

Hume, Kathryn. *Fantasy and Mimesis: Responses to Reality in Western Literature*. Methuen, 1984.

Ortiz, Fernando. *Contrapunteo Cubano del tabaco y el azúcar*. Cátedra, 2002.

Pennell, C. R. "Who Needs Pirate Heroes?" *Northern Mariner*, vol. 8, no. 2, 1998, pp. 61–79.

Pratt, Hugo. *Corto Maltese: The Ballad of the Salt Sea*. Universe, 2012.

———. *Corto Maltese: Under the Sign of Capricorn*. EuroComics, 2015.

Pratt, Mary Louise. *Imperial Eyes: Travel Writing and Transculturation*. Routledge, 1992.

Sabatini, Rafael. *Captain Blood*. Penguin, 2003.

Salgari, Emilio. *The Black Corsair*. ROH, 2016.

Skoptsov, Mikhail L. "Evoking History Through Fantasy: *Pirates of the Caribbean* and the Myths of the Golden Age." *Bringing History to Life Through Film: The Art of Cinematic Storytelling*, edited by Kathryn Anne Morey. Rowman & Littlefield, 2014.

White, Hayden. "The Historical Text as Literary Artifact." *Clio*, vol. 3, no. 3, 1974, pp. 277–303.

Williams, Raymond. *The English Novel from Dickens to Lawrence*. Hogarth, 1984.

7

Genealogies of Horror

Dario Argento's *Do You Like Hitchcock?* Or, Reading National Horror Against the Local

Fernando Gabriel Pagnoni Berns

When fans and film scholars think about Italian horror cinema, Dario Argento's name quickly comes to mind. He directed some of the most disturbing horror films, including classics such as *Suspiria* (1977) or *The Bird with the Crystal Plumage* (Italian title: *L'uccello dalle piume di cristallo*, 1970). While the former reinvented the Italian Gothic horror to new sensibilities, the latter was a blueprint for the Italian cycle widely known as *giallo* (Heller-Nicholas 60).

The Italian cycle of *giallo* (roughly, through the 1970s) has been conceptualized as an answer to Italy's cultural shifts when the nation changed from an agricultural country to a modern, cosmopolitan geography. The *giallo* narratives, focused on tropes such as a serial killer wearing black gloves, intricate plots, psychological trauma, and colorful but brutal murders, amount to a dilution of national fixity, now replaced by the gaze of tourism. Mikel Koven identifies this cosmopolitanism with violent impulses, these feelings tied to the anxieties brought by the encroaching modernity in postwar Italy.

Yet, even if tapping into social and cultural anxieties regarding the modernization of Italy, the *giallo* was not entirely vernacular, but the result of a transnational flux. Argento's 2005 TV horror film *Do You Like Hitchcock?* (Italian title: *Ti piace Hitchcock?*) plays with the genre's genealogies, tracing how audiovisual horror is not (and it never was) circumscribed to a nation; it is, in fact, a reinterpretation of previous global narratives, shaped to fit into social and cultural contexts of repressed fears and anxieties.

In *Do You Like Hitchcock?*, Giulio (Elio Germano), a college film student obsessed with the works of Alfred Hitchcock, investigates a murder committed in the apartment building across from his and suspects that his seductive neighbor hired a girlfriend to commit the deed. The film presents itself as an homage to the American master of the thriller. But the flux of the horror genre does not end there. Giulio studies German silent horror from the Weimar era, another cycle of films preoccupied with the gaze and spectacle (Barzilai 55). Further, the film's puzzling opening, with a young Giulio spying on two witches sacrificing a chicken, has nothing to do with the story's main plot but points to the genre's supernatural roots and *stregheria*, Italian witchcraft.

This chapter will trace the genealogies of the horror genre as depicted through the complex plot of Argento's *Do You Like Hitchcock?*, an overlooked film predicated on the disruption of the local/global dyad. Argento's film addresses the intricate fluxes of tropes and images inherent to horror cinema and demonstrates how this genre navigates between the local (tapping into social and cultural contexts) and the transnational.

Horror Cinema: The Local, the Transnational, and the Supranational

Tackling the broader significance of investigating Italian horror cinema would lead film scholarship and historians to a better understanding of the peculiarities of Italian cinema and its place on the global cinema map. The *giallo* is a transnational and supranational cycle that was crystalized in Italy because the social context of the time found in this cycle the perfect vehicle to channel collective social and cultural anxieties of the 1970s. In other words, the *giallo* is a vernacular cycle that metaphorizes, following horror scholar Robin Wood, the instability of national identity in a way that genres considered more "realistic" could not.

Robin Wood, in his "An Introduction to the American Horror Film," written in the middle of the 1970s, makes a psychoanalytic approach to horror films to argue that the monster in genre cinema works as a materialization of our collective nightmares. Wood argues that horror movies metaphorize anxieties, fears, and collective traumas existing in a given time and society. Following Wood, society drives all its efforts and energy into productive forms of work that serve to keep the hegemony of the capitalist and patriarchal system. There is, however, a "plus" (Wood 111) of libidinal energy that cannot be subsumed under the logic of capitalism (in its two aspects: work and controlled recreation), and it is this vital energy that leads us to want "something else" from life: that nonproductive, potentially subversive energy must be repressed. That energy is first and foremost anti-social; it does not obey market logic.

Wood then explains his concept of repression and oppression: the libidinal plus must be repressed by the subject. If this repression is insufficient, then oppression intervenes. The subject who cannot or does not wish to repress their vital impulses must then be oppressed to prevent this "symptom" of abnormality and malaise from becoming generalized in society (Wood 109). Any person who is a deviation from the status quo will be punished through a conversion into an "Other," textually embodied in a monstrous figure. Female sexuality, homosexuality, non-Western religions, and non-mainstream ideologies, among other characteristics, are configured as Otherness and turned into monsters within horror cinema. The real theme of horror films in general is the negotiation with these social anxieties. The monster is a conglomerate of repressed social and cultural anxieties that come to light and must be defeated in order to return them to a state of repression. The monster, in short, is a *symptom* of the repressed made grotesquely corporeal.

Following the symptomatic reading and the "monster turn" propagated by Wood in the 1970s, Jeffrey Jerome Cohen argues that the monster is a personification of the Otherness within culture. In this sense, then, each culture begets its own monsters (3) according to the parameters with which each society erects its figures of Otherness and normality. Cohen establishes seven theses to delineate the monster as cultural production. The first states that the monster's body is a cultural body (3) since the monstrous creature is made up of elements that society rejects as abnormal. This abjection, however, is not casual or universal: it responds to a certain culture and historical time. The monster's body is inextricably tied to its production context. Jack Halberstam agrees: "Monstrosity (and the fear it gives rise to) is historically conditioned rather than a psychological universal" (6).

Film scholar Adam Lowenstein goes beyond the monster in his studies and states that the horror film functions as an allegory. Allegory is derived from the Greek *allos* (other) and *agorein* (to speak publicly), and, as such, speaks obliquely of what a particular society and culture has repressed in a particular historical time (Lowenstein 15). For example, George Romero's *Night of the Living Dead* (1968) has been discussed as an allegory on the Vietnam War (Williams 26), without the film discussing said war explicitly in any moment. Within images of shock, dread, and gore, horror cinema taps into social and cultural fears, presenting them to viewers through the distorted mirror of genre conventions.

The thesis here exposed, of horror cinema being an allegorical moment that stages cultural and social anxieties through a deformed mirror led by a monster that is, in turn, a metaphor of what a society has repressed, is pertinent as an analytical tool to studying cinema. There is, however, a problem: coproductions and transnational cinema. In a film such as Robert Eggers's *The Witch* (2015), this approach might be problematic. The film is a coproduction between Great Britain, the United States, and Canada. As such, Eggers's story invites scholars following the symptomatic approach as studied by Wood or Lowenstein to wonder about what national anxieties are allegorized into the fantastical story of a witch cursing a family in New England. Those of the United States? Of Canada? Of Great Britain? All different countries united only by the English language; it is not clear how to approach this film in terms of the repressed symptom. The film stages the national fears and anxieties of the country where the film was most localized during the process of filming (Canada)? Or the director's native country (United States)?

There are many more examples, including the phenomenon now known by scholars as "Euro-horror," meaning that the horror cinema produced and directed within Europe has its own qualities and tropes, all different from that produced in, for example, the United States or Latin America. Yet, Euro-horror is not a cohesive set of images and cinematic fears. Peter Hutchings suggests that Euro-horror is an umbrella term that consists not in a cohesive totality, but in the absence of this totality. European horror consists instead, of a variety of different aesthetic and ideological practices with "no geographical centre and no core identity" (22). Still, there are some common tropes uniting the disparate productions of classical (through the late 1950s to the earlier 1980s) Euro-horror; according Danny Shipka, these common elements include a taste for "exploitation," while relying "on shocking and titillating audiences with as much nudity and violence as they could handle, all the while setting this mayhem in the best locations that Europe had to offer" (5).

The problem with the symptomatic approach when studying Euro-horror is that a common element shaping this European phenomenon is the regime of coproduction. Many of the films made during the heyday of Euro-horror were coproductions made between two or more countries. Even cycles considered as "purely" national as the Italian *giallo* were made, more often than not, backed by other countries such as Germany and Spain. Further, the idea of "original" was somehow lost in Euro-horror, as directors like Spaniard Jesus Franco filmed different versions of his films of erotica and horror; depending on the degree of freedom of each country, the film's version contained more nudity and gore and, sometimes, even hardcore scenes (Shipka 186).

The transnational problem does not foreclose the symptomatic perspective, but it favors more nuanced readings. It is worth remembering that even the cycle that started horror cinema, the American films made by Universal Studios, was not entirely "national": Tod Browning's *Dracula* (1931) depended on an Irish source (the novel and the play) and was led by a Hungarian star (Bela Lugosi). James Whale's *Frankenstein* (1932) was even "less" American, with the director and main stars (including Boris Karloff) of British origin. In fact, American horror cinema was predicated on the knowledge and expertise of many filmmakers, directors of photography, cameramen, among others, running away to America from the horrors of the Great War. "American horror cinema profited from such émigrés as Karl Freund or Val Lewton. Consequently, there is nothing new in Hollywood's [contemporary] import of directors" (Hantke xvi).

Horror cinema was transnational in nature, produced by a global flux of artisans, ideas, images, cycles, aesthetics, and ideologies. Yet, it remains to be investigated if said circulation was international, transnational, or supranational in perspective. Natasa Durovicová, in her introduction to her edited collection *World Cinemas, Transnational Perspectives*, argues that scholars in film history must distinguish between the concepts of international, transnational, and supranational. For the author, international is a problematic term, as it is "predicated on political systems in a latent relationship of parity, as signaled by the prefix 'inter' " (Durovicová x). Within the idea of "international" lies the erroneous concept that every nation has participated, in the same degree, in the production and circulation of a cultural artifact. Thus, the author prefers the term "transnational," which "acknowledges the persistent agency of the state, in a varying but fundamentally legitimizing relationship to the scale of 'the nation.' At the same time, the prefix 'trans-' implies relations of unevenness and mobility. It is this relative openness to modalities of geopolitical forms, social relations and especially to the variant scale on which relations in film history have occurred that gives this key term its dynamic force" (Durovicová x).

Investigating the transnational nature of most of Spanish and Italian horror cinema, Rui Trindade Oliveira argues for the "supranational" adjective. The supranational still lacks a definitive definition, but Oliveira uses it to point to a common identity that unites disparate nations, producing, for example, "Italian-Spanishness." This takes place when different nations share "cultural preoccupations" in common and, "secondly, industrial, socioeconomic, and political contexts of film production and distribution" (xiii). Thus, regions sharing a common geographical space—for example, the Baltic region, the Mediterranean, among others—political contexts—Latin America—or film productions and distribution—Spain and Italy in the 1970s—can be part of a supranational identity that surpasses borders and national definitions. For example, the *giallo* cycle was born in Italy but it was soon adopted by Spain, as both countries shared preoccupations regarding the influx of modernity and a new consumerist society—in the 1950s in Italy, in the 1960s in Spain—into their nations, even if Spain and Italy were widely different in terms of politics through the 1970s.

Do You Like Hitchcock? can be read in terms of symptomatic analysis, transnational cinema, and supranational flux. Following Wood, the film's monster embodies what Italy has repressed, now brought to light in the form of a killer. Which cultural anxieties are embodied in the film's main monsters? In the film, Giulio is forced to confront three young criminals, all prone to murder in exchange for money. In this scenario, it might be argued that the film codes the decline of youth's morals, as the killer(s) is/are young people. Further, the decline of parental values might be interpreted as another repression brought to the textual surface, as family (and the destruction of) it is an important issue within the film. Intrafamilial violence instigates murder (Shasa and her mother seem to hate each other). Giulio resolves the case with the help of his family. The benefits of the nuclear family are a novel theme for Argento, never used as much here as elsewhere.

The preceding readings are pertinent, but horror cinema is never "allegory of X," the X representing a univocal societal fear. The horror film is open to multiple interpretations. In this essay, I will read *Do You Like Hitchcock?* as marking a particular return of the repressed: the "traumatic" recognition that national cinema never has been completely local, but transnational or supranational of origin. Not even a cycle considered as proudly Italian as the *giallo* should be considered completely vernacular, but the consequence of the influxes of horror tropes and ideologies, a conglomerate of cultural elements navigating between the local and the transnational.

The Hitchcock Connection

Argento's *Do You Like Hitchcock?* was celebrated as a return to top form for the director after the critical and box office failures of *Phantom of the Opera* (1998) and *The Card Player* (2004)—with the well-received *Sleepless* (2001) in the middle. An homage to both, Alfred Hitchcock's career and Argento's stylistic *gialli* (plural for *giallo*), the film was considered an attempt from the Italian director to return to his "roots" and come "full circle" (Met 205), meaning, paying due respects to the man who inspired the *giallo* cycle.

But what is a *giallo* film?

The genre *giallo* does not lend itself to concrete definition, preferring rather the ambiguous and playful. In Italian, *giallo* means "yellow." The term refers to the bright colors of early mystery paperbacks published in Italy by the Milanese Mondadori. These paperbacks, which began publication in the late 1920s, mostly offered vernacular translations of authors such as Agatha Christie or Edgar Wallace. As Koven explains, "A few years earlier, Mondadori had achieved success with a series of romance novels published with bright blue covers, and so their *giallo* series was an extension of this color-coding of popular literature" (2). Soon enough, *yellow* signified "crime" for Italian readers. Through the 1970s, this label extended to cinema, when Italian (and, later, international) film audiences adopted it as the name for a peculiar Italian subgenre of thriller that emphasized atmosphere and the killings over the case's resolution.

Giallo was rapidly recognized by a series of striking features, and narrative and visual conventions. First and foremost, the murder itself. In contrast with the killings in classical crime cinema, mostly bloodless gunshots, the murders in *gialli* are depicted through sophisticated, cruel, bloody set pieces that, in the case of auteurs such as Dario Argento or Mario Bava, work almost autonomously from the main narrative. Long in length and filled with excessive, intricate detail, the murders are not just a plot point but a masterclass on the art of filmmaking. The *gialli* presented another set of recognizable conventions: amateur sleuths, close shots of hands (that of the murderer) covered by black gloves, repressed memories, bold music scores, and lengthy titles such as *The Strange Vice of Mrs. Wardh* (dir. Sergio Martino, 1971) or *The Case of the Bloody Iris* (dir. Giuliano Carnimeo, 1972). Also, shots of J&B Whiskey, a marker of sophisticated cosmopolitan life. The *giallo* was a response to Italy's "economic miracle" that changed the country's topography and cultural life from the agrarian to the modern after the nation opened to global tourism. Hence the travelogue narrative and the recurrent presence of airports, cars, and roads scattered throughout the films. In this latter point the *giallo* cycle was, in terms of Mikel Koven, vernacular, as the films were a distorted answer to the rapid changes made within the geography and landscapes of traditional Italy, now turned a cosmopolitan destination loved by the international jet set.

Notably, the Italian "economic miracle" refers to Italy's speedy and striking reconstruction following the Second World War and the fascist regime of Benito Mussolini. Even if the period of high economic growth ran from the early 1950s to the early 1970s, the famed "economic miracle" encompassed 1958 to 1963. The boom was supercharged by Marshall Plan program funding, which supported Italian economic policies. Italy invested these funds everywhere—but especially in the underdeveloped south. The Italian miracle was part of a global "golden age" of capitalism, "which created a new world market for consumer goods and forced Italians into a modern, industrial world" (Foot 138). The increasing prosperity brought a new consumerist society, then a real novelty; many Italians acquired consumer goods such as cars or home appliances like fridges, televisions, or washing machines (Foot 138). Urbanization and industrialization transformed the Italian landscape, producing "a shift of power away from the traditional 'structures in dominance'—that is, the essentially regionalist bourgeoisie and intellectual class—toward the 'emergent structure' centered on the technocrats," the latter a new class whose essential features were "a new mobility across the national space" (Restivo 46). Spain adopted the *giallo* because all the conditions that gave rise, within Italy, to this cycle, were also fulfilled in Spain, including an opening to the outside world (in the 1960s) due to the scarcity of foreign currency, which brought, in turn, a modern wave of progressive thinking that threatened to collapse the solid supports of national conservatism.

To this scenario of instability, the *giallo* cycle answered back with stories sustained on the ocular; the new influx of tourism—wandering the streets as the flaneur does (Koven 94)—and the abrupt changes in the national landscape made the eye and the gaze constitutive tropes of the *giallo* film. Argento's first *giallo*, *The Bird with the Crystal Plumage*, is built on the main hero witnessing a botched murder; yet the key to resolving the case lies in what he saw (and how he misreads what he saw). Argento's *Do You Like Hitchcock?* plays like any traditional *giallo* in this regard. Giulio is a young film history student working on his thesis about German expressionism. One night, bored and aroused, he starts to spy on his beautiful neighbor Sasha (Elisabetta Rocchetti) while she disrobes. Trapped by the excitement of the gaze, he looks for her every day, thus learning about Sasha's fights with her mother and her friendship with Federica (Chiara Conti), a young woman suffering sexual harassment in her job. When Sasha's mother is brutally killed, Giulio starts to suspect that both women are the culprits.

The preceding synopsis describes a traditional Italian *giallo* involving an amateur detective (Giulio) being drawn into investigating a shocking murder. In this case, the amateur is spurred into action when others do not believe his theory about Sasha and Federica exchanging victims in the same way that Bruno Anthony schemed to "crisscross . . . switch crimes" with his tennis hero, Guy Haines, in Hitchcock's *Strangers on a Train* (1951). Thanks to Giulio's theory and role as an amateur detective, *Do You Like Hitchcock?* plays as a traditional *giallo* while simultaneously acknowledging the *giallo* cycle's debt to the British master of suspense.

The *giallo* has three origins, each one solidifying the tropes of the genre. Arguably, it all began with Mario Bava's *The Girl Who Knew Too Much* (1963), a film revolving around Nora (Leticia Roman), a young woman who travels to Rome and witnesses a murder after, accidently, consuming some drugs. The police do not believe her since a corpse cannot be found. Several more murders follow, turning Nora into an amateur sleuth. *The Girl Who Knew Too Much* established some of the cycle's tropes, chief among them the eye and vision as untrusted apparatuses. Even Nora is uncertain about what she saw and if the murder really took place. Following this black-and-white film, Bava crystallized the conventions with his groundbreaking *Blood and Black Lace* (1964) where a masked, black-gloved killer starts murdering various fashion models. Finally, the *giallo* got all its definitive tropes with Argento's *Bird with the Crystal Plumage.*

The film that started it all, *The Girl Who Knew Too Much*, pays obvious homage to Hitchcock via its title, which evokes a film Hitchcock made twice: *The Man Who Knew Too Much* (1934 and 1956). It may be argued that the Italian cycle of *gialli* started via imitation of Hitchcock; it is worth pointing again to the origins of the yellow color: the Mondadori cheap paperbacks publishing authors who, in turn, were read by Hitchcock. Further, Argento "made it a habit in his films to don the black gloves himself in these sequences, partially as an homage to Alfred Hitchcock's cameos" (Koven 101). As with Hitchcockian films, the mystery's resolution was not as important as the presence of mistaken identities, creative murders, and inventive camerawork. The *giallo* film began as Hitchcockian mysteries that, eventually and slowly, developed into a very vernacular cycle after blending with the social and cultural characteristics of Italy through the 1960s and 1970s. Philippe Met calls this phenomenon "crisscrossing and/or cross-fertilization" (197). Hitchcock himself will look for inspiration in Europe—looking with special interest to the French thrillers made by Henri-George Clouzot—after feeling that he was repeating himself with his crime films.

This "crisscrossing and/or cross-fertilization" continues after the death of the *giallo* cycle at the beginning of the 1980s (due to Italy's general decline in global film geography and the end of the American grindhouse circuit, a venue that offered many efforts from the Euro-horror tradition). The *giallo* inspired and influenced one of the most American film cycles: the slasher, popular stories that dominated the horror market in US in the latter 1970s and 1980s, especially after the success of the *Friday the 13th* franchise. Mikel Koven argued that the *giallo* cycle introduced "several of the tropes and devices that became ubiquitous in these films [the slasher] by the end of the decade. We have the isolated location; beautiful girl students; a prototype of the Final Girl . . . ; and the discovery of all the bodies in one location" (162). In another case of transnational flux, the *giallo* served American ideology, especially through the Reaganomics of the 1980s, with youth seemingly falling, to the conservative mind, into the dangers of sex, drugs, and criminality. Thus, the United States finds that one of its most popular and "national" cycles, the slasher, is as complex in its construction as the *giallo*. If the *giallo* is a complex agglomeration of Hitchcockian influences, the American slasher finds its roots in the Italian *giallo*, one and the other disproving any idea that a national film cycle is authentically autarchic.

From a strictly narrative perspective, Argento has fashioned a highly typical *giallo* narrative with his homage to Hitchcock. Yet, the film addresses its debt to Hitchcock in an explicit way, making constant references to the director's corpus of films and style. But, yet again, the film is typically vernacular, a story that fills all the expected boxes of the *giallo* film. Following Wood and Lowenstein's symptomatic analyses, *Do You Like Hitchcock?* can be read as the return of the Italian repressed. But what has been repressed here? Perhaps the sense of generational dislocation and disenchantment youth suffer at the turn of the new millennium in Italy? In this film, Argento makes an unusual move toward family and its powers of emotional support. Both Federica and Sasha seem to be young women suffering from a loss of ties with their families: Federica is alone to contend with her boss, while Sasha is unable to talk with her mother except through fights. On the other hand, Giulio has a girlfriend, Arianna (Cristina Brondo), and a mother (Elena Maria Bellini) who help Giulio in his investigation, even if the young man's thesis about the murder sounds to both women a little far-fetched. It is hinted that Giulio is not completely happy with his mother's new boyfriend (his future stepdad): still, Giulio's stepdad comes to his rescue when he is attacked by one of the film's real culprits, video club owner Andrea (Iván Morales), who tries to drown Giulio in his bathtub. While Giulio is a healthy young man—the film's hero—with a supportive family, all the suspected characters seem to have no family or problematic ones. The Italian symptom of repression that the film offers appears to be a wake-up call about how traditional family ties, so dear to Italy, are becoming increasingly ephemeral in the new millennium. In the end, the family is presented as a saving institution. This message, somewhat conservative for horror cinema, is tempered by the inclusion of the main assembled family, signaling an acceptance of new ways of understanding this bond outside of traditional Italian norms.

Still, at the end, what *Do You Like Hitchcock?* brings to the surface is the acknowledgment that Italian horror is indebted to the American thriller, which, in turn, will be indebted to European horror in the form of the slasher cycle. This "crisscrossing and/or cross-fertilization," however, is not the only influence delineating Argento's film.

The German Flux

Bafflingly, Giulio's thesis revolves around German expressionist cinema rather than Hitchcock, the obvious choice in a film that pays homage to the British master of suspense. Still, this choice is coherent with the film's thesis: horror has never been purely local but is born of transnational influences and feedback. One of the *giallo*'s roots is the *krimi* film, a German corpus of crime films. The *krimi* cycle was another transnational phenomenon, with West Germany (later with influx from Spain, the UK, and/or France) making a series of films inspired by the novels of Edgar Wallace. These narratives draw their name "from a line of paperbacks known as *Taschenkrimi*, the paperback form of the *Kriminalroman* that the society read in prodigious numbers" (Sanjek 84). From 1959 to 1972, more than forty West German films were adapted from Wallace's works, the majority produced by Rialto Films. As David Sanjek noted, both the *gialli* and the *krimi* films shared common tropes, the most important being an emphasis on the murders, an ironic look to society's evils (including social mobility), and black-gloved killers. The *krimi* and the *giallo* resemble each other in a supranational way "in their interpolation of established national and extranational visual and narrative codes" (Sanjek 84). The influence of Italian money investments and artistic input slowly derived from the German *krimi* into the *giallo* cycle, now firmly located in Italy. Julian Grainger noted that "the Italian *giallo* mixed the *krimi* with the police procedural and added a twist of its own; an almost fetishistic attention to the murderer and the killings he (and sometimes she) perpetrated" (118).

The connection with the *krimi* cycle is not the only element connecting *Do You Like Hitchcock?* with German horror and crime cinema. Giulio has been trapped by what he has seen and cannot let the case die. This investment in the gaze is prototypical of the *giallo*; still, Weimar macabre cinema, the one Giulio investigates, is embedded in the power of the gaze. German expressionist cinema was preoccupied with the gaze and, like the *giallo* cycle, with the changes brought by modernity to the social and cultural landscape. Electricity, the increasing velocity of trains and cars, and new inventions abounded even as cinema changed how people looked at their surroundings (Killen; Guerin). For German medical culture, the abrupt changes brought by modernity and the difficulty in processing them all were causes of nervous breakdowns, chronic fatigue, and fits of hysteria. The citizenship was reeling from the traumas of the Great War and the strains of adapting to a new reality. In this scenario, it is not coincidental that expressionist art flourished, inviting the Germans to watch reality through a deformed lens. Preoccupation with the traumatic aspects of modernity and the effects of shell shock brought by the Great War were predicated on the psyches and, materially, on the eyes: victims of the Great War returned mute, their eyes completely vacant. Further, hypnotism was an accepted tool to cure war's victims, thus enhancing the power of the gaze (Andriopoulos). Not coincidentally, German macabre cinema emphasized extreme close-ups of eyes, in films such as the aptly titled *The Mummy's Eyes* (Ernst Lubitsch, 1918) and *The Cabinet of Dr. Caligari* (Robert Wiene, 1920). The two scenes of German horror depicted through *Do You Like Hitchcock?* concern the gaze: one illustrates the use of optical effects, with the vampire dissolving slowly at the coming of dawn in *Nosferatu: A Symphony of Horror* (F. W. Murnau, 1929). The second is a close shot of the golem's eyes in *The Golem: How He Came into the World* (Paul Wegener and Carl Boese, 1920). Argento's film returns to primal preoccupations with the gaze before the birth of the *giallo*, reminding audiences that the gaze has been central to macabre cinema since its earliest days.

Return to the Italian Locale

There is yet another baffling aspect of the narrative structure of Argento's *Do You Like Hitchcock?*—an opening that seems thematically disconnected from the rest of the film. A young Giulio, a boy of eight or nine, follows a couple of young women through the forest. The women arrive at an isolated cabin. Watching them from a window, young Giulio is amazed at the spectacle before his eyes: the women kill a chicken and bathe in its blood. The women are young witches, and Giulio watches one of their bloody rituals. The women discover the young boy watching them and hunt him down through the forest; fortunately, Giulio escapes unscathed. Based on this opening, viewers might understandably assume that Argento has returned to his classic theme of witchcraft and is making one of his *Three Mothers spiritual* sequels to *Suspiria*. But any viewers who would assume this would be incorrect. Certainly, the witches do not return once the opening segment ends, and the story quickly abandons supernatural elements. Ultimately, *Do You Like Hitchcock?* revolves around human killers, not witchcraft.

And yet, this incongruous opening is integral to the story, since it returns to the classic *giallo* theme of the voyeuristic gaze. Thus, the opening fits squarely into the mold of the *giallo* cycle and its preoccupation with the gaze. But why witches, of all monsters? The answer is twofold. First, because witches are arguably the only vernacular Italian monsters. Italy has a tradition of witchcraft and dark arts. As Marina Montesano has explained, witchcraft in Italy is as old as ancient Rome, not in myth and oral legend as in ancient Greece, but already "the product of literary creativity" (37). Witchcraft and the presence of powerful witches were vital in Italy's history, filled as it is with "*sortilegi* (sorcerers), *auguri* (augurs), *arioli* (diviners) and *incantatores* (spellbinders)" (Montesano 67).

The second reason is *Suspiria*. The Italian director was widely known for the huge success of *The Bird with the Crystal Plumage*. Yet, the box office hit that turned him into a transnational Master of Horror was *Suspiria* (1977), a story revolving around the presence of female witches in a German dance academy. Thus, the opening of *Do You Like Hitchcock?* captures a tradition of Italian female witchcraft, both in a historical sense as artistic, with Argento himself gaining global recognition due his film on witchcraft. It can be argued, then, that *Do You Like Hitchcock?* comes full circle, drawing from the sources of Italy's history of witchcraft and Argento's most successful horror film, while, at the same time, bringing the Hitchcock connections to the fore. Returning to our supranational approach, we can affirm that the obsession with witches, even if the aforementioned "national monster," is characteristic of Argento's cinema. The director is world famous for his *Three Mothers* trilogy, which includes *Suspiria*, *Inferno* (1980), and *The Mother of Tears* (2007), making his name synonymous with witchcraft. The "threatening woman," a figure to whom Argento will dedicate so much celluloid, is not a purely Italian obsession either: Alfred Hitchcock was already known for his recurrent use of female stereotypes. Hitchcock used a certain kind of blond female character in his movies so frequently that she eventually received her own nickname: "The Hitchcock Blonde," opening the path to accusations of misogyny (Shelley 17).

Spanish *giallo*, and even Italian horror cinema in general, was not characterized by the presence of witches as the main threat. *Do You Like Hitchcock?* is, then, the product of foreign influences (silent horror cinema, Hitchcock), the supranational (the *giallo*), and the authorial (Argento's own universe). At the same time, the supranational includes the social and particular context of Italy, even if this is valid for other countries that have taken up the *giallo*, such as Spain, France, or the United States via auteurs such as Brian de Palma and Quentin Tarantino. And so, while the *giallo* is a vernacular cycle crystallized in Italy, this fact does not preclude acknowledging that the cycle has deep roots in the long history of international horror and crime cinema. It can be said, then, that the *giallo* is a cycle transnationally shaped but crystallized in its perfect form within the Italian historical context, through the intervention of authors such as Mario Bava or Dario Argento.

Conclusions

It is noticeable that Argento returns to Germany again after *Suspiria* with *Do You Like Hitchcock?* Germany is where, arguably, horror cinema started, amid the lights and shadows of expressionist cinema. Scott Poole argued that horror cinema began in the aftermath of the Great War, when the landscapes were soaked with blood and corpses, and first Europe and then the world suffered severe trauma in terms of space and time. It seemed as if the world suddenly got small in size, many disparate countries now united by the horrors of war. Patriotism and nationalism were replaced, in only a few short weeks, by horror. The macabre cinema of the Weimar, with its distorted mise-en-scènes, supernatural moods, and stories of deranged criminals quickly seeped into America and gave birth to the modern horror tale. With this new horror film, Argento addresses not only the debt that the Italian *giallo* has to Hitchcock, but with the source of all horror cinema, meaning, the silent output of the Weimar Republic.

Do You Like Hitchcock? ends with the revelation that Federica was another culprit all along. In the climax, she is defeated by both Giulio and Arianna in a scene that heavily evokes Hitchcock's *Rear Window* (1954), another story sustained by the ocular. Federica, using a black vinyl overcoat and wig, fits into the *giallo* cycle and in any Hitchcock film as well. A coda reveals that Giulio, after the dangers caused by his voyeurism, changed the subject of his thesis now to Soviet cinema. Soviet culture mistrusted the fantastic, communist Russia had almost no horror cinema—except rare incursions such as the folk tale *Viy* (Konstantin Ershov and Gueorgui Kropatchev). Giulio has escaped to safer geographical and filmic zones.

There is one final global commentary subtly embedded in the film. For a movie that pays homage to horror cinema, *Do You Like Hitchcock?* contains little that is "cinematic" here. Most of the action and exchanges between the different characters takes place in the video club owned by Andrea. Nobody is depicted going to cinema theaters, neither is any movie seen on a big screen. German expressionism or Alfred Hitchcock's works are watched on DVDs in the safety of homes. Further, Andrea agreed to participate in the killing of Sasha's mother because he was paid good money.

Andrea explained he needed the money since his video rental business was nearly bankrupt because people had stopped renting films. Dario Argento glimpsed the future of movie viewing, with the globe now dominated by streaming and the death of the physical medium. Still, streaming allowed viewers worldwide to appreciate many foreign horror films that would pass unnoticed otherwise, leading spectators to understand that horror cinema was, and still is, transnational and supranational in nature.

Works Cited

Andriopoulos, Stefan. *Possessed: Hypnotic Crimes, Corporate Fiction, and the Invention of Cinema*. U of Chicago P, 2008.

Barzilai, Maya. *Golem: Modern Wars and Their Monsters*. New York UP, 2016.

Cohen, Jeffrey Jerome. 1996. "Monster Culture (Seven Theses)." *Monster Theory: Reading Culture*, edited by Jeffrey Jerome Cohen, U of Minnesota P, pp. 3–25.

Durovicová, Natasa. "Preface." *World Cinemas, Transnational Perspectives*, edited by Natasa Durovicová and Kathleen Newman, Routledge, 2010, pp. xi–xv.

Foot, John. *Modern Italy*. Palgrave Macmillan, 2003.

Guerin, Frances. *A Culture of Light: Cinema and Technology in 1920s Germany*. U of Minnesota P, 2005.

Grainger, Julian. "*Deep Red*." *Art of Darkness: The Cinema of Dario Argento*, edited by Chris Gallant, FAB Press, 2000, pp. 115–25.

Halberstam, Jack. *Skin Shows: Gothic Horror and the Technology of Monsters*. Duke UP, 1995.

Hantke, Steffen. 2010. "Introduction: They Don't Make 'Em Like They Used To." *American Horror Film: The Genre at the Turn of the Millennium*, edited by Steffen Hantke, UP of Mississippi, pp. vii–xxii.

Heller-Nicholas, Alexandra. *The Giallo Canvas: Art, Excess and Horror Cinema*. McFarland, 2021.

Hutchings, Peter. "Resident Evil? The Limits of European Horror: *Resident Evil* versus *Suspiria*." *European Nightmares: Horror Cinema in Europe Since 1945*, edited by Patricia Allmer, Emily Brick, and David Huxley, Wallflower, 2012, pp. 13–24.

Killen, Andreas. *Berlin Electropolis: Shock, Nerves, and German Modernity*. U of California P, 2006.

Koven, Mikel. *La Dolce Morte: Vernacular Cinema and the Italian Giallo Film*. Scarecrow Press, 2006.

Lowenstein, Adam. *Shocking Representation: Historical Trauma, National Cinema, and the Modern Horror Film*. Columbia UP, 2005.

Met, Philippe. "'Knowing Too Much' About Hitchcock: The Genesis of the Italian *Giallo*." *After Hitchcock: Influence, Imitation, and Intertextuality*, edited by David Boyd and R. Barton Palmer, U of Texas P, 2006, pp. 195–214.

Montesano, Marina. *Classical Culture and Witchcraft in Medieval and Renaissance Italy*. Palgrave Macmillan, 2018.

Oliveira, Rui Trindade. *Supranational Horrors: Italian and Spanish Horror Cinema Since 1968*. Lexington Books, 2022.

Poole, Scott. *Wastelands: The Great War and the Origins of Modern Horror*. Counterpoint, 2018.

Restivo, Angelo. *The Cinema of Economic Miracles: Visuality and Modernization in the Italian Art Film*. Duke UP, 2022.

Sanjek, David. "Foreign Detection: The West German *Krimi* and the Italian *Giallo*." *Spectator*, vol. 14, no. 2, 1994, pp. 82–95.

Shelley, Peter. *Grande Dame Guignol Cinema: A History of Hag Horror from* Baby Jane *to* Mother. McFarland, 2019.

Shipka, Danny. *Perverse Titillation: The Exploitation Cinema of Italy, Spain and France, 1960–1980*. McFarland, 2011.

Williams, Tony. *The Cinema of George Romero: Knight of the Living Dead*. Wallflower, 2003.

Wood, Robin. "An Introduction to the American Horror Film." *Planks of Reason: Essays on the Horror Film*, edited by Barry Keith Grant and Christopher Sharrett, Scarecrow Press, 2004, pp. 107–41.

8

"That Ghastly Whiteness"

Dino Battaglia Adapts Poe and Melville to Comics

Davide Carnevale

Beginning in the 1930s, the Italian comic book industry began to look overseas, especially to the United States, for models for renewal. In the same period when Italian literary figures like Vittorini and Pavese looked to the prose of Hemingway, Faulkner, and Steinbeck for a path out of the swamp of the fascist regime's rhetoric, comic artists such as Giovanni Scolari, Rino Albertarelli, and Carlo Cossio began to imitate the style of American comics legends like Alex Raymond, Harold Foster, and Milton Caniff. Publishing their strips in the most popular periodicals, these Americans freed comics from the prejudice that they were products aimed exclusively at a children's audience. Instead of relying upon captions as the sole textual component of their work, these artists added thought and word balloons. The scenes they drew in panels grew increasingly dynamic and cinematic. Soon, Italian artists began producing new comic serials inspired by the more adult genres of American popular fiction. Inspired by the noir and detective pulp genre, Vincenzo Baggioli and Carlo Cossio created *Dick Fulmine* (1938–1955). Italian science fiction comics of the era included *Saturno contro la Terra* (1936–1946) by Cesare Zavattini and Giovanni Scolari and *Virus, il mago della foresta morta* (1939) by Federico Pedrocchi and Walter Molino. American western films inspired their famous

Italian comics counterpart, *Tex* (1948–1967) by Giovanni Luigi Bonelli and Aurelio Galleppini, as well as *Il grande Blek* (1954–1967), *Capitan Miki* (1951–1967), and *Comandante Mark* (1966–1990), all created by "the EsseGesse collective" of Giovanni Sinchetto, Dario Guzzon, and Pietro Sartoris.[1] During that same period, Dino Battaglia (Venice 1923–Milan 1983) transitioned from children's illustrator to comics artist because of the growing popularity and significance of the comics medium in Italy. As he recalled: "My encounter with comics was completely accidental. In the post-war period, it was the only field in which you could work. Black-and-white illustration—as it was understood in 1929 and '30—disappeared, and American-style comics were emerging. I, too, drew inspiration from those models: The prototypes were Caniff, Foster, and Raymond. Shortly thereafter, Hugo Pratt told me that I had managed to resemble those I admired and that it was time to do something personal" (Battaglia, *Edgar Allan Poe* 4–5). After World War II, Battaglia's new generation of artists developed a mature language of comics, expressing new forms of narration and confronting serious prose literature on equal terms. They also created new labels to describe their comics art, as Hugo Pratt pointedly described himself as "an author of 'drawn literature.' " He added, "My drawing tries to be a writing. I draw my own writing, and I write my own drawings" (Pratt and Petitfaux 166),

It is no coincidence that the Italian scene of the second half of the twentieth century is populated by a large number of artists involved not only in the creation of original stories and characters (many of which endure), but also in adapting to comics several important literary works, paying particular attention to American fiction. Among the era's graphic adaptations of literary works are Sergio Toppi's translations of Jack London's works, *L'amore alla vita* (1976), *Una volta sola nella vita* (1977), the Edgar Allan Poe tales drawn by Guido Crepax (the internationally famous creator of the *Valentina* series), and *two* adaptations of *Moby Dick* by Franco Caprioli (1965–1975).

Notably, *Moby Dick* was a work that inspired several Italian comics adaptations. Crepax himself tackles the novel in an ironic and irreverent way in his *Bianca. La casa matta* (1969). It was Dino Battaglia, however, who published the first comic translation of Melville's masterpiece in the pages of *Sgt. Kirk* magazine in 1967. Based on a script by his wife, Laura De Vescovi, Battaglia's adaptation is thirty-one pages, condensing the story into a handful of emblematic scenes, for which "the narrative essentiality is obtained through a systematic stripping down of the original text," while "the drawings take care to translate the rich but immaterial consistency of the descriptions" (Schiavo). The density of the drawings and the exiguity of the verbal component, completely insufficient to translate Melville's overwhelming text on its own, make this approach immediately evident. It is in this first attempt to translate a classic of literature that the Venetian artist experiments for the first time with many of those unusual drawing techniques that will soon make his style unmistakable, beginning the long reflection on the absolute linguistic value of comics that runs throughout his work.

However, we are still far from the stylistic tension and experimentalism that characterize Battaglia's most mature works, as he uses here a conventional panel layout on his pages—"a succession of small frames that only rarely open up to a real illustration inserted in the context" (Piano 31). Nothing here suggests the profound subversion of the traditional compositional canons that Battaglia will later carry out by arranging the drawings—often free from the contours of the panels—on the page in a very unusual way. The first hint of the artist Battaglia will later come in the last panel of his Melville adaptation, which condenses the entire story of the novel into a single illustration, bringing together the figures of Ahab, the ship *Pequod*, and Moby Dick "to form a significant cross" (Piano 32).

What is already fully evident, however, is the important expressive value that white has in Battaglia's drawing. The whiteness of the sails of whalers, seagulls, sky, and sea—often divided only by a thin trace of ink—merges with the neutral background of the page, opening the reader's eyes to the boundless landscapes scanned by Ahab. Readers see with Ahab's obsessive eyes as he strains to see another white sign on the horizon, that of the monstrous body of his nemesis, "that ghastly whiteness," which becomes an indicator and symbol, in its ambiguous indecipherability, of a repulsive and uncanny emotional tension: "there yet lurks an elusive something in the innermost idea of this hue, which strikes more of panic to the soul than that redness which affrights in blood. This elusive quality it is, which causes the thought of whiteness, when divorced from more kindly associations, and coupled with any object terrible in itself, to heighten that terror to the furthest bounds" (Melville 179–80). Far from constituting an absence of meaning, for Melville white, "by its indefiniteness," acts as an "intensifying agent" (187), an emotional catalyst, a lesson that Battaglia will make his own and will explore in his later works, carrying out a profound theoretical reflection that explains his elevation of the practice of transposition. This is a category to which a good part of his production can be ascribed, as an ideal terrain of stylistic experimentation and, above all, of comparison between a purely verbal form, literature, and a "verb-visual," to use the definition coined by Umberto Eco to indicate the hybrid nature, at the same time narrative and figurative, of comics.

Known for his comic adaptations, the Venetian artist returned to Poe's works often because he saw in this writer from Boston a kindred spirit, equally inclined to the macabre and a "nocturnal" irony. Battaglia published eight Poe adaptations in the pages of *Linus*. This famous magazine, founded in 1965 by Giovanni Gandini, was the first to publish new comics by Italian creators like Crepax, Pratt, and Battaglia alongside reprints of acclaimed international comics. The high quality of the works found in these pages elevated the reputation the comic medium held in Italy. Interestingly, all of the Poe adaptations Battaglia published in *Linus* are concentrated in the last phase of the artist's professional career, between 1968 (the date of publication of *Re Peste*) and 1981 (*Le straordinarie avventure di Hans Pfall*). This final work came out just two years before his death, during the most mature phase of his career, when the stroke of the drawing and the technique of composition of the page, in their combination with the written text, had reached an unmatched refinement both in terms of style and narration.

These are works that, in their presentation of different formal solutions to the problem of adaptation, offer an exhaustive and fascinating sample of the representative techniques used by Battaglia to recreate the fantastic indeterminacy. These works may be subdivided on the basis of their range of action through *figurative* techniques, *compositional* techniques, and *textual* techniques. The *figurative* techniques concern everything related to Battaglia's design, characterized by unusual stylistic choices for comics and by a particularly elaborate and metaphorical trait. His *compositional* (or "syntactic") techniques refer both to the layout of the single panel—its images and point of view—and to the distribution of the panels on the page, where the sequence of images marks the rhythm of the narration. His *textual* techniques go beyond what the comics industry calls "lettering"—overcoming a merely typographic approach in the graphic rendering of letters—and involves his use of the "drawn word." His textual techniques also include the ways in which he fits the written components of the comics onto the page, establishing an indissoluble complementarity between text and images.

The presentation of the gloomy manor as a central piece of the events narrated in *La caduta della casa degli Usher* immediately offers some interesting points of analysis. The slow approach of the anonymous protagonist of Poe's story to the house becomes, in Battaglia's work, a significantly condensed scene in the splendid opening page (fig. 8.1), rendered in two vertical panels. The first panel shows the figure of the solitary traveler as he crosses the swamp on which the property of the Usher family stands. The second panel shows the detail of a thin crack on a wall, which serves as a metaphor for the house's impending ruin. Aside from a blurred image of the house's outline, its shape partially illuminated by the storm unleashed at the end of the story, this crack is the only clue to the appearance of the house that the artist grants to the reader.

Figure 8.1. Opening page of *La caduta della casa degli Usher*. *Source:* Dino Battaglia. Edgar Allan Poe, © heirs of Battaglia © Solone srl—Edizioni NPE for the Italian edition, courtesy of the publisher.

By directing the reader's attention to the disturbing crack—and forcing the reader to imagine the rest of the building—Battaglia's visualization of Poe's prose captures the same descriptive vagueness present in the original work. Poe does not write more than Battaglia shows us, although it may seem the opposite; the writer's long lingering on the final meters that separate the protagonist from the house of his childhood friend, which occupies almost a quarter of the pages of the story, does not leave room for a direct description of its appearance, which can only be deduced from the anguished sensations that his direct vision raises in the narrator. The representation of the dilapidated palace is left to the indeterminacy of such terms like "melancholy," "dreary," "insufferable gloom," "desolate," "terrible," "iciness," all referable to a semantics of emotions that leaves the aspect of the house to the reader's imagination. The disturbing house, except in the case of the crack that runs through it, is almost invisible to sight. From its roof to the foundations, it is more of a premonition than a concrete structural lesion, yet it is meticulously described as "a barely perceptible fissure, which, extending from the roof of the building in front, made its way down the wall in a zigzag direction, until it became lost in the sullen waters of the tarn" (Poe 182).

In the same way, in the comic version, the thin crack is confused between the lines of the bricks and the other details of the wall, a barely identifiable trace in a panel that seems to serve as the frame of the central caption, where extracts from the incipit of the story are provided. No specific mention of the crack is made, which makes the drawing the only clue of its presence. Therefore, this seemingly negligible element becomes, both for Poe and Battaglia, so important as to connote the entire house. The crack is the very symbol of that omen of decay that permeates the whole story, and that will find fulfillment at its end, when the fissure, which has become a chasm so large that the viewer can now glimpse the chillingly white moon through it, reappears in both works, with a substantial identity of representation.

The coexistence of a great variety of graphic techniques used on the first page, many of which are completely unusual in comics, is an indication of the extreme versatility and richness of Battaglia's drawing. Battaglia uses a mixture of different styles and methodologies to give the image of the narrator on horseback a depth of meaning that goes far beyond mere direct representation, involving an unprecedented approximation of the drawn sign to the written sign. While the rotting vegetation of the swamp is recreated with rough nib lines drawn in such a marked way as to stand out in the foreground as something indistinct—a solution that recalls the use of the brush in the Japanese tradition—the foliage that covers the twisted branches of the tree standing in the upper part of the panel is just hinted at by the slight trace of "sponging"—a use of the pad that recurs frequently in Battaglia's drawings, so much so that it can be considered one of his stylistic traits through which he reaches a variety of grays so broad that it perfectly covers the richness of color shades.

In contrast, the figure of the rider in the middle of the scene is far more defined than the context in which it is placed, especially considering the details of the coat and the animal. Still, the dense weaving of white lines—obtained by the comics artist literally by "scratching" the ink off the sheet with a razor blade—makes the image rarefied, evanescent, almost hidden from the observer by an ethereal diaphragm that amplifies the distance. Specifically, if this choice can find an explanation in the desire to reproduce the thin mist exhaled by the unwholesome waters of the swamp into which the protagonist is entering, it is far more difficult to explain the frequent repetition of the same technique in the pages that follow, not to mention in almost all the artist's works.

For example, the sudden appearance of the specter of the Red Death, presumably the apex of the fantastic tension of the story, is relegated to a corner of the page in a position of secondary importance even to the upper panel, which shows only the empty interior of one of the halls of the party, while occupying roughly half of the entire page. As Battaglia himself noted, the scene is so veiled by the "scratched" texture that the spectral figure seems to emerge from nowhere in the white background, from an indeterminacy to which it belongs. And so, the drawing of a ghost feels like the ghost of a drawing that, while seeming to be almost completely canceled, is destined to return. This is a perfect representation of that dulling of the senses and that gnoseological uncertainty that is closely linked, in the fantastic narrative, to the irrational breakthrough. Critic Daniele Barbieri adds validity to this interpretation by describing Battaglia's use of the color white as "a metaphor, at the same time, of the indeterminacy (and therefore of the mystery) of the figures it weaves, and of the narrator's reticence in the direction of whose dimension the figures seem to vanish" (*Il pensiero disegnato* 119).

By using "white" as a sign, Battaglia transfers to his works the emotional tension that constantly supports the fantastic tale: the wavering of reason in the presence of the inconceivable, the inexplicable. His artistic whiteness erases in dazzling splendor every detail of the reality enclosed within the confines of the panel that, however limited they may be, still determines a portion of that paradigm to which every mimetic representation refers. Where the logic of the uncanny then foresees an increase in darkness, Battaglia shines a ghostly luminosity that seems to illuminate everything, yet surprisingly performs a "blinding" function. The shroud that envelops the incarnation of the Red Death, therefore, appears made of pure light. Here, the whiteness is a metaphor for the splendor of death that washes over the man who places himself before it—a slender shadow on the point of being overwhelmed by the unsustainable glow before the ghost may reach it. Similarly, the night seems to flood the deserted streets of the mysterious Venice presented in the drawings of *La scommessa*. Battaglia repeatedly draws the devil as little more than a diaphanous, intangible reflection, a Lucifer who hastens to rejoin the light from which he'd emerged once he's won his grisly prize, as the last panel suggests (fig. 8.2).

Figure 8.2. Page 9 of *La scommessa. Source:* Dino Battaglia. Edgar Allan Poe, © heirs of Battaglia © Solone srl—Edizioni NPE for the Italian edition, courtesy of the publisher.

In *La caduta della casa degli Usher*, even Lady Madeline Usher—who in life was nothing more than a simple shadow in motion—is barely hinted at by the trace of the sponging technique. On escaping from her death bed, she is illustrated as a chilling apparition of ghostly light. She is a screaming banshee torn from Irish legends, standing out with terrible power against the black background, before throwing herself on her brother in a deadly embrace. In Battaglia's comic, as in the original Poe story, Madeline shows herself as being more concrete as a murderous ghost than she ever was when she was alive.

But it is another panel of this adaptation that offers an unexpected link between Poe's story and the particular use that Battaglia makes of the white color. The panel is the last on the right of the fourth page (fig. 8.3),

Figure 8.3. Page 4 of *La caduta della casa degli Usher*, panel 5. *Source:* Dino Battaglia. Edgar Allan Poe, © heirs of Battaglia © Solone srl—Edizioni NPE for the Italian edition, courtesy of the publisher.

and it is significantly reproposed in a substantially identical way, but in a specular position, on the eighth page. On this panel, the protagonist and Roderick Usher are shown carrying the coffin of the latter's sister along a narrow staircase inexplicably invaded by such an intense luminosity as to allow only the figures of the two men and the details of their steps. It is an image that finds a curious counterpart in Poe's description of one of the paintings made by the lord of the house of Usher:

> A small picture presented the interior of an immensely long and rectangular vault or tunnel, with low walls, smooth, white, and without interruption or device. Certain accessory points of the design served well to convey the idea that this excavation lay at an exceeding depth below the surface of the earth. No outlet was observed in any portion of its vast extent, and no torch, or other artificial source of light was discernible, yet a flood of intense rays rolled throughout, and bathed the whole in a ghastly and inappropriate splendor. (187)

There is an impressive coincidence between Roderick's painting and Battaglia's drawing that is so perfect that it leaves no doubt as to its intentionality. The artist seems to be taunting Poe's readers by drawing exactly what the latter described but hiding the result in the folds of the story to reach a total, temporary cancellation of the distance between the literary representation of a figurative work and the figurative representation of a literary work. This authorizes us to consider "a ghastly and inappropriate splendor" as the most effective and evocative definition of the brightness of Battaglia's graphic sign.

In a poetic played on contrasts, the white color acquires particular relevance in the lettering, as for the title of *La caduta*, subtracted from the black background that encloses it. Battaglia uses white again in the onomatopoeia of the sounds that terrify Roderick during his last night, distinguishable only thanks to the outlines of the large letters that cross the panels. The outlines visually reproduce both the vagueness of the noises and the profound disturbance that these arouse in the two protagonists. In Battaglia's art, whiteness constitutes a "versatile and effective semantic tool" (Barbieri, *Il pensiero disegnato* 119) capable of regulating the emotional intensity of narration. The whiteness keeps the ambiguous and disturbing charge constant, strengthening it when it seems to run out and dampening its most exasperated tones, all the while feeding the fantastic effect of Battaglia's "visual tales."

His use of whiteness is also significant in its most amorphous use: as a neutral background of the page. In this negative space, the artist seems to rely on his obstinate commitment to unhinge the traditional construction of the page. His refusal of the usual montage of images involves a full-fledged *deconstruction* of the sequentiality on which the spatial and temporal order within the comic normally rests. This collapse of two organizing principles seen as indispensable to the cohesiveness of comics narratives finds a perfect equivalent in the fantastic literature genre. This deconstruction also undermines every acquired certainty, in that continuous erosion of the rationalist perspective that constitutes its essential trait. Thus, the panels lose their closed determination, expanding seamlessly in the background, until in many cases they invade each other. One example of this is found on the first page of *La scommessa*, where different moments and situations are confused in a seemingly unified drawing. And yet, upon careful observation, this drawing proves to be composed of several "fragments" of images. In these fragments, the protagonist, depicted several times with always different frames, moves ever closer. Battaglia acts without worrying about possible limits between the parts, as he does in an even more evident way on the last page, taking a run-up that allows him to overcome without any obstacle the clear walls represented by the margins of the panels (fig. 8.2).

On the top of page 8, in a panel that acts as the fusion between two different scenes, the protagonist finds himself having to talk to an interlocutor who is both behind and in front of him; as if the drawing wants to suggest to the reader the ubiquitous and "diabolical" nature of the mysterious passerby. The total or partial omission of the border that delimits the panels implies that the preservation of their precise autonomy and distinction from the absence of meaning of the background is upheld by the white color in the latter, which Battaglia reuses to overcome the conventional architecture of the page. As the orderly arrangement of the images in a sequence that gives the illusion of the passing of time and displacement in space, Battaglia's rule-breaking images and layout shift the reader's attention from the single scene to the page in its entirety. Consequently, the story's atmosphere is heightened. Also, its internal rhythm is modulated from time to time by compositional forms that vary based on the needs of the narration, pressing fragmentation on the reader and instilling a feeling of uneasy anguish.

In short, the white space is used by the Venetian master to magnify the drawing, amplifying its emotional and narrative impact on the page throughout the eight-page length of *La caduta*. In illustrating a close-up of Madeline Usher's chilling gaze, Battaglia presents a small panel devoid of outlines, yet highlighted by both the unusual horizontal cut and the large margin that separates it from the rest of the images. These elements isolate the figures from their context, lowering them into an indefinite nothingness. By placing his figures in an evocative absence of shapes and color, Battaglia demonstrates how his drawings are "no longer an illustration of the story, but a real way to tell it linguistically" (Cremonini and Frasnedi 120).

Note

1. On the influence of American comics on the medium's evolution in Italy, see Nicola Paladin's essay "The American Revolution in Italy: From EsseGesse to Hugo Pratt" (2016).

Works Cited

Barbieri, Daniele. *Breve storia della letteratura a fumetti.* Carocci, 2014.
———. *I linguaggi del fumetto.* Bompiani, 1991.
———. *Il pensiero disegnato.* Coniglio Editore, 2010.
Battaglia, Dino. *Edgar Allan Poe.* Nicola Pesce Editore, 2016.
———. *I cinque della Selena.* Ivaldi Editore, 1982.
———. *L'uomo del New England.* Nicola Pesce Editore, 2016.
———. *Moby Dick.* Lo Scarabeo, 2022.
———. *Totentanz.* Libri Edizioni, 1972.
Becciu, Leonardo. *Il fumetto in Italia.* Sansoni, 1971.
Brunoro, Gianni. "Che luminosa levità in quei cupi grigi . . ." *Edgar Allan Poe.* Nicola Pesce Editore, 2016.
Cremonini, Giorgio, and Fabrizio Frasnedi. *Vedere e scrivere.* Il Mulino, 1982.
Dallavalle, Sara. "Esperienze grafiche di Dino Battaglia e Sergio Toppi." *Lo spazio bianco*, 28 March 2015. Accessed 24 Apr. 2024. https://www.lospaziobianco.it/esperienze-grafiche-dino-battaglia-sergio-toppi/.
Eco, Umberto. "All'ultima storia capì: Corto Maltese sono io." *La Repubblica*, 7 Aug. 2005. https://www.repubblica.it/2005/h/sezioni/spettacoli_e_cultura/ecopratt/ecopratt/ecopratt.html?ref=search. Accessed 25 Apr. 2024.
———. *Apocalittici e integrati.* Bompiani, 1964.
Faeti, Antonio. *Guardare le figure. Gli illustratori italiani dei libri per l'infanzia.* Einaudi, 1972.

Festi, Roberto, Odoardo Semellini, and Alfredo Castelli. *Maestri del fumetto europeo*. Little Nemo, 2004.

Fresnault-Deruelle, Pierre. "Le verbal dans les bandes dessinées." *Communications*, vol. 15, no. 1, 1970, pp. 145–61.

Lazzarin, Stefano. "Fantastico: il caso italiano." *Il fantastico. Tradizioni a confronto*, edited by Roberto Colonna, Arcoiris, 2015, pp. 45–72.

McCloud, Scott. *Understanding Comics: The Invisible Art*. Tundra, 1993.

Melville, Herman. *Moby Dick or the White Whale* [1851]. C. H. Simonds, 1922.

Paladin, Nicola. "La Rivoluzione Americana in Italia: dagli EsseGesse a Hugo Pratt." *Il fumetto: fonte e inteprete della storia*, edited by Nicola Spagnolli, Claudio Gallo, and Giuseppe Bonomi. Betelgeuse Editore, 2016.

Peeters, Benoît. *Leggere il fumetto*. V. Pavesio, 2000.

Piano, Carlo. "Moby Dick: adattamento a fumetti. Dino Battaglia." *Moby Dick*. Lo Scarabeo, 2022.

Poe, Edgar A. *The Works of Edgar Allan Poe*, vol. 1, edited by John Henry Ingram. A. & C. Black, 1899.

Prandi, Marco, and Paolo Ferrari, eds. *Dino Battaglia: Le immagini parlanti*. Editori del Grifo, 2010.

Pratt, Hugo, and Dominique Petitfaux. *All'ombra di Corto*. Rizzoli, 1993.

Rastelli, Simone. "Otto passi nel delirio: il Poe di Dino Battaglia." *Lo spazio bianco*, 13 Sept. 2016. Accessed 25 Jan. 2024.

Schiavo, Carlo. "Letteratura e fumetto—Dino Battaglia, o Philosophy of transposition." *Argo*, no. 2, 2001. Accessed 19 Jan. 2024.

Interlude

Weird Italy: Dante and Italian Genre Fiction

Dominique Musorrafiti and Matteo Damiani

To grasp the intricate relationship between Italian culture and Dante, it's essential to first elucidate the precise meaning of Italianità (Italianness). Italianità is a relatively recent concept, primarily developed during the Risorgimento period. This idea was shaped and nurtured by the intellectual and political elite of that era, solidifying over the last two centuries. However, it's crucial to emphasize that this notion of Italic identity, often perceived as homogeneous and monolithic, actually clashes with the historical complexity and diversity of Italy.

Thanks to its extremely favorable position, situated right in the heart of the Mediterranean, and blessed with a relatively mild climate in certain regions, the Italian peninsula has always been inhabited by a melting pot of entirely distinct populations. Over the millennia, migratory waves have relentlessly followed one another, impacting the region, altering, overturning, or merely influencing local customs and practices.

A quick glance at the genetic map of the modern local population reveals how this supposed Italian identity is rather the result of a relatively recent artificial effort (Fiorito et al.)

Each of these peoples has left more or less significant traces on the country's culture. Over the millennia, countless populations such as the Etruscans, Sabines, Samnites, Celts, Latins, Sardinians, Greeks, Phoenicians, Carthaginians, various Germanic peoples (including Vandals, Lombards, and Goths), Normans, Arabs, Slavic populations, and peoples from the borders of the Roman Empire, pushed by other populations from the Euro-Asian steppes and plains, have settled on the peninsula.

During the Roman Empire alone, goods and knowledge from everywhere converged in Rome, allowing unprecedented cultural and economic development in the Mediterranean. The Romans made enormous efforts to build road networks for the sharing of goods, to facilitate military movements, and to accelerate communications. The very life of the empire depended on the speed of this information and goods traveling like impulses along this nervous system. Inevitably, ideas and new religions from the East, such as those of Egypt or Mithraism before, and Christianity later, spread throughout the empire. Like an imaginary funnel, Rome, and Italy, absorbed, digested, and later reinterpreted all these influences.

Part of the strength of Italian culture has been its ability to reprocess, sometimes even originally or entirely unconsciously, notions and ideas from distant lands. Take pizza, for example, which, without the American tomato, introduced to Europe through the Columbian exchange, could never have become the quintessential symbol of contemporary Italian cuisine; or the Sicilian citrus fruits, whose distant Eastern origins have been forgotten by many; or coffee, which arrived in Italy from Mocha in Yemen (from which the name of the famous Italian coffee pot derives) and from where ships laden with coffee set sail for the West around the sixteenth century, thanks solely to the commercial inclination of the Most Serene Republic of Venice. Cities like Venice, Rome, and Naples were crucial in spreading coffee culture, with their historic cafés becoming cultural and social icons. Around these establishments, like the historic Caffè Pedrocchi in Padua, intellectuals and artists often gathered, actively contributing to the political and cultural development of the era.

Italian politicians and marketing specialists daily stuff public speeches and countless advertisements with keywords like "Italian," "local," "sovereign," and variants, to artificially and grotesquely outline a traditional national identity that seems immutable and indestructible, but which, when scrutinized, proves incorrect. They play with concepts and rules that establish an invented and easily understandable Italian identity solely to win a few more votes or sell one more *panettone*. In the end, it's all just marketing.

The issue of constructing an Italian identity is a modern concept cultivated by a sphere of enlightened intellectuals and politicians during the Risorgimento, who saw Petrarch and Dante as the epitome of Italianness. This concept was born under the influence of the French Revolution, whose principles inspired generations of young Italians, in reaction to the Napoleonic invasion and the control of foreign powers over the territory. This conception of Italy was not yet well defined, and even the members of the cultural elite did not agree on the extent of the territory or how circumstantial this nation was (Limes Club Verona).

As with the entire discourse on the creation of Italian identity, even the famous phrase "we have made Italy, now we must make Italians," attributed to Massimo D'Azeglio, has an uncertain origin, or at least it is probably a not particularly faithful synthesis made by Ferdinando Marini, a politician and governor of Eritrea. In any case, this approximate quotation helps to identify the urgency felt by that political class, which sensed the need to create a unified people who shared a common culture, could defend themselves and fight, and would come together in times of need and crisis.

This idea of Italianità reached and spread among the popular and rural classes much later and was constructed by the Italian state, and not vice versa as the patriots of the Risorgimento would have hoped. Very effective tools were used, such as compulsory education (which facilitated access to the study of Dante, Manzoni, Ariosto, Boccaccio, Torquato Tasso, Petrarch, and other fathers of Italian literature), the Catholic religion (whose centuries-long influence on the territory has left traces far more pronounced than the awareness of a national identity), mandatory military conscription (a rite of passage for countless Italian youths, which allowed generations of young people to travel and serve the state in places far from home, encouraging them to get to know the country and the identity of their fellow soldiers), the Italian diaspora (for example, miners who migrated to Belgium had, for the first time, the opportunity to interact with Italians from other parts of the country and learn about their customs, traditions, and cuisines), public administration (which served to enlist and provide a certain and secure job to masses of citizens as well as to share common laws throughout the territory, protecting, at least theoretically for the first time, the common citizen from local abuses), and later also radio and television, which allowed millions of illiterate Italian citizens, accustomed to speaking exclusively in local dialects, to listen and learn the Italian language. To better define this identity, Italian intellectuals like Benedetto Croce chose to look at the common past, and to the question "What is the character of a people?" Croce answered: "Its history: all its history and nothing but its history. The coincidence is, in this case, perfect, or, rather, it is not a matter of coincidence but of identity" (Croce 291).

The study of Dante Alighieri and *The Divine Comedy* was incorporated into Italian education starting from the nineteenth century. However, Dante's presence in educational programs was formally included in the curriculum during the period of the establishment of the unified Italian state in 1861. With the formation of the Italian state, there was a growing interest in cultivating a sense of national identity and unity among citizens. From this moment, Dante was effectively considered one of the founding fathers of the Italian language and literature. When in 1827 Alessandro Manzoni decided to write *The Betrothed* (*I Promessi Sposi*) to reaffirm his linguistic choice, he emphasized the fact that he went to Florence to *risciacquare i panni in Arno* (literally, "to rinse clothes in the Arno"), referring to the process of refining the language by taking as a model the purity and elegance of Florentine language and literature; the Arno is the river that flows through Florence. This choice profoundly influenced the birth of conventional Italian in the newly formed Kingdom of Italy, thanks to the report that Manzoni himself sent, in 1868, to the Minister of Education Broglio for the teaching of Italian in state schools. Dante Alighieri's work acquired a status of cultural and national importance over the years, and its presence in the curriculum was promoted through educational reforms. The same fate was shared by Manzoni's work, *I Promessi Sposi*. It was during this period that the Italian tricolor flag became a unifying symbol for the Italian people, who until then had always been fragmented and now under a single emblem found a common national identity and values. Carrying this flag, Giuseppe Garibaldi gathered a group of volunteers known as the Thousand in an expedition to liberate Italy from Bourbon rule and unify it as an independent nation.

Consolidation of Italian Identity Through Cinema and TV

Over the decades, an array of tools of varying effectiveness have been used to outline and strengthen this identity: from the unified use of a single national language to the construction of a mythical Italian identity, pure and the sole heir to the greatness of the Roman Empire. This strategy involved historical and cultural figures of great significance but also had long grotesque and dystopian phases, like the forced Italianization of language during fascist Italy, the racial laws, and Tuffolino, the alter ego of Mickey Mouse from the fascist era.

The inconclusive nationalist efforts of the fascist regime and the excessive pomp that accompanied its spread led, for some decades, to a deflation of Italic pride, introducing the image of the opportunistic *italietta* (small Italy) post-World War II, still a scarred victim of inappropriate pride that brought the country to ruins, weak and unreliable, subservient to the powerful and overbearing to the weakest. The term *italietta* was initially used by nationalists against the Italy of Giolitti, then by fascism that dreamed of an Italy with nationalist fervor, to finally acquire its modern connotation in the postwar period.

To distance themselves from this unflattering image of the country, in the first phase, Italian authors, not only in the fantasy genre, up until at least the early seventies, sometimes sought to obscure the Italian origin of their works. They masked their credits with Anglophone or foreign pseudonyms (Terence Hill, pseudonym of Mario Girotti; Bud Spencer, aka Carlo Pedersoli; Sophia Loren, aka Sofia Villani Scicolone; Patty Pravo, aka Nicoletta Strambelli, et al.) to reach the widest possible audience. They collaborated with foreign stars and actors (Clint Eastwood, Lee Van Cleef, Vincent Price, Christopher Lee, Boris Karloff, Barbara Steele, et al.), often in foreign locations (Spain, Africa, South America, United States, Germany, etc.), using new and still partially unexplored languages (spaghetti western, horror, *giallo*, thriller), not shying away from innovative and personal exploration of the cinematic media. They also accepted experimental collaborations with directors or industry specialists from other nations, utilizing avant-garde photographic techniques and visual effects (Vittorio Storaro, Carlo Rambaldi, et al.), internationally appreciated craftsmanship (Milena Canonero, Piero Gherardi, Gabriella Pescucci, et al.), and award-winning composers (Ennio Morricone, Nino Rota, Piero Umiliani, Giorgio Moroder, et al.) to give their works as international (and least provincial) an aura as possible. This experience and tendency toward internationalization led many of these exponents to later work and start collaborations that continue to this day.

Some aspects of this internationalization also had grotesque consequences. Since various exponents of the nascent Italian music scene had adopted exotic stage names like Bobby Solo (pseudonym of Roberto Satti), Little Tony (aka Antonio Ciacci), Mogol (aka Giulio Rapetti), among others, to increase their international appeal, a segment of the young Italians began to mimic attitudes and behaviors to appear as intriguing foreigners in their own country. This desire to distance themselves from the poor Italian suburbs, feeling shame and embarrassment for their social condition, and thus trying to present themselves with flashy names or to act like Americani, was ridiculed by Renato Carosone with the famous song "Tu vuo' fa l'Americano" ("You Want to Be American") in 1956.

Geretta Geretta, an American actress, director, screenwriter, and producer who worked on many horror films, including *Murder Rock* by Lucio Fulci (1984) and *Demons* by Lamberto Bava (1985), reflecting on her time spent on sets, said, "This is a movie, we did it in Italy. I'm American, I have an Italian name, my family is Italian, but I went there, I was a model, I made a bunch of Italian movies. . . . We sound funny and our lips are moving in funny directions but not mine because I am actually speaking English when we shot the movie." This amusing anecdote she shared explains why many films of that era had audio out of sync with the lip movements of the protagonists. Often actors and artists, who, as we have already mentioned, came from different parts of the world and did not speak Italian, were dubbed. Geretta also added, "You don't really go in and do something. First of all, they cast by picture because they go by look first. So if you look the part then that's enough for them because they figure they can direct and can get you to do what they want you to do, and it's very rare everyone would be speaking the same language on the set, so really what difference does it make your mumble?" (Ultimate Rabbit).

While some genres like spaghetti westerns, horror, or *giallo* succeeded in their aim to achieve success in territories outside national borders, Italian science fiction and fantastic genre in cinema never fully bloomed, leaving only a few albeit famous examples, like *The Tenth Victim* (*La Decima Vittima*), by Elio Petri (1965). This contrasts with other media such as comics (Sergio Tamburini, Tanino Liberatore, Bonelli comics, Bonvi, Magnus & Bunker, Pino Zac, Andrea Pazienza, Hugo Pratt, Guido Crepax, Paolo Eleuteri Serpieri, and even the Mickey Mouse comics created by Italian artists and writers, etc.), literature (Dino Buzzati, Italo Calvino, Gianni Rodari), and even philology and criticism (Umberto Eco, Oreste del Buono), which have embraced, explored, and analyzed the fantasy genre, adventure, and science fiction in more natural, personal, and original ways, managing to achieve global circulation.

Paradoxically, this period of introspection on nationally shared flaws and the aspiration to transcend provincialism for a complex and cosmopolitan society, intermingled with the economic boom of the era, did more than just foster the development of significant literary and cinematic genres like neorealism, *giallo*, and Italian-style comedies. These genres, while critically examining authority and adeptly engaging in self-analysis, simultaneously fortified the sense of national identity by embracing and appreciating diverse regional identities.

Amid this cultural renaissance, the archetype of the Italian citizen emerged, transcending the mediocrity that typified the average inhabitant of the peninsula, as portrayed in the narratives of various authors. This new Italian was marked by several unifying traits: a deep-rooted exposure to Catholic education began to encounter challenges with the advent of communist ideology, prompting a reassessment of traditional beliefs. This ideological shift is epitomized in the tragicomic escapades of characters like Peppone, a seasoned communist and atheist mayor, and Don Camillo, a dynamic and astute country priest adept at countering his counterpart's political activism. Both characters, ingeniously crafted by Giovannino Guareschi and vividly portrayed by Gino Cervi and Fernandel in film adaptations, represent diametric ends of the sociocultural spectrum. Yet, they are ultimately bound by a shared, loftier goal, managing to collaborate despite their pronounced differences—a narrative that resonates strongly with Dante's nuanced discourse on spirituality and earthly matters.

In the postwar era, Italians, having learned to read and write and becoming increasingly exposed to television, grew curious and eager for novelty, culture, and fresh ideas. In this context emerged the Italian American Mike Bongiorno, who significantly impacted Italian entertainment. His ability to connect with viewers made him a familiar face in many households and brought an increasing number of Italians in front of their TVs, dreaming and hoping for a better future. Mike Bongiorno was also known for iconic and surreal interviews, like those with Dave Gahan of Depeche Mode and musician Alberto Camerini, a child of Italian immigrants in Brazil. Upon returning to Italy, Camerini became a symbol of the Italian global citizen, thirsty for multiculturalism and influenced by the futurism of Kraftwerk and the Dadaism of David Bowie. Creative productions soared due to a high demand for content, leading to new projects and the reinterpretation and renewal of past artistic creations.

In the 1950s, Adriano Celentano emerged as a dominant figure whose influence spanned music, cinema, and television. With his innovative and often provocative approach, Celentano shaped the landscape of Italian light music. In the seventies, "Prisencolinensinainciusol" became one of his most famous songs for its uniqueness: the lyrics are in a made-up language, nonsensical gibberish resembling a form of broken English, with only a few phrases slightly reminiscent of actual English words, but not enough to form any coherent sentences. This artistic experiment playfully engaged listeners, leading non-English speakers to believe the song was in proper English, while some English speakers might experience auditory apophenia.

In the 1970s, the versatile singer and dancer Raffaella Carrà burst onto the scene with her dynamic presence and charisma, setting trends in style and fashion. On television, she and her international, multiethnic dance troupe performed dynamic choreographies in pioneering costumes that would influence future trends, set against fantastic and futuristic backgrounds. Her image reflected the evolution of Italian society during the sixties, seventies, and eighties, a period marked by significant cultural and social changes. Carrà also became an icon and a point of reference for the LGBT community due to her open-mindedness, inclusive attitude, and support for sexual diversity issues. Her ability to communicate with the audience and entertain contributed to the popularity of her shows in Italy and abroad. Her influence is evident in the choreography of Bianca Li in Daft Punk's "Around the World" and Blur's "Music Is My Radar," where references can also be seen to the costumes from *The Tenth Victim* by Elio Petri, designed by Giulio Coltellacci and crafted by Sorelle Fontana.

Tony Renis, whose pseudonym was derived by combining the names of Guido Reni and Tony Curtis, was a singer, composer, record producer, and actor. He performed in the nightclubs of Milan and later in Milanese theaters, often alongside his childhood friend Adriano Celentano, where they impersonated Dean Martin and Jerry Lewis, respectively.

In 1978, Tony Renis embarked on a new journey as the host of *Stryx*, a television variety show whose name was a playful twist on the Latin term *strix*, denoting an owl or owl-like creature. It also referred to the mythical owl-like beings known as *strige*, associated with woodland and cave-dwelling witches. A demonic sanctuary was the backdrop for the show, where mischievous devils, alluring pagan priestesses, enchanting fairies, mysterious witches, and wandering minstrels performed. This bizarre show made a lasting impression on Italian television culture known for its innovative and groundbreaking nature, challenging the status quo with its social commentary and encouraging creative expression and sensual exploration. Stryx, by combining various artistic forms such as music, cabaret, and stunning visual performances, boldly defied the traditional limits of televised entertainment.

An audacious idea that blended sensuality and devilry was conceived by the show's creators, Alberto Testa, Enzo Trapani, and Carla Vistarini. They based their work on old European pagan rituals, symbols of superstition, and vivid and impressive scenery by Ennio Di Maio. They also employed intricate costumes by Gianna Sgarbossa to create a juxtaposition between the modern and the medieval, invoking a hellish vision of Dante.

The occult and pagan scene, with a touch of satanic charm, was dominated by influential personalities who led bacchanalian ceremonies. They included Grace Jones, Amanda Lear, Anna Oxa, Patty Pravo, Mia Martini, Gal Costa, Asha Puthli, who were joined by the playful bard elf Angelo Branduardi and the cosmo-devils called the Rockets.

All this lengthy preamble is to say that the term "Italian" does not identify something well defined or delineated; this is a simplification. To be Italian, whether willingly or unwillingly, means to be heirs of a fluid and permeable culture that has absorbed elements seemingly in conflict with each other, creating a complex and multifaceted culture, which is almost always unaware of its ancient and intricate origins—a concept at times elusive or even contradictory.

Our words, our thoughts, and the grammatical structures of our sentences are much older than the average citizen might assume. Often, people attribute their linguistic and cultural heritage solely to the Greco-Roman and Judeo-Christian traditions. However, this perspective is somewhat narrow. For example, a significant portion of the words used in these pages are derived from the Indo-European language family (this concept is always true regardless of whether you speak any Indo-European language such as Italian, English, French, etc.), not directly from Latin or Greek, as many Italians might presume. This misconception is partly due to the Italian educational system, which sometimes fails to elucidate this millennia-long historical evolution clearly. Similarly, our aesthetic taste, our thirst for the fantastic, the mysterious, the journey, and the exploration of magical, enchanted, or alien places stem from an ancient past, whose echoes have reached us, often transported by cultural waves that have crossed time and space in unexpected ways.

Inferno

Dante Alighieri is a pivotal figure in the history of Italian culture. Through his work, he revolutionized the linguistic landscape. The choice to write in the Florentine vernacular rather than Latin had a significant impact on the formation of a unified language. Prior to Dante, Italy was a mosaic of regional dialects; through his work, a common linguistic identity gradually began to take shape.

Through his verses, Dante explored universal themes that resonate with the human experience, thereby contributing to the development of a more cohesive Italian cultural identity. His work has had a lasting influence on Italian literature, art, and culture, establishing a linguistic and stylistic model that has influenced generations of writers and thinkers.

However, Dante's influence goes far beyond this. His ability to interweave universal themes, the psychological depth of his characters, and the complexity of the plot in *The Divine Comedy* laid the foundations for modern genre fiction.

Nevertheless, what interests us here is how his vision of the afterlife, especially the concept of hell, has inspired and shaped not only religious, literary, and philosophical imaginings but also the realm of fantasy. In reality, even Dante, despite being a fundamental figure in the global literary landscape, is himself part of a cultural relay that has roots extending far back in time and space.

The *Inferno*, in contrast to *Paradise* and *Purgatory*, holds a particular allure for artists and readers. The *Inferno*, with its arid and hellish landscapes and rich iconography, presents a broad and diverse canvas for artistic expression. While *Paradise* and *Purgatory* are associated with notions of serenity and redemption, themes that offer fewer ideas for dynamic stories, the *Inferno* stimulates the imagination with its visions of torment and punishment. This descriptive and emotional vividness offers artists a wide scope to explore universal themes such as good versus evil, justice, and human suffering.

Furthermore, the *Inferno*, with its hierarchical structure of circles and detailed characterization of its inhabitants, provides a dramatic narrative and inherent tension that captivate readers. The depiction of punishments and sinful figures evokes profound reflections on human nature and morality, themes that resonate deeply in both literature and visual art.

Dante and the Church

Dante Alighieri's relationship with the Catholic Church and its historical context deeply influenced his work. *The Divine Comedy* is firmly rooted in Christian theology, and Dante draws extensively from his theological and biblical knowledge. The poem explores themes such as divine justice, redemption, free will, and the afterlife, reflecting the medieval understanding of Catholic theology on which he bases his depictions of Hell, Purgatory, and Paradise. For instance, the three-realm structure mirrors medieval Christian cosmology, which included Hell as a place of damnation, Purgatory as a place of purification, and Paradise as God's abode.

Dante openly criticizes the corruption and immorality within the Church of his time. In his journey through Hell, Dante places many corrupt clergymen and simoniacal popes among the damned. This criticism reflects his concern for the moral degradation of the Church of his era. The poet populates his work with numerous characters that hold theological, political, or moral significance. Some figures, however, are also praised for their integrity and virtue. In the poem, he is guided by Virgil through Hell and Purgatory, representing human reason. Dante appeals to the Catholic faith as the foundation for his epic journey through the afterlife.

Despite the decline of religious influence in many aspects of contemporary society, the Catholic Church has always played a significant role in Italy's territory and the shaping of its culture. This influence is seen through the Church's active involvement in various social and ethical issues since its early establishment. From the early days of the Christian era, the spread of Catholicism has molded culture, influencing beliefs, values, and social practices. The Church has been a prominent patron of the arts, supporting artists such as Michelangelo, Leonardo da Vinci, and Raphael, who created some of the most renowned works of the Renaissance. Sacred art has been a means through which the Church communicated its teachings and instructed the illiterate. Religious architecture, with its churches and cathedrals, is a significant artistic expression and spiritual gathering place for the population. These buildings, which have also contributed to defining the appearance of cities and towns, have become destinations for pilgrimage and cultural tourism.

In the Catholic tradition, the use of images and artwork to express and teach the faith has been a practice aimed at conveying theological messages through art, using visual iconography to communicate spiritual concepts. The Church promoted and emphasized beauty and harmony through artworks as reflections of divine creation. Artists were encouraged to create works that inspired a sense of the divine and contributed to liturgical worship. However, it should be noted that the relationship between the Church and artists was complex and marked by tensions, especially during historical periods when conflicts of opinions occurred or when artists sought to interpret religious themes in a personal manner.

Christianity and the Synthesis of Paganism

Of significant value is the crucial role that the Church has played in education and learning. Schools operated by the Church have contributed to the dissemination of knowledge and literacy. Additionally, the Catholic Church exerted significant influence on social and political life. It contributed to shaping cultural traditions through religious festivities. Celebrations such as Christmas and Easter have become integral parts of Italian culture, influencing daily life, family traditions, and the holiday calendar. On February 24, 1582, the Gregorian calendar was introduced by Pope Gregory XIII through the papal bull *Inter gravissimas*. This reform primarily addressed the dating of Easter and rectified the accumulation of temporal errors caused by the difference between the tropical year (the time it takes the Earth to complete one full orbit around the Sun) and the calendar year. These rules maintained the correct alignment of the equinoxes and consequently integrated pagan nature-related festivals that the majority of the population celebrated.

To understand Dante's work, it's important to remember that the Catholic Church inherited and absorbed many elements from pagan religions while introducing new, distinct teachings and practices that set it apart from previous traditions. The continuity with these religions often involved adaptation and reinterpretation rather than pure continuity, thus entailing a transformative process. The Catholic Church incorporated various elements from preexisting religions. The hierarchical structure in the Catholic ecclesiastical organization inherited the concept of authority and hierarchy from earlier models, such as the administrative structure where the division of the empire into provinces and dioceses became a template for ecclesiastical organization. The use of councils and synods for making important decisions paralleled Roman senatorial practices, and the adoption of Roman titles and honors, such as "Pope" for the Bishop of Rome, further reinforced this structure. This hierarchy, as will be discussed later, has permeated into the realm of fantasy literature, including Dante's severe infernal tribunals.

Many sacred rites and ceremonies of the Catholic Church, such as liturgy, sacraments, and rituals like the Mass, have influences that can be traced back to ancient pagan religious traditions. In some cases, Christian churches were built on ancient temples or places of religious significance to the Romans, perhaps for purely practical reasons—such as utilizing existing foundations—but they also contributed to a sense of continuity with the past. The liturgical calendar of the Catholic Church, with its festivals and celebrations, incorporated some preexisting Roman and pre-Roman festivities. For instance, many dates of Christian festivities coincide with ancient celebrations, often in an attempt to Christianize existing observances.

The traditional date of the birth of Jesus Christ, Christmas, was set on December 25th to coincide with various pagan festivities, including the birthdate of Mithras, the winter solstice, and Roman celebrations associated with the god of the sun, Sol Invictus. Candlemas on February 2nd is associated with the presentation of Jesus at the Temple, a day that aligns with ancient Roman celebrations, such as those honoring Februa, the goddess of purification. Christian Easter, which commemorates the resurrection of Jesus, is linked to the ancient Jewish Passover but occurred during the period of pagan celebrations related to spring, the awakening of nature, and fertility deities. The feast of St. John the Baptist on June 24th overlaps with the summer solstice, connecting to ancient pagan celebrations. The Lemuria or Lemuralia festivals of ancient Rome, designed to exercise the spirits of the dead, the lemures, were replaced by Pope Boniface IV in 609 with All Saints' Day, now celebrated on November 1st. Even the Roman festival of Parentalia, honoring deceased family members, became a Christian celebration to honor one's departed loved ones. The Catholic feast of the Assumption of Mary, which celebrates Mary's ascension to heaven, can be associated with earlier traditions related to Greek goddesses, such as the ascension of the goddess Artemis.

Even some Christian symbols and iconographies have roots in ancient religions. For instance, the use of the cross as a Christian symbol dates back to a pagan past and later came to represent the crucifixion of Christ, using a Roman cross where the condemned were punished by death. The "magic hands" of Sabazius, from which, according to some, the gesture of blessing is derived, and so on. The concept of the veneration of saints, where human figures are revered and invoked, can be seen as a continuation of Roman religious practices where some divinities, *lares*, *penates*, heroic figures, or ancestors were honored. Even certain metaphysical concepts, such as the battle between good and evil and the immortality of the soul, are shared with Mithraism.

The figure of the Virgin Mary in Christian tradition incorporates various characteristics and qualities that evoke certain Greek, Roman, and Italic deities, albeit with significant theological differences. Mary is commonly known as the Mother of Jesus and the "Mother of God," but she is also referred to as the "Virgin Mary." This duality of motherhood and virginity is reminiscent of some mother goddesses in Greek and Roman mythologies, such as Demeter and Cybele (Bona Dea, the Latinized version of Cybele; Terra, a Roman mother goddess; and Ops, of Sabine origin, representing local variations of the Great Mother), who were revered as goddesses of fertility and motherhood.

Mary is seen as a figure of intercession between human beings and God, akin to Athena in Greek mythology. The Madonna is described as devout and humble, much like the Roman goddess Vesta, venerated as the goddess of home and family, who is characterized by an aura of purity and devotion. Catholic traditions assert that Mary was assumed into heaven after her death, similar to the ascension of some deities in ancient mythology. She is honored with titles such as the "Queen of Heaven," somewhat evoking the image of queen goddesses like Hera in Greek mythology or Juno in Roman mythology. Furthermore, the iconography of the Virgin Mary, especially in artistic representations, echoes some images of ancient classical goddesses. The associations of Mary with mythological deities do not represent a direct transposition of beliefs or practices, but rather symbolic influences and parallels that have emerged throughout history. Some scholars have attempted to identify these correspondences.

Psychologist Carl Gustav Jung suggested that the figure of Mary could be a manifestation of broader archetypes, which may bear similarities to ancient mother goddesses. Authors like Merlin Stone in *When God Was a Woman*, archaeologist and historian Margaret Murray in *The Witch-Cult in Western Europe*, scholar of religions Mircea Eliade in *Patterns in Comparative Religion*, and other works, as well as anthropologist of religions Raphael Patai, have written on themes related to representations of the Great Mother in various religious traditions, exploring analogies between Mary and mother goddesses from other cultures.

Some historians, such as Maria Tasinato, have also noted how Greek and Roman religious figures, over the centuries, were stripped of their initial positive qualities and began to transform into demons, specters, monsters, torturers, and tempters. *Maladea* by Nicola Pasqualicchio analyzes how the figures of classical deities become malevolent phantoms that haunt the corridors of the mind, leading to the need for an exorcism, which consists of psychological rationalization of the fantastical, reducing it to a pathology of the imagination and offering hope of recovery. These figures that insinuate themselves into visions and dreams become agents of torment, deserving punishment themselves.

Similarly, certain characters from classical Greek and Roman mythology no longer retain their heroic status in Dante's Christian vision of the afterlife. In *Inferno*, we find Ulysses, along with Diomedes, being punished for his cunning and accused of giving misleading advice during his lifetime, deceiving others. Achilles and Paris, on the other hand, are considered traitors to their homeland and are placed in infernal circles. Just as the Catholic Church has hierarchies, *Inferno* also follows a hierarchy of regions, each designed to punish specific types of sinners. Demons act as executors of the punishments inflicted upon those who have committed specific sins. They enforce divine laws, inflicting tortures proportionate to the sins committed, representing the punitive and judgmental aspect based on one's actions during earthly life. Dante's *Inferno* also incorporates creatures like the Furies, vengeful mythological beings tormenting the damned. They reside in the infernal circle dedicated to violent sinners, especially those who have committed murder.

Dante's contemporary Church is corrupt, and this corruption continues for centuries, as also denounced by Alessandro Manzoni, who criticizes its hypocrisy and degradation. Despite a faction of the Church seeking to connect with the local population by preaching the charisma of poverty, humility, and service to others, as exemplified by the Franciscans, founded by Saint Francis of Assisi in the thirteenth century, or the Benedictine Order, founded by Saint Benedict of Nursia in the sixth century, known for its monastic rule and communal life based on prayer, labor, and stability, whose founders Dante places in Paradise, moral decay remains constant. It is they who communicate with the majority of the population that does not live in luxury and opulence, a lifestyle enjoyed by only a small part of the nobility.

Dante's Legacy: Between the Sacred and the Profane

Dante's influence on the cultural landscape following the release of *The Divine Comedy* is undeniable. In the fourteenth century, the visual interpretations of Dante Alighieri's works were chiefly focused on sin and the torments of hell. These artistic representations, rich in paintings and sculptures, were imbued with a profound sense of transcendence, underscored by the prevalent use of religious symbolism and martyrdom scenes. Artists such as Giotto di Bondone and Duccio di Buoninsegna epitomized this trend, infusing their works with deep spirituality and humanity, while vividly portraying the Dantean themes of suffering, devotion, and sacrifice.

The emergence of Sandro Botticelli signaled a transformative era. His renditions of Dante's oeuvre, particularly the renowned series of illustrations for *The Divine Comedy*, diverged from the transcendental to embrace a more humanistic and rational interpretation, accentuating the characters' humanity and emotional depth over divine retribution.

Federico Zuccari, a notable outlier in the portrayal of Dantean themes until the nineteenth century, set himself apart through the use of distinct techniques for each section of *The Divine Comedy*.

Even though they are not explicitly Dantesque, the depictions of Hell by Hieronymus Bosch are inspired by Dante's poetry. The same holds true for Michelangelo's *The Last Judgment*, where the torments suffered by the damned are drawn from the vivid and gruesome descriptions found in Dante's *Inferno*.

Michelangelo's representations, inspired by Dantesque themes as seen in his *The Last Judgment* in the Sistine Chapel, are characterized by a lesser emphasis on religiosity and a greater interest in human anatomy. In *The Last Judgment*, Michelangelo's figures, while marked by detailed and powerful musculature, are not mere expressions of physical form; they embody profound spiritual and ethical implications, evoking themes of judgment, redemption, and damnation that resonate with Dante's journeys through Inferno, Purgatory, and Paradise.

In the nineteenth century, there was a new development in the visual interpretation of the *Divina Commedia* due to the attraction of the Romantics, the English Pre-Raphaelites, and the German Nazarenes active in Rome at the beginning of the nineteenth century, toward the Middle Ages and its literature. Artists such as Henry Fuseli, William Blake, and Eugène Delacroix left a personal stamp in illustrating the Dantesque poem, marking an era of transition from Neoclassicism to an artistic expression laden with emotionality and romanticism. Their works, imbued with drama, intense emotions, and symbolism, emerged powerfully, as in his pencil and watercolor sketches that encompass Blake's *Inferno*, *Purgatory*, and *Paradise* (Frey). The Romantic period saw a further flourishing in interpretations of the *Divina Commedia*. For instance, Gustave Doré, with his famous cycle of illustrations, had a profound and lasting impact on the visual perception of the poem. His engravings, characterized by attention to detail and a majestic use of chiaroscuro, profoundly influenced the collective vision of Dante's work.

The English Victorian poet and painter Dante Gabriel Rossetti was also a member of the Pre-Raphaelite movement, and he drew inspiration from medieval and Renaissance themes. Rossetti also translated the poem and used it as a source of inspiration for some of his works. T. S. Eliot acknowledged having a deep interest in Dante's work, which was a starting point for reflecting on themes related to spiritual search and the exploration of human existence.

The twentieth century witnessed a rich diversification in the artistic interpretation of *The Divine Comedy*. Dante Alighieri's influence extended beyond the visual arts, notably inspiring James Joyce's *Ulysses*. This work mirrors the poem's tripartite structure, cementing its status as a modern epic. Jorge Luis Borges, the Argentine literary maestro, often wove metaphysical and philosophical themes into his narratives, drawing inspiration from Dante's masterpiece, particularly in works like *The Aleph*, which directly references the epic.

In the realm of cinema, Dante's narrative made its silver screen debut in 1911 with *La Divina Commedia*, directed by Giuseppe de Liguoro. Esteemed as one of the pioneering Italian feature films, it also stands as one of the initial cinematic forays into Dante's transcendent universe. This film sparked a trend of Dante-inspired cinematic adaptations, not strictly adhering to the original narrative but creatively echoing its themes, symbols, and concepts. Henry Otto's *Dante's Inferno* (1924) brought a silent portrayal of a man's descent into Hell, while Harry Lachman's version (1935) offered a narrative backdrop of *The Divine Comedy* to chronicle Dante's life. The 2007 documentary by Sean Meredith, ingeniously combining animation with live-action, explores the epic through diverse artistic perspectives. Meanwhile, Ron Howard's *Inferno* (2016), inspired by Dan Brown's novel, reimagined Dante's infernal realms. Finally, *Dante's Hell Animated* helmed by Boris Acosta (2013) vividly animated the depths of Dante's Hell, showcasing the narrative's enduring appeal and versatility across mediums.

In 1950, Salvador Dalí was commissioned to illustrate Dante's work, resulting in a series of lithographs that reflected unique aesthetics for each section of the poem: a surreal Inferno, an expressionist and existential Purgatory, and a Paradise characterized by traditional composition and an almost sacred aura. Concurrently, artists like Robert Rauschenberg and Renato Guttuso brought the *Commedia* into modern contexts by merging artistic styles, symbolism, and social critique. Rauschenberg incorporated contemporary figures and magazine imagery, while Guttuso infused his critical, Marxist perspective through vibrant colors and texts from the poem. Similarly, though unsuccessfully during his lifetime, Pier Paolo

Pasolini attempted this modern reinterpretation with *La Divina Mimesis*, published posthumously in 1975. Pasolini reimagined the Divine Comedy for the modern age, turning the Inferno into a portrayal of the neocapitalist world, aimed at chastising contemporary figures such as conformists and the petit bourgeoisie.

More recently, Dante's work has continued to inspire across cultural boundaries, as evidenced by the illustrated version by Japanese manga *Go Nagai* (1994–1995), which demonstrates the ability of Dante's masterpiece to transcend cultures and generations.

Recipe for Success

In his work, Dante reprocesses, blends, and narrates hundreds of stories of characters originating from vastly different cultural and historical backgrounds, yet connects them through common elements and motifs.

It's easy to focus on the similarities with modern fantasy literature rather than the differences, which are equally significant. *The Divine Comedy* is a text saturated with allegories and metaphors, an intellectual work demanding extensive cultural knowledge for full comprehension and digestion. It's a mystical text and, at the same time, a strongly political one, addressing earthly issues and complex metaphysical problems, discussing universal matters as well as deeply personal stories.

Once more, it's essential to acknowledge that the poem is deeply embedded in the medieval theological and philosophical context. Dante uses his work not only to navigate spiritual and moral themes but also to comment on and critique the society of his time. Demons, as well as other characters and elements of the work, are multifunctional: they represent both literal entities in the universe of the *Comedy* and symbols of broader concepts such as justice, sin, and redemption.

This complexity, which can certainly intimidate readers unaccustomed to this genre of literature, including all Italian students exposed to Dante during their high school years—among whom are almost certainly future horror directors, and authors of fantasy books and comics—is markedly distinct from the accessibility of the pop fantasy culture it inspired. What has been most transmitted to the fantasy genre are the most striking, theatrical, and easily comprehensible elements. Paradoxically, Dante has influenced both sophisticated theologians and satanic metalheads in equal measure, each selecting elements that best suited their own sensibilities.

Given that studying Dante is mandatory in Italian schools, as mentioned, every student, willingly or not, has been exposed to this imagery. They had to read and attempt to interpret, often reluctantly and under the threat of poor grades, sonnets written in a language partially incomprehensible, whose text necessarily had to be deciphered with the teacher's explanations and the dense footnotes accompanying the text at the bottom of each page.

For most young people, *The Divine Comedy*, especially the *Purgatorio* and *Paradiso*, represented moments of almost transcendental boredom. However, the *Inferno*, with its grotesque and terrifying depictions, often managed to captivate the attention even of the most inattentive students.

The first-person narrative used in the story allowed for a higher level of immersion, a narrative device later also found in modern Gothic exponents, from Poe to Lovecraft. In these works, the narrator, sometimes on the brink of madness, having lived through an extraordinary and seemingly incredible event, invites the reader to heed their warnings and apocalyptic visions. This occurs despite the limitations of human vocabulary, which fails to adequately describe the unspeakable realities or truths that have been revealed to them:

> O voi ch'avete li 'ntelletti sani,
> mirate la dottrina che s'asconde
> sotto 'l velame de li versi strani.
> (Alighieri, *Inferno* IX, vv. 61–63)

> O ye who have undistempered intellects,
> Observe the doctrine that conceals itself
> Beneath the veil of the mysterious verses!
> (Alighieri, *Inferno* IX, vv. 61–63)

. . . and . . .

> Allor mi dolsi, e ora mi ridoglio
> quando drizzo la mente a ciò ch'io vidi,
> e più lo 'ngegno affreno ch'i' non soglio,
> perché non corra che virtù nol guidi;
> sì che, se stella bona o miglior cosa
> m'ha dato 'l ben, ch'io stessi nol m'invidi.
> (Alighieri, *Inferno*, Canto XXVI, vv. 19–24)

Then sorrowed I, and sorrow now again,
When I direct my mind to what I saw,
And more my genius curb than I am wont,
That it may run not unless virtue guide it;
So that if some good star, or better thing,
Have given me good, I may myself not grudge it.
(Alighieri, *Inferno*, Canto XXVI, vv. 19–24)

The Hero's Journey

In *The Divine Comedy*, Dante embarks on a journey that is simultaneously physical, metaphysical, and psychological, traversing the afterlife and interacting with supernatural entities. This narrative framework profoundly influenced subsequent literature, evolving into a kind of narrative archetype akin to the "hero's journey" found in many tales.

"The Hero's Journey" is a narrative model proposed by Christopher Vogler, building upon the theories of Joseph Campbell as presented in his work *The Hero with a Thousand Faces* (1949). This model has consistently resonated with fans of fantasy tales and has formed the foundation, whether consciously or not, for countless stories and sagas. It outlines a typical journey that many heroes across various cultures embark on in their narratives, such as Jason's quest for the Golden Fleece leading the Argonauts, Odysseus's return to Ithaca, the epic of Gilgamesh, and Beowulf's attempts to defeat Grendel and his mother, among others.

The journey commences with the hero's departure from their ordinary world, followed by their initiation into an unfamiliar or magical realm, where they face trials, encounter allies and foes, and confront their darkest aspects. The journey culminates with the hero's return to the ordinary world, transformed and enriched by the experiences they have undergone. Although this framework is not rigid, it serves as a foundation for analyzing and constructing narratives, demonstrating its significance across a wide spectrum of cultures and epochs.

In this light, the journey of an Italian migrant mirrors the hero's journey. Unaware of his fate, he begins a journey where he must confront a tortuous spatiotemporal path filled with many uncertainties, while also undergoing a bureaucratic process to reach his destination. There, he will have to muster all his effort to succeed in the endeavor.

Dante Alighieri's *Divina Commedia*, despite having some peculiarities due to its nature and the era in which it was written, follows this pattern as well. The persistence and universality of Dante's journey highlight his ability to capture the fundamental structure of the heroic path.

In *Inferno*, Dante finds himself lost in a dark wood, symbolizing his spiritual loss. This marks the beginning of his call to adventure, guided first by Virgil, the author of the *Aeneid* who in his epic described Aeneas's journey to the realm of the dead. There is no explicit refusal from Dante, but his initial hesitation and fear might be interpreted as a reluctant acceptance of the call. Virgil, Beatrice, and Saint Bernard act as supernatural guides assisting Dante in his journey through Inferno, Purgatory, and Paradise. Dante's entrance into Hell signifies the crossing of the first threshold, initiating his journey into the afterlife. He encounters various damned souls, demons, angels, and blessed spirits, representing the challenges to overcome, allies, and enemies in his spiritual growth journey. The poet's arrival at the Earth's center, where he meets Lucifer, represents the darkest and deepest point of his journey, akin to the approach to the innermost cave in Vogler's model. Dante's ultimate trial is his ascension through Hell and Purgatory and his ascent to Paradise. The reward is the vision of God, signifying ultimate understanding and redemption. Symbolically, Dante's journey ends with his return to Earth and his preparation to write his work, sharing his experience and teachings. Dante's resurrection is spiritual. His return with the elixir manifests in the composition of the *Divina Commedia*, imparting wisdom and warnings to his contemporaries and future generations.

In contemporary literature, we can see the echoes of Dante's structure and themes in works such as *The Lord of the Rings* by J. R. R. Tolkien, where Frodo's journey is both physical and inner, filled with trials, allies, and enemies, akin to Dante's path. Similarly, the complex cosmology and demonic figures of the *Divina Commedia* can be seen as precursors to the intricate worlds and fantastic creatures found in series like *Harry Potter* by J. K. Rowling.

It's clear that all the elements of a fantasy adventure, tinged with a hint of horror, are present: monstrous characters, terrifying demons, parallel universes, and then the hero, who traverses the entirety of Hell and rises, purifying himself along the path until he reaches Paradise, the coveted destination and abode of divine light, after having literally and metaphorically crossed the entire realm of the afterlife, a shadow and reflection of our everyday life.

The way Dante characterizes the infernal figures, endowing them with depth and nuances, paves the way for a more complex and multifaceted representation of evil, as seen in the ambiguous and multidimensional characters in the works of authors like Stephen King or George R. R. Martin.

Gruesome details, despairing specters wandering through hellish lands, and demons that incessantly torment the souls of the damned populate the pages of the *Divina Commedia.* These vigorous images have captured the imagination of generations, captivating many youths and at times even disturbing the more sensitive students in their nocturnal nightmares. Dante, with his use of allegories and personifications of demons, has opened a gateway for many into a wild and shadowy world, yet simultaneously intriguing. This universe, filled with sounds, dripping with blood, and oppressive atmospheres, reveals its raw intensity in Dante's narrative.

The entrance to Hell marks the beginning of a transcendental journey. Located in a dark forest, a symbol of spiritual bewilderment, the entrance is guarded by Charon, the ferryman of souls. The words engraved on the access arch, "Abandon all hope, ye who enter here," warn visitors of the irreversible despair that permeates this realm. Dante, accompanied by the poet Virgil, thus embarks on his journey through the circles of Hell, exploring the depths of the human condition and divine justice.

Dante's clever use of the gate to Hell has smoothly flowed into the collective imagination of cinema and fantasy, from Lucio Fulci's *Inferno* trilogy of the early eighties, to *Dylan Dog*'s Golconda, from the multidimensional portal in *Under the Chinese Restaurant* by Bruno Bozzetto (1987), to the hellish door in the film adaptation of the haunting Valentina, *Baba Yaga* by Corrado Farina (1973), and culminating in the Upside Down of *Stranger Things*, which directly mirrors and evokes Dante's inferno, ruled by a corrupted version of the chosen angel, now fallen into this spectral world, just as Lucifer falls to the center of Hell. A portal opening to another dimension, where the laws governing our world are contradicted or overturned, as literally happens in *Through the Looking-Glass* by Lewis Carroll, is a well-established literary device for starting a story, for initiating a protagonist's journey of redemption and purification, as in the *Divina Commedia*, or for the loss of one's sanity, as in gothic literature (Cassini). The door to parallel worlds in the *Twilight Zone* was thus first opened by Dante.

Demons are also keepers of secrets and unspeakable truths protected by barriers or infernal gates. In Dante Alighieri's work obstacles such as doors, guardians, and barriers play a key role both literally and metaphorically. These narrative elements, in addition to acting as physical obstacles, represent spiritual, moral, or psychological barriers. They symbolize the divisions between the different levels of sin and consciousness, once again highlighting the hierarchical and moral structure of Hell.

This wealth of imagery is not solely the product of his genius. In delineating Hell in his *Divina Commedia,* Dante did not limit himself to a mere exercise of imagination. Rather, he skillfully collected and reworked material from various cultures and epochs, some even very distant in time. As we have seen, in the creation of Hell, Dante did not hesitate to blend elements of Greek tradition with those of Christianity. The resulting image carries traces of the Greek tradition, like Hades or Plato's myth of Er, the Apocalypse of Paul (Visio Pauli), which provides detailed descriptions of Hell and Heaven as experienced through the visions of Saint Paul (Silverstein), but also of the Jewish Gehenna, the Arabic Jahannam, underscoring significant parallels with the hell of Dharmic religions, Naraka, the Sumerian Kur, and so on, at least indicating that this archetype has been attracting human attention for a very long time.

Fantastic Journeys, Bureaucracy, Demons, and the Supernatural

The concept of demons inflicting specific punishments on the souls of the damned, a kind of poetic justice or *contrapasso*, is reflected in various cultures. This is clearly seen in the multilevel structure of Hell, a feature present both in the Chinese version of Diyu, with its eighteen levels, and in the Indian version, as well as in Plato's myth of Er, asserting a newfound moral responsibility for one's fate after death, a concept that was somewhat foreign to traditional Greek notions up to that point.

These observations prompt reflection on how the archetype of Hell, with its punishments and hierarchical structure, is a theme that has fascinated humanity for centuries, across different cultures. Dante, with his erudition and poetic skill, has managed to weave these different strands into a work that, while rooted in his time and culture, engages with a much broader and more universal heritage. These images have survived over the millennia and have smoothly converged into our common imagination in a completely fluid and often unconscious manner, much like when we live and grow within a cultural or religious context: we are not always aware of the influence we receive from our surrounding environment, which often conditions every thought we have, even the most personal ones.

Demons, with their grim and horrific appearance, not only instill fear but also serve to convey moral lessons, admonishing us not to sin and to steer clear of temptations that constantly lurk in everyday life. In various cantos of *Inferno*, demons are depicted as the custodians of the various punishments and torments inflicted upon the damned. In the fifth *bolgia* of the eighth circle of Hell, the demons known as Malebranche guide Dante and Virgil. These demons punish the barrators (those guilty of corruption and fraud) by immersing them in boiling pitch.

This moral teaching, in its simplest form, has flowed into countless modern horror films where the young are punished for taking refuge in a cabin near a lake to use drugs, listen to rock music, and have fun despite the warnings received, as occurs in *Friday the 13th* by Sean S. Cunningham (1980), *The Burning* by Tony Maylam (1981), *Sleepaway Camp* by Robert Hiltzik (1983), *The Cabin in the Woods* by Drew Goddard (2011), *The Fear Street Trilogy* by Leigh Janiak, among others.

The demons, described with monstrous and grotesque detail, such as to create repulsion and terror in the reader, from Charon to Pluto, through Cerberus and Phlegyas, are also guardians and judges of the infernal *bolgias*.

> Stavvi Minòs, orribilmente, e ringhia:
>
> essamina le colpe ne l'intrata;
> giudica e manda secondo ch'avvinghia.
> (Alighieri, *Inferno*, Canto V, vv. 4–6)
>
> There standeth Minos horribly, and snarls;
> Examines the transgressions at the entrance;
> Judges, and sends according as he girds him.
> (Alighieri, *Inferno*, Canto V, vv. 4–6)

This concept is epitomized by Minos, the king of Crete and son of Zeus, who is situated in the second infernal circle, where the lustful reside (Canto V). His task is to judge and assign the sinners to their designated place of punishment. When a damned soul appears before him, it fully confesses its sins, and Minos, having determined the appropriate infernal location, wraps his serpent tail around himself as many times as the circles the damned must descend to reach their eternal dwelling (Bernstein).

In Dante's work, bureaucracy is utilized as a metaphor to express social and political critiques. This critique suggests that earthly structures of power and control are inadequate and corrupt compared to divine judgment. Dante's idea of pairing the fantastic journey with a lengthy or frustrating bureaucratic process predates many stories where administration and formalism govern magical or spacetime adventures that can host elements of magic, the supernatural, or complex inner experiences. An example is Kafka's narrative *The Trial*, which also serves as a literary model for all subsequent works, or *Hospital* by Han Song, where the narrator, like Dante, is accompanied by three female counterparts and finds himself unwillingly trapped in a labyrinthine city built around a dystopian hospital system.

These imaginative concepts have been reinterpreted in various ways in many films, including *Heaven Can Wait* directed by Warren Beatty and Buck Henry (1978), *Brazil* by Terry Gilliam (1985), *Beetlejuice* by Tim Burton (1988), *Switch* by Blake Edwards (1991) adapted from *Goodbye Charlie* by George Axelrod (1959), *The City of Lost Children* by Marc Caro and Jean-Pierre Jeunet (1995), *The Devil's Advocate* by Taylor Hackford (1997), *Men in Black* series (1997–2019) based on the Marvel Comics by Lowell Cunningham, *Dogma* by Kevin Smith (1999), *The 13th Floor* by Josef Rusnak (1999) adapted from *Simulacron-3* by Daniel F. Galouye (1964), *The Matrix* franchise by the Wachowskis (since 1999), *Don't Tempt Me* by Agustín Díaz Yanes (2001), *Bruce Almighty* directed by Tom Shadyac (2003), *The Hitchhiker's Guide to the Galaxy* by Garth Jennings (2005) adapting the franchise created in 1978 by Douglas Adams, *Evan Almighty* directed by Tom Shadyac (2007), *The Imaginarium of Doctor Parnassus* by Terry Gilliam (2009), *The Adjustment Bureau* by George Nolfi (2011) adapted from *Adjustment Team* by Philip K. Dick, and *Oh My God* directed by Umesh Shukla (2012).

These themes are also evident in TV series such as *Supernatural* created by Eric Kripke and produced from 2005 to 2020 for fifteen seasons, *The Good Place* created by Michael Schur (2016–2020), *Happy!* created by Grant Morrison and Brian Taylor (2017–2019) based on the comic of the same name written by Morrison and illustrated by Darick Robertson, *Nobody's Looking* created by Daniel Rezende, Carolina Markowicz, and Teodoro Poppovic (2019), *Servant* created by Tony Basgallop (2019–2023), *Good Omens* directed by Douglas Mackinnon (2019) and based on the novel by Terry Pratchett and Neil Gaiman (1990), *Sandman* by David S. Goyer and Allan Heinberg (2022) inspired by the comic book series by Neil Gaiman, with various events set in a Hell largely derived from Dante, *Loki* created by Michael Waldron (2021–2023), *Severance* created by Dan Erickson and directed by Ben Stiller and Aoife McArdle (2022), and various episodes of *Star Trek* in different shows and seasons.

As well, between the fantastic and bureaucracy are the film *Lemony Snicket's "A Series of Unfortunate Events"* directed by Brad Silberling (2004) and the Netflix production *A Series of Unfortunate Events* by Mark Hudis (2017–2019), both inspired by the books of author Daniel Handler.

In addition are video games like *Grim Fandango* (1998), *Psychonauts* (2005) and *Psychonauts 2* (2021) by Tim Schafer, and *Afterparty* (2019) by Night School Studio. While in some cases the hero's journey of purification finds a positive ending, in *Inside*, created by Playdead in 2016, there is no redemption: the misadventures of a boy forced to traverse a completely gray and desolate world, managed by a company conducting a series of mind control experiments, will find a dramatic and hopeless end.

The Folklore of Horror

Dante's epic reflects not only the theology and philosophy of the time but also the popular beliefs, superstitions, and myths that were deeply rooted in medieval culture. In many Italian regions, particularly in rural areas and more traditional communities, a cultural syncretism developed, merging official religious beliefs and practices with ancient pagan or superstitious traditions. This fusion led to a coexistence of superstitious practices and religious rites. The official Catholic Church promoted a doctrine based on Christian faith and the Holy Scriptures, but in some regions of Italy, it was possible to observe a coexistence of superstitious traditions, popular beliefs, and religious practices. The Catholic Church did not always manage to keep the more remote rural areas under its "control," partly due to the geographical configuration of the territory. In these areas, practices such as the use of amulets, herbs, belief in omens, or consultation of traditional healers have roots that were never eradicated and have grown in local and cultural traditions. Many practices have persisted regardless of the directives of the Church. The relationship between superstition and the Catholic Church in Italy is a complex and multifaceted phenomenon. In some cases, the celebration of patron saint festivals often includes processions, blessings of sacred objects, and practices that, although they have a religious basis, include superstitious elements. Some cults of saints may blend with more folkloristic devotional practices, as still happens in Cocullo with the Festival of the Snake-Catchers (*Festa dei Serpari*). The veneration of particular saints for protection from specific events or diseases can take on superstitious traits, although this may vary from community to community. In some cases, the Church has had to adopt a more flexible pastoral approach toward popular practices, trying to understand and integrate local cultural elements without compromising fundamental doctrine.

Many superstitions are related to beliefs about lucky or unlucky days, objects that bring good or bad luck, and practices to ward off the evil eye or protect against negative forces. The culture is rich in symbolism and mythology, for example, iron, salt, and the eye are often considered protective elements. Some superstitions are also tied to specific events or celebrations and require practices to attract good luck. Protecting oneself from negative influences or attracting divine benevolence are the same, so recourse to "amulets" or spells can be made. Superstitions are also intertwined with folklore and local narrative. Tales of mythological creatures, such as deities that have become the new demons, witches, or elves, added to the already demonic figures of incubi and succubi from Roman tradition, have influenced the superstitious beliefs of communities.

In the Middle Ages, and later, the concept of witchcraft was common and often associated with pagan practices and, especially after the publication of the *Malleus Maleficarum* (*Witch's Hammer*, 1486), with heresy and the demonic. However, in the *Divina Commedia*, Dante does not explicitly mention witches. The two figures that most closely approach this vision are Manto, the soothsayer daughter of Tiresias in Canto XIX of *Inferno*, and Erichtho, a necromancer mentioned in Canto IX, for whom Virgil in the past had traveled to the lowest circle of Hell to retrieve a soul for one of her necromantic rites, who could be considered close to the image of witches because, like them, they can evoke and manipulate the dead.

In this context, witchcraft can be understood in various ways, from popular traditions of magic to beliefs related to black magic or the occult, providing inexhaustible material for the entire fantasy genre. In a territory rich in folkloristic and magical-religious traditions dating back to ancient times, it's crucial to distinguish between witchcraft as a traditional magical practice and popular perceptions of witchcraft linked to negative stereotypes. During the period of the Inquisition, between the sixteenth and eighteenth centuries, there were episodes of persecution of people accused of witchcraft. The Catholic Inquisition sought to eliminate practices considered heretical or contrary to the doctrine of the Church. Many innocents were persecuted and executed in this context.

For instance, the Benandanti believed that witches sought to harm crops and the community through malefic practices. Consequently, they felt that going out at night in spiritual form would allow them to combat them. It's said that during their nocturnal outings, they participated in mystical rites, during which they could assume animal forms or interact with other supernatural entities. According to the Italian historian and essayist Carlo Ginzburg, unlike tales of witchcraft, the actions of the Benandanti were aimed at defending, not harming. However, in different parts of Italy, other traditions, beliefs, and magical practices present similarities or parallels to these figures. In many regions of Italy, there was a widespread belief in witches, who could be considered as evil as they were benevolent. The Janara is a witch from southern Italian folklore, feared for bringing sickness, famine, and death. To prevent her entry, locals would place a broom or salt by their doors, forcing her to count each thread or grain until sunrise made her powerless. On the contrary, the Befana is a witch who brings sweets and treats to children and is still celebrated today, every year on January 6th, while in some localities the Three Wise Men who bring gifts to baby Jesus are celebrated.

There were figures, similar to the Benandanti, who could be perceived as healers or individuals capable of defending the community from negative influences. In some communities, there were beliefs related to lunar cycles, full moon nights, or specific dates of the year. These beliefs often involved rituals and mystical activities during certain periods. Some traditions in rural areas could include beliefs in "nature spirits" or supernatural entities that influenced daily life. The perception of these entities varies, appearing either benevolent or malevolent based on the context.

Italian horror cinema has often drawn inspiration from the country's rich literary and cultural tradition, synthesizing pagan elements with Dante's work. The directors create their films in a daily context where the devil and holy water meet, the blessing and the inquisition. Films that could be interpreted in this light or that present symbolic elements traceable to the poet's work include *Black Sunday* (*Nella maschera del demonio*, 1960) directed by Mario Bava, featuring representations of evil and dark forces typical of Dante's *Inferno*, with an addition of local folklore starring a witch seeking revenge after being condemned for witchcraft and executed; Dario Argento's *Suspiria* (1977), known for its surreal and dreamlike atmosphere, echoing some descriptions of Hell and recurring themes of darkness. Also by Dario Argento is *Inferno* (1980), associated both by its title and through certain evocative sequences where elements of witchcraft and supernatural forces can be found. Lucio Fulci's *The Beyond* (*L'aldilà*, 1981) has supernatural and apocalyptic elements that can be interpreted in light of Dante's visions. Although not a traditional horror film, *Salò or the 120 Days of Sodom* (*Salò, o le 120 giornate di Sodoma*, 1975), an extremely disturbing drama directed by Pier Paolo Pasolini, is sometimes associated with the concept of Hell due to its cruel and perverse representations. The distinctive aesthetics of horror cinema often incorporate symbolic and visual elements that evoke Dante's infernal imagery. Pupi Avati created *The House with Laughing Windows* (*La casa dalle finestre che ridono*, 1976) with a dark and unsettling atmosphere, where a sense of mystery and horror constantly grows. *The Black Cat* by Lucio Fulci (*Gatto nero*, 1981), inspired by Edgar Allan Poe's tale, features a series of supernatural and disturbing events that evoke a hellish atmosphere. Landscapes that recall the idea of Hell or present dark and disturbing atmospheres are found in *Cemetery Man* (*Dellamorte Dellamore*, 1994) directed by Michele Soavi, where elements of horror and supernatural phenomena create a surreal, often disturbing, and romantic atmosphere.

Supernatural, demonic, and occult elements clashing with forces of good and thus subject to divine justice, for example, are found in *Don't Torture a Duckling* (*Non si sevizia un paperino*, 1972) directed by Lucio Fulci, where the theme of evil within a community and accusations of witchcraft are explored. In the film, the protagonist confronts dark forces to solve a series of murders. Fulci again, in *The House by the Cemetery* (*Quella villa accanto al cimitero*, 1981), explores the themes of the supernatural and evil through the story of a family moving into a house with a dark past. *Demons* (*Demoni*, 1985) by Lamberto Bava, produced by Dario Argento, features demonic creatures emerging during a film screening, leading to a clash between evil and those trying to survive, wrapped in a frantic atmosphere. Michele Soavi in *The Church* (*La chiesa*, 1989) takes viewers to an ancient church built on a site of ancient satanic rites, where the conflict between dark forces and benevolent forces begins. Again Soavi, in the film *The Devil's Daughter* (*La Setta*, 1991), addresses the theme of demonic possession and the clash between good and evil within a demonic cult.

Films more distinctly marked and incorporating elements of mysticism, satanic possession, or conflicts between the supernatural and faith include *The Nun* (*La monaca*, 1965) directed by Damiano Damiani, whose plot is based on a seventeenth-century news story about a young nun accused of moral corruption. The film addresses themes of sin, guilt, and religious repression.

Witches, clashes between pagan deities and Christian figures, elements of black magic, occultism, folklore, and mythology are found in *The Witch in Love* (*La strega in amore*, 1966), a film by Damiano Damiani, the story of a witch who falls in love with a Nazi officer during World War II. Renato Polselli in the film *Black Magic Rites* (*Riti, magie nere e segrete orge nel trecento . . .*, 1973), also known as *The Reincarnation of Isabel*, tells an eccentric and surreal story involving elements of witchcraft and reincarnation. While Lamberto Bava, in *The Ogre* (*Il mostro*, 1989), following a young woman who discovers she is a descendant of a lineage of witches, addresses the theme of magical heritage and clashes with dark forces.

The modern imagery of the afterlife, as well as its metaphorical interpretations, over the centuries, has been shaped by Dante's infernal and paradisiacal visions and this influence, in all its declinations, more or less consciously, appears cyclically in every representation.

The *Divina Commedia*, with its universal exploration of the themes of feelings, vices, and human inclinations, has continued to be a relevant work for readers and artists of every era. Dante created a work that captures the essence of the human condition, serving as a timeless vade mecum. It speaks to readers across historical and cultural contexts, offering universal messages and inexhaustible inspiration for artists.

Through the poem, artists can explore profound themes, while maintaining their uniqueness and artistic originality. Dante's work thus becomes a stage where different artistic interpretations manifest, each reflecting the time, culture, and personal vision of the artist. In this way, the *Divina Commedia* not only survives but thrives through the centuries, continually renewing itself in the hands of those who interpret it.

Authors' note: Some readers might argue that this chapter overemphasizes Church-related themes, while others might point to a lack of broader representation. We would like to offer some clarifications in response to these concerns.

Dominique, an Italian Caribbean woman born in the Veneto region and classically educated in Italy, can confirm that the vast majority of the Italian society, at least until the 1980s, was almost entirely white and partially rural, aside from larger cities like Turin, Bologna, Milan, Rome, and Florence. A Christian-Jewish cultural component served as the sole unifying element in the young country, as neither the language nor traditions were the same across all regions. In Italian history, there are few examples of significant multiethnic and multicultural friendships, such as the one between Giuseppe Garibaldi and Alexandre Dumas père. Since these are primarily transient and entirely personal stories, no sufficiently large groups of other ethnic and cultural identities have formed to provide opportunities to tell stories from different perspectives, with the exception of small enclaves in Italian territory of Greek, Albanian, Croatian, Tyrolean, and other origins, which, however, have focused on preserving their own identity. Black and Muslim Italians were almost completely absent, and second generations only began to appear toward the end of the 1990s.

Anecdotally, growing up in Padua during the 1980s and 1990s, in the industrious Veneto region, neither of us had classmates of non-European origin. Today, however, the reality of Italian society is markedly different. A recurring discussion among us is that, despite the presence of many children of Afro, Arab, Muslim, and Asian origin in Italian schools by the late 1990s—who are now adults—they remain almost invisible in contemporary television and film.

Over the past twenty years, family units from various Eastern European countries have increased across Italy. As the process of inclusion often takes time, new stories and traditions are likely to emerge in the near future. Representation is still largely limited to sports or activism, with few exceptions in recent television productions such as *Zero* (2021), *Uonderbois* (2024), and *Citadel: Diana* (2024).

Moreover, since the late 1980s, funding for genres like horror, fantasy, and science fiction in Italian film and television has significantly declined. This combination of factors has resulted in very few Afro/Arab representatives in these fields. Second and third generations are still fighting for their rights.

Hence the need for the global societal changes argued for in part 3 of this book, which begins in the following pages . . .

Works Cited

Alighieri, Dante. *The Divine Comedy*. Translated by Henry Wadsworth Longfellow, 1867. https://www.gutenberg.org/ebooks/1004.

Bernstein, Alan E. *The Formation of Hell: Death and Retribution in the Ancient and Early Christian Worlds*. Cornell UP, 1996.

Cassini, Andrea. "Dante weird: il pioniere dello 'strano' letterario." *L'Indiscreto*, 29 Apr. 2019. https://www.indiscreto.org/dante-weird-il-pioniere-dello-strano-letterario/.

Croce, Benedetto. *Teoria E Storia Della Storiografia*. 1866.

Fiorito, Giovanni, Cornelia Di Gaetano, Simonetta Guarrera, Fabio Rosa, Marcus W. Feldman, Alberto Piazza, and Giuseppe Matullo. "The Italian Genome Reflects the History of Europe and the Mediterranean Basin." *European Journal of Human* Genetics, vol. 24, 2016, pp. 1056–62. https://doi.org/10.1038/ejhg.2015.233.

Frey, Angelica. "Dante's Divine Comedy and Its Influence on Art History." *Art & Object*, 24 May 2021. https://www.artandobject.com/articles/dantes-divine-comedy-and-its-influence-art-history.

Limes Club Verona. "L'Identità italiana e la storia. Conversazione con il prof. Ernesto Galli della Loggia." *Limes*. https://www.limesonline.com/limesplus/l-identita-italiana-e-la-storia-14655505.

Silverstein, Theodore. *Visio Sancti Pauli: The History of the Apocalypse in Latin Together with Nine Texts*. Christophers, 1935. https://archive.org/details/visiosanctipauli0000silv/page/n5/mode/2up.

"Stryx." Wikiwand. https://www.wikiwand.com/en/articles/Stryx.

The Ultimate Rabbit. "Geretta Geretta Looks Back on 'Demons' at New Beverly Cinema." *The Ultimate Rabbit*, 12 Aug. 2019. https://theultimaterabbit.com/2019/08/12/geretta-geretta-looks-back-on-demons-at-new-beverly-cinema.

Part 3

Reimagining Italian America

Artifacts of Anti-fascist and Ecofeminist Fantastika

Being Italian isn't about where you're from. It's about what you value.

—Giancarlo Esposito, speaking to Spike Lee
in FIAT 500e commercial (May 1, 2024)

In a post-emancipation world, everyone's humanity must be reissued and prescribed a meaning that grants everyone enfranchisement. . . . Justice can only be obtained when people strive to imagine and create a world order that does no harm.

—Kellie Carter Jackson

Reimagining Italian America

9

"The Ocean Inside Her"

C. L. Herman's *The Drowning Summer* as Italian American Young Adult Speculative Fiction

Lisa Marie Paolucci

"The first thing Stella Zanetti did when Mina got home from the hospital was make stuffed artichokes" (Herman, *Drowning* 380). Most individuals reading this passage from C. L. Herman's *The Drowning Summer* (2022) would be surprised to learn that sixteen-year-old Mina, short for Marina Elena, had been injured by a glass-shard-toothed demon in a local community center on Long Island. Indeed, this "atmospheric, magical" work might cast Mina's Italian American identity as a minor detail in a story about a family of spirit-conjuring mediums and the mysterious deaths of three teenagers—the Cliffside Trio—during "the drowning summer" (CLHerman.com). However, Herman's novel can be viewed as a site of female, bisexual Italian American identity development.

Herman, a bestselling author of several YA speculative fiction works, dedicated *The Drowning Summer* to her "grandmother Carmella Parrinello, who taught me everything I know about the Sound, Italian food, and making the most of the time you've got" (Herman, *Drowning*). Herman's reference to her grandparents' "dining room" and their "world-class Italian food" in *The Devouring Gray* (360), also hints at a cultural linkage.[1] These ties to Italian heritage emphasize food, which plays a large role in Mina's relationship with her mother, Stella. Stella's catering business features Italian American fare, and cooking is central to their home life. This chapter considers food, fashion, sustainability, identity formation, and culture in *The Drowning Summer.*

The Drowning Summer as Young Adult Speculative Fiction

Valentina Adami describes the functions and values of YA literature as connecting the most pressing issues of society to an adolescent quest for identity (130). In YA speculative fiction, "the dystopian content makes the protagonist's quest even harder, further highlighting the interconnectedness of the political and personal" (130). These works show "young adults that they have the power to do something in the world" (131) and "educate them into being better and more active citizens" (131). Anthony D. Boynton and colleagues describe a "recenter[ing] of the adolescent as a critical social figure" when speculative fiction "merg[es] with the genre of young adult literature" (7). For Frederick Luis Aldama, speculative fiction "wakes us to new ways of existing in mind/body, socioeconomics, politics, and ecogeographies" (ix). These perspectives accurately support this analysis of *The Drowning Summer*, as discussed below.

Mina and her friend Evelyn, another teenager also coming to terms with her identity, choose functional strategies based on what Aldama might call "creative cocreat[ion]" (ix) and their environment, to save the world. "Imagini[ing] a world that could be," Mina and Evelyn pursue occupations that emphasize sustainability in the face of climate change (Kröger and Anderson 293). Yet, Mina and Evelyn have essential differences. By candlelight Mina rips stitches from a "flawed design attempt" (7) and considers her outsider status in a key element of Zanetti identity: "Most of the Zanettis had a little something extra, a connection to the spirits they could either nurture or ignore. The dead called to her family, and her family answered them, guiding ghosts from this world to whatever came next" (8). Mina's mother, Stella, and her brother do this work while Mina and her cousin Sergio look on.

Physical descriptions of Mina and Stella highlight their differences. Mina's hair is "bleached blond and brittle" while Stella's is "dark, wavy, and improbably long, falling almost to her waist" (9). Mina's fragility contrasts with Stella's vibrant lushness. Mina "weakly" convinces her mother to take her along to Sand Dollar Cove. Stella wears "a highly impractical outfit to talk to the dead—a flowing maxi dress and her favorite opal headband twined through her dark hair . . . standing tall and regal in the surf, as ethereal and unknowable as the spirits she guided from the earth to their final resting place," while Mina wears "waterproof boots" (11–12).

As a small blue light takes "humanoid form," Mina enters the ocean. Mina's senses are assaulted by loud humming, the "smell . . . of salt and brine with an edge of rot, so powerful, she nearly gagged" (15). Screaming voices of spirits emerge in "an agonizing assault of noise" (15). Tossed by the ocean "like an errant seashell," she falls. Stella then asserts that "someone *else* called a spirit" (18) and readers learn that Mina's wrist injury is actually a "bluish-green sand dollar the size of a quarter" that causes extreme pain (18). The rest of the novel will trace Mina's path to learning about her own identity as a young bisexual woman, an Italian American, and a medium. Mina's literal and figurative relationship to the ocean parallels her eventual development into a practicing medium.

The Drowning Summer and Italian American Women's Writing

Several themes in Italian American women's writing appear relevant to *The Drowning Summer*. One such theme is a tension between individual and shared identities. As Marianna De Marco Torgovnick writes: "When Italian American daughters rebel, their 'I-ness' comes through loud and strong—but so too does their remembrance of the 'we.' They feel the lure of family and community—the thrill of self-sacrifice. The 'I' is a heady release conflicted by a potent nostalgia" (153). Mary Jo Bona emphasizes that "Italian American women writers produced works that make individual women's development central, often through sexual and educational exploration" ("Rich" 92). Rose De Angelis also describes how these "women succeed in redefining themselves as active agents" (114). Fred Gardaphé, too, identifies "novel[s] of self-awakening that record the efforts of a young woman to achieve her own identity amid the chaos that accompanies her family's disintegration" (140–41). The "remaking of the self" runs through *The Drowning Summer* and is supported by the speculative content.

Stella and Mina seek fulfillment through creative expression, another common theme in Italian American women's writing. For Stella, creativity takes place in the kitchen, exemplifying what Edvige Giunta and Louise

DeSalvo have written about "cooking and eating . . . [being] central to the work of Italian American authors" (11). While Daniella Gioseffi's analysis pits creative expression against life in the "symbolic kitchen prison" (15), for Stella, the kitchen is connected to what Louise DeSalvo describes as "ceremony in cooking" and Edvige Giunta characterizes as "sacramental" and "ritualistic" (104). Bona emphasizes that the "respect and devotion to food and the pride taken" makes the kitchen "a sacramental place for Italian Americans" ("But" 101), while Annie Lanzillotto describes the relationship between family members and food as "communion. Transmogrification" (235) that connects generations. Laura Ruberto's analysis of films and the Italian American experience also identifies artistic interpretations of "home-food-woman—a positive, alternative space . . . a liberating space" inviting "creativity" (167–68). Indeed, Giunta and DeSalvo have noted the "cultural power" of food wielded by Italian American women "food-makers" who held "sensory and sensual ties" to traditional recipes (1). "Stella's rapid movements around the kitchen and the "massive pot on the stove, boiling like the contents of a cauldron" (199), contribute to a picture of someone who speaks to ghosts, taking a subject that has been "a staple of Italian American literature" and "reinscrib[ing]" it with deeper meaning (Giunta 91). Mina also works in the kitchen, supporting these creative endeavors, but struggles to gain agency in both mediumship and fashion design.

Food and/as Identity

For Mina, playing an active role in the kitchen is one way she can begin practicing family rituals. Plans for Mina to observe a summoning begin with Stella preparing fresh clams. "Food was Stella's love language, and the kitchen was her workshop. . . . Her mother's cooking had nothing to do with the supernatural, but it was good enough to feel like it" (49). Far from inhabiting a "symbolic kitchen-prison," Stella's creative mastery redefines her role in the kitchen, and even the nature of food itself (Gioseffi and Oberdan 15). Mina recognizes cooking as one way Stella achieves self-actualization: "One day, Mina wanted people to talk about her clothing designs the way they talked about her mother's olive-and-escarole bread or her marinated artichoke hearts" (50).

After steaming for a few minutes, "the [clam] shells had opened little by little until her mother could finally pry out the meat inside" (52). The symbolism of the clamshell further underscores Stella's desire to control Mina's mediumship, and just as she expresses an approving "that's my seashell," she uses a "slotted spoon . . . [to] pull out a clam, cracked wide open" from the large pot and "extract the meat effortlessly with a fork" (56). It is the way she is used to handling Mina—steaming out any stubbornness until she bent to her will. At the same time, Stella seeks answers her daughter will not provide. By the end of the chapter, Stella has invited Mina to come to their next summoning under certain conditions. Mina thinks of "the place in [her] mind where she went to feel safe. An ocean—her ocean, where the water was always calm and smooth as glass, and the bottom was so far down, no one had ever found it. Her and Evelyn's . . . [past, when they summoned a spirit as childhood friends] belonged on the seafloor. She would do anything to keep it there" (55). This metaphor of the ocean pervades the novel, representing Mina's way of handling the world around her and her relationship with an estranged friend, Evelyn.

Environmentalism and *The Drowning Summer*

The Drowning Summer also emphasizes the importance of environmentalism. Climate fiction can have a significant impact on young adults. Adami considers it "one of the most relevant threats to our future . . . used by much contemporary speculative fiction to set up future dystopian or post-apocalyptic scenarios" (131). She notes that works of YA speculative fiction "ultimately inspir[e] creative thinking and action" (135). Marc DiPaolo writes of the importance of climate fiction, "proving literature to be a surprisingly valuable tool in collective efforts to address global warming" (2).

While Mina struggles to become a medium, her estranged friend Evelyn MacKenzie seeks to address climate issues, noting that "it was impossible to care about marine ecology without also caring about rising sea levels and fossil fuels" (34–35). Evelyn "had spent her childhood spying on the organisms that chose to make their homes here, in the intertidal zone, where the harsh extremes of the tides and the temperatures made for hearty creatures that didn't take any bullshit" (28). It is arguable that Evelyn herself is symbolically located in this intertidal zone, facing major challenges, but surviving, nevertheless.

Evelyn had hoped to earn an internship with the Coastal Wildlife and Conservation Research Society as a way into college, but when she helps her boyfriend cheat on an exam, it springboards her return to Mina

Zanetti. Cheating could cost her the internship. Evelyn finds a "crumbling" (25) seashell on a necklace with directions for a spell Mina gave her to call a spirit, then heads to Sand Dollar Cove, exactly where readers saw Stella and Mina and where the Cliffside Trio had been found six years earlier, drowned, lying in a cave, with sand dollars over their eyes. The crime was blamed on Evelyn's father, Greg, a linkage between family, history, and the environment.

Evelyn calls a spirit to take away the cheating incident. The chapter concludes with a weeping Evelyn grateful that "the magic had found her again, just when she needed it most" (32). However, Mina finds Evelyn and reveals the sand dollar mark, making Evelyn feel "cornered and exposed—a tide pool in the sun, a mollusk cowering as a predator approached" (41). Evelyn is out of place, in danger, without the benefit of a safe shelter. After their confrontation, Mina leaves and Evelyn apologizes to the spirit that she summoned; suddenly the smell of the ocean intrudes. Evelyn's summoning fails to secure her internship, and she remains a "tiny insignificant organism in a tiny insignificant tide pool who would stay trapped there until she died" (62).

Again, Evelyn sees herself in a kind of in-between zone, vulnerable to the elements. She registers a sound of loud crying that isn't her own, and smells the sea and then watches as the bathroom sinks suddenly begin to spurt water. But this time, "something hovered between the sink and the grimy tile wall, a humanoid figure, wispy and indistinct, made of the murky greens and browns of the ocean floor. In the place where its eyes should have been were two sand dollars. It disappeared between one blink and the next" (63). These continued, unplanned, involuntary summonings send Evelyn back to Mina, and so begins what a *Booklist* review refers to as "increasingly convoluted" events (Hutley 50).

The Ocean and Mina's Identity

References to the ocean often serve as metaphors for Mina's identity development. When Mina observes the summoning of Salvatore Giacomo for his wife, in the saltwater pool in the basement of the Shorewell Community Center, she learns that the six "blue-green hands" that pulled Giacomo down into the water were the Cliffside Trio (77). Later, Stella explains that this is "the unraveling," in which "an unsettled spirit will absorb ghosts that are ready to move on and continue to run off the power of their souls. The more spirits they devour, the more dangerous they become" (81). Stella acknowledges that the appearance of a demon would be "catastrophic . . . on par with a natural disaster" (82). Though Mina's feelings of "frustration," terror, and anger threaten to have her lose her cool, she "forced all of it down" (84–85).

"In Mina's mind, she was a sailor in a boat. A net floated behind it, scooping up bits and pieces that did not belong on the water's surface. She took the truth about demons and Stella's *no* [to allowing Mina to help] and her own secrets. Caught them in that net. Kept her ocean calm and gentle" (85). Again, the metaphor of the ocean conveys much about Mina's character. In this case, she cannot bear to grapple with disruptive elements and clears them from the surface.

Later in the novel, after Mina tries and fails to find a scrying focus with which she connects, a necessity to become a medium, her mood darkens and, "that night, Mina's imaginary net was very full. She scooped up her guilt, her shame, her fear, then pulled them into her tiny boat. Her catches wriggled there, sharp, spiky things, some oozing, some rotting, some snarling at her with too many mouths. She picked up the net to stare at them—and then she shoved them into an iron chest coiled with silver chains. Mina took a deep breath and pitched it over the side" (121). Although Mina looks directly at the negative feelings, she tries to lock them down and ensure that they stay out of view, even to herself.

Mina and Evelyn begin to collaborate and discover unique viewpoints. Evelyn makes connections to "abnormally fluctuating sea levels . . . coastal erosion" and the destruction of the "creatures whose lives were tied to the Sound" (132). As they consider how spirits behave in alignment with the tides, Evelyn wonders if climate change, with its resulting "extreme tides" due to "changing sea levels" could change how the spirits act (33). Mina considers that this could be why Stella had been noticing more "unstable" behavior among the spirits—that they "need[ed] that cycle, too—highs and lows" (133). Mina and Evelyn's interactions begin to reveal that there could be novel methods for medium practice. For example, Evelyn accidentally finds her scrying focus, a seashell, while trying to assist Mina in finding her own. Envy created "ripples in Mina's ocean. . . . Soon they'd be large enough to disturb those dozens of chests she'd sunk to the bottom" (143). Their collaboratively developed insights begin to indicate the creative power that eventually imbues their union.

Mina has a vision, removing her from her literal surroundings as if the "sand dollar on [her] wrist [were] tugg[ing] her mind forward"

(152). She feels a strong "yearning" that she interprets as coming from whichever ghost was present and also from herself. This is a major turning point for Mina, as she acknowledges a powerful feeling that does not fit inside her normally controlled world (151). She later admits to Evelyn that she does not want to ask Stella for any help until she is prepared to begin mediumship, putting on a "false smile," which solidifies for Evelyn that the "perfect[ion]" that Mina always put forward, whether through her physical appearance or school achievements, was "a well-crafted adaptation" (157).

Mina and Evelyn learn about the Blue Tide Management Plant, a waste management site developed in the 1970s, and the significant pollution it had caused in the Long Island Sound for years. Pictures convey "a hideous diluted orange" much like the rotten-smelling orange appearing during their interactions with spirits. Evelyn realizes that the waste management plant was "hurting the dead" (177). Mina tries to question Stella, but she can get nowhere with her mother. Later that evening, as she begins to summon a spirit, "yearning met with yearning" (189). Although she cuts this activity short, it solidifies for Mina that she is in fact a medium. "Stella was still treating her like a child" though, and Mina decides that she must take matters into her own hands.

When Stella learns that Evelyn is a medium, and Mina admits to her mother that she and Evelyn had summoned spirits years ago, "it felt as if one of her many chests at the bottom of the ocean had cracked open, leaking poison into her carefully curated sea" (205). As Stella and Mina share truths, Stella admits that Mina had been "cursed," which is what the sand dollar on her wrist signifies (206). Mina used some of her blood in the summoning when she was a child, which allowed spirits Stella thought were the Cliffside Trio to "siphon some of [her] life force." In learning these truths, Mina feels that her mother's love is "like a hand holding her beneath the water. . . . That kind of love—stifling, smothering, terrifying—was the only kind Mina knew how to give. Stella had taught her that the same way she's taught her to steam a lobster" (209). The discussion ultimately ends with Mina needing some space, the first time that she has stood up to her mother. That night, at a beach party with many of their friends and acquaintances, Mina and Evelyn begin to acknowledge an attraction for each other. Arguably, Mina's efforts to gain agency in her own life, illustrated through the metaphor of the ocean, allow her to act on her previously identified sexuality as well.

Bisexual Identity in *The Drowning Summer*

Mina and Evelyn's bisexuality blends into the work, a departure from past YA books. Michael Cart writes that, even going back to the nineties, "too many [novels] . . . continued to focus narrowly on the coming-out experience and too few dealt with the realities of living as an out teen" (189). In addition, as Antero Garcia has noted: "Questioning women and men of color, bi-sexual teens and transgender individuals have very few options to read about characters that are, in terms of sexuality, like them" (90). Cart still points to the significance of literature in which LGBTQ identity is "simply a given" (194). Herman describes Mina and Evelyn's coming-out experiences, then depicts them within groups of family members and friends who accept their bisexuality, several of whom also " 'just happen to' " identify within the LGBTQ community themselves (Cart and Jenkins 165).

The narrator introduces Evelyn's sexual orientation through a coworker's offer to set her up: "You're bi right? Because I really think you'd get along" (37).

> Evelyn had come out on social media the year before . . . she *had* gotten an anonymous comment calling her fake once she started dating Nick. Saying she'd "claimed to be bi" only for the attention, that if she was dating a guy, she was straight. She'd deleted it right away, but the memory still stung. It was nice to talk to somebody about it who treated it like it was no big deal, because it wasn't. (37)

Herman's treatment of Evelyn's bisexuality as "no big deal" while acknowledging incidents of bias and cruelty, especially challenging for young people, exemplifies Cart's aforementioned description. For Mina, "com[ing] out as bi . . . after talking it through with Stella for weeks" had been "an act of vulnerability that she was unsure she'd ever be capable of again" (89). But the remainder of the novel demonstrates otherwise, as Mina continues to evolve alongside her deepening relationship with Evelyn.

With Mina's decision to function independently of her mother, fulfilling her own desires, she attempts to summon a spirit in the ocean when the moon is full. Both Evelyn and Nick witness it. Mina is transported to another place where she sees a familiarly shaped building and a girl who tries to get her to take a sand dollar. Mina discovers that the sand dollar mark on her wrist is her scrying focus. In the middle of these discoveries, Mina and Evelyn spend the night at Nick's, with Evelyn internally acknowledging a "massive crush" on Mina (257). In the next chapter, Mina, too realizes how Evelyn has made her feel: "The girl she was now understood for the first time how *alive* the sea was during a storm. How that wind and rain and lightning could change an ocean into something absolutely mesmerizing. Something beautiful" (265). Evelyn helps Mina realize her own beauty and power, and her work with Evelyn aims toward self-actualization (265).

After continued research, Evelyn, Mina, and Nick realize that the girl in Mina's vision is Annette Shorewell, who had tried to spread awareness about the dangerous pollution caused by Blue Tide. Annette vanished in the late seventies, and when Mina coughs up a "thick slimy blockage," she realizes that she is not being haunted by the Cliffside Trio, but by Annette, who is trying to become a demon (281). They then learn that the Cliffside Trio had been investigating the Blue Tide plant and Annette Shorewell, which explains many convoluted plot twists. For Mina, the additional element of sustainable fashion bolsters the emerging themes of self-actualization through creativity, her Italian American identity, and sexuality.

Sustainable Fashion and Identity in *The Drowning Summer*

Mina realizes her fashion design is "boring. . . . bland, uninspired pieces with no heart at all" (203) and that the fashion industry contributes to climate change. Later, Mina shows Evelyn her redesigned collection. She has reused and reworked fabrics so as not to continue wasting, and they become tangible versions of the ocean that is herself, "the rich pink of the sunset reflecting off the water," "trousers . . . as silky and ephemeral as foaming waves . . . a tiny glimpse into the world . . . through the lens of her ocean" (302). The jewel of the collection is a dress that Mina makes for Evelyn, meant to represent "the ocean after dark," "black, dark bluish-green, golden moons and stars, metallic beads" (304). Evelyn puts it on and becomes "sea-foam and starlight . . . the moon's reflection," and the two kiss (304). Evelyn, who had always felt stuck in the intertidal zone, small and powerless, unable to move, symbolically expands into what feels like the entire ecosystem—ocean, sky, stars, unable to be confined or held down.

In part, Mina uses an originally designed garment as a way of draping Evelyn with her affection and admiration. This action connects to Edvige Giunta and Joseph Sciorra's observation that "weaving and needlework were implicated in the practice and beliefs of love magic" in their study of women's needlework in the Italian diaspora (8). But it also comes to symbolize Mina's agency, creativity, and future direction. As Giunta and Sciorra write: "needlework . . . can function as an artifact of the imagination, a repository of dreams, hopes, disappointments" (5). While Mina at first hides her collection from visitors, by the end of the novel she is proud to have it on display, which can be seen to echo Giunta and Sciorra's description of Italian women's process of working on their textiles in a courtyard in view of others (8).

Integrating Identity in *The Drowning Summer*

As Mina's newly discovered agency emerges in separating from her mother, Torgovnick's earlier words about "want[ing] the 'I' to linger along with the 'we' " return to mind (153). Herman's novel does not conclude with the severance of the Italian American mother-daughter relationship. Through a conversation over "antipasti . . . cheese, prosciutto, roasted red peppers . . . olives," Mina learns that Stella has known all along that Annette Shorewell is haunting them. Stella had had no choice but to deal with Annette's ghost after Mina, as a child, had offered her own blood. Annette feeds off Mina's life force, a bargain Stella made to save Mina's life. In the face of Mina's anger, Stella attempts to make a new deal to have Annette steal her spirit completely, sacrificing herself to release Mina. Stella washes up to shore in "some kind of coma" and is hospitalized (331), which pushes Mina to confront her fear and to try to save her mother's life.

Mina and Evelyn develop a new ritual that includes "two vials . . . a new kind of ward . . . the Zanetti glass and the Mackenzie natural world mixed together" (353). Their combined efforts in creating something new ultimately change their lives. This is arguably related to Alexis Lothian's belief that "there is a powerful speculative element in the move from deconstructing existing binaries to visualizing . . . how the world might be changed by those binaries' subversion or destruction" (5). To some degree, literally coming together in a relationship as two bisexual teenagers while figuratively merging, they perform what Maria Gurevich and colleagues describe as "unsettl[ing]" or "disassembl[ing]" previously accepted categories (44). They summon Annette, whose ghost emerges from the pool in the basement of the Shorewell Community Center: "sand dollars pressed over Annette's eyes, seaweed, candy wrappers, and cigarette butts twined in her hair . . . fingernails were barnacles . . . teeth shards of broken glass . . . smell[ing] . . . strongly of rot . . . orange, corrosive light . . . inside her sternum" (356). Mina convinces Annette to break the bond with Stella and allow Mina and Evelyn to help her ascend. Through a series of complicated events that involves the betrayal of Mina's cousin Sergio, Mina and Evelyn banish Annette. Both wake up in the hospital, injured, but sure to survive, while Sergio has died. Stella is revived, and at home over stuffed artichokes, they agree that Stella will respect Mina's autonomy and make contact with the rest of the Zanetti family so that she can continue to learn about mediumship. Evelyn and Mina develop independence and creative agency, breaking out of their previous prisons. Evelyn starts the Cliffside Bay Conservation Initiative, while Mina will develop sustainable fashion.

In *The Drowning Summer*, a bisexual Italian American teenager empowers herself to attain independence, self-actualization, and creative agency by allowing the integration of elements of her identity. This takes place with and through a critical view of the crisis of climate change and the need for young people to collaborate, creatively, to devise innovative solutions. At the conclusion of the novel, Mina and Evelyn are together in the ocean. Mina "now . . . welcomed the surge of emotion. She would no longer be afraid to immerse herself in it. And she wouldn't sink. She wouldn't drown. She would swim" (399). As a work that can be viewed as part of Italian diasporic speculative fiction, *The Drowning Summer* contributes the character of a self-actualized bisexual Italian American teenager who has created her own resources to thrive in a constantly changing environment.

Note

1. I make no assumptions about Herman's attitudes or assumed heritage. Herman could not be reached for comment on these topics.

Works Cited

Adami, Valentina. "The Pedagogical Value of Young-Adult Speculative Fiction: Teaching Environmental Justice Through Julie Bertagna's *Exodus*." *Pólemos*, vol. 13, no. 1, Apr. 2019, pp. 127–47.

Aldama, Frederick Luis. "Dreaming Latinx Realities." *Speculative Fiction for Dreamers: A Latinx Anthology*, edited by Alex Hernandez, Matthew David Goodwin, and Sarah Rafael Garcia, Mad Creek Books, 2021, pp. ix–x.

Bona, Mary Jo. " 'But Is It great?' The Question of the Canon for Italian American Women Writers." *Multiethnic Literature and Canon Debates*, edited by Mary Jo Bona and Irma Maini, State U of NY P, 2006, pp. 85–110.

Bona, Mary Jo. "Rich Harvest: An Overview of Italian American Fiction." *Teaching Italian American Literature, Film, and Popular Culture*, edited by Edvige Giunta and Kathleen Zamboni McCormick, Modern Language Association of America, 2010, pp. 87–96.

Boynton, Anthony D., Benet Pera, and Doug Dluzen, eds. "From the Editors." *Journal of Science Fiction*, vol. 5, no. 2, May 2022, p. 7.

Cart, Michael. *Young Adult Literature: From Romance to Realism*. 3rd ed. Neal-Schuman, 2016.

Cart, Michael, and Christine A. Jenkins. *The Heart Has Its Reasons: Young Adult Literature with Gay/Lesbian/Queer Content, 1969–2004*. Scarecrow Press, 2006.

CLHerman.com. "About Me." Last modified 4 Feb. 2023. https://www.clherman.com/about.

De Angelis, Rose. " 'Stripping Down' Gender Roles in Italian American Fiction by Women." *Teaching Italian American Literature, Film, and Popular Culture*, edited by Edvige Giunta and Kathleen Zamboni McCormick, Modern Language Association of America, 2010, pp. 109–14.

DeSalvo, Louise. *Crazy in the Kitchen: Food, Feuds, and Forgiveness in an Italian American Family*. Bloomsbury, 2004.

DiPaolo, Marc. *Fire and Snow: Climate Fiction from the Inklings to "Game of Thrones."* State U of New York P, 2018.

Garcia, Antero. *Critical Foundations in Young Adult Literature: Challenging Genres*. Sense, 2013.

Gardaphé, Fred. *Italian Signs, American Streets: The Evolution of Italian American Narrative*. Duke UP, 1996.

Gioseffi, Daniela, and Angelina Oberdan. *Pioneering Italian American Culture: Escaping La Vita Cucina*. Bordighera Press, 2013.

Giunta, Edvige. *Writing with an Accent: Contemporary Italian American Women Authors*. Palgrave, 2002.

Giunta, Edvige, and Joseph Sciorra, eds. *Embroidered Stories: Interpreting Women's Domestic Needlework from the Italian Diaspora*. UP of Mississippi, 2014.

Giunta, Edvige, and Louise De Salvo, eds. *The Milk of Almonds: Italian American Women Writers on Food and Culture*. Feminist Press at CUNY, 2002.

Gurevich, Maria, Helen Bailey, and Jo Bower. "Querying Theory and Politics: The Epistemic Dis)location of Bisexuality Within Queer Theory." *Bisexuality and Queer Theory: Intersections, Connections, and Challenges*, edited by Jonathan Alexander and Serena Anderlini-D'Onofrio, Routledge, 2012, pp. 43–65.

Herman, C. L. *The Devouring Gray*. Hyperion, 2019.

Herman, C. L. *The Drowning Summer*. Titan Books, 2022.

Hutley, Kristy. Review of *The Drowning Summer* by Christine L. Herman. *Booklist*. 15 Apr. 2022, www.booklistonline.com.

Kröger, Lisa, and Melanie R. Anderson. *Monster She Wrote: The Women Who Pioneered Horror & Speculative Fiction*. Quirk Books, 2019.

Lanzillotto, Annie. "Food Voice Narrative: *Cosa Mangia Oggi*." *Gastropolis: Food & New York City*, edited by Annie Hauck-Lawson and Jonathan Deutsch, Columbia UP, 2009, pp. 233–51.

Lothian, Alexis. *Old Futures: Speculative Fiction and Queer Possibility*. New York UP, 2018.

Ruberto, Laura E. "Where Did the Goodfellas Learn How to Cook? Gender, Labor, and the Italian American Experience." *Italian Americana*, vol. 21, no. 2, Summer 2003, pp. 164–76.

Torgovnick, Marianna De Marco. *Crossing Ocean Parkway*. U of Chicago P, 1996.

10

"True Blue" Humanities

Madonna's EcoFantastika

Drago Momcilovic

One of my earliest memories of Madonna is actually the memory of a scent—the fragrance of patchouli oil that infused the audio cassette cover of her 1989 album *Like a Prayer*. Given the themes of family, guilt, sexuality, and eroticism that she explores on that record, I imagine that the addition of patchouli was intended to simulate the sensory experience of a church service or the larger Roman Catholic culture, so vital to her as an artist of Italian descent. Having been raised in the Serbian Orthodox Church myself, I could certainly appreciate the magical lure of incense. But in my thirteen-year-old heart, the perfumed packaging connected me less to Madonna's well-known Catholicism and more to the new-age counterculture of the 1960s that she sometimes channeled in her work. I was especially intrigued by Madonna's tourism of hippie culture and its reverence for Mother Earth. In that moment, I saw Madonna through the lens of other pop culture icons of flower power that I had secretly admired in the 1980s—including Susanna Hoffs, lead singer of the Bangles, whose video *In Your Room* was a joyous aesthetic tour of 1960s psychedelica; and Olivia d'Abo, the British actress who played the defiant American teenager Karen Arnold in the ABC sitcom *The Wonder Years*. Both *In Your Room* and *The Wonder Years* premiered in 1988, so

I couldn't help but experience *Like a Prayer* through the prism of these colorful archetypes. But Madonna was no cliché. Appearing on the cover of her album wearing a waistcoat embroidered with flowers, while a zipper necklace studded with crystals dangled from her neck like a pagan rosary, Madonna seemed like an environmental prophetess with a whole new terrain to explore. And she did.

Madonna has always promoted herself as a "true blue" lover of love, to quote her 1986 album title. But does her work not also speak to what we might call a "true blue" humanities, one that celebrates the individual as well as the natural landscapes that have nurtured her growth and self-reflection over her multiple decades as a successful recording artist and especially as a visual storyteller? And in an age when the environment as such has shifted in the cultural imaginary from a source of wonder and inspiration, on the one hand, to an object of terrifying concern, on the other, would it not be wise and worthwhile to start thinking of Madonna as not just a fantasist but an ecofantasist? In this essay, I want to highlight Madonna's often-overlooked and ecologically inspired music videos, which have always percolated with a fantasy element that reveals the artist's growing interest in creaturely and elemental forms of life and vitality. I also want to highlight Madonna's own trajectory from a popular artist with a deep and abiding interest in the enchanting alterity of the environmental domain to an environmental activist of sorts whose fantasy worlds and speculative visions are much more attentive than ever before to environmental disaster and planetary degradation.

Fantasy, Fantastika, and EcoFantastika

Is fantasy literature, by its very nature, ecologically oriented? That is the guiding question that inspires American science fiction author Ursula K. Le Guin's definition of fantasy, which she understands in relation to the antithetical influences of realism: "What fantasy generally does that the realistic novel generally cannot do is include the nonhuman as essential. . . . To include an animal as a protagonist equal with the human is—in modern terms—to write a fantasy" (87). Le Guin goes on to suggest that America's great work of nineteenth-century realism, Herman Melville's philosophical novel *Moby-Dick; or, The Whale* (1851), actually includes a strong "fantasy element," represented by the physical and conceptual largesse of the whale, and invites further scrutiny about fantasy and its place in American (and global) literature (87). Le Guin's characterization is notable because, as Mariah Larsson reminds us, fantasy can also produce a powerful "ecocentric" awareness of the nonhuman realm and the obscenity of "anthropocentric" narratives that we so often project onto it (128).

But such ecocentric awareness is not exclusive to fantasy or the realist narratives with a "fantasy element." It also extends to other speculative modes and genres of storytelling that fall under the general category of Fantastika, a neologism first coined by American literary critic John Clute. Fantastika—which groups together fantasy literature with science fiction and even horror—opens readers onto landscapes in crisis, horizons that strip us of our epistemological certainty and undermine, or muddy, or reject outright the things we know about ourselves and the world around us. American fantasy author Paul Di Filippo applauds Fantastika for this very reason. In the preface of his 2018 short story collection *Infinite Fantastika* Di Filippo argues that this storytelling tradition "[encompasses] . . . all the counterfactual, impossible, heretofore-unknown, magical, as-yet-unrealized scenarios stretching from before the Big Bang to beyond the Heat Death of the universe" (x).

In his theorization, John Clute relies on an important distinction between the *world* we believe to have conquered and the *planet* we inhabit and share with other creaturely and nonhuman forms and forces. The world, according to Clute, is a modern theoretical construction, carefully curated through four centuries of intellectual and scholarly rigor. It is an expression of "Apollonian . . . beauty of the intensely described, a beauty achieved through refusal and exclusion and measure and argument" (21). In his sense of world, the figure of the autonomous and rational human subject establishes authorial dominion and drives the larger cultural project of Western Enlightenment. The planet, by contrast, cuts the disproportionately influential figure of the human being down to size. It renders the individual subject as one of many different types of creaturely and elemental life that share and cocreate our various terrains. The planet reasserts its forgotten power over us by reminding us, via speculative visions of past and future, that we are "a species clinging to a ball that may one day spin us off" (23–24). In this way, Fantastika retains a timely and urgent connection to contemporary anxieties about climate change, global warming, pollution, and the loss of biodiversity, all of which mark the appearance of what Nobel Prize winners Paul J. Crutzen and Eugene F. Stoermer refer to as the Anthropocene epoch, an immanent phase in our geological development marked by the unprecedented impact of collective human activity and industrial development on planetary ecosystems and processes.

The line between fantasy and Fantastika is obviously a fine one. In fact, the speculative modes of literary representation, as Le Guin and Clute discuss them, often bring stories about the ordered, anthropocentric world into uncomfortable proximity with narratives about the more volatile planetary domain, creating a larger corpus of work that I want to call ecoFantastika. I offer this term for two reasons. First, the prefix eco-, which derives from the Greek root word *oikos* and evokes the etymological image of a house or household, brings together a wide range of speculative narratives for us to consider—from the subtleties of the nonhuman "fantasy element" that Le Guin traces in realism and other mimetic traditions, to the planetary spectacles of crisis and cataclysm that Clute traces in Fantastika. And second, the term "ecoFantastika" calls attention to a more widespread cultural anxiety about humanity's relationship to the nonhuman Other, an anxiety that ignites and implicates different modes and mediums of storytelling, including visual and audiovisual narrative.

This second point is particularly important when we look at one of the more surprising and enduring popular artists to popularize ecofantastika as a form of mass entertainment, Italian American pop star and music video artist Madonna. Over the last four decades, the singer, in collaboration with other artists, producers, directors, and stylists, has released collaboratively authored video clips that reveal her as a curator and purveyor not only of erotic fantasies—like those featured in her infamous *Sex* book, photographed by Steven Meisel and published in 1992, and accompanied by seemingly handwritten erotic stories inspired by the fiction of French writer Anaïs Nin and crafted in the voice of a fictional narrator of her own invention, named Dita Parlo—but also of ecofantasies, both seductive and alarming. In earlier iterations of her Ecofantastika, Madonna projects images of an eroticized world that allows her to engage and explore public perceptions of her own identity as a rising star and proud representative of Italian American culture in the so-called MTV age of the 1980s. After the year 2000, however, Madonna's Ecofantastika, which continues to draw upon those themes, refracts the hallmarks of her brand through a more environmentally conscious sensibility, one that pits her notion of world, of *her* world, against the notion of planet, of *our* planet. In the remainder of this essay, I argue that the Madonna of the 1980s, and indeed the Madonna of today, forge speculative visual narratives that bring together these conceptions of world and planet. In so doing, Madonna is able to raise questions about the human subject's variable presence within and impact upon these domains. To this end, I offer close readings of two groupings of Madonna's most important eco-fantastic music videos—*Burning Up*, *Like a Virgin*, and *Cherish* from the 1980s, which articulate Madonna's sense of world and its engagements with various types of nonhuman otherness; and *Love Profusion*, *Get Together*, and *4 Minutes*, which explore notions of chaotic elemental planetarity.[1] These music videos establish Madonna as an important figure of Italian American ecoFantastika, one who exercises her humanism, and especially her erotic humanism, at the very borders of the human.

Reimagining Madonna's Material World

Madonna is an important figure of what I call erotic humanism, by which I mean two things. First, Madonna's creative work chronicles shared human experiences about love, affection, and desire. In centering and eroticizing the figure of the beloved, and reflecting the diversity of romantic entanglements in the world she chronicles in her work, Madonna broadens the concept of the erotic altogether to include compassion, empathy, trust, and respect. Second, Madonna's artistic offerings emanate from her own fantasies and experiences, even if her stories are not strictly autobiographical. Madonna stressed this second point during a panel discussion with American visual artist Marilyn Minter at the Brooklyn Museum in 2017. In that conversation, Madonna described her work as a form of humanist self-portraiture that records all her pain and joy, much like the magical realist portraits of Mexican painter Frida Kahlo whom she has frequently cited as a creative muse.

Scholars have frequently noted Madonna's interest in fantasy as a vehicle for such concerns relating to her erotic humanism. John Fiske, for instance, retains the importance of fantasy in his sociological analyses of Madonna's music videos and their impact on the young "wannabe" fans who emulate her looks and movements. Marking the rise of what has come to be known informally in academia as Madonna studies, Fiske writes that Madonna "offers her fans access to semiotic and social power . . . through fantasy" (257). Camille Paglia also highlights the power of fantasy by lauding the star's work in the 1980s for its unapologetic eroticism and its reimagining of different archetypes of female sexuality. She celebrates

Madonna's *Open Your Heart* (1987, directed by Jean-Baptiste Mondino), in particular, for its recreation of the "risqué peep-show format" and the capacity of such a reinvented format to offer audiences a "brilliant mimed psychodrama of the interconnections between art and pornography, love and lust" (10). Anthony Julian Tamburri offers close readings of Madonna's two more controversial videos, *Like a Prayer* (1989, directed by Mary Lambert) and *Justify My Love* (1990, also directed by Mondino), arguing that they form a corpus of music video narratives that offer glimpses into Madonna's larger sociological imagination. Her videos, he explains, are often preoccupied with questions of "sexuality, religion, and race . . . [which] serve as integral components of Madonna's *visione del mondo*" (56). I situate Madonna's ecoFantastika within this longer and well-documented tradition of the artist's imaginative overtures, and I discuss them in relation to her persistent interest in eroticism, sexuality, and Italian cultural identity and belonging. In this way, I am indebted to the work of more recent scholars like Charity Marsh and Melissa West, who argue in 2003 that both Madonna and Björk are important figures in contemporary electronic dance music because they "narrow the culturally constructed division between nature and technology" (182). Their work marks an important point of departure for me as I extend these environmental and technological considerations to Madonna's music videos before and after 2003 and use her ecoFantastika as another way of conceptualizing her growth across decades as an artist in the public sphere.

Madonna's music videos of the 1980s introduce a polysemic "fantasy element" that allows the artist to engage questions of erotic desire and Italianness through artful representations of a rich and magical natural world. Three videos, in particular, offer speculative visions of the artist herself as she comes into close and often meaningful contact with non-human others. In fact, the second video Madonna ever filmed, *Burning Up* (1983, directed by Steve Barron), emerges as the earliest example of the singer's interest in ecoFantastika. Despite the song's lyrical references to fire, the video turns on the symbolic power of water and uses that element in creative ways to tell the story of her own erotic self-actualization. The video defamiliarizes and eroticizes the urban space of downtown Los Angeles, flooding it with nocturnal waters that disappear and reappear. Madonna, as star, navigates these waters in ways that reflect her own material position as novice in an overtly regulated music industry. She is first cast adrift in a boat that sails along the currents underneath her. The only images of agency and movement that we see in the video are shots of her partner, played by then-boyfriend Ken Compton, who drives a marine-colored Amphicar. By video's end, however, Madonna wrangles control over the relationship and even appears behind the wheel of the car. Her aquatic fantasy is thus a fable about the female recording artist gaining control over the elemental domain, or at least learning how to maneuver herself through the matrix of its forces. As a type of ecofantasy, *Burning Up* fulfills what Jenny Price describes, in her own search for nature in Los Angeles, as a "premier source of human meaning."

Madonna's next and perhaps more memorable waterscape—*Like a Virgin* (1984, directed by Lambert), filmed on location in New York City and Venice, Italy—allows her to engage more directly the question of her Italian ancestry.[2] The video—which helped catapult Madonna to international success and gave the artist her first and, for many years, her longest-running number-one song on the official US Billboard Hot 100 singles chart—emerges as an imaginative self-portrait of a star who finds global success in New York City while also vicariously asserting her Italian cultural roots and her untroubled access to those landscapes. The opening moments of *Like a Virgin* reimagine New York City as a distant and peaceful skyline stretching along the banks of the East River, whose currents twinkle with opportunity. The video also rewrites Madonna's own Italian origins. Though her paternal family hails from the landlocked village of Pacentro in the province of L'Aquila, Madonna's Italian cultural roots are mobilized in the video through shots of the islands and canals of Venice, whose historical wealth, booming trade industry, and economic interest in other cultures and their industries derived primarily from its position on the Mediterranean Sea (Ferrero 9–10). In making this move, the video frames Madonna as one of the most glorified success stories of the MTV era, a figure whose unimpeded mobility and transnational movements will help shape public perceptions of environmental crisis in the years to come.

Madonna's erotic self-portraiture in *Like a Virgin* also features the artist holding court alongside many different images of a lion. One might make the argument that the lion is a mere instrument in the singer's vanity project, a tabula rasa upon which she projects her own idealized image as a seductress with a strong sexual appetite, or perhaps a personification of her astrological sign in the Western zodiac, which corresponds to the constellation of Leo. However, the lion is also a mythical composite with several different functions and meanings in the story. It is, first and foremost, a real animal that prowls along the perimeter of San Marco Piazza, while a longing Madonna adorned in a bridal gown and matching veil waits for her lover in the baroque hall of the Palazzo Ca' Zenobio. It is also a meaningful totem for Madonna's love interest, an aristocratic bridegroom who shifts repeatedly between animal and human states and who conceals his human face with a Venetian eye mask adorned with patches of a lion's mane. Finally, it is a powerful emblem of the city itself, whose founder, Saint Mark the Evangelist, was represented in Early Christian practice as a winged lion. Madonna's use of creatures and waterscapes as "fantasy elements" in the video allows the artist to stage in speculative terms a primal scene of her own parthenogenesis. Out of her Venetian daydream, she becomes a star of her own making.

Six years later, Madonna returns to the twin themes of elemental waters and creaturely life with the music video *Cherish* (1989, directed by Herb Ritts), the third single from her *Like a Prayer* album. The video casts Madonna as an interloper of sorts, entering a supernatural domain populated by four mythical mermen and finding a sense of shared intimacy with them. Unlike the more commonly known mermaid, whose plaintive longing for terrestrial happiness Hans Christian Andersen popularized in his Romantic fairy tale "The Little Mermaid," the magical mermen in *Cherish* form an insular and elusive community unto themselves, continually disappearing from her, and our, visual field with splashes of water. Media scholar Carol Vernallis offers a compelling reading of these images as expressions of the "central theme [of invisibility] in the gay experience" (234). These mermen, I would add, create a visible and prominent space for queer male subjectivity in a landscape that Madonna and Ritts rearrange in more elementally forward terms. Consequently, the imaginative geography of *Cherish* recalls the fond memory of Madonna's first mentor, ballet teacher Christopher Flynn, who introduced her to art and the gay subculture of metropolitan Detroit.[3] The video's self-referentiality allows Madonna to imbue her sense of world with mythic recreations of the people she lost, including Flynn, to AIDS and AIDS-related complications. In this way, the mermen represent vital life, frolicking and moving freely, and the video itself uses ecofantasy to promote more widespread and attentive forms of mourning and remembrance, particularly for the anonymous, disinherited, estranged, and unhoused victims of the AIDS crisis.

The video also invokes the images of the supernatural creature and the magical sea in ways that challenge the strict and dogmatic Catholicism of her upbringing and its heteronormative and procreative views of human sexuality. The release of "Cherish" as the third single from *Like a Prayer* is significant. Her first single release from that record, "Like a Prayer," and its accompanying video generated some of the most intense controversy of Madonna's career and provoked accusations of blasphemy. According to Marc DiPaolo, the song eroticizes her relationship with Christ amid personal crises with the other men in her life, including her father and her ex-husband Sean Penn (xlv). Consequently, Madonna counters the reactions of conservative religious critics with a blue-toned seascape where the singer is free to explore divergent and perhaps more folkloric notions of sexuality, exuberance, compassion, and remembrance.

Madonna's World Storm

In the years following the release of *Burning Up*, *Like a Virgin*, and *Cherish*, Madonna's ecoFantastika takes a more explicitly planetary turn. As she awakens to the growing concerns and cultural fears about the increasing frequency of natural disasters and the cumulative and deleterious effects of climate change and global warming, her creative work responds in kind. Her videos in the new millennium, in particular, gravitate toward a more radically speculative set of tropes and forms that displace the figure of the nonhuman Other with the increasingly urgent figure of the planetary Other, conceived in various ways as an unstable and dangerous domain. Three events, in particular, mark the appearance of this more ecocentric Madonna. The first is the star's participation in a global charitable effort known as Live Earth, a series of benefit concerts orchestrated in 2007 to raise awareness about climate change and to launch an action campaign to combat the environmental crisis. Madonna composed the theme song for the event, a ballad called "Hey You," and performed the song for the first and only time at Wembley Stadium in London. Her involvement in Live Earth hearkened back to her appearance onstage in 1985 as part of Live Aid, a global charity concert designed to combat African famine; as she took the stage, she performed "Love Makes the World Go Round," one of the songs that would appear on *True Blue* (1986). The second event, which elaborates some of the intentions of the first, was an image overhaul staged by *Vanity Fair* for its May 2008 issue, the annual green issue. Promoting the release of her most recent album *Hard Candy*, whose lead single "4 Minutes" was originally titled "4 Minutes to Save the World," Madonna appeared on the cover of the magazine wearing a skintight bodysuit designed by Dolce & Gabbana, an Italian fashion brand she patronized throughout her career, and struck a pose as a modern recreation of the mythological Titan god Atlas, who is condemned to hold the weight of the heavens on his shoulders for eternity. In the photo, taken by Steven Meisel, Madonna stands, hunched slightly toward the camera with her arms outstretched, in front of the eighty-pound polystyrene globe behind her. The image, which celebrates her physical and creative vitality at the age of fifty, also brings the myth of Madonna into more intimate contact with environmental concerns and highlights her own standing as a woman with enough power and privilege to raise such awareness. The third event was a devastating earthquake in Italy in 2009, which killed more than two hundred people in the Abruzzo region of Italy, including residents of the village of Pacentro where the star's paternal grandparents had lived until 1919 (Byrne). Her donation to relief efforts, which totaled almost half a million dollars, generated headlines in the popular press that made explicit references to the artist's genealogical connection to those Italian landscapes. Together, these historical events and their representations in popular news media structure Madonna's turn to more radically speculative stories about the volatile planet and our complicity in damaging it, even as she continued to promote her erotic humanism and celebrate her ancestral Italian roots.

Madonna's first foray into the planetary realm is the animated video clip *Love Profusion* (2004, directed by Luc Besson), whose lyrical content and initial video premise suggest a deceptively optimistic story about a woman in the first throes of love. The video enacts the singer's own shifting interest from the world to the planet by showcasing Madonna navigating a seemingly self-contained and beautifully ordered global environment. The computer-generated images of nature reveal an orbed sense of world, bordered above and below by curved aerial and oceanic horizons through which Madonna moves, quite effortlessly and rather magically, in a pair of red high heels that invite comparison to Dorothy traveling the famed yellow brick road in *The Wizard of Oz* (1939). Madonna's character defies the material and mechanical constraints of her environment, stretching and crawling across the glassy surface of ocean waves without sinking under them, and later, walking along a carpet of flowers that form a beautiful ribbon in the sky.[4] The song reproduces this sense of euphoria as she whispers a familiar refrain—"I've got you under my skin," the title of a Cole Porter song that fellow Italian crooner Frank Sinatra popularized in 1966. However, her tour of the planet is soon interspersed with shots of a more menacing urban landscape. As she walks down bustling streets, a catastrophic gale gusts in her direction, causing paper and other debris to swirl around her as the city lights flicker and the camera shakes. These visual details hearken back to the traumatized landscapes of Manhattan following the collapse of the World Trade Center.

Interestingly, both the utopic aerial and aquatic environments as well as the chaotic urban landscape of *Love Profusion* ultimately expel Madonna, who had navigated the former so joyously and weathered the latter so confidently. By video's end, a digital flutter of silver fairies envelops her, only to disband suddenly, leaving behind no visual trace of the artist. The sense of planetarity that she projects in this video raises key questions not only about Madonna's uncertain standing in an equally uncertain music industry facing the digital turn, but also about the status of humanity in general as it must now cope with environmental cataclysms capable of displacing and dispossessing the human world. The final image of the clip raises just such a fear. The video ends with a shot not of Madonna but with a computer-generated view of an abandoned stretch of sandy beach, perhaps a Mediterranean coastline like the canals and islands of *Like a Virgin*. The video captures this beautiful but empty vista from far above the earth's surface, as if to suggest that the overhead shot is a projection of divine spectatorship, a sign that God bears witness to a sixth and final mass extinction. The Madonna that emerges here cannot disengage herself fully from the Catholic beliefs and iconography that have been so central to her mythology. As Thomas J. Ferraro reminds us, Madonna's work between 1985 and 1991 reveals the singer's "radiance" in which "Italian Catholicism informs just about everything Madonna does" (153). But the video also charts new terrain, as she extends her affective relation to Italian culture and imagery to the reinvented and ambiguous landscapes of her planetary imagination.

Two years later, Madonna released a second animated music video that presents an even more volatile view of the planetary domain. The European version of *Get Together* (2006, directed by Logan Studios) features animated images and a color palette that are both inspired by the erotic illustrations of Italian comic book artist Milo Manara.[5] However, the video transforms a song about the excitement of meeting a new lover into a visual story about seismic disturbances plaguing both figure and ground.[6] The clip enhances live footage from Madonna's promotional club tour, which she created to promote her disco album *Confessions on a Dance Floor* (2005), to forge the vision of an unstable planetary horizon that moves and shifts around her. Branching trees, for instance, quickly morph into fiery splashes of lava and sink into a terrain suspended between solid and liquid states. Amorphous shapes pass across Madonna and her dancers with great speed, separating into curls or droplets and reforming once more as larger clouds and waves. Roads and ledges cut colorful streaks through the landscape in ways that resemble both microscopic nerve endings and axonal pathways and macroscopic projections of elemental landscapes seen from afar. The planetary domain shuffles unpredictably between solidity and fluidity, disintegration and aggregation, the atomized and the boundless. Although Madonna remains in partial or compromised view throughout the video, she, too, becomes part of the unstable visual architecture of this futuristic landscape. The video's final image captures Madonna in a potentially triumphant pose as she perches herself on top of a skyscraper and stares into the giant moon above. But the camera soon pulls away, and her figure disappears amid the pulsating chaos of the elements. The video illustrates the true and often disavowed power of the elemental world, as Jeffrey Jerome Cohen and Lowell Duckert describe it: "The elements circulate, spark dense and light effusion, turbulent narrative, a vorticular and disanthropocentric perspective of force as much as matter" (17). If *Love Profusion* casts a prophetic eye at the world following environmental disaster, then *Get Together* approximates the sensory experience of a singular moment within that disaster.

Perhaps Madonna's most radically unsettling example of ecoFantastika is her third animated music video, *4 Minutes* (2008, directed by Jonas Euvremer and François Rousselet), which costars Timbaland and Justin Timberlake, who cowrote and coproduced her record. The video, released four years after the 2004 earthquake and tsunami in the Indian Ocean, captures a landscape that disappears progressively under a mysterious tidal wave of darkness. This wave, however, is not an abstraction of nothingness; it appears as a cascade of interconnected black planar surfaces that spread through space like an animated Cubist painting by Pablo Picasso. This darkness washes over various scenes of urban consumption. Shoppers at the supermarket, families at the dinner table, consumers in the parking lot, and lovers in the bedroom all meet their fate when the tidal wave engulfs them. The video recalls the drama of the ancient flood narrative. But this flood is not divinely sanctioned, as the Great Deluge is in the stories of Noah and Utnapishtim. Nor is the video's diluvial disaster tied in any explicit way to the virtue of an archetypal Favored One, divinely selected to rebuild the world after the flood. In fact, the flood envelops everyone in its path—not just the apathetic consumers who are taken unaware, but also Madonna and Timberlake, figures of privileged means and unimpeded mobility who resist the enveloping tide as long as they can through artful choreography and blocking; eventually, they, too, run out of time. The flood is thus an inherent part of the landscape itself, a preprogrammed kill switch that allows the planet to collapse rather than self-correct. The final moments of the video signal this fate: Timberlake's flesh peels away from the left side of his torso, exposing a single rib in a cataclysmic recapitulation of the Judeo-Christian story of the first human beings; while the flesh over Madonna's right cheekbone, a symbolic expression of her beauty and age, metrics applied rather unfairly to female performers in the music industry, begins to disintegrate.

The world outside the music video is implicated in this crisis as well. On the one hand, Madonna's peeling face is an allegorical indictment of our collective consumption habits, which so often include a heightened sense of scrutiny. As an artist and a woman of a certain age, Madonna literally faces these challenges, which social media and on-demand streaming amplify. Released in April 2008, four months before the star would turn fifty, *4 Minutes* caught the attention of critics and fans alike who counted down the days, as if her age were some kind of signal marking an end to her reign as the Queen of Pop. On the other hand, the video literally frames Madonna as a morally ambiguous figure with an equally ambiguous position in the environmental movement. Could she have brought this disaster on herself? Our first glimpse of Madonna—pushing against a black Cadillac while moving slowly into the distance, away from the camera, away from us—is structured as an act of partially obscured spectatorship. The amorphous darkness stands between her and the camera through which we watch. This shot composition reveals two Madonnas: the first, shunning the darkness and doing everything within her power to escape it; and the second, drawing it forward, deliberately, into the world of wasteful consumerism where it can, and does, lay waste to everything and everyone, including herself. Certainly, the latter is true, in a manner of speaking, if we consider the carbon footprint incurred by the rise of multimillion-dollar music video production—a trend in which Madonna and other superstars of the 1980s are certainly implicated—since the launch of MTV in 1981. Framing herself as both ecoactivist and a contributor to the problems of wasteful consumption, *4 Minutes* relies on an ambivalent heroics that accords with Dipesh Chakrabarty's view that "we may not experience ourselves as a geological agent, but we appear to have become one at the level of the species" (221). For figures of privilege and influence like Madonna, furthermore, the planetary crisis she reimagines in her video "cannot be reduced to a story of capitalism . . . there are no lifeboats here for the rich and the privileged" (221).

Furthermore, Madonna's ambivalent presence in her own ecoFantastika becomes more prominent when we consider her work alongside the material realities of the locales she reimagined in her earlier videos. Madonna's Venice, for instance, so fondly mythologized in *Like a Virgin*, recently became the blank canvas upon which sculptor Lorenzo Quinn, son of Mexican American actor Anthony Quinn, projected his vision of an Italian landscape that has become increasingly vulnerable to the effects of climate change, including pollution and rising sea levels. Quinn's nine-meter-tall marble installation, *Support* (2017), depicts a pair of oversized hands, presumably belonging to a child and possibly referring to abject and disempowered communities that disproportionately suffer the effects of global environmental catastrophes. Quinn affixes the hands to the edifice of the Ca' Sagredo luxury hotel in Venice, near the same Rialto Bridge where Madonna famously cavorted in a gondola in *Like a Virgin*. The pose of the hands, the way they literally support the physical structure of the hotel, calls to mind the urgent necessity of collective and meaningful action, as well as our failure to orchestrate such responses or deal effectively with the fallout. In the years following the sculpture's debut, the image of children's hands emerging from the water are haunted more so than ever by media images of the growing refugee crisis, particularly in Italy. Both Madonna's video and Quinn's sculpture use elements of fantastic, the surreal, and the magically realistic in order to tell visual stories about human and planetary upheaval. Madonna's reformulations, which read as well-intentioned stories calling for change, also showcase some of the systemic problems that contribute to such environmental distress in the first place.

Four Minutes to Save the Planet?

EcoFantastika circulates stories as well as images that proliferate within the public sphere and structure our collective fantasies about our actions, histories, and place in the world. These texts visualize and reimagine tensions that are already beginning to appear between the human world, on the one hand, and the elemental and creaturely forms and forces and planetary horizons that continue to degrade or resist our attempts at mastery. Madonna emerges in this tradition as an unlikely but extremely sympathetic and illuminating figure. Although her videos chart her various interests in anthropocentric concepts like sexuality, erotic desire, and Italian cultural identity and belonging, her explorations of selfhood are rarely the narcissistic vanity projects that detractors and critics may describe. Motivated by different humanist and posthumanist concerns in different phases of her career, Madonna opens herself to the otherness of speculative storytelling—and the radical otherness of planetary crisis, as we see in her most recent work—in order to make room for the world and the planet in her own self-portraiture. Her work reveals, among other things, a form of self-portraiture that is both optimistic in its commitments to erotic humanism and Italian pride, and simultaneously cautious and critical of the traditions, institutions, practices, and ways of thinking that have fueled the rise of the Anthropocene and Anthropocene-related anxieties. If we can speak of Madonna as an ecofantasist whose work moves us from the sugary love songs on her 1986 album *True Blue* to a "true blue" humanist inspired by growing concerns about our planetary health and future, then we can give truth to the closing statement on that same album: love makes the world go round.

Notes

1. For the sake of clarity, I will italicize all titles of music videos and place in quotation marks the names of the songs they promote.

2. It is worth noting here that Madonna actually belongs to two different diasporas, possibly three. She is the daughter of Silvio Ciccone, the son of Italian immigrants, and of Madonna Fortin, whose ancestors migrated from France to Québec in 1650 and to Michigan two centuries later. It is her Italian ancestry, however, that becomes a recurring theme in many of her music videos, particularly *Papa Don't Preach* (1986, directed by James Foley). Viewers will remember the famous slow-motion sequence featuring Madonna in Tappen Park in Staten Island, wearing her famous black t-shirt bearing the artist's presumed statement of Italian pride, "Italians Do It Better." The video, a fictional melodrama about an unwed mother-to-be played by Madonna herself, structures the singer's fantasies of reconnection to her Italian heritage by setting the story within the context of a strict Italian Catholic family headed by Madonna's on-screen father, played by Italian American film actor Danny Aiello. The video is also shot on location in various Italian neighborhoods in Staten Island, from Bay Street to Richmond Terrace, thus reinforcing the historically significant image of the borough as the

adopted home of "the largest percentage of Italian Americans in any congressional district in the country," as James Molinaro once described it. For Molinaro's full statement, see Mele (7).

3. See Gus Van Sant's interview with Madonna about her first directorial project, the feature-length film *Filth and Wisdom*, which features a character, a blind professor played by British actor Richard E. Grant, inspired by Flynn (Madonna).

4. Madonna's invocation of a rationalized global space challenges the cosmic mysticism she embraces in a similar video, *Ray of Light* (1998, directed by Jonas Åkerlund), which compresses the global events of a single day and the frenetic activities of urban and rural spaces into the modest time span of four minutes. The video positions Madonna alongside many other figures and actions that fill the tapestry of human life over the course of a day, suggesting that her influence or importance is no greater or lesser than anyone or anything else.

5. In 2020, Manara created a lithograph, *Femme de Vitruve, Hommage Léonard de Vinci*, that transforms the main subject of Leonardo da Vinci's *Vitruvian Man* into a nude woman. Her wavy hair emulates Madonna's famous coiffure on the cover of the green issue of *Vanity Fair*.

6. I describe *Get Together* as a visual narrative about Anthropocene violence. However, the video also embraces aspects of the art video genre, which Diane Railton and Paul Watson describe as a genre that "appeals to notions of art and aesthetics" (51) and that "works as an aesthetic complement to the song or vies with it for artistic consideration" (52).

Works Cited

Byrne, Fiona. "Madonna Donates 'Substantial Sum' to Earthquake Victims." *NME*, 8 Apr. 2009. https://www.nme.com/news/music/madonna-259-1315070.

Chakrabarty, Dipesh. "The Climate of History: Four Theses." *Critical Inquiry*, vol. 35, Winter 2009, pp. 197–222.

Clute, John. *Pardon This Intrusion: Fantastika in the World Storm*. Beccon, 2011.

Cohen, Jeffrey Jerome, and Lowell Duckert. "Introduction: Eleven Principles of the Elements." *Elemental Ecocriticism: Thinking with Earth, Air, Water, and Fire*, edited by Jeffrey Jerome Cohen and Lowell Duckert, U of Minnesota P, 2015, pp. 1–17.

Crutzen, Paul J., and Eugene F. Stoermer. "The Anthropocene." *IGBP [International Geosphere-Biosphere Programme] Newsletter*, vol. 41, 2000, p. 17.

Di Filippo, Paul. *Infinite Fantastika*. WordFire Press, 2018.

DiPaolo, Marc. "Introduction: Meeting Madonna and C. S. Lewis Again, for the First Time." *Unruly Catholics from Dante to Madonna: Faith, Heresy, and Politics in Cultural Studies*, edited by Marc DiPaolo, Scarecrow Press, 2013, pp. xxvii–lii.

Ferrero, Joanne M. *Venice: History of the Floating City*. Cambridge UP, 2016.

Ferraro, Thomas J. *Feeling Italian: The Art of Ethnicity in America*. New York UP, 2005.

Fiske, John. "Madonna." *Reception Study from Literary Theory to Cultural Studies*, edited by James L. Machor and Philip Goldstein, Routledge, 2001, pp. 246–58.

Ilari, Alessandra. "Madonna: Great Material." *W*, 31 Jan. 2010. https://www.wmagazine.com/story/madonna-dolce-gabbana.

Larsson, Mariah. "Bringing Dragons Back into the World: Dismantling the Anthropocene in Robin Hobb's The Realm of the Elderlings." *The Enduring Fantastic: Essays on Imagination and Western Culture*, edited by Anna Höglund and Cecilia Trenter, McFarland, 2021, pp. 124–39.

Le Guin, Ursula K. "The Critics, the Monsters, and the Fantasists." *Wordsworth Circle*, vol. 38, no. 1–2, 2007, pp. 83–87.

Madonna. "Madonna." Interview by Gus Van Sant. *Interview*, 3 May 3 2010. https://www.interviewmagazine.com/music/madonna. Accessed 8 Feb. 2023.

Marsh, Charity, and Melissa West. "The Nature/Technology Binary Opposition Dismantled in the Music of Madonna and Björk." *Music and Technoculture*, edited by Ren Lysloff and Leslie C. Gay Jr., Wesleyan UP, 2003, pp. 182–203.

Mele, Andrew Paul. *Images of America: Italian Staten Island*. Arcadia, 2010.

Paglia, Camille. *Sex, Art, and American Culture*. Vintage, 1992.

Price, Jenny. "Thirteen Ways of Seeing Nature in LA: Part I." *The Believer*, 1 Apr. 1 2006. https://www.thebeliever.net/thirteen-ways-of-seeing-nature-in-la/.

Railton, Diane, and Paul Watson. *Music Video and the Politics of Representation*. Edinburgh UP, 2011.

Tamburri, Anthony Julian. *Italian/American Short Films and Music Videos: A Semiotic Reading*. Digital-I Books, 2002.

Vernallis, Carol. Experiencing Music Video: Aesthetics and Cultural Context. Columbia UP, 2004.

11

Guillermo del Toro's *Pinocchio*

Reconceptualizing Italia, Italian Americans, and Fantastika Through a Wooden Boy's Questions

DANEL OLSON

It is easy to forget that Pinocchio is one of Fantastika's most enduring Outsiders, an immigrant who never becomes native. The famous wooden boy—this *burattino*—is scorned and exploited because he is an alien among us. A stranger in a strange land without resources, Pinocchio has little to declare but his unguarded reactions and impulses. Not human until the very end of Carlo Collodi's book, Pinocchio never becomes a real boy in Guillermo del Toro's *Pinocchio* (2022), a stop-motion, cinematic reimagining from North American creators, inspired by del Toro's discovery of acclaimed illustrator Gris Grimly's iconic drawings of the magic puppet. Despite his lack of acceptance, little Pinocchio will help anybody else in need, just as is his wont to pepper the powerful and privileged with questions, many of which are unanswerable. Pinocchio can be hoodwinked and hornswoggled, and even hanged and left for dead in the original book, but this only comes from his efforts to help those he loves. In his openness is a purity of heart. Del Toro's Pinocchio does not transform to human, but his words and behavior teach us what it is to be humane in a time when protections of the vulnerable are at their lowest. Pinocchio's questioning and compassion are set in fascist Italy, but the movie released in America between one MAGA term and another. The ACLU, *The New York Times*, *The Washington Post*, Human Rights Watch, occasional US Justice Department reports, and even conservative outlets like *The Wall Street Journal* detailed the institutional intimidation, bullying, and cruelty (through presidential executive orders, new restrictive laws from Congress, Supreme Court rulings, unlawful deportation and inhumane detention, and overzealous actions by ICE and US Customs and Border Protection agents). The human rights abuses, sometimes addressed by Guillermo del Toro himself on X, were especially directed against immigrants, women, children, and "outsiders" of all kinds in the USA.

Long before del Toro, of course, countless readers of Collodi's book and viewers of other *Pinocchio* film adaptations found themselves drawn to the little wooden boy's soulfulness. When Pinocchio expresses joy, despite his feelings of alienation and frequent hunger pangs (a constant refrain in Collodi's work that suggests how dire life was for average Italians in the nineteenth century), Pinocchio becomes a Wordsworthian "Father of the Man," able to lift the rest of us again. As Italian Americans, we who are descendants of those who left their native countries because of persecution or poverty may feel a kinship to Pinocchio because our ancestors, too, were striving to achieve a better life. Like Pinocchio, our ancestors were sometimes rebuffed, denigrated, objectified, targeted, manipulated, and denied. In the words of Emma Lazarus's famous Petrarchan sonnet on the Statue of Liberty, the Italian immigrants were "tired" as well as "poor, homeless, tempest-tossed." Unfortunately, those of us who have forgotten how much previous generations of Italian immigrants suffered are less likely to see in Pinocchio a moral exemplar whose guileless, expansive heart and limitless capacity for empathy are worth emulating today.

As hard to believe as it is, there were only 853 people of Italian descent in 1850 living in New York City (Cannistraro and Meyer). Twenty years later, that number of Italians had only grown in the Empire City by 1,947 more. Philip V. Cannistraro and Gerald Meyer point out a striking fact that many may have forgotten: "among all the new immigrant nationalities, the Italians had the most difficult adjustment. Their occupational and social patterns were the least adaptable to their new environment; and, unlike the Jews, for example, they had no sizable group of previously arrived compatriots to provide services and advocate for them. The Italian immigrants received the least hospitality and experienced the most insistent and pervasive hostility." It is also a fact that "American [immigration] officials accepted notions of southern Italian racial inferiority that had been propagated by anthropologists in Italy itself. Consequently, Italians were frequently not thought of as 'white'" (Cannistraro and Meyer 6). Most of the Italians arriving to American shores were from the impoverished Mezzogiorno, or Southern Italy, who had faced high child mortality in their families, hunger, limited chances for education, and few opportunities to afford land to farm or a shop to make crafts. The second largest group hailed from Veneto, which may come as a surprise to moderns when we consider its wealthy cities of Verona, Padua, Vicenza, and Venice (Hooper 8–10).

The Italian American story could be an inspiring saga to anyone. It certainly is to me, as I have an ancestor from Sardinia. Italian Americans asked for fairness and what America had vowed belonged to all in its founding documents. Resistance to domination by hegemonic power has a greater efficacy when marginalized groups and immigrants band together as a force multiplier, and Italian Americans showed skill at uniting to ask for respect and push for reforms. A key blessing of the nineteenth- and twentieth-century Italian immigrants to America was their Pinocchio-like drive to get answers to questions, their push for change, and their demand for a reason why things were as they were. Many of them left Italy because of dire poverty and all the factors that follow (poor nutrition, susceptibility to disease, abuse by the wealthy and the criminal elements). They were often land-poor peasants (Contadini) and craftspeople (Artigiani), or those who worked with "ceramics and terracotta, hide and leather, metal, wood, marble and stone works, fabrics, lace and embroidery, glass and mosaics" (Cordovani). They became the Italian Americans who would face so many disadvantages in the New World yet would also heroically fight against ossified power structures, expose the suffering, and storm for change and a more egalitarian state. This existence of an impulse by Italian Americans to awaken the country and reform it may surprise some of our students today, but as Marcella Bencivenni convincingly reminds us, "despite their present conservative image, Italian Americans have a vibrant and rich radical past" ("Review"). We can consider, for instance, keen Italian American efforts at leading and participating in labor movements and stop-work actions. Consider, Bencivenni notes, "the Lawrence textile strikes of 1912 and 1919, the Paterson Silk Strike of 1913, the Mesabi Iron Range strikes of 1907 and 1916, and the New York City Harbor strikes of 1907 and 1919, as well as coal mining strikes. They also made important contributions to American labor unions, especially the revolutionary Industrial Workers of the World, the International Ladies'

Garment Workers' Union, and the Amalgamated Clothing Workers of America" ("Review"). Bencivenni adds that Italian immigrants and their sons and daughters, on the cultural front, were creating and preserving an alternate culture from the hegemonic one, "their own political and social clubs, mutual aid societies, alternative libraries and press, as well as their own orchestras and theaters" ("Review").

Food and drink, fashion and music, dance and sex symbols, movies and comic books, art design and automobiles, religion and government, trials and legal victories, literature and colloquial language itself—can we think of one area of American life not shaped by the seductive energy of Italian Americans? I write of the five million Italians (Cannistraro and Meyer) who came to America in the nineteenth and early twentieth centuries. The Emigrazione Italiana waned during World War I and was restricted with the Immigration Act of 1924, when people from Germany, the UK, and Ireland instead were given 70 percent of available visas (Zapata et al.). I also write of the six hundred thousand Italians who have since 1945 become citizens of the US, and their descendants (Cannistraro and Meyer). Their presence in American culture is so deep it is immeasurable. To imagine what American culture would look, sound, and feel like without them and their legacy is mind-boggling. To imagine American film (live-action or animation) without Italian stories is also impossible. Yet Italian Americans have not merely given the US epic changes. They have questioned—with Pinocchioesque drive and insistence—things as they are, and why they are. In this spirit and on this path, Italian immigrants have carried with them to our shores their world-famous little friend, their darling *ragazzo* filled with questions. He is a character instantly identifiable (even if you have never read his whole story, as annotated by a cricket dandy) as any in the pantheon of iconic, needed Outsiders from other countries.

Pinocchio was created by Carlo Lorenzini, who renamed himself Carlo Collodi after his mother's village (which today is forty-five minutes from Florence by car). The Pinocchio stories appeared between 1881 and 1882 in one of the first weekly Italian magazines for children, *Giornale per I bambini*. These picaresque adventures were collected into novel form in 1883. Notably, Collodi wrote *Pinocchio* less than two decades after Italy united under one kingdom. Many of Collodi's adult contemporaries would recognize in the Pinocchio stories what their children were not politically aware enough to; Collodi used allegory and political satire to mock luminaries from the social and political map of the newly forged Kingdom of

Figure 11.1. Pinocchio's anti-fascist musical he composes all by himself. Il Duce stars as "Baby-poops-his-pants!" *Source:* Del Toro, Guillermo, dir. *Guillermo del Toro's Pinocchio*, 2022; New York: The Criterion Collection, 2023. Blu-ray Disc, 4K UHD.

Italy. Today some of Collodi's intended targets, high and low, may be as lost to most readers as the real-life personages satirized by Jonathan Swift in *Gulliver's Travels* or by L. Frank Baum in *The Wonderful Wizard of Oz*.

It is true that Collodi's masterpiece is so frenetic that few films capture the boy's frantic spirit, but del Toro and his editing team come close, using lots of jump cuts featuring our tiny hero in action. Pinocchio wants to join and taste everything in equal measure, as excited at the mention of church as hot chocolate and treating them with the same wide-eyed wonder and delight. "For him, the world is entirely fresh, and every moment is an adventure," says the director who loves him (del Toro, "Introduction"). In fact, during a thirty-minute one-on-one chat my wife and I had with co-screenwriter Patrick McHale during the afterparty following the American premiere of this film at Hollywood's Grauman's Chinese Theater, I mentioned I loved it foremost for a personal reason: Pinocchio reminded me of my oldest daughter, Emily, at around five years old. The way Pinocchio sashayed about so carefree. How Pinocchio talks to everything—even if inanimate—reminded me of how my daughter would converse with flowers, and wave goodbye gently to them on taking her leave. Pinocchio's method is asking about everything, everywhere, and all at once. To my delight, McHale said he felt the same. He was writing the script with del Toro when his son was about the same age as the puppet and was influenced by his son's mannerisms. His son's joy, excitement, and endless questions were funneled into the film script. My daughter and his son: our children prove that not all Pinocchios we meet in this life are made of wood.

Without an awareness of the satirical dimensions of the novel, modern readers might fall into the trap of viewing Pinocchio solely as being a mouthy liar whose nose grows when he tells falsehoods. But the iconic image of the growing nose is merely the superficial hook—the moralistic lure that draws parents to impart Pinocchio's tales to children as a didactic corrective for children's tendency to become fabulists. The more vital and profound part of this grainy lad's nature is that he is constantly asking dangerous questions of the powerful and making dangerously guileless observations about society. Like the child hero of "The Emperor's New Clothes," Pinocchio cannot be shaken into doubting the proof of his own eyes no matter what the self-protecting adults say to him. Pinocchio is

Figure 11.2. The author and his wife with *Guillermo del Toro's Pinocchio* co-screenwriter Patrick McHale (*center*) at the American premiere afterparty. *Source:* Courtesy of the author.

a consummately kind interrogator, but he will exhaust you. He asks so many deceptively simple-sounding questions that reveal themselves as unexpectedly profound that the very listeners most convinced that they had all of life's answers at their fingertips do not know quite what to say in response. Pinocchio's ability to silence, dumbfound, and distract the ostensibly stronger is his strength. Once his spindly legs take him to the cobblestone streets of his village, Pinocchio shows no special love of age or rank. He will question anybody in del Toro's film, from parents to priests to shady employers to podesta to Il Duce. Pinocchio is a poker, jabbing holes into others' power-dykes. (He *is* made of sticks, after all.) Pinocchio's targets go as high as Mussolini and Death herself, and all have been exhausted by this little boy. Their reactions, which are as extreme as wanting him burned to death, shot, tossed off a cliff to sea, or eaten, speak volumes to their frustration.

It is not entirely the wooden boy's fault if some of these new people are unaccepting of him, as when the solemn priest and narrow-minded parishioners insult his maker in del Toro's film, screaming at Pinocchio that he's a demon, and casting him out on his first visit to the Roman Catholic church of the village. Still, forgiving Pinocchio will return to that same church to help his father repair its bomb-damaged crucifix, a

Figure 11.3. Benito Mussolini, aghast: "These puppets, I do not like. Shoot him!" *Source:* Del Toro, Guillermo, dir. *Guillermo del Toro's Pinocchio*. 2022; New York: The Criterion Collection, 2023. Blu-ray Disc, 4K UHD.

more soulful and giving boy than any of that lot turning up to church the Sunday before.

While many villains threaten and abuse del Toro's Pinocchio, none cause him more pain than his own maker. Geppetto expresses three sentiments to his creation that amount to a betrayal of the little boy: 1) I am not your father, 2) you are a burden, and 3) why can't you be like my lost son Carlo? It is difficult to forgive Geppetto for saying these things because Pinocchio is a fundamentally lovable boy, as well as a fantastical wonder who the Sprite of Life quickened with animation. We can also feel the pain reflected in Pinocchio's eyes in a motif that recurs in many of del Toro's films—the wounded, soulful eyes of a child rejected by its parents. Later in the film, Geppetto repents his treatment of Pinocchio. Some viewers may feel and share in Geppetto's guilt as much as they feel Pinocchio's pain, since many have shunned someone they loved and have been shunned by those they love. Some viewers may feel and share in Geppetto's guilt as much as they feel Pinocchio's pain, since many have shunned someone they loved and have been shunned by those they love. Significantly, Pinocchio's response to this shunning is the classic immigrants' response. Like them, Pinocchio goes far away, makes money, and sends that income back to his family. In a similar way, the lonely puppet boy will show that he was not such a burden after all by becoming a performer.

In a documentary on the making of *Pinocchio*, del Toro muses: "Most of my movies, one way or another, deal with me and my father." In his films, del Toro creates resonance by looking at lonely failures and how they wrestle with a sense of worthlessness. Viewers can see reflected in the eyes of his protagonists a haunted fear of the father figure. During the most physically and emotionally violent moments in his films, the eyes of the child reflect a lifetime of trauma, defeat, loss, and humiliation.

At his first twitching to life, we observe the wooden boy is sloppily fashioned on one side of his head and has just one ear. The reason? His maker was drunk at the time of woodcarving. Such physical imperfections somehow make Pinocchio a more perfect character to study and to gauge others' reactions. Bland handsomeness dulls us, but this knotty, naughty lad enthralls.

Pinocchio's questioning nature leads him into contact with Italy's religious-economic-political-judicial-legal strata. In del Toro's version, the pine boy contends with 1) the caviling village priest who morally caves in, 2) the crooked traveling-capitalist showman Volpe who hoards Pinocchio's earnings once promised to Geppetto, and 3) Il Duce himself, of Trumpian

Figure 11.4. Rome's Palazzo Venezia balcony where Mussolini gave speeches, including his proclamation of the Italian Colonial Empire (1936) and Italy's declaration of war on France and Britain (1940). On May 8, 1938, Adolf Hitler stood by Il Duce's side here, as Mussolini promised Italia's golden future. Seven years later, with Rome in ruins from both Axis and Allied bombings, American tanks rolled past the same balcony. *Source:* Courtesy of the author.

ego, who Pinocchio calls not "Benito Mussolini" but the most crapulous epithet a six-year-old can throw: "Baby-poops-his-pants!" The insult is heard, the Dictator gives the order, and the bodyguard promptly points and shoots his pistol, felling the boy, prompting wonderstruck Pinocchio to exclaim in the anteroom of Limbo: "I cannot die!" That exclamation leads us to the movie's metaphysics: What becomes of the philosophical nature of Pinocchio when he encounters Roman Catholicism?

What might strike readers of Collodi's short masterwork as an odd and conspicuous absence is that neither Church nor priest nor Pontiff nor Bible nor Ten Commandments are illustrated or mentioned in the original book. The lone religious reference in most editions is to the Franciscan Saint Anthony of Padua, patron saint of travelers and of lost and stolen articles (and Pinocchio is all of the above). Saint Anthony is also the patron saint of sailors and fishermen (who Pinocchio and Geppetto travel with), priests (who Pinocchio and Geppetto are alternatively employed and scorned by), and the poor (a demographic that again includes both the wooden puppet and his creator).

In taking hold of this classic Italian tale and making it his own, Mexican director Guillermo del Toro brings out of the story some of the very elements most calculated to help remind Italian viewers of Roman Catholic influences (for his part, the Catholic heritage is triple-concentrated in del Toro, coming from his Irish, Spanish, and Mexican roots). The anti-fascist filmmaker whose *Pinocchio* wins the 2023 Oscar for Best Animated Feature enriches his film with two obsessions that have a key role to play in both Mediterranean and Mexican culture: the Church and Death.

Del Toro's film opens with the bombing of a church that results in the loss of its roof, the arm of its wooden crucifix Jesus, and the flesh-and-blood son of Geppetto. Little Carlo dies in an explosion when WWI

Figure 11.5. Guillermo del Toro and one of thousands of handmade Pinocchio puppets coming alive in the stop-motion film that won the Best Animated Feature Oscar. *Source:* Del Toro, Guillermo, dir. *Guillermo del Toro's Pinocchio*. 2022; New York: The Criterion Collection, 2023. Blu-ray Disc, 4K UHD.

Italian biplanes return to base and drop bombs only to lighten their load before landing. Understandably, Pinocchio would later become transfixed by the sight of the broken crucifix, and by tales of Geppetto's lost son. In one of the most moving moments of the film, Pinocchio points to the massive, hanging crucifix that he and Geppetto are working to repair: "*Him*. They were all singing to him. He's made of wood too . . . Why do they like him and not me?" This mystery is not easily explained. A stammering Geppetto must change the subject because he cannot plumb all the reasons for instinctive human hatred and clannish rejection: "Come here, Pinocchio. People are sometimes afraid of things they don't know—but they'll get to know you—and like you. And—and for that . . . Are you ready for school?" (del Toro and McHale 42).

More than anything (except paternal rejection), Pinocchio is pained and confused by prejudice and injustice. Del Toro, who has consistently expressed empathy for the poor and outrage at the injustices committed by the powerful, shares in Pinocchio's perspective. On that critical level, del Toro seems to understand the enduring moral of Collodi's work far better than many modern-day Italians and Italian Americans seem to. Why don't we understand the message of our family's Coming-to-America story anymore? Why do we need a film adaptation helmed by del Toro to remind us what Pinocchio stands for?

Considering this often hostile and denigrating reception from the New World to Italians, these first-generation Italian Americans pushed back with impressive and understandable zeal against social, political, and economic limits placed on them in America. Indeed, many first-generation Italian American activists advocated for economic, political, social, ethnic, and racial equality for all Americans, helping move America forward to a more progressive future. These efforts stand in sharp contrast with the political activism of many of the most publicly recognizable Italian Americans of today, who have taken sharply conservative turns working in realms of government, the judiciary, and law enforcement. Several socially and politically powerful second- to fourth-generation Italian Americans have lost the "Pinocchio instinct" of their forebears and do not act, as the little wooden boy has always acted, to afflict the comfortable and comfort the afflicted. Many of these contemporary, archconservative Italian American officials are mired in a nostalgia for an imagined golden past instead of working actively to move all Americans, Italian and non-Italian alike, toward a more equitable and inclusive future.

Admittedly, there are effective contemporary Italian American leaders championing positions of reform, labor union defenses, immigrant rights, reproductive freedom for women, and guaranteed freedoms for the LGBTQIA2S+ communities. We may point, for instance, to the epically long service of Speaker of the House Nancy Pelosi who represented San Francisco. However, the fighting days of radical Italian American politics seem to have been eclipsed by a vigorous conservative movement, a fact reflected in the titles of several brilliant studies over the last few decades, often tracing the pattern of Italian Americans' politics and the construction of "Whiteness," including *The Lost World of Italian-American Radicalism: Politics, Labor, and Culture* (Marcella Bencivenni, 2011); *Italian Immigrant Radical Culture: The Idealism of the Sovversivi in the United States, 1890–1940* (Philip V. Cannistraro and Gerald Meyer, 2003); *Are Italians White? How Race Is Made in America* (editors Jennifer Guglielmo and Salvatore Salerno, 2004); *White on Arrival: Italians, Race, Color, and Power in Chicago, 1890–1945* (Thomas A. Guglielmo, 2004); *Whiteness of a Different Color: European Immigrants and the Alchemy of Race* (Matthew Frye Jacobson, 1999); *A Great Conspiracy Against Our Race: Italian Immigrant Newspapers and the Construction of Whiteness in the Early 20th Century* (Peter G. Vellon, 2014); *Working Toward Whiteness—How America's Immigrants Became White: The Strange Journey from Ellis Island to the Suburbs* (David R. Roediger, 2005); *The White Racial Frame: Centuries of Racial Framing and Counter-Framing* (Joe R. Feagin, 2013); *White by Law: The Legal Construction of Race* (Ian F. Haney-López, 1996); *White Identity Politics* (Ashley Jardina, 2019); *Desiring Whiteness* (Kalpana Sephardi-Crooks, 2000); *The Rise and Fall of the Caucasian Race: A Political History of Racial Identity* (Bruce Baum, 2008); *The History of White People* (Nell Irvin Painter, 2010); and *Fatal Invention: How Science, Politics, and Big Business Re-create Race in the Twenty-First Century* (Dorothy Roberts, 2012).

Compounding the problem, in recent years, Americans have witnessed a steady socio-politico-judicial-cultural revanchism of territory that more liberal citizens felt was safely held in a modern age, but decidedly was not. I would make a profile of such Italian American leaders in the judiciary (the Supreme Court Justices Samuel Alito and the late Antonin Scalia); the Department of Justice (Attorney General Pam Bondi and Associate AG Rudy Giuliani); State Department and intelligence (Secretary of State and CIA Director under President Donald Trump Mike Pompeo); and immigration (Florida Governor Ron DeSantis and Sheriff of Maricopa County, Arizona, Joe Arpaio). Since these Italian Americans have detrimentally affected the body politic, I suggest that what we need most of all is for

Pinocchio to come out of retirement and start ceaselessly interrogating all of them. Pinocchio needs to ask Alito, Bondi, Arpaio, DeSantis, Giuliani, and Pompeo the same kind of difficult questions in real life that he did in del Toro's film, when he hounded that "Guardian of Morality," the martial Podesta—the fascist-appointed mayor of Pinocchio's hometown.

One of the many powers of Fantastika is that it allows odd characters, small animals, and other misfits to speak out. Like literature that permits the fool, the joker, and the castle jester to mimic and to ask hard or taboo questions of all, we might wish that a Sebastian J. Cricket or Pinocchio could speak out about unfairness they see beyond Italy, as both would dependably speak up at any sign of injustice in del Toro's movie. We need their passion to be heard when there is callousness toward people. We need their questions. We need their outcry against injustice in the real world, whenever right-wing judges and lawyers actively roll back hard-fought victories in civil and human rights, swiftly returning us to earlier, more tyrannical times.

In 1836, President Andrew Jackson appointed the first Roman Catholic judge to the United States Supreme Court: Roger B. Taney. Since then, at time of writing, we now have seven Roman Catholic judges on the Supreme Court. Five of the seven belong to a strident, politically active brand of Catholicism that ascribes traditional roles to women, holds highly conservative views of birth and contraception, and is disdainful of progressive moves to liberalize sexual mores, either within the Church or secular society. Like the Podesta, these judges may be dubbed "Guardians of Morality." During their partisan congressional confirmation hearings, these jurists assured the American people that they rule from reason, and not their heart, ideology, or religious training and views. Certainly, Justices Antonin Scalia and Samuel A. Alito said so in their congressional hearings, when nominated by Presidents Ronald Reagan (in 1982) and George W. Bush (in 2005) (Gore et al.). In his hearing, Justice Brett Kavanaugh infamously referred to *Roe v. Wade* as "settled law," before going on to reverse forty-five years of precedent in gutting the ruling in June 2022. By sending the issue of abortion back to the states, the right-wing Supreme Court has created a national environment deeply hostile to female bodily autonomy. Rather than agreeing that women's bodies should be theirs to control throughout the US as a human right, predominantly male legislators have given command of their bodies to local legislators who pass laws that conform to their own religious views, and not to the dictates of "settled law" and the United States Constitution. As of 2024, "twenty-one states ban abortion or restrict the procedure earlier in pregnancy than the standard set by *Roe v. Wade*" (McCann and Walker 2024).

The first Italian American named to the Supreme Court was Antonin Scalia. He served from 1986 up until his death by natural causes at a shooting lodge in Texas in 2016. The second Italian American justice, Samuel A. Alito Jr., took his seat on the bench in January of 2006. There are deep connections between the two men: both were proud Italian Americans who grew up in Trenton, New Jersey, the sons of schoolteacher mothers and Italian immigrant fathers (Scalia's being from Sicily, where Cosa Nostro long corrupted politics, and Alito's from Calabria, plagued since 1860 by the vicious 'Ndrangheta). Both men were valedictorians and summa cum laude graduates, developed reputations for being argumentative public debaters, and became constitutional textualists and originalists, as well as active members of the libertarian Federalist Society. Both men were devoted Roman Catholics who were dissatisfied with the civil rights legacies of the 1960s and advocated for a return to traditional moral values. They both believed that a judge's personal, religious views could inform his judicial rulings, and they put that belief into action time and again in their rulings on the Supreme Court. Scalia argued that the death penalty was not a cruel and unusual punishment, as it had been deemed in 1972, but was constitutionally allowable. On the other hand, he believed that affirmative action was unconstitutional. Moreover, Scalia, a father of the modern conservative movement, proposed that nothing in the US Constitution protected same-sex unions and a woman's right to choose whether to carry a baby to term. For his part, Alito, before arriving on the Supreme Court, cast one of the few dissents over body-integrity privacy on the Third Circuit panel, arguing in *Planned Parenthood v. Casey* for the provision that had mandated married women must inform their spouses before seeking an abortion, even if the pregnancy was not from their spouse. Later, during confirmation hearings to the Supreme Court, the ACLU spoke out against what some saw as his feudal "willingness to support government actions that abridge individual freedoms," especially in connection to expanded surveillance of Americans, indefinite imprisoning of terror suspects without charge, support of the death penalty, and advocacy of prayer in public schools (ACLU). These warnings were well founded, as Alito would eventually write in the watershed *Dobbs v. Jackson Women's Health Organization* decision that "Roe was egregiously wrong from the start" (Alito qtd. in Liptak and Kantor). Alito would deliver his first public statement about *Dobbs* in Rome, as a keynote speaker at the Religious Liberty Initiative, sponsored by the University of Notre Dame Law School. All of the preceding demonstrates that Alito and Scalia couldn't be ideologically further from the progressive Italian American activists from one hundred years earlier in American history.

Meanwhile, in what is the mother country for the ancestors of the most conservative Supreme Court Justices, a place long thought to favor patriarchy, abortion became legal in Italy in May 1978, "when Italian women were allowed to terminate a pregnancy on request during the first 90 days" (Wanrooij). Before then, abortion was considered by Book 2, Title X of the Italian Criminal Code as a "crime against the integrity and the bloodline." In 1981, two referendums a couple of days apart targeted eliminating abortion rights but were "rejected by 88.4% of Italian voters" (Wanrooij). Unbelievably, America—a country and culture once thought to be looking to the future and not bound by ancient roots and customs—has shown less resolve to be modern than Italy and has become more traditional than the Old Country.

Moving to the even rougher world of politics, the former Mayor of New York City Rudy Giuliani, the man who led the Southern District of New York in a successful 1980s RICO prosecution breaking the grip of five Italian American mob families on the Empire City, once mused, "I was a tough as a kid, a boxer. Could I have become a Wiseguy? . . . *Sure*!" (Giuliani qtd. in *Fear City*). Full of contradictions, known for towering achievements and abysmal failures, once shrewdly strategic and now uncommonly garrulous, Giuliani was characterized recently by his lawyer Joe Sibley in a press conference: "Unfortunately, my client likes to talk, a lot."

Giuliani's toiling for President Trump at the White House is akin, through the looking glass that Fantastika affords us, to Pinocchio's planting his fortune into the "Field of Miracles." To a rube like Pinocchio, the fox and the cat *seemed* a good lot to throw in his fortune, when they promised the field would pay golden dividends, but when it came time to harvest the high yield, those golden coins were all gone. Giuliani's golden coins vanished, too, and will cost more, as he not only slandered Georgia election officials but has still not been paid all the legal fees he (at this chapter's printing) is owed by his stone-cold boss at the White House. A squawk at Giuliani's fate could come from the parrot in Collodi's book who laughs repeatedly at Pinocchio looking for his four planted gold pieces—that dupe who once said, "[Suppose if I find] one hundred thousand? Oh, what I fine gentleman I shall be then! I shall have a magnificent palace, and a thousand wooden ponies, . . . and a cellar full of lollies" (Collodi 126). The parrot admits his chuckling comes "at those simpletons who are silly enough to believe all the nonsense they hear, and who are always cheated by those who are more cunning than they are" (127). Wise is the tale—for wooden boys, for Wiseguys, and for a tough boy of Flatbush who would be celebrated on the cover of *Time* in 2001 as "America's Mayor" and nullified on *Times*' cover in 2019 as the "Secretary of Offense."

Giuliani as advisor and lawyer to President Trump called into the microphone on the White House Ellipse on January 6, 2020, for "Trial by Combat." Worse words and disrespect for the rule of law—that a call to arms bests a process of calm, slow, orderly justice—are imaginable from a lawyer who obtained so many victories in the courtroom before (including against the Cosa Nostra of New York—the Families Bonano, Colombo, Gambino, Genovese, and Luchese). Indeed, Giuliani once hated how New York Mafia families would prey on new Italian immigrants to America, with loan shark schemes, protection plans, and price fixing and bid rigging. Yet years later the New York Bar Association (justifiably) would disbar Giuliani for his violent rhetoric, unethical actions, and Pinocchio-penchant for lying. Giuliani has applied since for a $500 million bankruptcy. In Collodi's *Pinocchio*, the boy lost his money, too, and was given a ruling by a Gorilla Judge and hauled off by Mastiff Guards to a debtor's prison for four months, before arguing for early release by sneakily declaring himself a "rascal," just as a rascal-pardon had been declared by the king. Perhaps a pardon from an American King will come in time for Giuliani—or for the sake of Justice, not.

Other prominent Italian Americans active in the modern MAGA movement are Attorney General Pam Bondi, who received ethics complaints from law professors and judges over firing subordinates for not siding with President Trump, and Mike Pompeo, the proudly "anti-woke" Secretary of State for the Trump administration who infamously tweeted that multiculturalism is "not who America is" and "it makes the country weaker" (qtd. in Labott). Fueled by Trump's inflammatory accusations that the Chinese were intentionally spreading the "Kung Fu Flu," anti–Asian American sentiment spiked during the COVID-19 pandemic. Exacerbating the situation, Pompeo made a speech at the Nixon Library in which he made blanket accusations of industrial espionage against Chinese students studying in institutions of higher learning in the US: "Too many of them come here to steal our intellectual property and to take this back to their country" (qtd. in Wright). Traditionally, some of our top minds in Silicon Valley have come from China. Pompeo's speech pushed them away. In fact, his Cold Warrior posturing had several tangible results, lowering the number of student visas to China allowed by the US government, decreasing the number of Chinese who wanted to come to America, and stoking "yellow peril" fears that contributed to a post-2020 spike in hate crimes committed against Chinese Americans, Chinese nationals living in America, and anyone who even appeared to be Asian.

Former presidential hopeful Governor Ron DeSantis has chosen other vulnerable populations to scapegoat. In launching his "National Faith and Family Coalition," DeSantis assailed the LGBTQIA2S+ community via an attack on Disney World's inclusive policies in Orlando. After the governor threatened tax penalties for "wokeness," the Walt Disney Corporation pulled out of a planned campus construction in Florida, costing the state an estimated two thousand jobs. DeSantis has also ordered special transports to deliver asylum seekers who had come to Florida's shores to sanctuary cities in the northern US as punishment for their merciful immigration policies. Using FEMA funds, DeSantis has also opened the spectacle of an Everglades Alligator Alcatraz without air conditioning for five thousand detained migrants. In targeting gays, drag queens, and refugees, DeSantis has embraced an Us-versus-Them worldview and a strategy of vote-getting through the demonization of all outsiders. DeSantis's nativist policies are echoes of the same kinds of draconian campaigns launched against the Italian immigrants of generations back. His use of such tactics against the vulnerable peoples of today speaks at least to his embracing of historical amnesia, if not his cynical political hypocrisy. Since DeSantis willfully forgets the lessons of history, it is also no surprise that he has taken to banning the study of America's history in public schools. He does not want new generations of Americans to learn about either America's history of human rights violations or the history of the civil rights movements that fought to make the country live up to the ideals professed in its Constitution and Declaration of Independence.

Another lightning rod in America's contemporary immigration debates is Sheriff Joe Arpaio of Arizona. In 2017, a federal court found Arpaio guilty of violating the rights of Latinos in Maricopa County. Less than a month after his conviction, Arpaio was pardoned by President Trump. According to the ACLU, "Long before the Trump Administration erected a tent city detention camp for migrant children in Texas, Arpaio had his own 'Tent City,' a brutal, outdoor holding pen that he once proudly referred to as a 'concentration camp' " (Tashman). This detention system humiliated people and denied them "basic necessities and health care. For instance, female inmates reported that officers made them sleep in their own menstrual blood and assaulted pregnant women" (Tashman). The power of the Far Right—and the sense that these abuses do not matter if they are committed against nonwhite people—can be seen in the fact that this sheriff became a Republican primary challenger candidate for US Senator from Arizona against his party rival, incumbent Republican Senator Jeff Flake. Arpaio ultimately lost to Flake, but the fact that the "ex-sheriff's horrific tactics: attacking immigrant communities, defending racial profiling, and encouraging brutality from law enforcement" (Tashman) did not bar him from running speaks to how uncaring our times have become toward immigrants. Again, the irony of Arpaio, a son of immigrants, actively tormenting immigrants is galling and horrifying.

An immigrant himself, the imaginative weaver of Fantastika narratives Guillermo del Toro knows full well that the act of immigration involves imagination by necessity. Immigrants must have faith and imagination. They must believe that life in the new land will be—all things considered—better. Knowing that their journey to a new land means risking death, and leaving behind their family, homeland, and native food, music, and language, these immigrants must make the leap of faith anyway. Their dreams and practical plans to migrate involve making fantastic plans. Immigration involves immigrants believing the impossible and making a new story for their fates. Immigration inspires immigrants to write themselves into their own stories of Fantastika. Immigrants—and the descendants of immigrants who came from another place—have traveled far, like this questing boy, Pinocchio. Even today, we should all recognize ourselves in modern-day immigrants. We should also recognize this vulnerable wooden boy, for he is, "truly, all of us" (del Toro, "Introduction").

These prominent contemporary Italian Americans surveyed here—Giuliani, DeSantis, Arpaio, Alito, Pompeo, Bondi, and Scalia—all placed themselves on pedestals of moral authority. They named themselves guardians of morality, protectors of Roman Catholicism, and champions of traditional American family values. An unforgettable film like *Guillermo del Toro's Pinocchio* asks: Who watches these watchers? Who guards these guardians of morality? Clearly, we need it to be Pinocchio who keeps his eye on these despots posing as champions of freedom.

It is the voice of Pinocchio that should come back to us now, frenetic, sincere, searching, and unafraid. When Pinocchio sees unfairness, he ignores

Figure 11.6. Take your bow, Pinocchio—the wooden boy who reminds us what it is to be human! *Source:* Del Toro, Guillermo, dir. *Guillermo del Toro's Pinocchio.* 2022; New York: The Criterion Collection, 2023. Blu-ray Disc, 4K UHD.

the fascist slogans on his village walls of "Credere, Obbedire, Cambattere" (To Believe, To Obey, To Fight). He is forever asking . . . "*Why*?"

That is a question we all need to ask, time and again, in the face of oppression.

Works Cited

ACLU. "ACLU Opposes Nomination of Judge Alito." *American Civil Liberties Union*, 9 Jan. 2006. https://web.archive.org/web/20060113023700/http://www.aclu.org/scotus/2005/23308res20060103.html#1.

Bencivenni, Marcella. *Italian Immigrant Radical Culture: The Idealism of the Sovversivi in the United States, 1890–1940.* New York UP, 2011.

———. "Review of *The Lost World of Italian-American Radicalism: Politics, Labor, and Culture.*" *Monthly Review: An Independent Socialist Magazine*, 1 Jan. 2006, https://monthlyreview.org/2006/01/01/lost-and-found-the-italian-american-radical-experience/.

Cannistraro, Philip V., and Gerald Meyer. *The Lost World of Italian-American Radicalism: Politics, Labor, and Culture.* Praeger, 2003.

Collodi [Lorenzini], Carlo. *The Adventures of Pinocchio.* 1838. Translator unascribed, illustrated with interactive elements by MinaLima [Miraphora Mina and Eduardo Lima], Harper Design, 2020.

Cordovani, Marcello. "My Private Italy: Italian Craftsmanship, a Long History of Creativity and Passion." *VitorItaly*, 31 Aug. 2020. https://vitoritalytours.com/blog/item/54-my-private-italy-italian-craftsmanship-a-long-history-of-creativity-and-passion.html.

del Toro, Guillermo. "Introduction." *The Adventures of Pinocchio*. 1838. Translator unascribed, illustrated by Gris Grimly. Tor Classics, 2022.

del Toro, Guillermo, and Patrick McHale. *Guillermo del Toro's Pinocchio Screenplay*. Deadline, 2022. https://deadline.com/2022/12/guillermo-del-toro-pinocchio-script-read-the-screenplay-1235203733/.

Fear City: New York vs. the Mafia. Directed by Sam Hobkinson, Netflix, 2020.

Gore, D'Angelo, with Robert Farley and Lori Robertson. "What Gorsuch, Kavanaugh and Barrett Said About *Roe* at Confirmation Hearings." *FactCheck.org*, 24 Jun. 2022. https://www.factcheck.org/2022/05/what-gorsuch-kavanaugh-and-barrett-said-about-roe-at-confirmation-hearings/.

Guillermo del Toro's Pinocchio. Directed by Guillermo Del Toro, Netflix, 2022.

Guillermo del Toro's Pinocchio: Handcarved Cinema (a Making-Of Documentary). Directed by Guillermo del Toro, Netflix, 2022.

Heipel, Edie. "Supreme Court Justice Alito: Faith 'Should Affect the Way You Treat People' as a Judge." *Catholic News Agency*, 28 Sept. 2022. https://www.catholicnewsagency.com/news/252414/supreme-court-justice-alito-faith-should-affect-the-way-you-treat-people-as-a-judge.

Hooper, John. *The Italians*. Penguin, 2015.

Killough, Ashley, and Ed Lavandera. "Texas Supreme Court Rules Against Pregnant Woman Seeking Abortion as She Leaves State for Procedure." *CNN*, 13 Dec. 2023. https://www.cnn.com/2023/12/11/us/texas-woman-leaves-state-abortion/index.html.

Labott, Elise. "No Amount of Swagger Can Dress Up Pompeo's Legacy." *Foreign Policy*, 21 Jan. 2021. https://foreignpolicy.com/2021/01/21/mike-pompeo-stained-legacy-secretary-of-state-political-ambitions/.

Lazarus, Emma. "The New Colossus." 1883. *Poetry Foundation*, 2022. https://www.poetryfoundation.org/poems/46550/the-new-colossus.

Liptak, Adam, and Jodi Kantor. "Behind the Scenes at the Dismantling of *Roe v. Wade*." *New York Times*, 15 Dec. 2023. https://www.nytimes.com/2023/12/15/us/supreme-court-dobbs-roe-abortion.html.

Maccarone, Eleonora. "Italian Americans and Columbus: How the Controversies May Affect Their Vote." *Nuovo Mondo*, 30 Oct. 2020. https://lavocedinewyork.com/people/nuovo-mondo/2020/10/30/italian-americans-and-columbus-how-the-controversies-may-affect-their-vote/.

McCann, Allison, and Amy Schoenfeld Walker. "Tracking Abortion Laws Across the Country." *New York Times*, 2 July 2025. https://www.nytimes.com/interactive/2024/us/abortion-laws-roe-v-wade.html.

Olson, Danel. *Guillermo del Toro's "The Devil's Backbone" & "Pan's Labyrinth": Studies in the Horror Film*. Centipede Press, 2016.

Parks, Miles. "Giuliani Is Ordered to Pay $148 Million to Georgia Election Workers He Defamed." *NPR*, 15 Dec. 2023. https://www.npr.org/2023/12/15/1219048410/giuliani-defamation-trial-money-georgia-election-workers.

Pinocchio. Directed by Roberto Benigni, Melampo Cinematografica and Cecchi Gori Group, 2002.

Pinocchio. Directed by Norman Ferguson, T. Hee, and Wilfred Jackson, Disney, 1940.

Pinocchio. Directed by Matteo Garrone, Archimede and Rai Cinema, 2019.

Pinocchio. Directed by Robert Zemeckis, Disney, 2022.

Politico. "How Antonin Scalia Changed America: 19 Top Legal Thinkers on the Justice's Legacy for the Court, the Law and the Public." *Politico Magazine*, 14 Feb. 2016. https://www.politico.com/magazine/story/2016/02/antonin-scalia-how-he-changed-america-213631/.

Savage, David G. "Supreme Court Controversy Over Alito, Thomas Free Trips Began with Justice Scalia." *Los Angeles Times*, 21 June 2023. https://www.latimes.com/politics/story/2023-06-21/justice-scalia-showed-his-colleagues-how-to-take-free-trips.

Tashman, Brian. "Arizona Voters Deserve to Know Joe Arpaio's True Record of Brutality and Abuse." *American Civil Liberties Union*, 27 June 2018. https://www.aclu.org/news/criminal-law-reform/arizona-voters-deserve-know-joe-arpaios-true-record-brutality-and-abuse.

Tosches, Nick. "Introduction." *Nightmare Alley*. 1946. NYRB Classics, 2021. https://crimereads.com/william-lindsay-greshams-nightmare-alley/.

Wanrooij, Bruno P. F. "The Italian Republic." *The Continuum Complete International Encyclopedia of Sexuality*. CCIES, 2004. https://web.archive.org/web/20120218012553/http://www.iub.edu/~kinsey/ccies/it.php#contracep.

Weiss, Debra Cassens. "Nearly 20 Years Ago, Scalia Explained Why He Didn't Consider Jet Trip a Gift." *American Bar Association*, 25 Apr. 2023. https://www.abajournal.com/news/article/nearly-20-years-ago-scalia-explained-why-he-didnt-consider-jet-trip-a-gift/.

Wright, Thomas. "Pompeo's Surreal Speech on China." Brookings Institute, 27 July 2020. https://www.brookings.edu/articles/pompeos-surreal-speech-on-china/.

Zapata, Christian, with Amanda Onion, Missy Sullivan, and Matt Mullen. "U.S. Immigration Timeline." *History*, https://www.history.com/topics/immigration/immigration-united-states-timeline#White%20People%20of%20'Good%20Character'%20Granted%20Citizenship.

12

Race and Italian/American Identity in Dorothy Bryant's *Miss Giardino* and *The Kin of Ata Are Waiting for You*

Victoria Tomasulo

> The fabrication of an Africanist persona is reflexive; an extraordinary meditation on the self; a powerful exploration of the fears and desires that reside in the writerly conscious. It is an astonishing revelation of longing, of terror, of perplexity, of shame, of magnanimity. It requires hard work *not* to see this.
>
> —Toni Morrison, *Playing in the Dark*

Born in 1930 to immigrant parents from Balangero, a factory town near Turin, Dorothy Calvetti Bryant grew up in a working-class, ethnically diverse neighborhood in the San Francisco Bay area. She taught at Contra Community College, where she was the first woman to become chair of the English Department and the first faculty member to create a black studies course, but by 1976 she had given up her university career to devote herself fully to her writing. By 2007, she had published ten novels, three volumes of essays, and four plays, yet her work might have passed into obscurity had it not been recuperated by scholars of

Italian America who were interested in how differences of class, gender, ethnicity, and region have shaped her fiction. This essay looks at Bryant's early fiction through a different lens—that of race, which is crucial for understanding the Italian/American dimension of her work. My focus is on *Miss Giardino* (1976), Bryant's most autobiographical fiction and the only one whose protagonist is identified as Italian/American, and *The Kin of Ata Are Waiting for You*, a speculative fiction that has been marketed as "part love story, part science fiction, at once Jungian myth and Utopian allegory," which Alice Walker characterized as "one of my favorite books in all the world." Originally published as *The Comforter* in 1971, it tells the story of a male writer's spiritual salvation on the imaginary island of Ata, whose racially mixed inhabitants worship dreams and find contentment in a communal lifestyle. Against critics' characterization of the novel as a fantasy of white redemption and racial harmony, I argue that it offers a counternarrative to Italian American identification with whiteness by reimagining the myth of Columbus and highlighting a spiritual kinship between Italian and African diasporas.

My understanding of whiteness relies upon the theoretical framework of Jennifer Guglielmo, who, in the introduction of *Are Italians White? How Race Is Made in America* (2012), defines "White" as a category imposed by the US government on the first wave of Italian immigrants, the majority of whom were from impoverished Southern regions of Italy, and as "a consciousness they both adopted and rejected" (3). Guglielmo challenges the assumption that European immigrants in the late nineteenth and early twentieth centuries inhabited a liminal racial category, becoming white over time as they assimilated norms of US racism (12). Drawing from the scholarship of her brother, the historian Thomas Guglielmo, she distinguishes between race and color, categories used in immigration and census records, noting that Italian immigrants were considered "white on arrival" even as they faced discrimination and exploitation as members of the Italian race; they could vote, own land, marry other Europeans, serve on juries, and enjoy other benefits of citizenship. Their status as white did not protect them from discrimination since they were slow to understand how race operated in the New World; they "accepted work coded as 'black' by local customs, mobilized alongside people of color, and incited the wrath of white supremacists by their transgressions across the color line" (11). While the persecution of the "dagoes," as Southern Italians were then called, was not on par with the systemic disenfranchisement and violence African Americans faced, it should not be understated, nor should the parallels in their historical experience of racism be overlooked. In the 1890s, Southern Italian immigrant laborers worked alongside African Americans as indentured servants on plantations that they believed were Italian colonies. Between 1891 and 1915, forty-one Italians were lynched in seven different states; the most well-known lynching occurred in New Orleans, where eleven Sicilians were falsely accused of murdering the city's police chief (Vellon 217). Roediger's scholarship has shown how the racism directed at Southern Italian immigrants drew from the same discourses used to denigrate African Americans. Indeed, the epithet "guinea," a slur targeting Italians, especially those with darker skin, had once branded African slaves and their descendants ("Guineas" 655).

According to Jennifer Guglielmo and Salvatore Salerno, Italian/Americans began to "mobilize and identify as whites en masse" in the 1940s, when New Deal reforms amplified disparities in resources between white immigrants and people of color (13). Whiteness offered Southern Italian immigrants a social mobility that had been denied to them in postunification Italy, where they were deemed racially inferior to Northern Italians. As Jennifer Guglielmo explains: "In contrast to the Old World, southern Italians never occupied the lowest of social positions in the United States. This was because the United States had both racial *and* color categories, and if Italians were denigrated and exploited in the former, they were greatly privileged in the latter" (Guglielmo and Salerno 36). Claiming whiteness came with a price, however. In exchange for the benefits of American citizenship, Italian Americans had to renounce their ethnic identities (which were then understood as racial categories), sacrificing their languages, customs, and traditions (Gardaphé 189). Perhaps even more importantly, they needed to distance themselves from African Americans and other groups considered nonwhite, foregoing the possibility of an alliance rooted in class solidarity. "Whiteness," as I employ the term in this chapter, denotes a social position determined by America's racial hierarchies and a value system that accords with US capitalism, privileging individual success—as measured by material gains and professional accomplishments—over collective improvement and spiritual goals. It is often abetted by bootstrap narratives and myths of meritocracy that deny systemic racism, making whites seem more deserving than others.

While there is no consensus among scholars about when—or even if—Italian Americans began to identify with whiteness, most would agree that the myth of Columbus as "the first immigrant" whose voyage had laid the foundation for the social and economic advancement of millions was instrumentalized to give Italian Americans a central place in the national narrative. Shortly after the New Orleans lynching, in response to the Italian government's demand for reparations, President Harrison called on Congress to protect foreign nationals from mob violence. His decision to honor Columbus in 1892, one year after the lynching, has been seen as a conciliatory gesture directed toward the *prominenti*, a small group of elite Italian immigrants who "supported an upper-class notion of Italian national identity . . . based upon an imagined 'Italian' heritage of civilization and whiteness" (Vellon 3). These men, many of whom were from Northern Italy, encouraged working-class Italian immigrants to identify with Columbus to rehabilitate their public image. Yet their appropriation of the Columbus myth did little to staunch the rising tide of xenophobic sentiment against Italians. In 1911, the US Immigration Commission concluded that "certain kinds of criminality are inherent in the Italian race," including "crimes of personal violence, robbery, blackmail and extortion," an opinion that likely played a role in the decision to severely curtail Italian immigration in 1924. It was not until 1965 that Italian American organizations managed to pressure the government into overturning the racist quota system, using romantic fictions built around Columbus as ammunition for their cause (Staples).

Written in the early to mid-1970s, Bryant's early fiction offers us a window into the psyche of Italian America at a turning point in its history, when the inauguration of Columbus Day as a federal holiday coincided with the rise of the white ethnic revival (Ruberto and Sciorra). Italian Americans, along with other European groups whose ancestors had arrived on Ellis Island, were invested in an ethnic bootstrap narrative of immigrant history that seemed at cross-purposes with the goals of the civil rights and Black Power movements. *Miss Giardino* unsettles what the historian Matthew Frye Jacobson has called "the myth of the indomitable white ethnics," lamenting the conditions under which Italian immigrants lived and labored and the sacrifices involved in assimilating to white America. At the same time, it remained distant from BIPOC struggles. While Bryant participated in civil rights marches and would have considered herself an ally, her portrayal of black student activists in both *Ella Price's Journal* (1972) and *Miss Giardino* (1976) is condescending, reflecting her own belief as a former community college professor that they used "political slogans as an excuse for bad study habits" (*Literary Lynching* 106). Her ambivalence toward the racial issues of her generation might have been felt by many Italian Americans who, as Guglielmo has noted, alternated between adopting and rejecting whiteness.

Reading *Miss Giardino* through the lens of Toni Morrison's *Playing in the Dark: Whiteness and the Literary Imagination*, I find that disillusionment with the American Dream coexists with "a fabricated brew of darkness, otherness, and alarm that is uniquely American" (38). In *Playing in the Dark*, Morrison argues that "the major and championed characteristics" of early American literature have been informed by "a dark, abiding, signifying Africanist presence" (4). She proposes that we investigate the function of the Africanist character as a "surrogate and enabler," asking, "In what ways does the imaginative encounter with Africanism enable white writers to think about themselves?" (51–52). This question guides my reading of the two most significant black characters created by Bryant in the 1970s: Booker Henderson, a high school dropout who haunts the retired Italian American schoolteacher's dreams in *Miss Giardino*, and Augustine, the Atans' spiritual leader and the agent of the male narrator's salvation in *The Kin of Ata*. While both characters serve as surrogates and enablers, only Augustine literally and figuratively escapes an Africanist framework by walking into fire, a portal to another world that enables her to experience life in apartheid in South Africa and to participate in the civil rights movement.

Among the four novels that Bryant published in the 1970s, two of which were formally innovative—*The Kin of Ata* and *The Garden of Eros*—I have chosen to compare *The Kin of Ata* with *Miss Giardino* because both rely on Africanist characters to interrogate myths that have been adopted by Italian Americans when they identified with whiteness: the American educational system as a meritocracy, the ethnic bootstrap narrative, and Columbus as the heroic discoverer of the New World. Through this comparison, I seek to understand the role that genres play in shaping an Italian American writer's critique of whiteness. Since *The Kin of Ata* resists easy categorization, combining elements of science fiction, fantasy, and mysticism, I refer to it as Fantastika, John Clute's term, since 2007, for the wide range of genres that fall under the umbrella of the SF master text. In the first part of this chapter, I will discuss how Bryant's *Miss Giardino* represents the intergenerational trauma of migration and assimilation to white American society through a retired Italian American schoolteacher's remembered and imagined encounters with a black former student, an Africanist character. This discussion serves as a counterpoint to my reading of race and Italian/American identity in *The Kin of Ata*, which Bryant has described as a "Jungian religious fantasy inspired by my spiritual search and my reading in the literature in the mystics" (*Literary Lynchings* 106). I contend that by playing with what utopia studies scholar Tom Moylan in his article "The Locus of Hope: Utopia versus Ideology" has called "preconceptual images," Bryant was able to imagine alternatives to whiteness that eluded her in her more realistic fiction.

Africanism and the Madwoman Trope in *Miss Giardino*

Miss Giardino juxtaposes the postwar with the prewar periods: before and after Italian Americans mobilized in identifying with whiteness. Like *The Kin of Ata*, it begins with a life-changing accident: Anna Giardino, a retired schoolteacher in San Francisco who has been commemorated for forty years of service to Camino Real High School, awakens in a hospital bed with no memory of the incident that brought her there. A local newspaper article speculates that she was the victim of a robbery that took place in front of Camino Real High, where she was found unconscious on the sidewalk at 4 a.m. The novel unfolds over seven days, an allusion to the book of Genesis; the first chapter begins with "Monday" and the last chapter is titled "Sunday." Yet this linear narrative structure, which implies progress, the teleology of the immigrant success story, is undercut by the traumatic presence of the past in each chapter. Flashbacks of Anna's early childhood in an itinerant Italian immigrant family of miners are interspersed with memories of her experiences as a high school teacher, and a recurring dream sequence of Camino Real on fire ends the first five chapters, from Monday to Friday. Guided by her dreams, Anna Giardino reconstructs the events leading to her injury on that fateful night. By framing Miss Giardino's story as a drama of memory, Bryant hints at a cultural amnesia; she holds a mirror to Italian America and asks, What happens when we can neither remember nor forget our histories?

On the surface, Anna Giardino's life is a success story. Unlike her father, a coal miner whose slavish devotion to the American Dream leaves him crippled with lung disease in middle age, she learns English quickly and applies herself to her studies, earning from her father the scornful epithet "the American." Thanks to compulsory education laws and the support of various benefactors, she accumulates a cultural capital that translates into social mobility, distancing herself from her origins through education. The first in her family to attend college, Anna remains single and childless throughout her life and makes it her mission to save her students through literacy, using the essays of Bertrand Russell as a model. Her colorblind pedagogical approach is linked to the bootstrap philosophy that underpins capitalism in the US, according to which the individual and not the system is responsible for their success. While her methods work for some students—most notably, a Chicana student who will replace Miss Giardino as a teacher at Camino Real—they fail with her black students, who resist her attempts to educate them and accuse her of racism. Disillusioned yet seething, she retires.

One of these students, whose first name is an ironic allusion to Booker T. Washington, functions as her black doppelgänger. His haunting presence in her dreams, along with her memories of their antagonistic student-teacher relationship, leads us to suspect that he had robbed and assaulted her. However, in "Saturday," when Anna reconstructs the night of her robbery by physically returning to the crime scene, we learn that a different chain of events had transpired. Although Booker had reached for her purse, he stopped when he recognized her. Anna remembers striking him with all her force and scratching his face, possessed by hatred. When he pushed her in his struggle to escape, he unwittingly saved her by preventing her from acting on her secret plan to burn down the school. Since Miss Giardino has suppressed her memory of the incident, we discover her plan of arson when she does, in the novel's penultimate chapter. As JoAnne Ruvoli has noted, the novel subverts the stereotypes it has conditioned us to expect, casting doubt on Miss Giardino's reliability as a narrator (141).

Each of the first four chapters ends with a dream of the school building on fire. In Monday's dream, Miss Giardino is "the age as she had been when the school actually burned down, shortly before she graduated, in 1922" (21). As fire ravages the building's interior, Anna stands outside of Camino Real, wondering why its red bricks are unblackened. The school principal, Mr. Simson, explains that "the fire is too hot to make smoke, the fire is all outside and the outer shell shows nothing," yet when they move closer to the building and look at the flames through the window, she feels no heat (21). Mr. Simson wordlessly instructs her to tear the building down, brick by brick, adding, "Otherwise, my dear, we'll never get started building" (22). As he raises his flute to his lips, she begins her demolition project, yanking bricks out of the wall and tossing them over her shoulder, a bit dismayed that no one offers to help yet resigned to her task. This initial dream is self-reflexive, reminding the reader of the psychic demolition that it sets in motion: Miss Giardino's defensive ego, like the school building in the dream with its "cold fire" lodged inside, will need to be broken down for her to access her repressed rage. Freud has explained how the language of dreams articulates desires that have been deemed too dangerous to be admitted into consciousness in a disguised form, relying upon the metaphorical operations of condensation and displacement. That the school principal orders Miss Giardino to dismantle the building without telling her directly enables Miss Giardino to fulfill her secret wish while disavowing her destructive desire, projecting it onto an authority figure.

Thursday's dream signals a turning point in her self-awareness. No longer a calm spectator of her work on the outside of the burning building, she is now inside the same classroom where she has taught brown and black students for the last two years of her tenure at Camino Real, shouting at them to escape the fire; they ignore her, dancing in a "languid and sensuous" manner to the "harsh, hostile, mindless, furious" music of late capitalism or scrawling obscenities on the wall. Her emotional investment in the dream makes her unaware of its status as a fiction; she is so distraught that she forgets that she was supposed to "watch the dream so that she could understand." Only then does Booker's "deep black voice" emerge as a murmur "from somewhere in the dancing crowd," closing the chapter: "You get'n closer" (108), a casual observation that clarifies his purpose in the narrative—to guide Anna toward self-knowledge.

Miss Giardino's desire to burn down Camino Real recalls the "madwoman in the attic" trope formulated by feminist literary critics Sandra Gilbert and Susan Gubar, a metaphor of "the rebelliously diseased woman writer struggling to gain independence" whose presence can be traced in the works of nineteenth-century women writers (xxxviii). Gilbert and Gubar derive their paradigm from the eponymous protagonist of Charlotte Brontë's *Jane Eyre*, a poor, plain orphaned artist with a rebellious spirit who finds her way in Victorian society by becoming a governess at Thornfield Hall, the ancestral estate of the world-weary Mr. Rochester. The fire that Jane metaphorically snuffs out in her role as Mr. Rochester's governess tears through the mansion's walls at the end of the novel, when her doppelgänger, Bertha Mason, the "mad" Creole wife her employer and soon-to-be husband has confined to an attic decades ago, asserts her final act of agency by setting her prison on fire. Gilbert reads in Bertha's rebellion Jane's desire for freedom over her destiny and Brontë's desire to wrest control from a patriarchal literary tradition (339). Bertha's function as Jane Eyre's alter ego and her confinement to the shadows of Brontë's novel would later become the subject of postcolonial criticism after the 1968 publication of Jean Rhys's *Wide Sargasso Sea*, which gave Bertha Mason a voice and a history of her own—that of the Jamaican-born white Antoinette Cosway—while also exploring Rochester's perspective.

The madwoman trope is instructive for understanding the source of Miss Giardino's rage, her frustrated ambition as an English teacher who is destined not to make much of a difference in the lives of her multiethnic students. After she confesses to her on-again, off-again partner Arno her foiled plan of arson, she wonders if she is "crazy" and dismisses the thought, offering this rebuttal: "Yet, it had seemed logical. It was the institution itself, the conditions, The System, as Arno always put it, that was to blame. Not her or the students or even the teachers she most despised. To remove, to obliterate one structure of that system seemed like the only way to force a change" (144). Not only does this explanation seem too pat for a woman like Miss Giardino, but it begs the question: Which institution? The old one that insisted on student-teacher hierarchies and grammar lessons, or the new one that was underway in the late 1960s, which prioritized the socioemotional component of learning and legitimized the status of Ebonics as a language? Given Miss Giardino's scorn for progressive teaching methods, the new school would seem the more likely object of her hostility. However, in Monday's dream, she is tearing down the bricks of the school that burned down in 1922, suggesting that her target is the institution that shaped her own education. A servant of the System who has sacrificed her happiness to reap what Roediger has called "the wages of whiteness," the limited purchasing power of a "house on a hill," she may be more like Grace Poole, Bertha/Antoinette's hired captor, than Brontë's madwoman, despite their shared desire to escape confinement.

As Crista Baiada has persuasively argued, Miss Giardino "does not recognize the potential resistance of students who balk at adapting to the values she embodies . . . because this would require acknowledging her own ethical compromises and cultural losses" (22). Her inability to connect with her students of color and understand them on her own terms becomes apparent in her conversation with Arno in "Saturday," when she remembers Booker's refusal to learn from her. Recalling how he once sat in the back of the classroom, glaring at her with "death rays" in his eyes, she mentally berates him for not identifying with her own history as the daughter of an immigrant coal miner and for not working hard enough to overcome his laziness: "*If I told him my father was a slave to the System, would he listen? If I told him we are both victims? If I told him he is enjoying this in order to avoid the harder work of doing something about it? If I told him . . . no, I've tried, tried so many times, with so many. He won't listen. They never listen*" (30). This brief interior monologue is full of contradictions. By calling her father "a slave," Anna conflates America's dehumanizing system of chattel slavery with the exploitation of Italian immigrant laborers. By equating her struggle with Booker's, she ignores the status of Italian Americans as "whites on arrival" who were never subject to the systemic disenfranchisement faced by African Americans. Despite her belief that she and Booker are victims of systemic injustice, she separates the individual from the system, attributing a black student's failure to laziness rather than to racial politics; yet in the final two sentences, she reverses course, erasing Booker's individuality—"he" becomes an anonymous "they" who "never listen," who remain obstinately opposed to her attempts to save them.

Miss Giardino's memory of the role she played in Booker's life is also contradictory. While she blames Booker for not giving her class a chance, she also admits to Arno that she gave up on him soon after reading his first and only composition (129, 130). Her sudden resignation is puzzling given her assessment of his paper:

> The thought behind the paper was pure hate, but it was clear. All the errors were mechanical problems. There were no sentences that fall apart in the middle because the mind couldn't sustain a thought. There was no hopeless collapse or sudden emptiness or hysterical explosion. No one could understand without having read paper after paper and learned to recognize the mind so damaged that a teacher could do very little. Whatever damage Booker had suffered, and she was willing to admit that he had suffered much, it was reversible. He was still strong. (130)

Although Miss Giardino recognizes Booker's intelligence, she does not engage with the content of his essay. Instead, she marks all its grammatical errors and asks Booker to turn in a new draft, a grading approach that is opposed to the recommendations of the National Council of Teachers of English in their 1974 resolution, "Students' Right to Their Own Language"

(8). Furious that Miss Bryant refuses to acknowledge his ideas, Booker withdraws from the class, and eventually from the school. Even though she is blamed for his decision to drop out, Miss Giardino does not attempt to reach out to him. (In "Saturday," she calls his home for the first time, feigning concern for his well-being to glean information from his mother that will help her reconstruct her memory of the robbery.) She and Arno agree that the system scapegoated her instead of taking responsibility for its own failures; at the age of sixty-four, she needed more institutional support. While this may have been true, she conveyed unwillingness to adapt her teaching methods to the times, resisting collaboration with her more well-liked colleague, Stuart Warner, and telling the Black Students' Union that she was qualified to teach only standard English in response to their accusation that she did not respect black dialect (129). What is more alarming is the absence of a discourse of the civil rights movement. Miss Giardino's last year of teaching was 1968–1969, yet she never considers how Martin Luther King's death might have impacted her students. Although the text asks us to discount Booker's accusation of racism, to see it as a way for him to escape "the harder work" of learning to write in standard English, I find evidence to support his view—not in what she does as much as what she does not do.

Consistent with Morrison's discussion of the Africanist presence in early American literature as a surrogate for meditations on whiteness in *Playing in the Dark*, Booker is serviceable to Bryant only for what he reveals about her relationship with her Italian/American identity; he does not exist as a character in his own right any more than "Bertha Mason" does in Charlotte Brontë's novel. Bryant's own failure to imagine Booker as a subject is reflected in a scene in which Miss Giardino is unable to sustain her former student's image: "She concentrated on the image until she wore it out, blurred it. She was unable to call it up any longer, and she had gained nothing with it, *not a glimpse of herself with him*" (135, my italics). Although Booker is "the key to her [Anna Giardino's] memory," he is present only as a voice in a few dreams in which he utters a few words. He is most present in "Saturday" as the subject of Anna and Arno's conversation following her 4 a.m. excursion to Camino Real, Anna's final attempt to reconstruct the robbery. However, in contrast with Bryant's "model minorities," students from marginalized ethnic backgrounds whom Miss Giardino has managed to reach—Stephen Tatarin, the son of a Russian immigrant with whom Miss Bryant shared an unspoken erotic bond, who writes a panegyric letter to her decades later; Maria Flores, a Chicana who replaces Miss Giardino soon after her retirement and befriends her after her injury—we never hear from Booker directly; his discourse is always mediated by his former English teacher's. For instance, we know only that Miss Giardino thinks that Booker's composition is a hateful accusation directed against her; Booker's words, unlike Stephen Tatarin's, are withheld from the reader.

Like her author's, Miss Giardino's Africanist portrayal of Booker both enables and limits her self-knowledge. Miss Giardino's life work has been predicated on her assumption that she could save others through literacy, as she had been saved, earmarked for success as one who was deemed unlike those "other Italians." At some point during 1968–1969, she must have realized that her belief in education as a path to social mobility was, in Arno's words, "a comfortable fiction, a way to keep the poor in place" since it is dependent on only a few students "making it" (111). Despite what she tells herself about the need to force a systemic change (144), the target of her fantasized arson was her own investment in whiteness. At the end of "Saturday," Anna realizes that Booker's absorption of her rage has saved her from the fate of Bertha Mason: having displaced the "full force of her stored-up anger" onto him, she no longer fantasizes about burning down the school: "What should be done with an old woman capable of attempting to burn down a school in order to relieve her pent-up fury? She had no answer. She could not even imagine such a woman" (145). The chapter culminates in her epiphanic identification with her Old World father: "He had a vision of a better life and he had strained himself to the utmost to go after it. So had she. He had been used and abused by the forces in which he had put all his hope. So had she. He had become filled with hatred and bitterness and despair and had vented his hatred on the nearest targets. So, finally, had she" (146). Hence, Booker saves Anna Giardino in more ways than one, marking the boundary between life and death and madness and sanity, thereby allowing her to recognize herself and her father as "whites on a leash," the term used by the Italian American scholar Fred Gardaphé to describe the disdain and reluctance with which Italian immigrants and their descendants were allowed to integrate into white American society (189).

Aware that she has lost more than she has gained in assimilating to American culture, in "Sunday," the novel's final chapter, Anna attempts to escape whiteness in a more rational manner by abandoning her "house on a hill," an allusion to John Winthrop's sermon to the Pilgrims who had migrated to Massachusetts Bay Colony. Never a lover of travel, she turns down her friend David's offer to host her in a house in the south of France, a few hours from her mother's village in Piedmont, and makes plans to move to the Mission District, where she will write an ethnic history of Camino Real High. Italian American feminist literary critic Mary Jo Bona is somewhat hopeful that this writing project can engender a critical race awareness: "Perhaps forging a diasporan consciousness will enable Anna to reconsider social categories of gender and race in her understanding of not only her parents' and siblings' tragic encounters with America, but also of those of her students of color" (21). Given her inability to recognize Booker's racialized struggle and her own white privilege, I am more skeptical. Anna's last name, which translates as "garden," is as ironic as Booker's since her race blindness forecloses the possibility of a cross-racial alliance, preventing her from reclaiming her lost Italianità.

Italians and Africans as Spiritual Kin

Owing to its departure from realism, *The Kin of Ata* offers a more playful and subversive critique of whiteness than *Miss Giardino*. Its protagonist is an anti-hero, a selfish, materialistic young man who has achieved commercial success by exploiting wealthy young women for their connections. After accidentally killing his girlfriend Connie during a fight at 3 a.m. in which they are both stoned, he drives away from the crime scene and winds up driving off a bend in the road. Instead of dying, he is transported by the inhabitants of Ata to their island, which is invisible to the rest of the world. In Ata, he regains his mobility and is initiated into the ways of its people through its two leaders, Augustine and Salvatore, who behave toward him like surrogate parents. Their loving care enables his spiritual conversion.

In a study of three utopian novels published in 1970s America, Edward K. Chan has argued that Bryant, along with Marge Piercy and Samuel Delany, incorporates racial difference into her utopia without accounting for its remainder. Chan draws attention to how Bryant alternates between strategies of nonsignification and countersignification in her description of the Atans, at times suspending the racial semiotic and at other times calling it into question. While the typical Atan is "a medium composite" whose racial type is unidentifiable to the protagonist, a "large minority" of

Atans have a combination of Nordic, African, and Asiatic features (18–19). For Chan, these strategies serve to homogenize the subject, much like discourses of multiculturalism in a liberal democracy. Insisting that we are all kin, Bryant is unable to imagine a place that values the specificity of racial difference without resorting to essentializing stereotypes.

While Chan draws valid conclusions from the novel's initial description of the Atans, he overlooks the major role played by Augustine and Salvatore, the most spiritually evolved of the Atans, who are clearly marked by signifiers of racial and ethnic difference. Salvatore's name gives away his Italianità and his association with salvation. He is depicted as a bald, middle-aged man with brown skin, an indication that he is of Southern Italian origin, possibly Sicilian. His legs are "spindly," yet he is robust enough to lift the protagonist and carry him out of a cave (14). Although Augustine has "blue eyes," "sharp, pointed features," "a long nose," and "a long face with a pointed chin," her blackness is her most salient characteristic: her skin is described as "not just brown but *almost a true black*" (12, my emphasis), and she is referred to as "the black woman" five times in the narrative before the protagonist learns her name (13, 20, 28, 32, 45). Like her appearance, her name evokes a dual African and Italian heritage: one thinks of Augustine of Hippo, the Roman African whose theological writings influenced the Church, as well as Saint Augustine, who was born in North Africa.

Gender, like race, is fluid in Atan culture, yet Augustine's and Salvatore's roles complement each other in a traditional gender-based fashion. While Augustine assumes the role of the comforter, nurturing the protagonist through food and sex, Salvatore explains the rituals and belief systems of the Atans to the protagonist after he has learned their language. Both are archetypal characters who teach the protagonist spiritual discipline and open his eyes to different ways of being and knowing. By making an African character and a Southern Italian character the principal agents of the protagonist's salvation, Bryant links the two cultures through their indigenous roots, highlighting the superiority of folkloric ways of knowing that have been devalued both in the United States and in Northern Europe.

Each night, the Atans gather around a fire to recite their dreams, a sacred practice from which they derive the meaning of their existence, their foundation myths, and spiritual precepts. In a review of *The Kin of Ata* published online, Bogi Takács traces Bryant's inspiration for Atan dreams to Senoi dream theory. Popularized by West Coast Jungians in the 1960s and 1970s, the dreamwork movement drew upon the writings of anthropologist Kilton Stewart and psychologist Patricia Garfield, the author of *Creative Dreaming* (1974). Both Stewart and Garfield visited the Senoi, an aboriginal tribe who lived in the Malaysian jungle, and noted the importance of dreams in their everyday lives. According to these scientists, the Senoi had learned methods of controlling and shaping their dreams to conquer their fears and maximize their pleasure. Proponents of the dreamwork movement correlated the absence of violence and mental illness among the Senoi with their dream practices, claims that have since been debunked (Domhoff). Takács notes how Bryant's characterization of the Atans resembles these pseudoscientific discourses on the Senoi, citing the narrator's description of the Atans' attitude toward illness: "I never saw anyone ill. The people believed that ill health began with donagdeo—acts which would disturb or decrease their ability to dream, and resulted from accompanying states of imbalance. . . . Actually, the people did not believe in accidental injuries; and a person's illnesses were his own responsibility. I don't mean to imply some magical immunity from biological fate, only that illness was over with quickly, either through recovery or death. There was no chronic dis-ease." Finding "the fetishization of the enlightened Indigenous person who stays away from civilization and technology" problematic in Bryant's work, Takács suggests it is an attempt at a cultural appropriation that is a misreading of anthropology, history, and science.

Although Bryant may have had Senoi dreamwork in mind while she was writing *The Kin of Ata*, its frames of reference are slipperier than Takács has acknowledged, considering that indigenous people from a wide range of cultures took dreamwork seriously: the Hopi believed dreams were portals to other worlds, West African tribes saw them as a bridge between the living and the dead, and Southern Italians interpreted them as omens or blessings. In each of these cultures, the spirit and the body were seen as interdependent, and illness was often regarded as a spiritual malady. The elaborate rituals Bryant's narrator records with ethnographic fervor might have been unique to the Senoi—except for the deliberate attempts to control dreams (Domhoff)—but nondualistic epistemologies and alternative healing practices were far more widespread.

Since Salvatore and Augustine are the spiritual leaders of the island and serve as the novel's principal characters, aside from the narrator, I read their alliance as symbolic of a symbiotic exchange between Italian and African diasporas that can facilitate healing from the wounds of white capitalism. In *Flavor and Soul: Italian America at Its African American*

Edge, John Gennari has identified affinities between Italian American and African American cultures, emphasizing "common traditions of vocal and bodily performance marked by intensity of ear and eye," "a penchant for extroverted, charismatic presentations of the self," "a shared set of fluid gender dynamics that scrambles the schematic boundaries of the dominant culture," and "a pragmatic approach to the difficulties and cruelties of life, which leads paradoxically to a heightened capacity for indulgence and enjoyment" (12). Bryant endows the natives of her imaginary island with similar expressive capacities. The Atans privilege oral and kinesthetic modes of communication over the written word; language is secondary, a tool of communication rather than a vehicle of self-expression. The capitalist work ethic and a gender-based division of labor have no place on this island: men and women work alongside each other in the fields, breaking into dance every now and then, taking turns so that others could rest, and the entire community participates in childrearing. Young Atans explore their sexuality with multiple partners, as nothing is "donagdeo" (taboo). While monogamous couples exist, there is no possessiveness, no sense of an "I" who has a claim on another's body. Even while eating, the Atans take turns feeding each other until everyone is sated.

Notwithstanding its gender fluidity and communal spirit, it would be a mistake to regard Ata as a traditional utopia. I agree with Tom Moylan, who in *Demand the Impossible: Science Fiction and the Utopian Imagination* (1986) has categorized *The Kin of Ata* among other female-authored fictions written in the heyday of civil rights and feminist movements as "a critical utopia." Moylan identifies three characteristics that separate critical utopian texts from the traditional utopian fictions of the past, all of which describe *The Kin of Ata*: an "awareness of the limitations of the utopian tradition," relevance to our contemporary historical moment, and "the continuing presence of difference and imperfections within utopian society itself" that "renders more recognizable and dynamic alternatives" (10). In "The Locus of Hope: Utopia versus Ideology," Moylan argues that "the critical utopian text can be a valuable part of the opposition to the prevailing system" even if it does not offer "practical blueprints of an actual alternative society . . . as it provides pre-conceptual images that are generated out of opposition to what is." Conceiving of the genre as self-reflexive and open-ended, he adds that "the unresolved tensions in the text, the tensions and absences . . . become an important part of oppositional ideology" (sec. 3). By leaving the tension between the gender-conforming and the gender-queer aspects of Atan society unresolved, Bryant draws attention to Ata's status as a fiction and to the impasse she faces as an

Italian/American feminist writer whose desire for gender equality is at odds with the practices of Italian and African cultures.

Reimagining Columbus

In 1971, the same year that Bryant self-published *The Comforter*, Columbus Day was declared a federal holiday. It is unclear how Bryant felt about Italian Americans' appropriation of Columbus; I have not been able to locate any writings by her on the subject. While Bryant likely did not have Columbus in mind when she wrote *The Comforter*, which would be published by Random House five years later as *The Kin of Ata Are Waiting for You*, her narrator-protagonist evokes Columbus through his accidental discovery of a new world, his interest in finding gold, and his condescending attitude toward the natives. "I made the protagonist and narrator an opportunistic, materialistic success, blind to the values prized on Ata," Bryant wrote in a synopsis of the book on her website. The novel's dense tropical setting, which evokes Hispaniola more than the Malaysian jungles, also establishes its intertextuality with the Columbus myth.

Initially, the narrator views the Atans through an Orientalist gaze, seeing them as "a race of mental retardants," as ignorant and savage (47). Even after he learns their language and admits to himself that their communal culture is superior to the individualistic and exploitative one he has left behind, he is still unwilling to relinquish his imperialistic attitude; he attempts to rape Augustine and to convert the Atan children, in the hope that they lead him to the "precious stones and jewels" he is wrongly convinced they are harboring, so that he could return to his country "with a new name, a new identity, and plenty to live on for the rest of [his] life" (75). Soon after this scene, however, Bryant unwittingly inverts the myth that was so integral in the whitewashing of Italian American history, allowing a powerful counterstory to emerge. While the historical Columbus succeeded in colonizing the inhabitants of Hispaniola, driven by his desire for "a new name, a new identity," and Queen Elizabeth's lust for gold, Bryant's nameless narrator is gradually converted by the natives. By the end of the narrative, he has fallen in love with Augustine, fathered a child with her, and has no desire to return to Western civilization, which he now sees as hideous and corrupt.

Bryant's narrator undergoes several stages in his conversion. After he accidentally kills an old Atan, a crime that recalls his accidental murder of Connie, he waits for the mass vengeance he is sure will follow. When he realizes that the Atans have no desire for retribution, he repents in the *la-ka* (a hut), facing Augustine—"I have never done anything good. I am an empty man. Not a real person. I gave away what was real in me long ago. I sold it. For nothing. I am nothing. I am not fit to live" (89)—and is forgiven by the community. Although he stops trying to convert Atans and find a way back to America, he does not renounce his colonial project; instead, he substitutes brute force with acts of cultural imperialism. Falsely believing himself to be the first scribe on the island, he sets about trying to document the many different Atan legends of the creation of the world, using "a modified Italian alphabet which is almost perfectly phonetic" (162). He becomes obsessed with creating a grand narrative of Atan history, only to learn from Salvatore and Augustine what every postmodern critic knows: that contradictions do not make stories less true; that their meaning resides not in the black marks on the page, but in the play of possibilities activated by reading (164, 167). He realizes the futility of his mission when Salvatore educates him about the writing tradition in Ata. Salvatore's views on the inferiority of writing to speech recall those of African griots, who were notoriously reluctant to have their legends transcribed and circulated in Europe and America: "Instead of expressing the unknown, the carved word became a thing between the people and the unknown which it should symbolize" (202). According to Salvatore, oral tradition survived in Ata because it allowed "room for an infinite number of dreams, which could change and grow and become closer to the reality" (202).

Augustine's sacrifice marks the final stage of the narrator's conversion. On the first day of spring, it is customary for the Atans to gather before a fire in the *la-ka* and for the oldest Atan to repeat, "Has any kin been chosen?" One day, Augustine, who has spent all winter in a trance, fasting, stands up and walks into the flames. Incensed with grief, the narrator curses the Atans and disparages them as "savages." Later, through Salvatore, he learns that Augustine never died; her passage through fire transported her to the world he had left behind, where her suffering would redeem all kin (187). Instructed by Salvatore, the narrator finds a way of dreaming "higher dreams" that enable him to track Augustine's movements across the globe, from Northern Europe to South Africa, from Japan to South America: "she circled the world on her knees, scrubbing the floors of the powerful, succoring the oppressed" (193). His method requires him to live by the rhythm of the Atans' ceremonial dances; any distraction and he loses his focus. For seven years he watches, unobserved, as Augustine travels across the US, singing in poor storefront churches and participating in civil rights marches, until she is shot during a raid. As she lay dying on the sidewalk, Augustine and the narrator communicate for the first time since her disappearance from Ata:

> "You were to show me the way out," I said, without speaking.
> "That is what I have done."
> "Don't leave me, Augustine."
> "I will never leave you." And she was gone. (199)

The narrator's spiritual salvation, "the way out" for him, requires that he surrender his position of authority and bear witness to the struggles of the black diaspora. Shortly after his wordless conversation, he gives up his self-imposed role as scribe and devotes himself to Atan rituals, humbled by his devotion to Augustine: "I kept my rhythm, thankful for every day that I was able to not fall too short of nagdeo, especially considering the kind of man I am" (203). Through the narrator's transformation from cultural imperialist to historical eyewitness, *The Kin of Ata* suggests that healing resides in what critical race scholar Asao Inoue, in a different context, has called deep listening, a "deep and mindful attending to the other" that opens space for understanding (Inoue).

Reimagining Black Diaspora

In "Black to the Future" (1993), Mark Dery coined the term "Afrofuturism" to denote "speculative fiction that treats African-American themes and addresses African American concerns in the context of twentieth-century technoculture" as well as "African American signification that appropriates images of technology and a prosthetically enhanced future" (180). His essay poses the following conundrum: "Can a community whose past has been deliberately rubbed out, and whose energies have subsequently been consumed with the search for legible traces of its history, imagine possible futures?" Augustine's time travel offers a response: no possible future can exist unless the past is re-lived by one who is disciplined enough to submit to the trials of "re-memory," Toni Morrison's term in *Beloved* for the imaginative reconstitution of the past in the present.

In substituting the time-travel machines of the Western sci-fi tradition with Atan dreams, Bryant goes beyond Afrofuturism, embracing what the Nigerian American sci-fi writer Nnedi Okorafor has called Africanfuturism, a branch of speculative fiction rooted in African mythology and history that does not center the West. That dreams are communicated from Augustine to the narrator through Salvatore reflects the influence of an African-centered cosmology in which "there, at times, occurs the phenomenon of triangulation in dreaming where dreams originate from another source to give messages to the individual for the benefit of others" (Augustine 3). Representing Italianità as compatible with African cosmologies, Bryant positions Salvatore as the third point on a triangle that connects the narrator with Augustine. His spiritual mentorship permits the narrator to access the "higher dreams" that communicate Augustine's message visually (203).

It can be argued that Bryant reproduces Africanist tropes by making Augustine the agent of the narrator's salvation. Her transnational migrations are narrated in a cursory fashion; the narrator does not pause to dwell on the incidents of injustice she is forced to endure. For instance, we know only that her stay in South Africa, an apartheid state at the time of Bryant's writing, was "brief" and "terrible" (193). While Augustine lacks subjectivity, the novel's status as a work of Fantastika makes it difficult to determine whether this limits or enhances her power as a character; she transcends the limits of human experience. Her "archetypal errancy, itineracy, and mockery of bounded time and space" (Okonkwo 654) link her with the ogbanje of Igbo folklore, the part-human, part-divine children who are believed to be born repeatedly to the same mother. In "Ogbanje Phenomenon; Mother's Perception, and Childhood Morbidity," Onyinye and colleagues write that

> ogbanje children are believed to be committed to a shortened life span to the deities. With this commitment they receive an extraordinary appearance and psychic talent, but at the expense of human relationships. They are said to have spiritual companions with which they always communicate supernaturally, resulting in hallucinatory experiences or dreams. They are also said to arrange to die at an agreed time of a brief illness, usually at about puberty or a significant time in their life such as their birthday. (79–80)

In his conversation with the narrator, Salvatore clarifies that Augustine has not been killed by fire; she has been reborn into the human world, where she will witness and experience suffering: "We mourn for her, for her sufferings, for the suffering she has been chosen to take on herself" (187). The tears that streamed down her face when she discouraged the narrator from entertaining the idea of marrying her suggest that she was aware of her destiny, as did her erratic behavior after she gives birth to their daughter. Denying illness, she subjected herself to ardent spiritual discipline in isolation and worked harder in the fields; moved out of the ka she and the narrator shared and wandered from place to place; abruptly began and ended work as a healer; stopped eating and grew very thin. When during the Atans' spring ceremonial, in response to the usual question—"Have any kin been chosen?"—she stood up and walked into the fire, she did not seem to be acting of her own accord; rather, she appeared to be following the instructions of a deity who spoke to her in dreams (184).

Nigerian scholars have written about how the ogbanje has become a trope in postcolonial literary works for the migration and displacement of African peoples (Adeleke and Kehinde 6). Much like the ogbanjes of traditional Igbo culture, who were seen as a threat to a family's ancestral line, as "a poor, obscure black woman" (188) Augustine is treated like a pariah in each country she visits until she is accidentally killed in a race riot in Harlem. Sensing her presence in a sunset glimpsed from a cliff where the Atans leave their dead, the narrator feels glad that "she had been freed of her ordeal and allowed to go Home," apparently unaware of the ogbanje's infinite cycle of birth, death, and regeneration (199); he still thinks of these metaphysical entities in Judeo-Christian terms.

While Augustine's spiritual journey allows her to escape the Africanist framework in which she was portrayed as the narrator's comforter in the first half of the book, Salvatore becomes the vehicle of the narrator's self-awareness. After learning from Salvatore that the Atans had once engaged in a written culture and decided to revert to their oral tradition when they found themselves "no longer dreaming the high dreams," the narrator reflects on his mistaken beliefs about them:

> For now I knew them [the Atans] as they were, not a happy, primitive, innocent people, free from the cares of the world, but the sustainers, the sufferers who tried to counter-balance what was done by men like me. People waiting patiently since the beginning of time, resigned to going on until the end of time, knowing that they could look for no great progress, no sign of the coming fulfillment of their dream. (204)

The narrator's final insight allows for the possibility of a racial reconciliation the likes of which we do not find in *Miss Giardino*, whose protagonist remains uncritical of her Africanist fantasies of Booker. His realization that Ata is not a utopia and that he and other Westerners need to be held accountable for the suffering they inflict on the planet are signs of a new habitus. Discrediting Orientalist stereotypes of the Atans through the narrator's revelation that they are not "the happy, primitive, innocent" people he had believed them to be, Bryant emphasizes the spiritual discipline involved in preserving one's cultural values and refusing a postcapitalist order, with its unending cycle of greed and violence, victims and conquerors. She valorizes the Atans for what she and Miss Giardino were unable to do: abolish whiteness.

Having learned that "the greatest miracle of Ata," that its people "were no different from any other people in the world, subject to the same faults, desires, and temptations, but living each day in battle against them" (193), the narrator walks into fire, ready to return to Western civilization as a form of penance. In prison for the murder of his girlfriend, which he has confessed before a packed courtroom, he writes the book we read. The return to the grim realism of the narrative frame accentuates by way of contrast the life-sustaining possibilities of speculative fiction.

Conclusion

Although SF genres have received considerable attention for their complicity with Empire, they can also work in the opposite direction, as Tom Moylan's scholarship on critical utopian texts of the 1970s has shown. In comparing *The Kin of Ata Are Waiting for You* with *Miss Giardino*, I have sought to demonstrate how Bryant's early experiment with Fantastika enabled a more subversive engagement with American history. While in *Miss Giardino* Bryant confines her vision to the psychic dilemma of a retired Italian/American schoolteacher who has internalized whiteness, in *The Kin of Ata*, she creates an alternate version of the Columbus myth, one in which the "discoverer of the New World" is freed of his own imperialistic desires and learns more from the natives than they do from him. The novels' shared motifs serve very different purposes. Dreams are not mnemonic tools, texts we need to analyze to understand our past; they are Africanfuturistic technologies that permit the writer, "the subject of the dream" in Morrison's words, to travel outside of her social positioning and bear witness to black women's history. Fire is not synonymous with the senseless destruction, helplessness, and terror of white capitalism; it rebirths and permits mobility.

Far from an escapist fantasy of white redemption, then, *The Kin of Ata* critiques the Italian/American infatuation with whiteness and imagines salutary alternatives to Empire in an imperfect world. Departing from the colorblind worldview found in *Miss Giardino*, it invites a broader investigation of the role played by Fantastika in the Italian/American racial imaginary.

Works Cited

Adeleke, Israel Oluwaseun, and Ayobami Kehinde. "Theorizing the Abiku/Ogbanje Motif in Sefi Atta's *Everything Good Will Come*." *Postcolonial Text*, vol. 19, no. 4, 2024, pp. 1–16.

Augustine, Nwoye. "The Psychology and Content of Dreaming in Africa." *Journal of Black Psychology*, vol. 43, no. 1, 26 July 2016, pp. 3–26.

Baiada, Crista. "Interrogating Myths of Education: Dorothy Bryant's *Ella Price's Journal* and *Miss Giardino*." *Italian American Review*, vol. 13, no. 1, Winter 2023, pp. 13–32.

Bona, Mary Jo. "Why Amnesia? Migrant Memories in Italian-American Literature." *Letterature D'America: rivista trimestrale*, vol. 40, no. 179, 2020, pp. 5–28.

Bryant, Dorothy. *Ella Price's Journal*. Feminist Press, 1997.

———."Fiction." Website of dbmom! https://www.dorothybryant.com/fiction/. Accessed 20 Jan. 2025.

———. *The Kin of Ata Are Waiting for You*. Random House, 1997.

———. *Literary Lynching: When Readers Censor Writers*. Website of dbmom! https://www.dorothybryant.com/literary-lynching/. Accessed 20 Jan. 2025.

———. *Miss Giardino*. Feminist Press, 1997.

Chan, Edward K. "Utopia and the Problem of Race: Accounting for the Remainder in the Imagination of the 1970s Utopian Subject." *Utopian Studies*, vol. 17, no. 3, 2006, pp. 465–90.

Clute, John. "Fantastika in the World Storm." *Pardon This Intrusion: Fantastika in the World Storm*. Beccon, 2011.

Committee on CCCC Language: Background Statement. "Students Right to Their Own Language." *National Council of Teachers of English*, vol. 25, no. 3, 1974, pp. 1–18.

Dery, Mark. "Black to the Future: Interviews with Samuel R. Delaney, Greg Tate, and Tricia Rose." *Flame Wars: The Discourse of Cybercultures*. Duke UP, 1994.

Domhoff, G. W. "Senoi Dream Theory: Myth, Scientific Method, and the Dreamwork Movement." http://dreamresearch.net/Library/senoi.html. Accessed 20 Jan. 2024.

Gardaphé, Fred. "We Weren't Always White: Race and Ethnicity in Italian/American Literature." *LIT: Literature Interpretation Theory*, vol. 13, no. 3, July–Sept. 2002, pp. 185–99.

Gennari, John. *Flavor and Soul: Italian America at Its African American Edge*. Chicago UP, 2017.

Gilbert, Sandra M., and Susan Gubar. *The Madwoman in the Attic: The Woman Writer and the Nineteenth-Century Literary Imagination*. 1979. 2nd ed., Yale UP, 2000.

Guglielmo, Jennifer, and Salvatore Salerno. *Are Italians White? How Race Is Made in America*. Taylor & Francis, 2003.

Guglielmo, Thomas A. *White on Arrival: Italians, Race, Color, and Power in Chicago, 1890–1945*. Oxford UP, 2004.

Inoue, Asao. "How Do We Language So People Stop Killing Each Other, or What Do We Do About White Language Supremacy?" *Conference on College Composition and Communication*, Annual Convention, Pennsylvania, Pittsburgh, 14 Mar. 2019. https://tinyurl.com/4C19ChairAddress.

Jacobson, Matthew Frye. *Roots Too: White Ethnic Revival in Post-Civil Rights America*. Harvard UP, 2008.

Morrison, Toni. *Playing in the Dark: Whiteness and the Literary Imagination*. Vintage, 1993.

Moylan, Tom. *Demand the Impossible: Science Fiction and the Utopian Imagination*. Methuen, 1986.

———. "The Locus of Hope: Utopia versus Ideology." *Science Fiction Studies*, vol. 9, no. 27, 1982. https://www.depauw.edu/sfs/backissues/27/moylan.html.

Okonkwo, Christopher N. "A Critical Divination: Reading Sula as Ogbanje-Abiku." *African-American Review*, vol. 38, no. 4, pp. 651–68.

Onyinye, Anyanwu, Exeonu T. Chinonyelum, Ezeanosike B. Obumneme, Okike O. Cliford, and Ibekwe C. Roland. "Ogbanje Phenomenon; Mothers Perception, and Childhood Morbidity." *Alternate Medicine*, vol. 37, no. 1, pp. 79–82.

Roediger, David R. "Guineas, Wiggers, and the Dramas of Racialized Culture." *American Literary History*, vol. 7, 1995, pp. 654–58.

———. *Working Towards Whiteness: How America's Immigrants Became White—The Strange Journey from Ellis Island to the Suburbs*. Basic Books, 2005.

Ruberto, Laura, and Joseph Sciorra. "Recontextualizing the Ocean Blue: Italian Americans and the Commemoration of Columbus." *Process: A Blog for American History*, 4 Oct. 2017. https://www.oah.org/process/recontextualizing-the-ocean-blue.

Ruvoli, JoAnne. "Unreliable Dreamers: Restoring the Memory." *Framing Ethnicity: Storytelling in Italian American Novels*. Dissertation, University of Illinois, 2011, pp. 114–62.

Staples, Brent. "How Italians Became White." *New York Times*, 12 Oct. 2019, https://www.nytimes.com/interactive/2019/10/12/opinion/columbus-day-italian-american-racism.html.

Takács, Bogi. "QUILTBAG +Speculative Classics: *The Kin of Ata Are Waiting for You* by Dorothy Bryant." *Tor.com*, 16 Oct. 2019. https://reactormag.com/quiltbag-speculative-classics-the-kin-of-ata-are-waiting-for-you-by-dorothy-bryant/.

Vellon, Peter G. *A Great Conspiracy Against Our Race: Italian Immigrant Newspapers and the Construction of Whiteness in the Early Twentieth Century*. New York UP, 2014.

Wahala, Nnedi. "Africanfuturism Defined." *Nnedi's Wahala Zone Blog*, 19 Oct. 2019. https://nnedi.blogspot.com/2019/10/africanfuturism-defined.html.

13

Dorothy Fontana

The New Jersey "Secretary" Who Cocreated *Star Trek*

Marc DiPaolo

In the corporate, collaborative working environment of the production of a television series, the question of authorship is fraught, which is why *Star Trek* producer John D. F. Black has objected to Gene Roddenberry getting nearly sole credit for creating the classic series when a "collective" was truly responsible (Altman 46). Fan and historian consensus points to this collective including Roddenberry and Black, plus scriptwriter and editor Dorothy Catherine ("D. C.") Fontana, and producers Gene L. Coon, Robert H. Justman, and Herbert F. Solow. Accepting this collective as a given, efforts to determine conclusively which creator is responsible for which aspects of the series—and its broader franchise mythos—seem doomed to fail. This is especially true since the *Trek* teleplays were contributed by an array of science fiction luminaries and fan writers working on a freelance basis—and all these scripts were rewritten to one degree or another by members of the collective. Under these circumstances, it is difficult to assign credit to who did the most to "create" the original series (aka *TOS*, 1966–1969) and/or make the franchise writ large "what it is today." And yet, when Fontana died of cancer at eighty on December 2, 2019, she received mournful social media tributes and obituaries from news outlets worldwide that either hinted or stated outright that her contribution to the collective creation of *Trek* had been far more substantial than she has customarily been given credit for. Ryan Britt's testimonial for *SyFy.com* was the most glowing: "R.I.P. D. C. Fontana: The Most Important Writer on the Original *Star Trek*." This brazen headline would later be softened to "D.C. Fontana Gave the Original *Star Trek* Its Human Heart," but the article's text remained fervent:

> If not for Fontana, the *Star Trek* franchise would never have become the tender and relatable futuristic world we know today. . . . It's nearly impossible to quantify her importance to *Star Trek* and popular science fiction as a whole, but we can try. . . . When people speak in reverent tones about the optimism and prescient science fiction progressivism of *Star Trek*, original series creator Gene Roddenberry gets a lot of credit for crafting that hopeful status quo we'd all like to be beamed into. But when it came to making the characters who populated that future world believable people, the *Star Trek* franchise wouldn't have achieved orbit without the talents and insight of D.C. Fontana.

In his 1995 memoir, *I Am Spock*, series star Leonard Nimoy was similarly effusive, claiming that Fontana's exceptional writing consistently elevated the quality of the show. Noting that she was "a very talented, solid individual for whom [he had] the utmost respect," he explained: "If you put Dorothy's stories together as a group . . . she gave us, by far, the best stories where we interacted with women who have fully developed characters in their own right [unlike other stories, that were the product of the sexist sixties and objectified and stereotyped women]. Nimoy noted, "The Enterprise Incident," like most of her scripts, "had an edge to it, an adult level of complication, and social commentary. The characters' lives were being affected, their ethics violated, and even their spirituality touched. Scripts like these added to the moral structure of the *Star Trek* universe" (Nimoy 118).

During Fontana's tenure writing and editing *Star Trek* adventures—not only for *TOS*, but the vast array of spinoff television and web series, tie-in novels, comic book series, and video games it spawned—she wrote a surprising number of beloved stories. These episodes included "Charlie X," "Tomorrow Is Yesterday," "This Side of Paradise," "Journey to Babel," "Friday's Child," "The Ultimate Computer," "Yesteryear," "Encounter at

Farpoint," "Dax," and an uncredited rewrite of the most popular *TOS* adventure of all, "City on the Edge of Forever." Fontana also cowrote Activision's video game *Star Trek: Bridge Commander* (2002), with Derek Chester, as well as authored one of the franchise's best novels, *Vulcan's Glory* (1989), which depicted Spock's earliest days on the *Enterprise*.

Like other women science fiction writers of her era, including C. L. Moore and "James Tiptree, Jr.," Fontana wrote all her *Trek* stories using either her initials or a male pseudonym to disguise her gender. She'd submitted her earliest freelance teleplays with "Dorothy C. Fontana" on the cover, and her first six onscreen credits in the 1960s were under that name. However, she switched to submitting her work as the genderless "D. C." after the makers of the action series *Combat!* obstinately refused to even glance at a script written by a woman (Volk-Weiss). Fontana stuck to "D. C." throughout her career but broke the tradition for *The Streets of San Francisco* when producer Quinn Martin asked her to use her full name so he could show the world he hired women (Bowie). In one other exception to her practice of using "D. C.," she would place the male pseudonyms "Michael Richards" and "J. Michael Bingham" (after her brothers, Michael and Richard) on any script she felt had been despoiled by intrusive rewrites done by others, including several episodes she wrote for season 3 of *Trek* and the first season of its sequel series, *Star Trek: The Next Generation*.

Set in the 1950s, the *Star Trek: Deep Space Nine* episode "Far Beyond the Stars" (1998) paid tribute to Fontana through the inclusion of Kay Eaton (Nana Visitor), a character who could only get her science fiction stories published in a pulp magazine by posing as a male. When Kay dodged a writing staff photo shoot to avoid having her cover blown to the readership, the scene played as a sly reference to fans only discovering that the wildly popular "D. C." was a woman because of a surprising photograph in Stephen Whitfield's 1968 book *The Making of "Star Trek,"* published halfway through *Trek*'s third season.

Never part of any television show's official "writers' room," Fontana accumulated all her writing credits either as a script editor or by working freelance. Somewhat pigeonholed in the science fiction genre, she was *Logan's Run*'s script editor, and freelance writer for *Buck Rogers in the 25th Century*, *He-Man and the Masters of the Universe*, *Land of the Lost*, *The Six Million Dollar Man*, and *The Wild, Wild West*. However, her record writing westerns demonstrated that there was more to her than being the queen of *Star Trek*; she contributed to *The Big Valley*, *Bonanza*, *Frontier Circus*,

Kung Fu, *Lonesome Dove: The Series*, and *The Road West*. In addition, her work outside her two biggest genre specialties included her writing multiple episodes of *The Waltons* and *Dallas*. Impressively—and justifiably—Fontana twice won lifetime achievement awards from the *Writers Guild of America* (1997 and 2002), was inducted into the Museum of Pop Culture's "Science Fiction and Fantasy Hall of Fame," and was twice named to the American Screenwriters Association's Hall of Fame.

In the 1970s, Fontana joined a recently formed women's committee of the Writer's Guild because she was disappointed that women only comprised 10 percent of the membership. It was important to her that women "had a voice" in the organization. After the 1998 writers' strike, Fontana ran for the guild board and won, primarily to boost female representation on the board, and was elected to a second, nonconsecutive term (Cassel).

In interviews, Fontana repeated her hope that she would not be remembered as "a woman writer" but as "a damn good writer." Uncomfortable with being dubbed a trailblazer, she would deflect the praise by noting she wasn't an outlier, frequently mentioning Leigh Brackett by name and noting that her female contemporaries were regular contributors to comedies, romances, and daytime soaps, though predominantly working in tandem with a spouse or other male partner. Fontana was more unusual in claiming sole credit for most of her teleplays. Notably, Fontana also began a second career teaching screenwriting courses at the American Film Institute in 1998.

In 1979, she met her future husband, Dennis Skotak—the Oscar-winning visual effects cinematographer who worked on *Aliens*, *Batman Returns*, and *The Abyss*—when they collaborated on a TV Halloween special pastiche of *Alien*. They married in 1981 and were together until she died in 2019.

Since Fontana was Italian, she justifiably deserves inclusion in the feminist project of recovering Italian American women writers spearheaded by Helen Barolini in *The Dream Book* (1985) and continued in the scholarship of Mary Jo Bona, Edvige Giunta, and Tesi di Laurea. As both an author of Fantastika and an artist working in the television medium—which fought long and hard for credibility even within film studies—Fontana has been overlooked by Barolini's project until now. This essay is intended to correct her accidental omission from the canon of Italian American women writers.

Though she did not discuss herself as an Italian in interviews, at least one online celebrity genealogy website identifies Fontana as Italian.

In addition, the Fontana surname is traceable back to Bologna. Hoping to confirm her ethnicity, I contacted *Trek* historian John Tenuto, who replied: "We know her father was Carlo Charles Fontana, born November 23, 1912, in Haledon, New Jersey. He may have passed before 1950, likely because he is not listed on the 1950s Census. D.C.'s mom was Catherine, born February 20, 1916, in New Jersey. Charles worked at Harmon Color Works as a laborer during the 1940s. I always wondered if Charlie X was named for him. I think, although I cannot confirm, that her family name was actually Fontania and that her grandfather was Dominick Fontania who had a son named Charles. If that is right, then Dominick was from Italy" (email: 3 July 2023).

Fontana was part of a generation of Italians eager to enculturate and sometimes quick to Anglicize Italian family names once they reached Hollywood, yet she did not change her surname. Admittedly, by the time she was establishing herself, many with Italian surnames were well established in Hollywood and global cinema, including Sinatra, Fellini, Magnani, Borgnine, and Mineo. Still, it remains notable that she retained her father's surname when faced with this choice. Furthermore, Fontana ensured that the multicultural *Star Trek* universe included Italian characters, writing "Tomorrow Is Yesterday," an episode that introduced a twentieth-century Earth character named USAF Police Col. Fellini (Ed Peck). Fontana also edited the script of Gene L. Coon's teleplay for "The Devil in the Dark," which introduced USS *Enterprise* Security Chief Giotto (played by Barry Russo). These roles for Italian characters were small enough that those fans who sought after overtly Italian characters in *Star Trek* might blink and miss them as I did, sadly. Nonetheless, those characters appeared in the show, and Fontana worked on the teleplays that introduced them. Still more noteworthy, Fontana wrote the premiere episode of *Star Trek: The Next Generation*, "Encounter at Farpoint," in which she introduced a character conceived by David Gerrold, Lt. Commander Data (Brent Spiner), a sentient android who longed to become human. Noting that Data's desires made him akin to Pinocchio, the little wooden person who longed to become "a real boy," Fontana wrote dialogue for Commander Riker that makes this symbolic Collodi connection explicit. During his first meeting with Data, Riker jokingly nicknames him "Pinocchio." In these and other ways, the not-always-obviously-Italian Dorothy Fontana embedded elements of her heritage into the classic scripts she wrote for *Star Trek*.

Dorothy Catherine Fontana was born on March 25, 1939, in Sussex, New Jersey, and raised by a single mother in Totowa for nineteen years.

Her father, a roofer and sider, had left the family when Dorothy was ten, forcing her homemaker mother, Catherine Norman Fontana, to work as a saleswoman in the linen department of Two Guys from Harrison discount store. "Pretty much" never seeing her father again, Fontana was left to watch her two younger brothers after school while her mother worked. The boys were four and eighteen months at the time. "I loved it," she reminisced, matter-of-factly. "I didn't have a problem with it. That was our family. That was what we did" (Davis).

A self-described tomboy, Fontana enjoyed roller-skating, horseback riding, and reading the classics voraciously, starting with *A Christmas Carol*. From eleven to fourteen, she "spent a lot of time writing horror stories starring me and my friends," featuring ghosts and vampires. Fontana started a novel in high school, but money problems derailed the project. At sixteen, she took her first secretarial job to pay for schoolbooks. She graduated from Passaic Valley High School in 1957. When it was time to enroll in Fairleigh Dickinson University's Rutherford campus, Fontana's mother advised her to select a practical major to mitigate the risk of pursuing the financially unstable career of a writer. She earned an Executive Secretarial Associate of Arts degree while writing for the college newspaper on the side, graduating in 1959 (Beckerman and Biese).

She then moved to New York and became a secretary in Columbia Pictures' television wing. Ironically, this would be the first of multiple abbreviated and temporary secretarial positions, as her New York supervisor died, compelling her to move back in with her mother briefly before taking the risk of moving to Los Angeles without securing a job before departure. Within two weeks, Fontana landed a position in the typing pool at Revue Studios, working as one producer Samuel A. Peeples's administrative assistant and typesetting screenplays (including *Psycho*). "I was seeing scripts come across our desks for the various shows we had on the air at the time, and I thought, 'I can write this,' like so many fools before me," she said (Sky).

At twenty-one, she wrote a television story of her own, showed it to Peeples, and made a sale, inspiring her to continue freelance writing screen stories and teleplays. Since selling scripts only netted her around $1,000 a sale, Fontana felt compelled to draw a regular income from her daytime clerical work and confined herself to writing teleplays in the evenings. Still, she saw herself as a writer, not an administrative assistant. Problems arose when her producers and supervisors would consider her the reverse: a secretary playing at being a writer. Despite these challenges,

Fontana sold multiple story ideas and full teleplays made into broadcast episodes of westerns and medical dramas such as *The Tall Man*, *The Road West*, and *Ben Casey*. After a short period working with Peeples, whom she considered a key mentor figure in her developing writing career, Fontana changed supervisors. She began working for Del Reisman, a producer on the television series *The Lieutenant* (1963–1964). Shortly afterward, the secretary working for series creator Gene Roddenberry fell ill, so Reisman surrendered Fontana to Roddenberry as an emergency replacement. Fontana recalled her first impression of Roddenberry as a formidable physical presence: a six-foot-three, heavy-set, genial man puffing on a cigar.

"He was a lot of fun," she remembered.

The Lieutenant fell victim to studio censorship and cancellation when Roddenberry attempted to wrestle overtly with systemic racism in an episode starring Nichelle Nichols. After *The Lieutenant*'s failure, Roddenberry decided it would be easier to promote socially progressive ideas if he presented them to the public dressed up in a fantastical allegory, in the tried-and-true Aesop and Jonathan Swift fashion. *Star Trek* began to marinate in his head. Inspired by his enthusiasm for films such as *Forbidden Planet* (1958) and *Master of the World* (1961), and books including *The Voyage of the Space Beagle* (1950) by A. E. van Voght and the pulp magazine *Captain Future: Wizard of Science* (1940–1944) by Edmond Hamilton, Roddenberry designed *Trek* to implicitly critique the turbulent present day of 1964 and offer a road map for a better future by depicting a peaceful, spacefaring human society whose chief source of conflict was encountering alien races that were not yet as far along in their cultural evolution to abandon warfare. He wanted the show's main setting to be the bridge of a spaceship helmed by a crew that was as multiracial as those found in most World War II films. He also wanted this diverse crew to include Spock, an enigmatic, possibly satanic alien with red skin and pointed ears.

Instead of a tough-as-nails, Lee Marvin–type commander of the (vessel that would later be called the) *Enterprise*, Roddenberry wanted to present a more compassionate model of manhood to his audience. This ship's captain would be a thoughtful leader with a big heart who avoided conflict whenever possible but could still make difficult, heart-wrenching choices in a crisis. Roddenberry's model for this commander was C. S. Forester's naval commander hero Horatio Hornblower. Significantly, Hornblower embodied the compassionate masculinity and humanistic ethics cultivated at the London boarding school Dulwich College. Traits associated with the "Old Alleynian" graduates of this real-life Hogwarts may be found in the personalities and writings of its graduates, especially Forester, Ernest Shackleton, P. G. Wodehouse, and Raymond Chandler. Roddenberry imbued all three *Enterprise* captains he created over the years with this "Dulwich" moral fiber: Christopher Pike, James T. Kirk, and Jean-Luc Picard. To round them out, he seasoned them with some of his own, Leo-sign character flaws, including a tendency toward melodramatically hogging the spotlight and being dependent upon the admiration of women for a sense of self-worth.

When Roddenberry wrote up a twelve-page treatment for *Star Trek*, he showed it to his production secretary. Fontana was instantly intrigued by the character of Spock and delighted to hear that Roddenberry had already had their mutual acquaintance from *The Lieutenant*—Leonard Nimoy—in mind to play him. She told him he was on to something, and he moved forward with the idea, instinctively making equally inspired first-pick casting choices as he rounded out the crew. To prep for the potential new series, Roddenberry secured Fontana twenty-five anthologies of science fiction short stories and asked her to comb through them for material they could adapt into episodes. As Fontana read the stories, she planned to write *Trek* scripts should the show be greenlit.

Given how remarkable it was that Roddenberry brought his egalitarian vision to the screen, it should be no surprise that he faced some obstacles from skeptical studio executives in constructing his multiracial *Enterprise* crew. Stephen E. Whitfield describes an early series development meeting in which

> there were still those who were afraid of the consequences [of presenting a diverse cast to the world] from a strictly dollars-and-cents point of view. By putting a Negro in the crew they might lose the Southern states, by putting a Mexican in the crew they might lose Texas, Arizona, and parts of California . . . a Chinese crew member could lose sales for the show in Indonesia, etc., etc., etc. Gene began to realize that if he listened to all these people, the *Enterprise* would end up with an all-white, Protestant, Caucasian crew. This could then rebound with the same result in a great many foreign countries, because why should they believe that 200 years from now such a ship would be manned by an all-American crew? So many people became embroiled in so much controversy that they ended up leaving Gene alone to do it the way he wanted to. (127–28)

Of course, Roddenberry did not invent utopian science fiction. Aside from an ideal city posited in Plato's *Republic* (375 BCE) and other embryonic forms of utopian concepts, the genre arguably was born with the publication of Thomas More's *Utopia* (1516) and developed in texts such as Tommaso Campanella's *The City of the Sun* (1623), Edward Bellamy's 1888 novel *Looking Backward: 2000–1887*, William Morris's *News from Nowhere* (1890), and Oscar Wilde's Roman Catholic road map through the industrial age, "The Soul of Man Under Socialism" (1891). Roddenberry's male-dominated vision of a perfect society was arguably outdone in its egalitarianism both before and since *TOS*'s three-season run by feminist utopias of Charlotte Perkins Gilman's *Herland* (1915) and Marge Piercy's *Woman on the Edge of Time* (1976), plus multiple works by Joanna Russ, Alice Bradley Sheldon, and Ursula K. Le Guin.

Still, in the end, Roddenberry would be the right person at the right time to propose a utopian science fiction show for the 1960s television landscape, and Lucille Ball would be equally instrumental in purchasing the show for her company, Desilu.

As a secretary and personal assistant to Roddenberry during the development and production of *Star Trek*, Fontana saw up close how much time Roddenberry spent vetting spec scripts and rewriting accepted scripts. She helped him in this process by making script notes of her own. After reading several sets of Fontana's notes, another *Trek* producer, Bob Justman, was struck by "the intelligence and orderly thought processes [Fontana] revealed in her story analysis" and "convinced Roddenberry to give her a trial assignment to write the script of 'Charlie X' " (Solow and Justman 132). Rising to the occasion, Fontana wrote a suspenseful, character-driven piece that impressed the cast and production team, especially since Roddenberry had given up on his own story idea as lacking enough incident to be exciting. Fontana was invited to write another episode: "Tomorrow Is Yesterday."

While writing this second story, from an original idea of her own, Fontana began to fear she would wind up spending her entire time working on *TOS* doing scriptwriter and editor work with a secretary's title and for a secretary's pay. Hoping to oblige Roddenberry to grant her the recompense she deserved, Fontana took a gamble and resigned. Her cunning plan worked. Two weeks later, Roddenberry called and asked her to do an extensive rewrite of a problematic teleplay by Jerry Sohl as a tryout for the full-time script editor job. He was considering her for the position since she'd "been there from the beginning" and intuitively understood *Star Trek*'s expansive fictional universe, cast of characters, future technology, and egalitarian ideals.

Figure 13.1. Leonard Nimoy and Jill Ireland as Spock and Leila Kalomi in "This Side of Paradise." *Source:* Desilu/Paramount, 1967, publicity still.

Fontana transformed the script, unnerving Nimoy by challenging him to play the logical, austere Mr. Spock *in love*. Despite his initial reservations, Nimoy finished shooting the episode feeling enormous gratitude for the meaty, powerful role she'd written him. Meanwhile, the NBC executives shared Roddenberry's pleasant surprise that Fontana had succeeded in penning a love story that *no one had thought she could make believable*. The now-classic episode "This Side of Paradise" landed Fontana the script editor job. "I wasn't going to dance in the streets," she remembered, "so I went home and danced in my apartment."

With her hiring on December 19, 1966, at age twenty-seven, Fontana had become the youngest story editor in television history and one of only a few female story editors (Volk-Weiss). For Fontana, rising to the challenge of her new position was not difficult: "I learned to speak up more because I had to." Since there were no staff writers, she would solicit scripts, read ones submitted to the slush pile, rewrite the works of others, and write her own original scripts longhand on yellow, lined paper before typing them up.

On *Star Trek*, Fontana enjoyed collaborating with producer Gene L. Coon in developing the iconic friendship between Kirk, Spock, and McCoy. She and Coon also consciously added badinage to the teleplays that brought out William Shatner's natural gift for comedy and made his Captain Kirk more appealing. The fans responded well to the show's increasing use of humor, but the comedy irritated Roddenberry, who himself wrote scripts largely devoid of humor. The push and pull over the proper balance of humor and drama aside, Fontana consistently demonstrated the ability to provide scripts—either written by her whole cloth or revised from other writers' work—that satisfied Roddenberry, the actors, and fans alike because she knew the characters so well that writing them became second nature (Kreski and Shatner 230).

In addition to writing about love and relationships, the voracious reader of history books also worked little-known, real-life incidents into her teleplays throughout her career, from *Star Trek* onward. A foiled, long-forgotten plot to steal Abraham Lincoln's corpse inspired a story she wrote for *Babylon 5*. Fontana also created a villain for *Lonesome Dove: The Series* inspired by real-life murderer Susan Monica, who murdered two handymen on her Oregon farm, dismembered them, and fed them to her pigs. Most famously, the *Pueblo* incident, involving North Korea's capture of the USS *Pueblo*, a Naval intelligence vessel with eighty-three crewmen aboard, on January 23, 1968—inspired her to write an espionage adventure: "The Enterprise Incident" (and its comic book sequel, "The Enterprise Experiment"). In the *Star Trek* version of the *Pueblo* scandal, Kirk and Spock set about stealing a Romulan starship's invisibility cloak device.

Infamously, the teleplay Fontana had the most difficulty editing and revising was Harlan Ellison's acclaimed episode, "City on the Edge of Forever." In 1966, Ellison submitted a tragic story set during the Depression involving a time-travel catastrophe that hands Adolf Hitler victory in World War II, erasing the utopian Federation from history. In the teleplay's "trolley problem"-style dilemma, Kirk must choose between saving the life of a Dorothy Day figure he has fallen in love with and allowing her to die to restore the established course of history. In Ellison's first draft, Kirk freezes up at the climactic moment because he cannot bring himself to let Edith Keeler die. Kirk's failure to act leaves Spock to take up the burden and ensure her preordained end. After reading Ellison's script,

Roddenberry felt strongly that Kirk, as the main character of the show, had to be the one to resolve the crisis. After all, Spock had already compelled Kirk to make a similarly appalling personal sacrifice in "Where No Man Has Gone Before," and Kirk had not frozen up when he had to kill his best friend. Ellison's Kirk, however, anticipated the Kirk of *The Wrath of Khan*, who refused to believe in the "no-win scenario" and would invariably respond to an impossible choice between two disastrous outcomes by finding an infinitely preferable "third way" no one had considered. Ellison and Roddenberry both had legitimate takes on Kirk, especially this early in the show's development, but Roddenberry was in charge, so his view prevailed. This time, Abraham would have to see Isaac's death through.

As a friend and fan of Ellison, Fontana feared offending him and setting off his infamous temper. As she anticipated, Ellison went ballistic when he saw how much his script had transformed. In retaliation, Ellison tried to have his name removed from the screenplay, but Roddenberry allegedly threatened to blacklist him if he did (Solow and Justman 275–89). Declaring Roddenberry a lying bully, Ellison went from being one of *Star Trek*'s biggest supporters to one of its biggest detractors. He consistently railed against any future franchise adventures indebted to the concepts he introduced in "City on the Edge of Forever," including the apocalyptic time-travel comedy *Star Trek IV: The Voyage Home*.[1]

According to "The Trouble with Tribbles" screenwriter David Gerrold, Fontana didn't tell Ellison for "three decades that she had done the rewrite on it. She let him blame Gene." When Ellison finally found out Fontana was among the four writers who—as he put it—"took turns pissing in my script," he was shocked and disappointed. Still, Gerrold would later recall, smiling, Harlan "couldn't be mad at her. *Nobody* could be mad at Dorothy" (Volk-Weiss).

This would be the biggest controversy Fontana would have to handle during an otherwise reasonably smooth tenure as script editor.

"Family Is Sacred": How Fontana and Spock Hungered for Their Absent Fathers

In Gene Roddenberry's twelve-page Bible, Mr. Spock was described sketchily as a figure of mystery who might be part Martian. Between the production of the two pilot episodes, "The Cage" and "Where No Man Has Gone Before," Spock was merged with the scrapped series regular Number One (who had a clinical, logical personality) into a composite character. In other respects, Spock was a blank slate. Writers who crafted early scripts for Spock—especially Samuel A. Peeples, John D. F. Black, and Theodore Sturgeon—gradually established, episode by episode, that Spock had devoted his life to logic and strictly controlled his emotions. However, like other Vulcans, Spock was susceptible to extreme outbursts of emotion when under the influence of intoxicating or cyclical, hormonal stimuli. His potentially volatile emotional core was complicated further by his half-human heritage and conflicted racial identity. These writers' contributions aside, Nimoy developed the Spock character himself to such a degree that Roddenberry was jealous of Spock's ownership of the character he had conceived of. Nimoy established Spock as being averse to violence and conceived of the nonlethal, incapacitating Vulcan neck pinch. Nimoy also made elements of his Jewish background part of the character, such as the quasi-rabbinical gesture of the Vulcan salute.

Figure 13.2. Spock with his parents, human schoolteacher Amanda Grayson and Sarek, the Vulcan ambassador. Characters created by D. C. Fontana and pictured here in *Star Trek IV: The Voyage Home* (1986). *Source: Star Trek IV: The Voyage Home*, Paramount, 1986, publicity still.

Taking the aforementioned as a given, Nimoy nevertheless cited Fontana as the single writer who did the most to help him bring Spock to life. Fontana's scripts explored Spock's interiority, introduced his family background, and further developed a Vulcan society introduced by Sturgeon in "Amok Time" (1967). Fontana created Spock's parents, the distant Vulcan Sarek, who disowned Spock for eighteen years for leaving Vulcan to join Starfleet, and the witty, assertive human, Amanda Grayson, whose love for Spock never wavered. Fontana also created Spock's childhood pet, I-Chaya, the fanged, bear-like Sehlat he was forced to euthanize to shorten its painful death. Fontana also conceived of the Kahs-wan, a Vulcan coming-of-age ritual involving a trip across the desert terrain of Vulcan's Forge. Perhaps most importantly, Fontana established that Spock was frequently bullied at school by racist, "pureblooded" Vulcans, who mocked his human mother and Spock himself for being half-human. Fontana wrote all these elements into "Journey to Babel" and "Yesteryear," which remain popular and influential episodes. Significantly, Spock's parents would become iconic, centrally important supporting characters appearing in numerous *Star Trek* spinoff shows (including *Discovery* and *Strange New Worlds*), and multiple films (including I, III, IV, and VI, and J. J. Abrams's first reboot film), as well as the popular novels *Vulcan Academy Murders* (1984) by Jean Lorrah and *Sarek* (1995) by A. C. Crispin. All of these are landmark *Star Trek* adventures.

Fontana has maintained that none of her scripts are autobiographical, noting that "family is sacred" and too private to write about for television. And yet, perhaps the reason the story of Spock's falling out with his parents resonates so strongly with fans is that Fontana wrote "Journey to Babel" from the heart. Despite her protestations, Fontana's scripts appear to arise from her lingering feelings of abandonment over her father's leaving her family forever when she was ten.

Looking back upon the span of her career late in life, Fontana said of her body of work: "My writing style has changed over the years, not just from maturity, but also reflecting the world in which we live and how I see it. . . . What hasn't changed is that I generally still write about love—between parents and children, siblings, friends, lovers—love gained, lost, envied, stolen, used, thrown away. . . . It's all about human beings, isn't it? It's who we are; it's what we write about" (Wolfman).

While many scholars regard biographical criticism skeptically, the details of Fontana's case encourage such analysis. After all, consider just how many of her teleplays concern single mothers, absent father figures, and estranged or orphaned children:

- In "Charlie X," an unruly, orphaned teen with godlike powers fixates upon Kirk as a potential replacement father figure.
- In "Friday's Child," Julie Newmar plays a pregnant queen whose king is killed; she looks to Doctor McCoy to act as a replacement father for her unborn child.
- In "Encounter at Farpoint," Fontana established that teenage civilian Wesley Crusher's father, Jack, was killed in action serving under his best friend, Captain Jean-Luc Picard. Wesley's mother, Beverly, had always harbored secret feelings for Picard—and suspected that Picard privately felt the same way about her—but Jack had stood between them. (Even dead, the memory of Jack *still* stood between them.) Later, when Beverly unexpectedly applied to become the Chief Medical Officer of the *Enterprise*, to serve under his captaincy, Picard couldn't help but wonder if she did it so he could eventually become a replacement father figure for Wesley.

There is one more, notable, instance of absent fathers in Fontana's *Trek* scripts: Dr. McCoy. In one of her conversations with actor DeForest Kelley about how Doctor McCoy should evolve as a character during season 2, Fontana suggested that the Georgia physician was notably older than Kirk and could credibly have a full-grown son. Fontana felt surprised affection for Kelley when he gently suggested she make the child a girl. "Joanna," her final script for *TOS*, was about this eponymous daughter, "who has just become a registered nurse and was joining the Federation because she wanted to catch up to her father, who has been on these five-year missions, and she hasn't seen him, and they had lost touch" (Bowie).

Unfortunately for both Kelley and Fontana, producer Fred Freiberger objected to this concept on a fundamental level. He feared the storyline would age McCoy too much. He also worried Kirk might develop feelings for Joanna in a plot twist that would make Kirk look like he was cradle-robbing his best friend's child. Freiberger ordered the episode fundamentally reimagined, replacing Joanna with an ex-girlfriend of Chekhov's, and angering Fontana enough that she refused to place her name on what would later be called "The Way to Eden."

Interestingly, Fontana was able to seed references to Joanna into *Star Trek: The Animated Series* and her novelization of "Encounter at Farpoint."

Also, her planned Joanna story became so famous in *Trek* fandom that other writers took up her cause and either mentioned Joanna or gave Joanna a talking part in their stories. These works include *Crisis on Centaurus, Provenance of Shadows, The Autobiography of James T. Kirk, Shadows on the Sun*, and the *Legacies* trilogy. In the last years of her life, Fontana told interviewers she was still interested in adapting her original idea into a novel. Sadly, she died before she had the opportunity.

Fontana's scripts feel like fantasy solutions to an unsolvable, real-life problem she faced. Even if she could not be with her Italian American father in our imperfect reality, she could write a happier ending for Spock and have him and Sarek make peace. Was this fantasy of reunion also a way of dealing with her heritage, which her father may have "taken with him"—and away from her—when he left?

The difficult but loving patriarch who is confounded by his children of two worlds is a narrative spine of immigrant lit in general—and Asian American literature in particular—appearing in narratives such as Julia Alvarez's *How the García Girls Lost Their Accents*, Jhumpa Lahiri's *The Namesake*, Art Spiegelman's *Maus*, Laila Lalami's *The Other Americans*, C. Y. Lee's *The Flower Drum Song*, John Okada's *No-No Boy*, Chang-Rae Lee's *Native Speaker*, and Thi Bui's *The Best We Could Do.*[2] Fontana's stories of imposing and absent fathers remind us that the iconic, ambivalently portrayed immigrant('s) father figure is also a key element in Italian American literature. For example, Fontana's real-life father conjures images of the killed or absent fathers from *Christ in Concrete* and *The Fortunate Pilgrim*. In contrast, the formidable Sarek has more in common with the fathers in Mario Puzo's *Godfather* and John Fante's *Wait Until Spring, Bandini*. The "Fantastika" element in the Sarek story is the eventual embracing of the estranged child that Fontana depicts in her iterations of this father figure.

The thought of Fontana never reconciling with her Italian biological father is depressing. What may be more tragic still is the painful feud that would erupt between her and the other father figure in her life: Roddenberry. Much of their relationship was amicable over the years, but their rapport gradually deteriorated alongside Roddenberry's wavering health. As one might expect, the thorny issues at the heart of the coming rift between Fontana and Roddenberry would be over exactly how much pay Fontana deserved and how much credit she should be given for her contributions to his franchise.

The Animated Series, *The Next Generation*, and the End of a Beautiful Friendship

Following the cancellation of the first series, Gene Roddenberry spent decades stoking the show's growing fanbase and cult status to pressure the franchise's new owners, Paramount, into restoring his science fiction universe to life in a new television or film series. These efforts led to several false starts, but Roddenberry saw three revivals in his lifetime: *Star Trek: The Animated Series* (aka *TAS*, 1973–1974), the film series spearheaded by Nicholas Meyer, Harve Bennett, and Robert Wise that began in 1979, and *Star Trek: The Next Generation* (aka *TNG*, 1987–1994). Pigeonholed as a television writer and not a screenwriter, Fontana was not invited to participate in shaping the movie scripts—which was particularly unfortunate in the case of *Star Trek: The Motion Picture*, because that turgid, lifeless epic had needed her deft hand desperately. This oversight aside, Roddenberry did recruit Fontana to write scripts for both television revivals.

Roddenberry appointed Fontana associate producer and story editor of *The Animated Series*, giving her a studio office and most of the creative control. He would read the proposed scripts from the comfort of home, occasionally rewriting or vetoing them. United in purpose, Fontana and Roddenberry strove to win over vociferously skeptical fans who were concerned *TAS* would be a trivial kids' show. She allayed some of those fears by ensuring that the animation faithfully recreated the classic *Enterprise* exterior and interiors. She also soon realized that a "cartoon" would enable the production team to present exotic planets and unique aliens far superior to what had been achievable with the limited resources of the live-action series.

Fontana remembered confronting a room of dubious fans, hoping to turn them to her side: "I went to the World Science Fiction Convention in Toronto in September of 1973, with only the animated opening credits to show to an expectant [midnight] audience. When that familiar starship flashed across the screen in the old way, with the music, and with the names of the actors involved—there was a standing ovation" (Startrek.com).

Treating the cartoon as the de facto fourth season of *TOS*, Fontana rehired the original cast members, as well as many of the show's most popular writers, including Gerrold, who provided an animated sequel to "Trouble with Tribbles," and her old mentor, Peeples. Her most notable teleplay-writer recruits included renowned science fiction author Larry

Figure 13.3. Fontana wrote the animated series episode "Yesteryear," a sequel to both "Journey to Babel" and "City on the Edge of Forever." Left to right, from foreground to background: Mr. Spock, Dr. McCoy, Captain Kirk, and the Guardian of Forever. "Yesteryear." *Source: Star Trek: The Animated Series*, NBC/Hal Sutherland, 1973, duplicate 35mm transparency.

Niven and Native American writer Russell Bates. Bates wrote the episode, "How Sharper than a Serpent's Tooth," introducing the first Native American character in Starfleet—Dawson Walking Bear, a Comanche ensign. Bates has the distinction of penning the only *Star Trek* script to win a writing Emmy.

In another step forward for diversity in *Trek*, Fontana saw to it that Lt. Nyota Uhura (Nichelle Nichols) and Lt. Hikaru Sulu (George Takei) had far more extensive roles in *TAS* than *TOS* had allotted them. Indeed, when Nichols read a script in which Uhura got her first chance to command the *Enterprise*, she yelled out, "Finally!" In the documentary *The Center Seat* (2021) Nichols recalled this moment, smiling: "Uhura got to captain the damn bridge! It was so satisfying, and I loved it!" (Volk-Weiss).

The cartoon lasted two seasons.

In 1987, through the intervention of his lawyer, Leonard Maizlish, Roddenberry regained some of the creative control he had lost over his IP during the production of the first motion picture. This new control led to his acquiring the clout to become appointed creator and showrunner of *Star Trek: The Next Generation*. Unfortunately, it had taken too long for this long-simmering TV sequel project to reach fruition. Suffering from diabetes, high blood pressure, and alcoholic encephalopathy, the aging Roddenberry was not up to the rigors of making a weekly show (Engel). Worried, he brought Gerrold and Fontana back into the fold, hoping to lean heavily on them in the creation of an entirely new cast of characters and the writing of a raft of new scripts. He assumed they would understand that *Star Trek* was still *his* baby—not *theirs*—and that he was sickly and needed his old friends to shoulder much of the burden of making *TNG* for him. What did not occur to him was the possibility that they might resent being asked to work for free here, and for cut-rate wages there, all the while being denied onscreen writing and cocreator credits.

According to Roddenberry biographer Joel Engel, Roddenberry liked Fontana and Gerrold personally and wanted their help to make the best possible series for the fans, but was also jealous and frightened of them. They'd both enjoyed far more career success than he had, and their early contributions to developing *TNG* were impressing Paramount executives to such an extent that Roddenberry feared the studio would pluck *Trek* out of his hands once again and hand it over to his two former protégés.

Early on Gerrold had specific ideas about distinguishing *TNG* from *TOS* so the new show wouldn't feel like warmed-up leftovers. He ran them by Roddenberry, who would approve, tweak, or reject the ideas, and Gerrold wrote them into the series Bible. During the series development process, Gerrold pushed for Captain Julien Picard to be depicted as an older, statesmanlike figure to contrast with the more Hemingway-like Kirk. The substitute "Spock character" would be an inverse of the Vulcan: an android who sought to be more human, rather than less. Both Fontana and Gerrold had the idea of placing a Klingon on the bridge to show that the twenty-fourth-century society of *TNG* was more peaceful than the twenty-third-century milieu of *TOS*, but Roddenberry rejected the idea. As a Klingon alternative, the production team contemplated essentially poaching the popular character of Vasquez from *Aliens*, changing the name but keeping her a badass Latina and even retaining the same actress: Jenette Goldstein (Gross and Altman 57).

Fontana had several problems with these proposed characters, starting with Julien Picard's first name. ("What would they call him, 'Julie'? No. Jean-Luc is better.") She also had reservations about transplanting the brownface Vasquez from *Aliens* onto the *Enterprise* bridge, unaltered ("Jenette Goldstein, is not Latina. She is petite, blue-eyed, and freckle-faced.") Most of all, Fontana hated that the proposed character "Lt. Troi" was supposed to have four breasts. ("Do you know how much trouble women have with the normal number? Keeping them out of the way of things . . . ? Four?!") In general, Fontana objected to any attempt to oversexualize the female characters and would later have her name taken off "The Naked Now" script when Roddenberry's rewrites included scenes in which Crusher and Yar threw themselves at Picard and Data (see Vary; Engel 227, 245).

By the time the unsigned series Bible was completed and printed, Gerrold was inclined to see himself as the new show's primary architect. In contrast, Roddenberry considered himself the true author of the series Bible and perceived Gerrold as little more than his amanuensis (Gross and Altman 61–63). In controversial industry histories, comparatively little has been written or said about exactly how much say Fontana had in providing ideas for this Bible.

Upon its completion, the Bible was handed over to Fontana to use as a reference as she wrote the premiere episode: "Encounter at Farpoint." Fontana had one big challenge in introducing the new ensemble cast: she disliked how bloodless the characters seemed to be in comparison to the meatier figures from the classic series. Where were the friendships that defined the classic crew? The notes of romance, humor, and good-natured rivalry? It was all absent (Gross and Altman 61–62). On paper, only Geordi seemed capable of healthy interpersonal relationships. To correct these defects, Fontana established more intimate connections between the characters. She imagined a potential Picard-Crusher romance (that would, decades later, prove pivotal to *Star Trek: Picard*'s third season). In one of the most memorable scenes in the episode, Fontana has Commander Riker compare the android Data to Pinocchio, who shared his wish to become fully human. The salient literary reference instantly crystalized the new character and served as a nod to Fontana's heritage.

After Fontana completed and submitted the script, Roddenberry wrote a "prequel" segment to lengthen the originally mooted one-hour premiere into a ninety-minute pilot. The "prequel" introduced the mischievous, all-powerful Q, a character Fontana and Gerrold dismissed as a retread

Figure 13.4. Who created these characters? Was it Gene Roddenberry, David Gerrold, or Dorothy Fontana? Cast from left to right, back row: LeVar Burton as Geordi La Forge, Brent Spiner as Data, Michael Dorn as Worf, Jonathan Frakes as William Riker. Second row, left to right: Marina Sirtis as Deanna Troi and Gates McFadden as Beverly Crusher. Front: Patrick Stewart as Jean-Luc Picard. *Source: Star Trek: The Next Generation*, Paramount, 1989, publicity still.

of *TOS* villain Trelane. Roddenberry wrote all the scenes featuring Q, minimized Tasha Yar's part (since she was too mannish for his taste), and gave much of Yar's cut material to a new, undeveloped Klingon crewman named "Worf" he created on the fly (Shatner). All the rest of the material in the script remained Fontana's. And yet, Roddenberry took her name off the script and submitted it to Paramount as his work alone. Fontana disliked all his changes aesthetically, but she was enraged Roddenberry had plotted to cheat her out of all payment, residuals, and creative credit by claiming sole credit for the script.

WGA arbitration would later name Fontana and Roddenberry as coscriptwriters.

Remembering how Roddenberry had cut her weekly salary on *TAS* to finance a raise for himself, Fontana complained to Gerrold, "Working for Gene Roddenberry always costs me money" (Gross and Altman 67–68).

Immediately after the debacle with "Farpoint," Roddenberry again attempted to take both money and credit away from Fontana by asking her to write a complete script for "The Naked Time" and put his name on it alongside hers if he did a light edit after she submitted it. She adamantly refused to go along with this plan. Roddenberry retaliated against Fontana by moving her office

> into a cramped space outside of which was a large generator that pounded and roared all day; entry was through a heavily traveled corridor that housed photocopiers and other office machines; a busy—and noisy—elevator was next door.
>
> "Gene's anger at Dorothy really got to the point where it was cruel," [Robert Lewin, creative producer of *TNG*, said]. . . . In another meeting, [Roddenberry] tried to embarrass her in front of Lewin, saying, "When Dorothy had to make changes on her first *Star Trek* script [in 1966] she broke down and cried."
>
> "In your dreams, Gene," she replied. "I've never cried over a script in my life." (Engel 254–55)

"Because she'd once been his secretary," Lewin said, "he always treated her like one. He expected gratitude and devotion and unlimited adoration" (Engel 231).

Unfortunately, the toxic work environment grew even more dire for Fontana when Gerrold and Roddenberry had a falling out. Early in *TNG*'s development, Gerrold took the showrunners at their word the series would be progressive. As a gay man, Gerrold was invested in writing a powerful AIDS allegory in "Blood and Fire." Gerrold felt his script was ultimately killed by a homophobic producer in one of many production office actions that flew in the face of the just, egalitarian future *Trek* had purported to depict. When he finally realized that Roddenberry had been gaslighting him about who was really behind the decisions that had marginalized him on set, Gerrold went home and instantly called Harlan Ellison to tell him he was right about Roddenberry all along (Gross and Altman 146).

Tensions between Gerrold and Roddenberry reached a boiling point when Gerrold filed a grievance claim with the WGA requesting a "cocreated by" credit for *TNG* in recompense for being the primary, unpaid author of the series Bible. According to multiple sources, Gerrold was treated infamously throughout his tenure on the show, facing prejudice for being gay from a supposedly progressive production team and seeing his AIDS-themed screenplay "Blood and Fire" buried for being too controversial, not insufficiently artistically sound. Fontana was one of the few who stood by Gerrold, and she suffered for her enduring loyalty to him.

Roddenberry called upon Fontana to help him defeat Gerrold's claim, but she preferred to remain neutral, citing her uncertainty as to who *really* wrote the Bible. Engel observed it would have been in her best interests to side with Roddenberry, but she had too much integrity. A tape recording of one of their key arguments about Gerrold depicts a lifelong relationship unraveling:

> "You have *no opinion* on whether I created this show?" [Roddenberry asked.]
>
> "I don't know," said Fontana.
>
> "I find that remarkable."
>
> "I'm sure you do, Gene, but there are memos—"
>
> " . . . We have been associated for twenty-one years. . . . You have no opinion on whether I'm honest in saying I created it, huh? . . . I find this astonishing—astonishing, Dorothy . . . I gave you opportunities."
>
> "That's true," Fontana said. (Engel 253–54)

Surprisingly, there is an uncanny similarity between their real-life, volatile, decades-long relationship and the frenemy dynamics between advertising executive Don Draper and his protégé (and former secretary) Peggy Olson in the acclaimed television series *Mad Men* (2007–2015). Of course, the fictional *Mad Men* characters worked in an advertising agency, and the real-life Roddenberry and Fontana were making a television series together. Still, both relationships unfolded throughout the 1960s and exhibited startlingly similar professional, gender, and power dynamics. Odder still, the two men have nearly identical virtues and vices. In some ways, the women are strikingly similar as well. Matching Fontana's feelings about Roddenberry, Peggy was grateful to Don for discovering her but resentful of her pay scale and mortified by Don's decision to take credit for an idea of hers that won him a Clio Award. (And the wall between fiction and reality seems particularly semipermeable when one considers the resonant image of Peggy saddled with a terrible office next to a loud, busy photocopier.) Furthermore, Don and Peggy's most famous argument could have been ripped straight from the tape-recorded argument transcribed in Engel's book:

> PEGGY: I'm sorry. I was excited, and I heard there was an amazing assignment.
>
> DON: And you thought you'd come in here and ask for it because I never say no.
>
> PEGGY: You say no all the time.
>
> DON: What do I have to do for you, Peggy? Tell me. You were my secretary, and now you have an office and a job that a lot of full-grown men would kill for. Every time I turn around you've got your hand in my pocket. You want a raise. You want [recognition]. . . . Put your nose down and pay attention to your work, 'cause there's not one thing that you've done here that I couldn't live without. (*Mad Men*, s3 e1: "Seven Twenty Three")

The final, most extreme retaliation against Fontana involved *Encounter at Farpoint*, a novel adaptation of the first *TNG* adventure (Gross and Altman 143). Knowing she was upset with his changes to her script, Roddenberry assured her total creative freedom to write the novel any way she liked. She took him at his word and wrote a complete manuscript. Only after she finished did Roddenberry's lawyer capriciously announce that Gerrold would be asked to write the novel instead. For his part, Gerrold was horrified when he heard Fontana had already finished the job with which he'd just been tasked. Eager to right this wrong, Gerrold submitted Fontana's manuscript with his name on it and ordered the publisher to deposit all his royalties into her bank account. It was an imperfect way of mitigating an impossible situation, but the alternative would have been Fontana's book being left unpublished and her work unpaid. And so, there's a book out there that Fontana wrote with Gerrold's name on it (Gross and Altman; Volk-Weiss).

Fontana's contract with *TNG* concluded on October 9, 1987: "Throughout [my time on the show,] I was subject to personal harassment, to sexual discrimination, and to personal discrimination. . . . When I refused to go against my principles and Guild rules, I was punished with the killing of my novelization contract and also punished with harassment in regards to parking, my office, and to my work. All of the above appeared to stem from Leonard Maizlish, although Roddenberry himself was not innocent by any means" (Gross and Altman 143–44).

On August 28, 2023, Gerrold made an elliptical Facebook post that appears to be related to his and Fontana's time on *TNG*: "If you were not in the room, your opinion is probably irrelevant. (There are some people who have probably written thousands of words about how a certain TV show was created. They were not in the room . . .)"

Unsurprisingly, Roddenberry's son Rod has been upset by scandalous stories such as these that have come out in the wake of his father's death. Expressing sympathy for those whose contributions to creating *Star Trek* have gone largely unsung for too long, Rod nevertheless said he was ready for the wronged parties to "stop bashing my fucking father" (Altman and Gross 125). Accepting for the moment the idea that Roddenberry has been unfairly demonized by a multitude of *Star Trek* behind-the-scenes tell-all books and documentaries, even a charitable assessment of the man would have to conclude that, on multiple occasions, he did not live up to his own egalitarian, Starfleet ideals.

In contrast, in both her fictional narratives and real-world actions, Fontana consistently demonstrated a firm commitment to the ideals of the United Federation of Planets. Even after she was free and clear of the toxic work environment of *TNG*, Fontana continued to defend freelance writers from being exploited by the show's producers. She said, "There were [*TNG* producers] going out to conventions and taking in young amateur writers who had good *Trek* ideas. One of the [would-be fan writers] wrote to me and asked how he could get more than $1,500 for a *Star Trek* script. The first thing I did was copy his letter and send it to the WGA Legal Department with a note that said, "FIX THIS!" . . . At the time, the fee for a script was at least 20K; and, of course, [the fan writers names were being removed from their scripts, cheating them of] residuals, etc. [The producers] were doing *a lot* of shady things. It was stopped."

We All Deserve to Live in D. C. Fontana's Socialist Utopia

One of the most intriguing elements of Fontana's tenure as script editor on the first *Star Trek* series was reading through the deluge of fan mail delivered to her office. Mountains of letters arrived from college students and young professionals, some of which professed the expected adoration of Kirk and Spock or enthusiasm for specific stories. Many commented insightfully on the series' political and scientific concepts. Fontana didn't realize just how large a percentage of *Trek*'s fanbase was female until she attended the first convention, in 1969, and saw that half the audience were female high school and college students, married women, and young professional women (Baker-Whitelaw). Indeed, with Fontana's encouragement and participation, *Trek* fandom—which preceded geek culture as we know it today—was founded by female fans.

This information might surprise some since the stereotypical view of *Star Trek* is that it was a series created by child-men for child-men: part WWII submarine combat adventure whimsically transposed to outer-space, and part adolescent wet-dream featuring red-miniskirt-wearing yeomen and half-naked, green-skinned alien concubines. Those franchise elements notwithstanding, one might argue that *Star Trek*, in all its multimedia forms, has been *by* women writers *for* women fans all along.

Certainly, as the first woman to write *Trek*, excel at it, and establish much of the tone and series lore, Fontana cultivated both a fictional universe and a professional working environment welcoming to women. Indeed, the list of women writers who would follow in Fontana's footsteps and offer significant contributions to the franchise over the next several decades is substantial. Consider the other female identifying writers of the first series: Margaret Armen, Jean Lisette Aroeste, Judy Burns, Shari Lewis, and Joyce Muskat. They were succeeded by female teleplay writers on sequel series from *The Next Generation* (aka *TNG*) to shows of the present day, such as the popular and acclaimed *Strange New Worlds* (2022–). Jeri Taylor, producer of *Voyager* (1995–2001) and cocreator of the franchise's first female series lead, Captain Kathryn Janeway, is arguably the most noteworthy female successor to Fontana. Others include Julie and Shawna Benson, Kirsten Beyer, Lisa Schultz Boyd, Sally Caves, Akela Cooper, Deborah Dean Davis, Jane Espensen, Dana Horgan, Ann Kim, Lisa Klink, Jenny Lumet, Kathryn Lyn, Diandra Pendleton-Thompson, Hannah Louise Shearer, Melinda M. Snodgrass, Phyllis Strong, Sarah Tarkoff, and Robin Wasserman.

Furthermore, David A. Goodman and Peter David aside, the best *Trek* novels were by women: Diane Duane, Diane Carey, A. C. Crispin, Britta Dennison, J. M. Dillard, L. A. Graf, Barbara Hambly, Janet Kagan, Jean Lorrah, Vonda N. McIntyre, M. S. Murdock, S. D. Perry, and Kristine Kathryn Rusch—plus the duos Judith and Garfield Reeves-Stevens, and Josepha Berman and Susan Shwartz.

Without Fontana paving the way, it is hard to imagine *Trek* quietly developing such a strong feminist pedigree.

Gene Roddenberry died during the production of the third season of *Star Trek: The Next Generation*. In the years since his passing, the intellectual property he cocreated with Fontana and others has grown exponentially. As of now, *Star Trek* is a multimedia franchise of a dozen series (comprised of 880 episodes over forty-four seasons), more than two hundred original novels, and at least a dozen multi-issue comic book series. The collective story these narratives unfold paints a sprawling history of a fictional universe, spanning from (a now-counterfactual) 1996—when Earth was finally liberated from the reign of genetically engineered superhuman tyrant Khan Noonien Singh (Ricardo Montalban)—to the inspiring rebirth of the utopian ideals of the Federation after two centuries of galaxy-wide isolationism and strife, circa 3189. While some of these shows are more gothic and militaristic in tone and others more transcendentalist and hopeful, all versions of *Star Trek* depict characters striving to live out their lives in a deeply imperfect society according to the ideals the Federation represents.

Notably, the franchise itself continually strives to live up to Afrofuturism's modeling of a more racially equal future (Zamalin), instead of succumbing to the gravitational pull of the colonial roots of science fiction (Rieder).

In recent years, *Star Trek* has enjoyed a new Renaissance thanks to the streaming channel *Paramount+*, which has premiered a half-dozen new television shows in the franchise. Certainly, *Paramount+*'s business model has played a critical role in this resurgence. I would also argue that *Star Trek*'s current popularity is inextricably tied to its promotion of an uncommon, Antifa ethos in a contemporary political context of resurgent global fascism. Ever since the shooting of Trayvon Martin and the Brexit general election, the venerable franchise has garnered renewed attention from activists and scholars who have sought solace from its hopeful depiction of the future. Modern-day idealists, intellectuals, and activists look to *Star Trek* for inspiration in efforts to subdue the forces of reaction and make the Federation's socialist utopia a reality in the here and now. Books such as *Star Trek's Philosophy of Peace and Justice: A Global, Anti-racist Approach* by José-Antonio Orosco and *Exploring Voyager: Critical Essays* edited by Robert L. Lively are emblematic of these efforts. Indeed, *Star Trek*'s moral values are worth contemplating as they are depicted in episodes and storylines from the various shows. Those values are also worth contemplating as they become apparent in any study of the life and works of D. C. Fontana.

As a writer of Marxist-feminist Fantastika for mass audiences, the late Dorothy Fontana has become part of a generations-long tradition of Italian American humanists at the forefront of movements for egalitarian arts and politics. Other members of this honorable group include Sacco and Vanzetti, Ginny Apuzzo, Pietro di Donato, Ani DiFranco, Diane di Prima, John Fante, Kitty Genovese, Viola Liuzzo, Tom Morello, Mario Savio, Eleanor Smeal (née Cutri), Bruce Springsteen, and Carlo Tresca. In addition, the following organizations have attracted many Italians who have worked toward manifesting a more just and egalitarian future: the anti-fascist Sardines movement; CIAO (Canadian Italians Against Oppression); "Paisans for Kamala"; the Facebook group Leftists of the Italian Diaspora; and academic organizations such as the Italian American Studies Association (IASA), the Working-Class Studies Association (WCSA), and the Society for the Study of Multiethnic Literature of the United States (MELUS), These Italians, collectively, have made significant contributions to the effort to push our disappointingly dystopian society toward becoming more akin to the comparatively kinder future depicted in *Star Trek*. Like these Italian socialist moral exemplars, Fontana should be remembered as the kind of Italian who supported unions over union busting, gave an Emmy-winning writing opportunity to a Native American scriptwriter (instead of seeking to silence unruly indigenous voices), and fought for creator rights, equitable pay, and proper working conditions for all economically vulnerable writers and artists—*especially* for women.

Dorothy Fontana was an Italian American writer of Fantastika par excellence. Her life, her work, and her ethics are worth remembering, contemplating, and emulating.

Author's note: With thanks to Bill Murphy, Anthony Lioi, Christopher González, and Joe Kraus.

Notes

1. In a happier end to this story, Ellison's original screenplay was brought to life in a graphic novel by Scott and David Tipton and illustrated by J. K. Woodward in 2015, three years before Ellison's death. In his introduction to the adaptation, Ellison effused that he "could not have pictured it as perfect as it turned out," and he asked readers to "please enjoy this graphic novel one one-millionth as much as I do, because I'm over the moon."

2. I respect that many readers will resist this line of thinking because white and minoritized immigrants are supposed to be different because of race. However, whiteness is not an ethnicity, and my skills in pattern recognition inevitably draw my attention to cross-racial patterns shared by immigrants.

Works Cited

Altman, Mark A., and Edward Gross. 2016. *The Fifty-Year Mission: The First 25 Years*. St. Martin's Press.

Baker-Whitelaw, Gavia. "Original 'Star Trek' Writer D.C. Fontana Looks Back on the Show's 50th Anniversary." *The Daily Dot*, 8 Sept. 2016. https://www.dailydot.com/parsec/star-trek-fontana-interview-anniversary/.

Beckerman, Jim, and Alex Biese. "Dorothy Fontana, the Totowa Writer Who Helped Shape 'Star Trek,' Has Died." *NorthJersey.com*, 4 Dec. 2019. https://www.northjersey.com/story/entertainment/2019/12/03/star-trek-writer-d-c-fontana-has-died/2598093001/.

Bennett, Harve, Nicholas Meyer, Leonard Nimoy, and Robert Wise, creators. *Star Trek: The Original Motion Picture Collection*. Starring: William Shatner, Leonard Nimoy, DeForest Kelley, Released 1979 to 1991, CBS Studios, Inc., 2016, Blu-ray Discs.

Boucher, Ashley. "Trailblazing 'Star Trek' Writer D.C. Fontana Dies at 80: 'She Was a Pioneer.'" *People*, 3 Dec. 2019. https://people.com/tv/dc-fontana-dead-star-trek-writer-80/.

Bowie, Stephen. "An Interview with D.C. Fontana (1939–2019)." *Shout! Factory*, 11 Dec. 2019. https://shoutfactory.com/blogs/product-blogs/an-interview-with-d-c-fontana-1939-2019.

Britt, Ryan. "D.C. Fontana Gave the Original *Star Trek* Its Human Heart." *SyFy.com*, 3 Dec. 2019. https://www.syfy.com/syfy-wire/dorothy-dc-fontana-gave-the-the-original-star-trek-its-human-heart.

Cassel, David. "Boldly Going: The Life of Pioneering 'Star Trek' Writer D.C. Fontana." *The New Stack*, 22 Dec. 2019. https://thenewstack.io/boldly-going-the-life-of-pioneering-woman-star-trek-writer-d-c-fontana/. Accessed 16 Aug. 2023.

Davis, Elias. "The Writer Speaks: D. C. Fontana." The Writers Guild Foundation. *YouTube*, 11 May 2012. https://www.youtube.com/watch?v=CCSp8TnnbNU. Accessed 5 Aug. 2023.

Engel, Joel. *Gene Roddenberry: The Myth and the Man Behind "Star Trek,"* Hyperion, 1994.

Fontana, Dorothy, creator. *Star Trek: The Animated Series* (aka *The Animated Adventures of Gene Roddenberry's "Star Trek"*). Starring: William Shatner, Leonard Nimoy, DeForest Kelley. Aired: 1973–1975, on NBC. CBS Studios, Inc., 2016, Blu-ray Discs.

Gerrold, David, and D. C. Fontana, creators. *Star Trek: The Next Generation: The Complete Series*. Starring: Patrick Stewart, Jonathan Frakes, Gates McFadden. Aired: 1987–1994, in syndication. CBS Studios, Inc., 2022, Blu-ray Discs.

Gross, Edward, and Mark A. Altman. *The Fifty-Year Mission: The Next 25 Years from "The Next Generation" to J. J. Abrams*. St. Martin's Press, 2016.

Kreski, Chris, and William Shatner. *"Star Trek" Memories*. Harper Collins, 1994.
Nimoy, Leonard. *I Am Spock*. Hachette Books, 1995.
Rieder, John. *Colonialism and the Emergence of Science Fiction*. Wesleyan UP, 2012.
Robinson, Ben, and Ian Spelling. *Star Trek: A Celebration*. Eaglemoss, 2021.
Roddenberry, Gene, creator. *Star Trek: The Original Series: The Complete Series*. Starring: William Shatner, Leonard Nimoy, DeForest Kelley. Aired: 1966–1969, on NBC. CBS Studios, Inc., 2016, Blu-ray Discs.
Shatner, William. *Chaos on the Bridge*. Vision Films, 2014, DVD.
Sky, Joshua. "Going Boldly: Interview with D.C. Fontana." *Future Science Fiction Digest*, no. 3, 26 June 2019. https://future-sf.com/non-fiction/going-boldly-interview-with-dc-fontana/.
Solow, Herbert F., and Robert H. Justman. *Inside "Star Trek": The Real Story*. Pocket Books, 1996.
Startrek.com staff writers (uncredited). "EXCLUSIVE INTERVIEW: Dorothy Fontana: Part 1 and Part 2." *StarTrek.com*, 18–19 May 2013. https://www.startrek.com/article/exclusive-interview-dorothy-fontana-part-1.
Vary, Adam B. "Star Trek: The Next Generation—an Oral History." *EW.com*, 25 Sept. 2007. Accessed 16 Aug. 2023.
Volk-Weiss, Brian. *The Center Seat: 55 Years of "Star Trek."* Nacelle, 2021, DVD.
Whitfield, Stephen E., and Gene Roddenberry. *The Making of "Star Trek."* Ballantine, 1973.
Wolfman, Marv. "Speaking with . . . D.C. Fontana." *What the—?* http://www.marvwolfman.com/marv/Speaking_With_D.C._Fontana_Part_One.html. Accessed 17 Aug. 2023.
Zamalin, Alex. Black Utopia: The History of an Idea from Black Nationalism to Afrofuturism. Columbia UP, 2019.

Appendix

The Canon of Speculative Fiction of the Italian Diaspora

Dominique Musorrafiti, Matteo Damiani,
and Marc DiPaolo

Children's Books

Francesco Tullio Altan: *La Pimpa* (1975–1995)
Felice Arena
Giovanni Bertinetti
Dino Buzzati: *The Bears' Famous Invasion of Sicily* (1945)
Nicoletta Costa
Elisabetta Dami: *Geronimo Stilton*
Silvana De Mari
Tomie dePaola
Joel Gennari
Roberto Piumini
Gianni Rodari
Giovanni Francesco "Gianfrancesco" Straparola

Comics and Graphic Novels

Vittorio Accornero de Testa
Mario Alberti: *Morgana* (2002)
Giancarlo Alessandrini

Amelia (aka Magica De Spell of *Uncle Scrooge* and *Duck Tales*)
Enrica Eren Angiolini
Jim Aparo
John Arcudi
Furio Arrasich: *Alika* (1965)
Claudio Asciuti
L'Audace
Franco Aureliani
Brian Azzarello
Roberto Baldazzini: *Ines la ragazza pneumatica* (2002)
Tony Barbieri
Alessandro Barbucci: *Sky Doll* (2000)
Lorenzo Bartoli: *Alice Dark* (2011)
Dante Bastianoni
Dino Battaglia
Helena Bertinelli
Giulio Bertoletti: *Crist-031* (1975)
Giacomo Bevilacqua
Simone Bianchi
Roberto Bonadimani: *Cittadini dello spazio* (1977); *Uri* (1977); *Anyha* (1980)
Gian Luigi Bonelli: *I conquistatori dello spazio* (1940); *Yorga* (1945); *Judok* (1963)
Sergio Bonelli
Bonvi: *Cattivik* (1965); *Storie dello spazio profondo* (1970); *Cronache del dopobomba* (1973)
Luciano Bottaro
Lorenzo Bartoli
Annalise Bissa
Alfredo Brasioli: *Ulix* (1980)
Daniele Brolli
Max Bunker: *Gesebel* (1966)
John Buscema
Sal Buscema
Guido Buzzelli: *Alex l'eroe dello spazio* (1952); *I pionieri della Via Lattea* (1955); *La guerra videologica* (1978)
Paul Campani: *Misterix* (1946)
Antonio Canale
Barbara Canepa: *Sky Doll* (2000)
Ade Capone: *Lazarus Ledd* (1993)

Alessandro Cappuccio
Greg Capullo
Joe Caramagna
Adriano Carnevali: *I Ronfi* (1981–1995)
Pier Carpi: *Uranella* (1966–68); *Destinazione Andromeda* (1972); *Satan's Wife* (1979)
Alfredo Castelli: *Gli astrostoppisti* (1971); *L'Ombra* (1974); *Martin Mystery* (1982–)
Claudio Castellini
Onofrio Catacchio
Catwoman
Fabio Celoni
Guido Moroni Celsi: *S.K.1* (1935–1937)
Charlton Comics
Carlo Chendi
Giorgio Chiaperotti: *Cosmik* (1967)
Barbara Ciardo
Comic Arts (comic magazine active 1965–2000)
Didier Conrad
Carlo Cossio: *Ciclone* (1945); *Tanks l'Uomo d'Acciaio* (1945); *Mirko* (1947)
Gianmauro Cozzi: *Greystorm* (2009–2010)
Guido Crepax: *Valentina* (1965)
Jon D'Agostino
Santo D'Amico: *Atoman contro Killer* (1965–1966)
Andrea Da Passano
Roberto De Angelis
Dick DeBartolo
Enrico de Boccard: *Il mistero del satellite H-15* (1955)
Tom DeFalco
Nunzio DeFilippis
Elena de' Grimani: *Rigel* (1999)
Gabriele Dell'Otto
Gianni de Luca: *Paulus* (2008)
J. M. DeMatteis
Adriano Di Benedetto
Diane DiMassa
Paul Dini
Roberto Diso: *Atoman contro Killer* (1965–1966)
Andrea Di Vito

Andrea Domestici
Nick Dragotta
ElfQuest
Luca Enoch: *Morgana* (2002); *Lilith* (2008–)
Eternauta magazine
Al Fago
Vince Fago (aka Vincenzo Francisco Gennaro Di Fago)
Tito Faraci: *Brad Barron* (2005–2006)
Mario Faustinelli: *Kolosso* (1964)
Valeria Favoccia
Gallieno Ferri: *Maskar* (1949)
Jean-Yves Ferri
Simona Ferri: *Angel's Friends* (2007)
John Ficarra
Manuele Fior: *Celestia* (2019)
Anthony Flamini
Bill Fraccio
Gagy: *I corsari della galassia* (1955)
Domenico Gallo
Jose Garibaldi
Max Massimino Garnier: *Misterix* (1946)
Romano Garofalo: *Medium* (1974)
Frank Giacoia
Chris Giarrusso
Dick Giordano
Gipi
Girus (Giuseppe Russo)
The Goon
Elisabetta Gnone
Gabriele Goggi: *Nolan, il pioniere dello spazio* (1953)
Pia Guerra
Angela Guissani and Luciana Giussani: *Diabolik* (1962)
Harley Quinn
Hellboy
Horror (Italian horror magazine)
Carmine Infantino
Roberta Ingranata
Iron Man
Tony Isabella

Jacovitti: *Tom Ficcanaso* (1957–1958); *Gionni Galassia* (1958–1959); *Baby Rocket* (1963); *Microciccio Spaccavento* (1965); *Arcicomiche stellari* (1978)
Eros Kara: *Astrella* (1969)
Lak il giustiziere dello spazio (1970)
Lak Timo (1964)
Walter Lantz
Andrea Lavezzolo: *Ciclone* (1945)
Tanino Liberatore: *RanXerox* (1978)
Lube (aka Luciano Bernasconi)
MAD Magazine
Magnus: *I briganti* (1978)
Il Male (Italian satirical magazine)
Emiliano Mammucari: *Orfani* (2013)
Milo Manara
Giovanni Manca: *Pier Cloruro de' Lambicchi* (1930); *Il castello dei misteri* (1934)
Nicola Mari
Rocco "Rocke" Mastroserio
Pat Masulli
Adele Matera
David Mazzucchelli
Michele Medda: *Nathan Never* (1991); *Legs Weaver* (1994–2005)
Sara Michieli
Mike Mignola
Walter Molino: *Virus, il mago della foresta morta* (1938)
Arnoldo Mondadori
Francesco Mortarino
Pete Morisi
Ms. Marvel
Lisa Montalbano
Andrea Moretto
Attilio Mussino
Marcel Navarro: *Jorgo* (1969); *Wampus* (1969)
Ann Nocenti
Giancarlo Olivares: *Hammer* (1994)
Alberto Ongaro: *Asso di Picche* (1945)
Joe Orlando
Jimmy Palmiotti
Andrea Pazienza

Federico Pedrocchi: *Saturno contro la Terra* (1936); *Virus, il mago della foresta morta* (1938)
Celestino Pes: *Ines la ragazza pneumatica* (2002)
Carlo Peroni
Dante Pertuz
Elena Pianta: *Gregory Hunter* (2001–2002)
Sara Pichelli
N. Pietramella: *Il dottor Hodler* (1955)
Paolo Piffarerio: *Atomik* (1962)
Wendy Pini and Richard Pini
Piranha II: The Spawning (1982)
Silverio Pisu: *Cosmine l'atomica del sesso* (1973–1974)
Angelo Platania: *Razzo, l'uomo plastica* (1948); *Barbel* (1965)
Carlo Porciani: *Kolosso* (1964)
Hugo Pratt: *Asso di Picche* (1945); *Corto Maltese* (1967)
Psyco (Italian horror magazine)
The Punisher
Nadir Quinto
Stefano Raffaele
Joe Raiola
Giorgio Rebuffi
Don Rico
Don Rosa
Roberto Recchioni: *Orfani* (2013)
Roberto Renzi: *Roal, il Tarzan del mare* (1947); *Tiramolla* (1952)
Franco Ricciardiello
Pino Rinaldi
Valentina Romeo
John Romita
John Romita Jr.
Mario Rossi: *Hammer* (1994)
Marco Rostagno (aka Paul Savant)
Marco Rota
Antonio Rubino: *Pomponio, Dinamello e Tonto Tito* (1923)
Giovanni ("John") Santangelo
Danilo Santoni
Matteo Scalera
Romano Scarpa
Luciano Secchi: *Atomik* (1962)

Antonio Serra: *Nathan Never* (1991); *Legs Weaver* (1994–2005); *Gregory Hunter* (2001–2002); *Greystorm* (2009–2010)
Tiziano Sclavi: *Dylan Dog* (1986–); *Cemetery Man* (1991)
Paolo Eleuteri Serpieri: *Druuna* (1985)
She-Hulk
Silver
Mark Silvestri
Gigi Simeoni: *Hammer* (1994)
Cesare Solini: *Amok* (1946)
Viviana Spinelli
Giorgia Sposito
Roberto Sturm
Ferdinando Tacconi
Tony Tallarico
Stefano Tamburini: *RanXerox* (1978)
Julian Totino Tedesco
Giovanni Ticci: *Judok* (1963)
Peter Tomasi
Topolino (comic magazine, 1949)
I Tre Porcellini (comic magazine active 1935–1937)
Sal Trapani
Giorgio Trevisan: *Medium* (1974)
Alberto Aleandro Uderzo: *Asterix the Gaul*
Uncle Scrooge
Jim Valentino
Robert Venditti
Venus (1966)
Emma Vieceli
Stefano Vietti: *Hammer* (1994); *NEXT 02* (2006)
Bepi Vigna: *Nathan Never* (1991)
Sam Viviano
Yambo (aka Enrico de' Conti Novelli da Bertinoro): *Gli esploratori dell'infinito* (1906); *Ciuffettino* (1902–1916); *Robottino, omino d'acciaio* (1935); *Gli uomini verdi* (1935); *I pionieri dello spazio* (1936)
Gerard Way
Helena Wayne
Witchblade
Pino Zac: *L'Orlando Furioso* (1972)
Juan Zanotto

Zatanna
Zatara
Cesare Zavattini: *Saturno contro la Terra* (1936)
Nevio Zeccara: *Gli astrostoppisti* (1971)
Zerocalcare
Silvia Ziche

Fantasy Novels and Short Stories

Abrakadabra: Storia dell'avvenire (1864–1865) by Antonio Ghislanzoni
Elisa S. Amore
Danilo Arona
Barbara Baraldi
Dino Buzzati
Paola Capriolo
Francesco Dimitri
Francesco Falconi
Serena Fiandro
Livio Gambarini
Alberto Henriet
Luna d'Inverno (Winter Fe') (2020) by Ilaria Varese Gene Wolf
Davide Mana
Luigi Motta
Murderers I Have Known, and Other Stories (2010) by Marina Warner
Non mi uccidere (2005) by Chiara Palazzolo
L'ora dei dannati—L'abisso (2020) by Luca Tarenzi
Pan (2008)
Christopher Paolini
Pirate Freedom (2007) by Ilaria Varese Gene Wolf
The Professor and the Siren (1956–1957) by Giuseppe Tommasi di Lampedusa
Questo non è un romanzo fantasy (2015) by Roberto Gerilli
Cecilia Randall
Emiliano Reali
Emilio Salgari
R. A. Salvatore
La stiva e l'abisso (2010) by Michele Mari
Terra ignota (2013) by Vanni Santoni
Il tesoro del Bigatto (1980) by Giuseppe Pederiali

Licia Troisi
Wunderkind. Una lucida moneta d'argento (2009) by G. L. D'Andrea
Zappa e Spada—Spaghetti Fantasy (anthology of fantasy short stories, 2017)
Gianluigi Zuddas

Film

Alberto Abruzzese: *Anemia* (1985)
Sergio Agosti: *N.P.* (1971)
Gabriele Albanesi: *The Last House in the Woods* (2006); *Horror Show* (2010)
Luciano Albertini
Marcello Aliprandi: *La ragazza di latta* (1970); *Whisper in the Dark* (1976)
Silvio Amadio: *Il medium* (1980)
Don Ameche
Franco Amurri: *Da grande* (1987)
Jennifer Aniston
Marco Antonio Andolfi: *Cross of the Seven Jewels* (1987)
Marcello Andrei: *A Black Ribbon for Deborah* (1974)
Mauro Aragoni: *S'arena. A Tale from Nuraghes* (2016)
Asia Argento
Dario Argento: *The Bird with the Crystal Plumage* (1970); *Deep Red* (1975); *Suspiria* (1977); *Inferno* (1981); *Tenebrae* (1982); *Phenomena* (1985); *Opera* (1987)
Arrow Video
Armand Assante
Ovidio G. Assonitis: *Beyond the Door* (1974); *Tentacles* (1977); *Madhouse* (1981)
Paul Attanasio
Carlo Ausino: *Don't Look in the Attic* (1981)
Marcello Avallone: *The House of the Blue Shadows* (1986); *Specters* (1987)
Pupi Avati: *The House with Laughing Windows* (1976)
Morena Baccarin
Charles Bail: *Choke Canyon* (1986)
Stanley Baker
Gianfranco Baldanello: *Danger!! Death Ray* (1967)
John Baldecchi
Anne Bancroft
Charles Band: *Trancers* (1985)

Billy Barty
Aurelius Battaglia
Luigi Batzella: *The Devil's Wedding Night* (1973); *La Bestia in calore* (1977)
Lamberto Bava: *Demons* (1985)
Mario Bava: *The Day the Sky Exploded* (1958); *Black Sunday* (1960); *Black Sabbath* (1963); *Kill, Baby, Kill* (1966); *A Bay of Blood* (1971)
Maria Bello
Monica Bellucci
Marco Beltrami
Roberto Benigni
Luca Bercovici
Sergio Bergonzelli: *In the Folds of the Flesh* (1970); *Blood Delirium* (1988)
Giulio Berruti: *Killer Nun* (1979)
Francesco Bertolini: *L'Inferno* (1911)
Stefano Bessoni: *Imago mortis* (2008); *Krokodyle* (2010)
Luigi Bezzoni: *The Fifth Chord* (1971)
Andrea Bianchi: *Burial Ground* (1981)
Paolo Bianchini: *Massacre Mania* (1967); *The Devil's Man* (1967); *Superargo and the Faceless Giants* (1968); *Superargo and the Faceless Giants* (1968)
Danny Bilson and Paul De Meo
Rachel Bilson
Christian Bisceglia
Blue Underground
Antonio Boccacci: *Tomb of Torture* (1963)
Florinda Bolkan
Marco Bonfanti: *The Man Without Gravity* (2019)
Jon Bon Jovi
Barbara Bouchet
Bruno Bozzetto: *The SuperVips* (1968); *Allegro non Troppo* (1976); *Sotto il ristorante cinese* (1986)
Walter Brandi
Tinto Brass: *Il disco volante* (1964)
Rossano Brazzi
Alfonso Brescia (aka Al Bradley): *Cosmos: War of the Planets* (1977); *War of the Robots* (1978); *Star Odyssey* (1979); *La bestia nello spazio* (1980); *Iron Warrior* (1987)
Franco Brocani: *Necropolis* (1970)
Albert Romolo Broccoli (aka "Cubby" Broccoli)
Barbara Broccoli

Cara Buono
Steve Buscemi
Dennis Cabella
Nicolas Cage
Mario Caiano
Daniel Caltagirone
Augusto Caminito
Pasquale Festa Campanile: *The Sex Machine* (1975)
Bobby Cannavale
Peter Capaldi
Alessandro Capone: *Witch Story* (1989)
Tim Cappello
Frank Capra
Garibaldi Serra Caracciolo: *The Seventh Grave* (1965)
Linda Cardellini
Steve Carell
Giuliano Carnimeo: *The Case of the Bloody Iris* (1972); *Exterminators of the Year 3000* (1983); *Ratman* (1988); *Computron 22* (1988)
Ferruccio Casapinta: *The Doll of Satan* (1968)
Claudio Cassinelli
Castellano & Pipolo: *Mia moglie è una strega* (1980)
Enzo G. Castellari
Nino Castelnuovo
Liliana Cavani: *I cannibali* (1970)
Paolo Cavara: *Mondo Cane* (1962); *Black Belly of the Tarantula* (1971)
Giorgio Cavedon: *Ombre* (1980)
John Cena
Giuliano Cenci
Michael Cera
Tonino Cervi: *Queens of Evil* (1970)
Raffiella Chapman
Riccardo Chemello: *Dampyr* (2022)
Giovanni Cianfriglia
Giacomo Cimini: *Red Riding Hood* (2003)
Beppe Cino
Camille Coduri
Diablo Cody
Enrica Bianchi Colombatto (aka Erika Blanc)
Mario Colucci: *Something Creeping in the Dark* (1971)

Enrico Colombo
Chris Columbus
Sandro Continenza
Francis Ford Coppola
Roman Coppola
Sofia Coppola
Sergio Corbucci: *Baracca e burattini* (1954); *Super Fuzz* (1980); *Sono un fenomeno paranormale* (1985)
Adrienne Corri
Don Coscarelli: *Phantasm* (1979); *The Beastmaster* (1982)
Luigi Cozzi (aka Lewis Coates): *The Tunnel Under the World* (1969); *Starcrash* (1978)
Armando Crispino: *The Dead Are Alive* (1972); *Autopsy* (1975); *Frankenstein all'italiana—Prendimi, straziami, che brucio de passion!* (1975)
Quirino Cristiani
The Criterion Collection
Massimo Dallamano: *What Have You Done to Solange?* (1972); *The Cursed Medallion* (1975)
Joe Dallesandro
Timothy Dalton
Damiano Damiani: *The Witch in Love* (1966)
Enzo D'Alò: *Momo* (2001)
Joe D'Amato: *Death Smiles on a Murderer* (1973)
Joe Dante: *Piranha* (1978); *Gremlins* (1984); *Gremlins 2: The New Batch* (1990)
Louis D'Esposito
Frank De Felitta
Agostino "Dino" De Laurentiis
Raffaella De Laurentiis
Giuseppe De Liguoro
Alberto De Martino: *The Blancheville Monster* (1963); *The Antichrist* (1974); *Holocaust 2000* (1977); *The Pumaman* (1980); *Blood Link* (1982); *Formula for a Murder* (1985)
Paul De Meo
James DeMonaco
Robert De Niro
Ruggero Deodato: *Cannibal Holocaust* (1980); *Body Count* (1986)
Brian de Palma
Vittorio De Sica: *Miracle in Milan* (1951); *The Last Judgement* (1961)
Rossella de Venuto

Danny DeVito
Claudio Di Biagio: *Vittima degli Eventi* (*Dylan Dog* fan film, 2014)
Leonardo DiCaprio
Denise Di Novi
Gino Domeneghini: *La Rosa di Bagdad* (1949)
Vincent D'Onofrio
Kirk Douglas
Kat Ellinger
Marcello Ercole
Luciano Ercoli: *Death Walks on High Heels* (1971)
Chris Evans
Facets Video
Roberto Faenza: *H2S* (1969)
Eleonora Fani
Franco Fantasia
Corrado Farina: *They Have Changed Their Face* (1971); *Baba Yaga* (1973)
Ernest Farino
Gabriella Farinon
Jon Favreau
Federico Fellini: *Spirits of the Dead* (1968)
Anthony C. Ferrante
Abel Ferrara
Martin Ferrero
Giorgio Ferroni: *Mill of the Stone Women* (1960); *The Night of the Devils* (1972)
Claire Forlani
Linda Fiorentino
Jane Fonda
Claire Forlani
Maurizio Forestieri
Claudio Fragasso: *Monster Dog* (1986); *After Death* (1989); *Beyond Darkness* (1990); *Night Killer* (1990); *Troll 2* (1990)
Michelangelo Frammartino: *Le quattro volte* (2010)
David Franzoni
Valentina Frascaroli
Riccardo Freda
Lucio Fulci: *Lizard in a Woman's Skin* (1971); *Don't Torture a Duckling* (1972); *Psychic* (1977); *Zombie* (1979); *Warriors of the Year 2072* (1984)
Silvana Gallardo
Vincent Gallo

Ida Galli
Mario Gariazzo (aka Roy Garrett): *The Eerie Midnight Horror Show* (1974); *Eyes Behind the Stars* (1978); *White Slave* (1985); *Fratello dello Spazio* (1988)
Janeane Garofalo
Matteo Garrone: *The Embalmer* (2002)
Sergio Garrone: *Lover of the Monster* (1974); *The Hand That Feeds the Dead* (1974)
Ernesto Gastaldi: *Werewolf in a Girls' Dormitory* (1961)
Alberto Genovese
Gianfranco Giagni: *The Spider Labyrinth* (1988)
Giancarlo Giannini
Paul Giamatti
Tony Gilroy
Antony I. Ginnane
Domiziana Giordano
Giordano Giulivi: *Apollo 54* (2007); *The Laplace's Demon* (2017)
Skyler Gisondo
Ariana Grande
Frank Grillo
Emidio Greco: *Morel's Invention* (1974)
Ugo Gregoretti: *Omicron* (1963)
Luca Guadagnino: *Suspiria* (2018)
La guerra ed il sogno di Momi (1917)
Mino Guerrini: *The Third Eye* (1966)
Carla Gugino
Corrado Guzzanti: *Fascisti su Marte* (2006)
Terrence Hill
Troy Howarth
Anjelica Huston
Ciro Ippolito: *Alien 2: On Earth* (1980)
Jennifer's Body (2009)
Kino Classics
Mikel J. Koven
Aldo Lado (aka George B. Lewis): *The Humanoid* (1979)
Don LaFontaine
Richard LaGravenese
Frank LaLoggia
Mario Landi: *Patrick Still Lives* (1980)

Marla Landi
Frank Langella
The Last Man on Earth (1964)
Fabrizio Laurenti
Gabriele Lavia
Christopher Lee
Umberto Lenzi
Téa Leoni
Ugo Liberatore: *Damned in Venice* (1978)
Alessio Liguori: *Report 51* (2013); *In the Trap* (2019); *Shortcut* (2020): *Il viaggio leggendario* (2023)
Ray Liotta
Robert Loggia
Paolo Lombardo: *Lucifera: Demon Lover* (1972)
Mino Loy: *Flashman* (1967)
Michele Lupo: *The Sheriff and the Satellite Kid* (1979); *Everything Happens to Me* (1980)
John Lurie
William Lustig
Ralph Macchio
Gabriele Mainetti: *They Call Me Jeeg Robot* (2015)
Don Mancini
Angela Mancuso
The Manetti Bros.: *The Arrival of Wang* (aka *L'arrivo di Wang*, 2011); *Paura* (2012); *Zora the Vampire* (2000)
Silvana Mangano
Luigi Mangini (aka Henry Wilson): *The Hyena of London* (1964)
Guido Mannari
Guido Manuli: *Aida of the Trees* (2001)
Joe Mantegna
Kate Mara
Rooney Mara
Marcel the Shell with Shoes On (2021)
Antonio Margheriti: *Space Men* (1960); *Seven Deaths in a Cat's Eye* (1973)
Andrea Marfori
Penny Marshall
Elsa Martinelli
Sergio Martino: *The Case of the Scorpion's Tail* (1972); *Your Vice Is a Locked Room and Only I Have the Key* (1972); *Slave of the Cannibal*

God (1978); *Island of the Fishmen* (1979); *Scorpion with Two Tails* (1982); *Vendetta dal Futuro* (1986)
Gianni Martucci
Camillo Mastrocinque: *Terror in the Crypt* (1964); *An Angel for Satan* (1966)
Armand Mastroianni
Marcello Mastroianni
Bruno Mattei: *Robowar* (1988)
Mario Mattoli: *Mille chilometri al minuto!* (1939)
Lorenzo Mattotti: *The Bears' Famous Invasion of Sicily* (2019)
Margaret Mazzantini
Joseph Mazzello
Peppino Mazzotta
The Mechanical Man (1921)
Christopher Meloni
José Luis Merino: *7 eroiche carogne* (1969); *Scream of the Demon Lover* (1970); *The Hanging Woman* (1973)
Metal Gear Solid: Philanthropy (Italian nonprofit fan film series produced by Hive Division, 2009)
Liza Minnelli
Vincent Minnelli: *A Matter of Time* (1976)
Cristin Milioti
Emilio Miraglia: *The Night Evelyn Came Out of the Grave* (1971); *The Red Queen Kills Seven Times* (1972)
Alfred Molina
Mondo films
Mondo Macabro
Nanni Moretti: *Ecce Homo* (1969)
Tony Musante
Ornella Muti
Vincenzo Natali
Franco Nero
Rosalba Neri
Maurizio Nichetti: *Stefano Quantestorie* (1993)
Daria Nicolodi
Greg Nicotero
Alessandro Nivola
Nick Nostro: *Superargo Versus Diabolicus* (1966)
Enrico Novelli: *A Marriage on the Moon* (1910)
Laura Nucci

Steve Oedekerk
Oscilloscope Laboratories
Al Pacino
Adolfo Padovan
Panic (1982)
Dennis Paoli
Giulio Paradisi (aka Michael J. Paradise): *The Visitor* (1979)
Neri Parenti: *Fracchia contro Dracula* (1985)
Pier Paolo Pasolini
Alvaro Passeri (aka Al Passeri): *Creatures from the Abyss* (1994)
Lucas Pavetto: *The Perfect Husband* (2014)
Victoria Pedretti
Bernadette Peters
Elio Petri: *The 10th Victim* (1965); *Todo Modo* (1976)
Roberto Piazzoli
Raffaele Picchio
Francesco Picone: *Anger of the Dead* (*Apocalisse Zero*, 2015)
Luciano Pigozzi
Pier Francesco Pingitore: *Ciao marziano* (1980)
Achille Pisanti
Donald Pleasance
Renato Polselli: *Vampire and the Ballerina* (1960); *The Vampire of the Opera* (1964); *La verità secondo Satana* (1972); *Black Magic Rites* (1973)
Renato Pozzetto
Fabio Prat
Paula Prentiss
Vincent Price
Biagio Proietti
Federico Prosperi
Franco Prosperi
Domenico Massimo Pupillo: *Bloody Pit of Horror* (1965); *Terror-Creatures from the Grave* (1965); *La vendetta di Lady Morgan* (1965)
Giulio Questi: *Arcana* (1972)
Zachary Quinto
Carlo Rambaldi
Godfrey Reggio
Piero Regnoli: *The Playgirls and the Vampire* (1960)
Eva Renzi
Giovanni Ribisi

Christina Ricci
Tonino Ricci: *Encounters in the Deep* (1979); *Panic* (1982); *Thor the Conqueror* (1983); *Raiders of the Magic Ivory* (1988)
Alfredo Rizzo: *The Bloodsucker Leads the Dance* (1975)
Road to L. (2005)
The Rocketeer (1991)
George A. Romero: *Dawn of the Dead* (1978)
Brunello Rondi: *Il demonio* (1963)
Nello Rossati: *I'm a Zombie, You're a Zombie, She's a Zombie* (1979)
Isabella Rossellini
Giacomo Rossi
Terry Rossio
Sergio Rubini: *Soul Mate* (2002)
Mark Ruffalo
Anthony Russo and Joseph Russo (aka "the Russo brothers")
James Russo
Frank Sabatella
Dardano Sacchetti
Shane Salerno
Gabriele Salvatores: *Nirvana* (1997); *The Invisible Boy* (2014)
Susan Sarandon
Tom Savini
Leopoldo Savona: *Byleth: The Demon of Incest* (1972)
Greta Scacchi
Romano Scavolini: *Spirits of Death* (1972)
Vincent Schiavelli
Jason Schwartzman
Annabella Sciorra
Kaya Scodelario
Martin Scorsese
Scream Factory
Henry Silva
Gary Sinise
Igor Skofic
The Sleep of Death (1980)
Michele Soavi: *StageFright: Aquarius* (1987); *Cemetery Man* (1994)
Steven Soderbergh
Alberto Sordi: *Catherine and I* (1980)
Spirits of Death (1972)

Michele Imperato Stabile
Sylvester Stallone
Terrence Stamp
Barbara Steele
Joseph Stefano
Paolo Strippoli: *A Classic Horror Story* (2021)
Sergio Stivaletti
Ken Stott
Mark Strong
Synapse Films
Giuseppe Tagliavia (aka Roberto Mauri): *The Invincible Brothers Maciste* (1964); *Slaughter of the Vampires* (1972); *Madeleine: Anatomy of a Nightmare* (1974)
Giacomo Talamini
Quentin Tarantino
Dino Tavella: *The Embalmer* (1965)
Chris Terrio
Ubaldo Terzani
Duccio Tessari: *My Son, the Hero* (1966); *Per amore . . . per magia . . .* (1967)
Eugenio Testa: *The Monster of Frankenstein* (1921)
Camillo Teti
Ugo Tognazzi: *I viaggiatori della sera* (1979)
Marilù Tolo
Marisa Tomei
Dominic Toretto
Totò
John Travolta
Stanley Tucci
Paige Turco
John Turturro
Liv Tyler
Mark Valenti
Rudolph Valentino
Amber Valletta
Giuseppe Vegezzi (aka Nello Vegezzi): *Katarsis* (1963)
Milo Ventimiglia
Victoria Vetri
Alberto Viavattene: *Morgue Street* (2012)
Paolo Villagio

Monica Vitti
Jeanette Volturno
Warrior of the Lost World (1983)
Rachel Weisz
Piergiuseppe Zaia: *Creators: The Past* (2020)
Roberto Zazzara: *The Bunker Game* (2022)
Primo Zeglio: *Mission Stardust* (1967)
Robert Zemeckis

Folklore and Oral Literature

Aamon
Amphisbaena
Ammuntadòre
Anguana, the aquatic nymph (aka Agana and Longana)
Babau
Badalisc
Badalischio
Basilisk
La Befana
Bella 'mbriana
The Benandanti
Biddrina
Bisso Galeto
Bombasin
Bonnacon
Borda
Buffardello
Burn a Black Candle: An Italian-American Grimoire by Dee Norman
Caddos birdes
Catoblepas
Cogas or Bruxas
Compendium Maleficarum (1608) by Francesco Maria Guazzo
The Confined
Crusades
Di Inferi: The Underworld deities of the Roman religion
Diana Nemorensis
Dipsa

Erchitu
Faun
flagellants
Gata Carogna
Gatto Mammone
Gigat
Giubiana the Witch
Gnefro
Griffin
Incubi
The Inquisition trials and heresies
Jaculo (aka *iaculo* or the javelin snake)
The Janare witches
The Janas
Krampus
The Laùro (aka Laurieddhu or Scazzamurrieddhru)
Linchetto
Malocchio (the Evil Eye)
The Mask of Venice
Italian American Folklore by Frances M. Malpezzi and William M. Clements
Italian Folktales by Italo Calvino
Maciara (or *masciara*)
Maimone (aka Mamuthone)
Marranghino
Marroca
Masca
Maskinganna (aka S'Ingannadore)
Mazapégul
Mazaròl
Mazzamurello
Mommotti (aka Mobbotti)
Monachicchio
Munaciello
Orcolat
Ozaena
Pantafica
Parcae, the Three Fates
The Pentamerone (1634 and 1636) by Giambattista Basile
Pantàsema (aka Pantàsima, Fantàsima, Mammoccia, Signoraccia)

Pettenedda
The religion of the Etruscan people
The religion of the Greeks
The religion of the Latin people
Sa Femina Accabadora (The Lady of the Good Death)
Salamander
Snake catchers
Succubi
Sa Mama 'e su Sole
Scultone
Snake regolo
Su Ammuntadore
Strego
Strix
Giovanni Francesco "Gianfrancesco" Straparola
Tarantasio
Tatzelwurm
Thyrus
Trud
Unicorn
The Wild Man
Witches of Benevento
The Witches of Valcamonica

Histories, Historical Figures, and Documents

Giovanni Aldini
Alone of All Her Sex: The Myth and the Cult of the Virgin Mary (1976) by Marina Warner
The Borgias
Cagliostro
Catholic saint hagiography
Francesco Colonna
Fairy tales from Italy
Il Conciliatore (progressive biweekly journal, 1818–1819)
Aleister Crowley
Giuseppe De Rosa
Anton Francesco Doni

Teofilo Folengo
Frederick II
Paolo Gorini
Gruppo 63
Italian medieval grimoires
Joan of Arc: The Image of Female Heroism (1981) by Marina Warner
The Letters of Pope Celestine VI to All Mankind (1948)
Cesare Lombroso
The Manifesto of Futurist Cooking (1930)
Lorenzo Pignotti
Polifilo
Marco Polo
The Prince of San Severo and his anatomical machines
Count Ugolino
The Virus Paradigm (2021) by Roberto Marchesini
Lo zar non è morto (1929) Gruppo dei Dieci

Horror Novels and Short Stories

Ambrosio, the monk
Niccolò Ammaniti
Eraldo Baldini
Peter Benchley's *Jaws*
Enrico Brizzi
Max Brooks
Guy Anthony De Marco
Giorgio De Maria
Oreste del Buono
Craig DiLouie
Paolo Di Orazio
Dream House (2015) by Marzia Kjellberg
Valerio Evangelisti
Fantastic Tales (1869) by Igino Ugo Tarchetti
Filippo Fassio
Franco Forte
Count Fosco
Jimmy Juliano
Tommaso Labranca

Greye La Spina
Thomas Ligotti
Nicola Lombardi
Alessandro Manzetti
Count Montoni
Robert Morasco
Gianfranco Nerozzi
Aldo Nove
Tommaso Ottonieri
John Polidori
Luca Ragagnin
Isabella Santacroce
Tiziano Scarpa
Matt Serafini
Roberto Sturm
Alda Teodorani
Rebecca Zanetti

Literature

Dante Alighieri
Apuleius
Thomas Aquinas
Ludovico Ariosto
Andrea da Barberino
Giambattista Basile
Giovanni Boccaccio
Massimo Bontempelli
Giannina Braschi
Roberto Bui and the Wu Ming collective
Italo Calvino
Luigi Capuana
Giosuè Carducci
Catherine of Bologna
La città del Sole (1602) by Tommaso Campanella
La città felice (1553) by Francesco Patrizi
Codex Seraphinianus (1981) by Luigi Serafini
Carlo Collodi

Gabriele D'Annunzio
Bonvesin Da La Riva
Luigi da Porto
Rustichello da Pisa
Jacopone da Todi
Christine de Pizan
Giuseppe Tomasi di Lampedusa
"Dialogue between Frederick Ruysch and His Mummies" by Giacomo Leopardi
Rufus Suter
Umberto Eco
Estasi e rapimento sopra la Luna di Archerio Filoseleno (1763) by Biagio Caputi
Francis of Assisi
Emilio Gabbrielli
Giuseppe Gorgiano
"In morte di Giulio Verne" by Guido Gozzano
Galgano Guidotti
Hypnerotomachia Poliphili (1499)
Iago
Icosameron (1788) Giacomo Casanova
If on a Winter's Night a Traveler . . . (1979)
L'isola di Narsida (1572) by Matteo Buonamico
Philip Lamantia
Tommaso Landolfi
Menotti Lerro
Primo Levi
Lucian of Samosata
Paolo Mantegazza
Filippo Tommaso Emilio Marinetti
The Merchant of Venice (ca. 1597)
La moda (1746) by Giambattista Roberti
Il mondo della Luna (1750) by Carlo Goldoni
Il mondo della Luna (1767) by Diodoro Delfico (aka Saverio Bettinelli)
Petronius (aka Gaius Petronius Arbiter)
Antonio Pigafetta
Luigi Pirandello
Polenta and Goanna (2008) by Emilio Gabbrielli
Prodromo (1670) by Francesco Lana de Terzi

Antonia Tanini Pulci
La repubblica delle api (1627) by Giovanni Bonifacio
La repubblica d'Evandria (1625) by Ludovico Zuccolo
La repubblica immaginaria (1583–1590) by Ludovico Agostini
Christina Rossetti
Dante Gabriel Rossetti
Rafael Sabatini
La Tavola Ritonda (ca 1446)
L'uomo d'un altro mondo (1768) by Pietro Chiari
Maria Valtorta
Sandro Veronesi
Un viaggetto nella Luna di N.N. accademico tassoniano (1836) by Bartolomeo Veratti
Viaggi di Enrico Wanton alle terre incognite australi, ed ai regni delle scimie, e de' cinocefali di Zaccaria Seriman (1749; 1764)
Patrizia Vicinelli
Volo per lo spazio (1782) by Giovanni Battista Zappi
Volt: a.k.a. Vincenzo Fani Ciotti
Marina Warner

Music

Dominick Argento
Ataraxia
Luis Bacalov
Angelo Daniel Badalamenti
Richard Benson
Luciano Berio
Blonde Redhead
La Bionda (1981's "I Wanna Be Your Lover")
Angelo Branduardi
Ferruccio Busoni
Sylvano Bussotti
Alberto Camerini
Camillas
Canali
Casino Royale
CCCP and CSI

Madonna Ciccone
Stelvio Cipriani
Bill Conti
John Corigliano
Alessandro Cortini
Luigi Dallapiccola
De Angelis brothers
Manuel De Sica
Ani DiFranco
Giuseppe "Pino" Donaggio
Gaetano Donizetti's *Lucia di Lammermoor*
Ludovico Einaudi
Elvenking
Giovanni Lindo Ferretti
Fleshgod Apocalypse
The Frozen Autumn
John Frusciante
Domenico Gallo
Michael Giacchino
Marcello Giombini
Goblin
Kirlian Camera
Klein & M.B.O.'s "Dirty Talk" and New Order's "Blue Monday"
Anna-Karin Klockar
Lacuna Coil
Litfiba
Daniele Luppi
Henry Mancini
Dario Marianelli
Attilio Mineo
Claudio Monteverdi
Tom Morello
Giorgio Moroder
Ennio Morricone
Mario Nascimbene
Bruno Nicolai
No Doubt
Novembre
Riz Ortolani

Pankow
Mike Patton
Jacoppo Peri
Goffredo Petrassi
Berto Pisano
Ildebrando Pizzetti
Arnaud Rebotini
Ottorino Respighi
Rhapsody of Fire
Nino Rota
Jeff Russo
Alan Silvestri
Spiritual Front
Teatro Satanico
Gwen Stefani
Armando Trovajoli
Il Trovatore
Steven Tyler
Piero Umiliani
Riccardo Zandonai
Frank Zappa

Painting, Sculpture, and Illustration

Giuseppe Arcimboldo
Edward Ardizzone
Amico Aspertini
Giacomo Balla
Timothy D. Bellavia
Umberto Boccioni
Lee Bontecou
Caravaggio
Fernando Carcupino
Niccolò Circignani
Alfred D. Crimi
Olivia De Berardinis
Valeria De Caterini
Fortunato Depero

Ul de Rico
Gustave Doré
Barry Fantoni
Fillìa (aka Luigi Colombo)
Frank Frazetta
Laura Gascoigne
Antonio Ligabue
Fred Marcellino
Carla Carli Mazzucato
Amedeo Modigliani
Attilio Mussino
Enrico Prampolini
Pulcinella sulla Luna lithographs (1840)
Il rotoplano "3bis" (1910) by Giovanni Bertinetti
Antonio Rubino
Enzo Sciotti
Luigi Serafini
Gino Severini
Frank Stella
Joseph Stella
Emanuele Taglietti
Thayaht
Paolo Uccello ("The Miracle of the Desecrated Host" ca 1468)
Artemisia Gentileschi
Marco D'Agrate

Science Fiction Novels, Short Stories, and Periodicals

1994: La nudità e la spada (1990) by Ferruccio Parazzoli
Lino Aldani
Aliens—Rivista di fantascienza (science fiction magazine, 1979–1980)
L'allegra terza guerra mondiale (1977) by Virgilio Martini
Donato Altomare
L'anaconda (1966) by Giorgio Scerbanenco
Andromeda
L'Anno 3000 (1897) by Paolo Mantegazza
Paolo Aresi
L'areostato nero (1918) by Alberto Orsi

Astralia (fanzine, 1974)
Paolo Bacigalupi
Belmoro (1957) by Corrado Alvaro
Marie-Helene Bertino
I biplani di D'Annunzio (1995) by Luca Masali
Carlo Bordoni
Ben Bova
Gianfranco Briatore (aka John Bree)
Dorothy Bryant
Dino Buzzati
Davide Camparsi
Cancroregina (1950) by Tommaso Landolfi
Il racconto di un guardiano di spiaggia: Traduzione libera della "Battaglia di Dorking" Capraia 189 (1872) attributed to Carlo Rossi
Luigi Capuana
Un carro nel cielo (1965) by Luigi Naviglio
Vittorio Catani
Francesca Cavallero
Il cavallo venduto (1963) by Giorgio Scerbanenco
La città sottomarina (1940) by Renzo Chiosso
Coloni dell'Universo (Science fiction anthology, 2023)
La colonia felice by Carlo Dossi
The Coming Dark Age (1974) by Roberto Vacca
Franci Conforti
Cosmo collana di fantascienza
Cosmo Argento
Cosmo Oro
Alberto Costantini
Inisero Cremaschi
Vincenzo Croce
Vittorio Curtoni
Cyborg (cyberpunk magazine)
Dalla Terra a Marte (1895) by F. Bianchi
Dalla Terra alle stelle: Viaggio meraviglioso di due italiani ed un francese (1887) by Ulisse Grifoni
Daniele D'Anza
Il Romanzo d'Avventure (1924–1936) by the publisher Sonzogno
Keith R. A. DeCandido
Delta

La disfatta dei mostri (1940) by Gustavo Reisoli
Dissipatio H.G.: The Vanishing (2020) by Guido Morselli
Antonio Dikele Distefano
Una donna con tre anime (1918) by Rosa Rosà
Dopo il trionfo del socialismo italiano. Sogno di un uomo di cuore (1907) by Ulisse Grifoni
Editrice Nord
L'elenco telefonico di Atlantide (2003) by Tullio Avoledo
"The End of Eternity" (1965) by Ernesto Gastaldi
Franco Enna
Eva ultima (1923) by Massimo Bontempelli
Lanfranco Fabriani
La fabbrica degli uomini alati (1945) by Guido Pusinich
Cesare Falessi
Fantacollana
Fantapocket Longanesi
La Fantascienza
Emiliano Farinella
Clelia Farris
Terri Favro
La fine del mondo (1949) by Emilio Garro
La fine del secolo XX (1906) by Giustino L. Ferri
D. C. Fontana
Futuria Fantasia (Fanzine)
Futuro (1963–1964)
Galassia (Italian science fiction book series, 1961–1979)
Galaxy magazine
Garibaldi a Gettysburg (1993) by Pierfrancesco Prosperi
Il gigante dell'apocalisse (1930) by Giovanni Bertinetti
Marcello Giombini
Il giro del mondo in 30 giorni (1899) by Ulisse Grifoni
Gog (1931) by Giovanni Papini
Francesco Grasso
La guerra del 2000 (1935) by Camillo Nessi
Christine Lynn Herman
House in the Sky (1928) by Gastone Simoni
Lorenzo Iacobellis
L'inattesa piega degli eventi (2008) by Enrico Brizzi
Giulia Iannuzzi

L'impero restaurato (2014) by Sandro Battisti
The Invisible Fence (1929) by Gastone Simoni
Ipergenio il disinventore (1931) by Giovanni Bertinetti
Peter Kolosimo
Lukha B. Kremo
Kronos (fanzine, 1973)
I Libri di Robot (1978–1979)
Ugo Malaguti
Memorie di un cuoco d'astronave (1997) by Massimo Mongai
Mauro Antonio Miglieruolo
Marco Milani
Mille metri sotto il Sahara (1938) by Francesco Pestellini
Miraggi di silicio (1995) by Massimo Pietroselli
I misteri politici della Luna (1863) by Guglielmo Folliero de Luna
Mondi astrali (1955)
Il mondo non è nostro (1989)
Giorgio Monicelli
Gianni Montanari
Rita Carla Francesca Monticelli
Alessandro Montoro
Maico Morellini
Gilda Musa
I navigatori del cielo (1925) by Renzo Chiosso
Nel 2073! Sogni d'uno stravagante (1874) by Agostino Della Sala Spada
Nero italiano (2003) by Giampietro Stocco
Next Magazine
Nicolas Eymerich, inquisitore (1994) by Valerio Evangelisti
Piergiorgio Nicolazzini
Numeri Unici (formerly *Nuovi Orizzonti*, fanzine)
Oltre il Cielo
Omega SF
Le orecchie di Meo (1908) by Giovanni Bertinetti
Oscar Fantascienza
Giovanni Papini
Il paese senza cielo (1939) by Giorgio Scerbanenco
Sandro Pergameno
Renato Pestriniero
Daniela Piegai
Il pianeta irritabile (1978) by Paolo Volponi

Ivo Prandin
Renato Prinzhofer
Bill Pronzini
Il prosciugamento del Mediterraneo (1923) by Calogero Ciancimino
Pierfrancesco Prosperi
Pulsar (1972) Fanzine
Roberto Quaglia
Roberta Rambelli
Il re del magazzino (1978) by Antonio Porta
Franco Ricciardiello
Davide Del Popolo Riolo
La rivolta del 2023 (1924) by Nino Salvaneschi
Robot, Rivista di fantascienza (1976–1979; 2003–)
Il Romanzo d'Avventure (1924–1936)
Rosa Rosà
Mary Doria Russell
Saga
Emilio Salgari
Sandro Sandrelli
Danilo Santoni
John Scalzi
Giorgio Scerbanenco
Scienza Fantastica—Avventure nello spazio, tempo e dimensione (science fiction magazine, 1952–1953)
Selene (science fiction and comic magazine, 1965)
Il sentiero delle ombre (1933) by Eugenio Prandi
Sezione π^2 (2007) by Giovanni De Matteo
Sigma
Il signore del tempo (1902) by Giuseppe Lipparini
Laura Silvestri
Sirenide (1921) by Nino Salvaneschi
The Sixth Day and Other Tales (1966, 1971, 1990) by Primo Levi
Il sogno di un pazzo (1940) by Ada Maria Pellacani
Sonzogno
Star Trek—La pista delle stelle (1978–1979)
Bruce Sterling
Giampietro Stocco
Storia di domani (1949) by Curzio Malaparte
Storia filosofica dei secoli futuri (1859) by Ippolito Nievo

Lo strano settembre 1950 (1950) by Donato Martucci and Uguccione Ranieri
La Terra senza sole (1948) by Virgilio Martini
Dario Tonani
Brian Trent
Silvia Treves
Trilogia di Occidente (2001–2006) by Mario Farneti
L'uomo di fil di ferro (1932) by Ciro Khan
L'uomo è forte (1938) by Corrado Alvaro
L'ultimo degli Atlantidi (1932) by Gastone Simoni
Urania magazine
Gli universi di Moras (1989) by Vittorio Catani
Riccardo Valla
Nicoletta Vallorani
VenCo (2023)
La Verita sul caso Motta (1941) by Mario Soldati
Francesco Verso
Viaggio alla luna (1857) by Ernesto Capocci
Il viaggio nell'universo (1838) by Francesco Viganò
Gianni Vicario
Alessandro Vietti
Il volo alle stelle (1931) by Roberto Mandel
The Worldwide Machine (1965) by Paolo Volponi
The World Without Women (1971) by Virgilio Martini

Television and Streaming Series and Miniseries

A come Andromeda (1972)
Admiral Al Calavicci (*Quantum Leap*)
The Adventures of Pinocchio (1972 miniseries)
Natasha Allegri
Piero Angela
Angel's Friends (2009)
Avatar: The Last Airbender and *The Legend of Korra*
Scott Baio
Joseph Barbera
Donald P. Bellisario
Greg Berlanti
Ed Bianchi

Steven Bochco
Flaminio Bollini
John Boni
Natasha Liu Bordizzo
Bu-Bum! La strada verso casa (2016)
Calimero (1963)
Joseph Campanella
Duane Capizzi
Gina Carano
Bill Carraro
David Chase
Anthony Cipriano
Citadel Diana (2024)
Nick Confalone
Vittorio Cottafav
Curon (2020)
Alexandra Daddario
Enzo D'Alò
Daniele D'Anza
James Darren
Deputy Seraph (1959)
Daredevil: Born Again (2025)
Michael Dante DiMartino
Sophia Di Martino
Paul Dini
ESP (1973)
Giancarlo Esposito
Extra (1976 miniseries)
Fantaghirò (1999–2000)
Il fascino dell'insolito (1980–1982)
Il fauno di marmo (1977 miniseries)
Jack D. Ferraiolo
Lou Ferrigno
Dave Filoni
The Flash (1990–1991)
Dorothy Fontana
Shea Fontana
Gamma (1975)
Michael Garibaldi (*Babylon 5*)

Gastone (aka Harold, a talking dog helper of Mr. Rossi)
I giochi del diavolo. Storie fantastiche dell'Ottocento (1981)
Grisù il draghetto (1975–1976)
Heroes (2006–2010)
Jack Huston
Armando Iannucci
Angela LaManna
Natasha Leggero
Robert Longo
Luna Nera (2020)
Silvio Maestranzi
Matt Maiellaro
Joe Manganiello
Alessandra Martines
Martin Mystery (2003–2006)
Glen Mazzara
Kate Micucci
Cristin Milioti
Anthony Minghella
Dominic Minghella
Max Minghella
Salvatore Nocita
Tig Notaro
The Odyssey (1968 miniseries)
Peter Onorati
Joe Oriolo
Nino Pagot and Toni Pagot
Adrian Paul
Penguin (2024)
"Madame" Maria Perego
Tom Perrotta
Robert Picardo
Racconti fantastici (1979 miniseries)
Rob Renzetti
Ritratto di donna velata (1975 miniseries)
Franco Rossi
Theo Rossi
Sandokan (TV series)
Chris Savino

Dario Scardapane
Margaret Scarpello
Piero Schivazappa
Adam Scott
Christian Marie Serratos (born Bernardi)
Sergio Sollima
Sound (1988)
Star Trek (especially the original series, *The Animated Series*, *Deep Space Nine*, *Voyager*, *Discovery*, and *Prodigy*)
Star Wars television shows on Disney+
Eric Stefani
Iginio Straffi
Stryx (1978)
Supergulp! (1972, 1977–1981)
Alessandro Taini (aka Talexi)
Topo Gigio (1959)
La traccia verde (1976)
Un marziano a Roma (1983)
Uonderbois (2024)
Valentina (1989)
Indira Varma
Thomas Vitale
Jon Vitti
Winx Club (2014)
W.I.T.C.H. (2004–2006)
Zero (2021)
Marouane Zotti

Theater

Luigi Antonelli
Guillaume Apollinaire
Eugenio Barba
Umberto Boccioni
Massimo Bontempelli
Anton Guilio Bragaglia
Breasts of Tiresias (1903)
Sophia Anne Caruso

Enrico Cavacchioli
Luigi Chiarelli
Bruno Corra
Rodolfo De Angelis
Ennio Flaiano
Dario Fo
Filippo Tommaso Marinetti
Un marziano a Roma (1960) by Ennio Flaiano
Minnie la candida (1926) by Massimo Bontempelli
La nuova colonia (1928) by Luigi Pirandello
Ettore Petrolini
Luigi Pirandello
Enrico Prampolini
Luca Ronconi
Pier Maria Rosso di San Secondo
Brian Siano
Six Characters in Search of an Author (1921)
Teatro degli Indepenti (1890–1960)
Teatro Grottesco

Video Games

La Abadía del Crimen
Alkimya: Memories of the Last Alchemist
Andrea Angiolino
Anna (2012)
Assassin's Creed II
Assassin's Creed Brotherhood
Chris Avellone
Bolt
Castlevania: Bloodlines
Christian Cantamessa
Dante's Inferno
Daymare: 1998
Dead or Alive's Leon
Duck Tales: Remastered
Dylan Dog: Horror Luna Park
Earth: 2140

Ezio Auditore da Firenze
GioGio's Bizarre Adventure
Glory of the Roman Empire
Grezzo 2
Stefano Gualeni
House of Da Vinci
The House of the Dead 4
Indiana Jones' Greatest Adventures
Joe Dever's Lone Wolf
JoJo's Bizarre Adventures: Eyes of Heaven
Journey to the Center of the Earth
Kingdom Hearts 3D: Dream Drop Distance
Lego Batman 3: Beyond Gotham
Mario's Time Machine
Martha Is Dead
Merchant Prince
NAPS team
Nemesis of the Roman Empire
Overwatch and *Overwatch 2*
Ovosonico
Pang
Paolo Pedercini
Pinocchio
Profexia
Rampage series (*Rampage 2, Rampage Through Time, Rampage World Tour*)
RedBit games
Redout
Remothered: Broken Porcelain
Remothered: Tormented Fathers
Santa Paravia en Fiumaccio
Secret Agent Barbie
Serious Sam 4
Serious Sam Double D
Kunos Simulazioni
Simulmondo
Sonic Unleashed
Street Fighter's Rose
Super Mario Bros.
Tomb Raider 2

Tomb Raider Chronicles
Tomb Raider: Prophecy
The Town of Light
Uncharted 4
Vampire Survivors
Zombie Army 4: Dead War
Zone 66

Web Resources

Weird Italy

Contributors

Marc DiPaolo has written the roman à clef *Fake Italian* for Bordighera Press (2021), and the monographs *Fire and Snow: Climate Fiction from the Inklings to "Game of Thrones"* (2018) and *War, Politics, and Superheroes* (CHOICE Outstanding Academic Title 2011). He has edited three additional American Studies books, including *Unruly Catholics from Dante to Madonna* (2007). He has been interviewed on NPR, BBC4, and in the AMC docuseries *Robert Kirkman's Secret History of Comics* (S1 E4, 2017). DiPaolo is Secretary for the Society for the Study of the Multi-Ethnic Literature of the United States and currently teaches global, multicultural humanities courses at Moraine Valley Community College. He has also served as a tenured Associate Professor of English at Southwestern Oklahoma State University (2016–2024), Visiting Associate Professor of Film, English, and Honors at Oklahoma City University (2009–2016), and as Assistant Professor of Journalism and New Media at Alvernia University (2005–2009).

Anthony Lioi is Professor of English in the Liberal Arts faculty of the Juilliard School, where he teaches composition, American literature, and the environmental humanities. He is the author of *Nerd Ecology* (2016) and numerous articles in the field of ecocriticism. He is coeditor of *Regeneration: Environment, Art, Culture.*

Fernando Gabriel Pagnoni Berns is a professor at Universidad de Buenos Aires–Facultad de Filosofía y Letras, where he teaches courses on international horror films. He is director of the research group on horror cinema, Grite; has authored a book about the Spanish horror TV series *Historias para no dormir*; and has edited books on horror directors James

Wan, Wes Craven, and an upcoming book on Dario Argento. He is the director of Terror: Estudios Críticos (Universidad de Cádiz), the first-ever horror studies series in Spain and is currently coediting the Routledge volume *Critical Readings on Hammer Horror Films.*

Davide Carnevale earned his doctorate in Italian Studies at the University of Rome "La Sapienza," in 2021. He has published the monograph *Narrating the Invasion: Trajectories and Renewal of the Twentieth-Century Fantastic* (2022) and wrote the introductions to the comics *La Mummia* by Dino Battaglia and *Il Collezionista* by Sergio Toppi for Nicola Pesce Editore. Since 2016, Carnevale has been the editorial secretary of *Novecento Transnazionale* journal and has been a member of the GEF (Grupo de estudio sobre lo Fantástico) since 2021.

Matteo Damiani is an Italian sinologist, photographer, author, and motion designer. Matteo lived and worked for ten years in China. He is the founder of CinaOggi.it, China-underground.com, Weirditaly.com, and RetroFuturista.com.

Alec Follett is a settler scholar living in Canada with Calabrian heritage by way of his mother's family. His research focuses on environment and colonialism in North American and Indigenous literature. Most recently, Alec has published scholarship on Cherokee author Thomas King's mystery novels, in which the hardboiled genre's indebtedness and resistance to oil and petromobility is examined. Alec holds a PhD in literary studies from the University of Guelph and is Professor of Communications at Conestoga College.

Ciro Incoronato received a PhD in bioethics from the University of Naples "Federico II" and is a PhD candidate in Romance Studies at Duke University. His areas of specialization are Italian and Italian American culture, Mediterranean and European Studies, and medical humanities. His first monograph, *Homo artificialis: dall'umanesimo della purezza ai neoumanesimi dell'ibridazione* (2016), explores the theoretical core of posthumanism. His current research project explores the economic and biopolitical role Italian organized crime plays in the Mediterranean area. He uses literary texts, movies, newspapers, and scientific publications, as well as concepts from philosophy and the social sciences, to investigate the evolution of the Neapolitan Camorra and its economic and environmental impact.

William Q. Malcuit is Associate Professor of English at the University of Wisconsin–Milwaukee, where he teaches classes in writing and literature. His research interests include poetry (both American and Italian), science fiction, and African American literature.

Drago Momcilovic is Senior Lecturer in Comparative Literature at the University of Wisconsin–Milwaukee. His teaching and research interests include contemporary literature and cinema, horror, gothic tradition, popular culture, music video, the environmental humanities, and posthumanism. His articles have appeared in the journals *Gothic Studies* and *Humanities*.

Dominique Musorrafiti is a cocurator of the website *Weird Italy*. Her father was an Italian chemical engineer and high school teacher of Greek and Polish heritage. Her mother is a Haitian high school language teacher of Dominican, Spanish, French, Portuguese, African, and Native American heritage. Being a mix of races and ethnicities makes her desire to understand different cultures and lifestyles. She grew up in Italy, lived for a few years in Haiti, then lived seven years in China, and six in Spain and Great Britain.

Danel Olson is a professor of Gothic fiction and cinema who has taught film, rhetoric, and literature courses in Palestine, Canada, China, and Lone Star College in Houston. Three-time finalist for the Bram Stoker Award and winner of a Shirley Jackson Award and two World Fantasy Awards, he earned his PhD at the University of Stirling, Scotland. His recent books include *9/11 Gothic: Decrypting Ghosts and Trauma in New York City's Terrorism Novels* (2021) and *Gothic War on Terror: Killing, Haunting, and PTSD in American Film, Fiction, Comics, and Video Games* (2023). Joyce Carol Oates describes the latter as "terrifically interesting with riveting material fastidiously assembled. A major work. Amazing . . . brilliant . . . all-encompassing. Should be required reading." *The Washington Post* calls his work on cinema "a major contribution to film history and scholarship." His forthcoming titles are *Diabolical Motherhood* for Bloomsbury and *Rosemary's Baby: Studies in the Horror Film* for Centipede Press.

Lisa Marie Paolucci holds a PhD in English Education from Columbia University. She is an assistant professor and Chair of Education at St. Francis College in Brooklyn, New York, and previously taught high school English in the New York City public school system.

Umberto Rossi, Honorary Fellow (Cultore della materia) at Sapienza University of Rome, is the author of *The Twisted Worlds of Philip K. Dick* (2011) and *Il secolo di fuoco* (2008), an introduction to twentieth-century war literature. He coedited the 2015 special issue of *Science Fiction Studies on Italian SF* (with A. Saiber and S. Proietti) and organized the 2019 International Pynchon Week in Rome, Italy, with Paolo Simonetti. Rossi is also a member of the Science Fiction Research Association and the secretary of the International Comparative Literature Association's Standing Research Committee on Graphic Literature and Comics Studies.

Cristian Soler is a PhD candidate in Iberian and Latin American Studies at Stanford University with a PhD minor in philosophy, literature, and the arts. He also holds a BA in philosophy and literature from Los Andes University (Colombia) and a master's in Medieval and Renaissance Studies from Columbia University. His work explores topics such as aesthetics and art theory, art therapy, epistemology, and cybernetics. He has taught courses on Hispanic comics, the history and philosophy of computation in the Middle Ages, and on Latin American contemporary art.

Victoria Tomasulo is Doctoral Lecturer of English at Queensborough Community College and a former first-generation student with working-class Italian and Polish roots. She received a PhD in comparative literature from CUNY Graduate Center in 2016 and a certificate in Italian Diaspora Studies from the Calandra Institute in 2019. Her scholarship explores intersections of class, race, gender, and ethnicity in contemporary women's literature in the US and Italy.

Index